The Game Trinity

Faraz Anwar Khan

INDIA • SINGAPORE • MALAYSIA

ISBN
Paperback 979-8-89610-735-4
Hardcase 979-8-89632-752-3

Dedication

I dedicate my first book to my late grandfather Ahmed Saeed Malihabadi, MP Rajya Sabha, a great Urdu writer, journalist, social worker and Islamic scholar of International fame.

Introduction

When it comes to the true nature of this world and the universe, the "ugly truth" is that there is no such thing as morality and justice. In the Bhagawat Gita, Lord Krishna said to Arjuna, that the whole of Existence is only a "Leela," that is, a divine Game. He told ARJUNA that as long as we live, we must keep playing according to the laws and rules that either we must discover ourselves or will be given to us by a teacher who wants us to become the "new participants" or contestants in the Gaming Universe.

Who is a real teacher? This question has been asked by the philosophers and the education reformers for thousands of years. Well, the answer is; a real teacher is the one who informs you as soon as possible after giving you the foundational knowledge of mathematics and the various sciences, that in order to survive and prosper in this world, you must become a Gamer. If you do not decide to or if you do not have the ability to do so, you will face the two greatest evils in this world; poverty and ridicule from all the Gamers. In addition to this, you will also not receive the metaphysical object that is desired by all the men and women in this world, Honor

If you are a non-gamer, you will remain poor for your whole life if you have been born in a poor family. On the other hand, if you have been born in a rich family and inherit a large amount of wealth from your parents, you will become poor very soon if you are a non-gamer because in the first case, you will not have any knowledge as to how to protect your wealth from the robbers that will be swarming around you like flies and in the second case, you will not have any knowledge as to how to use your wealth in order to accumulate even greater wealth through "game theory".

Before I talk about the Game Trinity, which forms the core of the universe, I must discuss about the various qualities of a Gamer. I will talk about the qualities in various numbers in each chapter of my book.

Chapter 1

Quality 1: During the game, he is never in a state of confusion

Comment: After "poor health", confusion is the second greatest enemy of a gamer. It arises from a low amount of intelligence, a timid nature, and a non-deterministic nature. If a man is not determined to make his life better through the acquisition of wealth or power, then he would never be able to take firm and unchanging decisions. Thus, only a person of normal intelligence and a bold and perseverant nature can become a Gamer

Quality 2: He protects his "plans" through a great amount of security

Comment: In a game, both the contestants must never get to know everything about each other's "game plans". Thus, the Gamer does all he can to prevent his rival from getting to know everything about his "game plan" either before the game begins or during the gaming period. It is true that during the gaming period, both the contestants will come to know a lot about each other's "game plans" (if both are individuals of normal intelligence), but not everything. The security methods include the creation of firewalls and passcodes (if the plans are on a computer) or the creation of spies and watchdogs.

Quality 3: Before and during the gaming period, he does not do anything that increases the "laziness" of his partners.

Comment: A gamer must be a very active individual, mentally and physically. Plus, he must always play a game with multiple "like minded" individuals. If he is the leader of his group, then it is purely his responsibility to make sure that neither he/she nor any of his partners becomes more and more lazy or loses his health. If he begins to get lazy and continues that path, then defeat is certain to him/her and the group. The causes of laziness are two; poor health and pessimism. Poor health arises from a poor manner of eating, living in a polluted environment and having a genetic syndrome (this is the reason as to why the people of the developed nations are better "gamers" than those of the developing nations). Pessimism arises from stoicism and nihilism. Stoicism says that your lifetime is nothing but a tiny blip or a flash of lightning on the geologic and cosmic timescales. Thus, according to it the world is nothing but a "circus" and the right man is the one who does not participate in it and just stands away and observes it. On the other hand, nihilism says that everything in this universe, including you, is "meaningless". Thus, it says that since nothing has any ultimate meaning, then you should never "strive" for the conquest of anything.

Quality 4: He never does anything or creates those conditions through his own actions which eventually lead to a "mutiny" in his group.

Comment: As has been said before, united we stand and divided we fall, the gamer always makes sure that the unity of his group members remains strong and everlasting. In order to achieve this, he takes "as much care" for their mental and physical health as he does for himself. In addition to this, he makes sure that they are always kept in an environment where the availability of energy and leisure is high and the possibility of getting diseases is low. Through his actions, a great gamer eventually manages to extract this statement from his group; you are a treasure to us. You are our teacher and our source of life. If you die, then we will all die.

Quality 5: He can see into the "future" of his rival or enemy and regards "plan creation" as more important than "group creation".

Comment: The individual who can knows the future, is as powerful as God. However, we can never see "everything" that is going to happen in the future because we have not created this world and this universe. We can only see a small fraction of it and in addition to this, make predictions. The small fraction is a product of "logical" thinking that is based on the laws of mathematics and physics and the predictions is a product of a "simulation". Thus, a great gamer is not only very good in mathematics and physics, but also creates simulations in collaboration with his almost equally intelligent and learned partners. His knowledge of the future set of actions of his enemy are based on; the nature of the mind of the enemy and its own group and the velocity with which the environment around it is changing. In order to get more knowledge of the mind of his enemy, he sends spies, diplomats, and bureaucrats into its territory. On the other hand, in order to get knowledge of the environmental conditions in which his/her enemy is placed, he sends reconnaissance probes and satellite analysis.

The great gamer knows that before you start playing, you must have a plan. He knows that by getting excited by the invitation of the enemy and just "jumping blindly" into its "gaming zone", you are committing suicide both for yourself and your group members. Thus, both sides refuse to give in to the initial "come and play" calls. They know that it is a trap. Both thus create a plan that is based on mathematics and science and the joint agreement of all the group members. As the gaming continues, their plans keep on changing or "evolving".

Quality 6: He first uses the "indirect" methods of achieving victory and makes sure that all the troubles that "hit" him group come only from the enemy group and nowhere else

Comment: As the great Chinese philosopher Sun Tzu said in his book "the art of war"; the real fighter wins a battle without any fighting. Thus, a great gamer, in order to prevent the large-scale use of his personal resources and that of his group members, he tries to play and achieve victory via the indirect methods. These include the assassination of the leader of the enemy group in a "top secret" manner through a brilliant spy, the artificial changing of the weather over the enemy's territory, the deployment of a deadly pathogen in the enemy's territory and the sucking out of all the wealth of the enemy and its partners through innovative economic techniques.

When it comes to all the problems that hit his group, the great gamer always tries to do all that he can to make sure that they all come from his enemy. However, in the real world, this is impossible since both the rivals have been placed in a universe that they did not create. Thus, in the wars between the nations of the Earth, troubles not only come from other nations, but also from hurricanes, floods, droughts, earthquakes, volcanoes, tornadoes, heat waves and cold waves.

Quality 7: He does not practice "passive resistance" for too long

Comment: A great gamer and all his group members are not followers of Jesus Christ, who said that if your enemy slaps you on your left cheek, you should give him the right cheek for another slap. However, the trouble with this doctrine is that after slapping you right cheek, the enemy will give you a powerful punch in your belly and if you still display "passive resistance", it will give you a kick in your balls. As has been said by all the wise men for thousands of years, if you do not stop "evil" after a certain point, it begins to believe that it is as free as God and can do anything it wants to. All evil people in the world have no sense of compassion or remorse. If not stopped, they will go to the limits of their evil fantasies. Thus, in the beginning, a great gamer and his group display passive resistance in order to know more about the mind of their enemy and its firepower, but when the necessary data has been acquired, the philosophy becomes; tit for tat.

Quality 8: He considers it his duty to stop, through courage increasing talk, one of his group members who have decided to flee the gaming zone due to irrational fears.

Comment: A member of the leader's group might decide not to play and to escape the gaming zone due to the onset of some beliefs that are the opposite of the rest of the group. These beliefs are purely the result of the person's unique mind. They can arise due to three causes; pessimism, stoicism, and nihilism. The quitter starts to believe that even if their group wins the game against their enemy, they are still insignificant and meaningless with respect to the universe. The universe can easily exterminate all the happiness that they would gain from the victory and would then proceed to kill all of them. Thus, when the leader is successful in catching his group member before he leaves the gaming zone, his purpose is to exterminate the three causes of fear and resignation and to increase the courage of the quitter. But the great gamer only keeps up his effort for a fixed time period (that is pre-decided by him). If the quitter refuses to change even after the fixed time period of lecturing, the leader sends him back to his home and replaces him with a new gamer.

Chapter 2

Quality 1: He moves according the enemy's desires if he has nothing for his self-protection

Comment: The great gamer knows how to preserve his own life far better than any normal man or a saint. Thus, if his enemy manages to capture him in a state of powerlessness and threatens him with death for disobedience, then he becomes a servant of the enemy only as long as the arrival of the proper opportunity. When the proper opportunity arrives, he wastes no time and with a 100% determined mind and with the full use of his intelligence and cunning, moves up either to get back his freedom via the use of the enemy's weapons (which the enemy provides him through its own carelessness) or to kill the enemy either by the use of his own weapons (which were placed beforehand at a location that was unknown to the enemy) or by the use of the enemy's weapons. As has been said before by a wise man; remain a sheep only as long as it is necessary and when it is no longer so, try your best to become a lion. The great gamer always desires to be the Shepard and not the sheep.

Quality 2: He retreats when it is rational to do so but makes his enemy follow him via seductive bait

Comment: if your enemy loses interest in you, then the game will end automatically. Thus, there would not be a winner and a loser. It would be a stalemate situation. A great gamer, does everything he can in order to avoid the birth of a stalemate. He retreats either to his "home base" or to a new location that was behind the one that he is playing in purely based on rational thinking. When he begins his retreat, he does not want the enemy to lose its enthusiasm in both the game and its rival. Thus, bait is used and its nature is purely according to the mind of the enemy. If the enemy is licentious, then the bait is a beautiful woman and if it is power hungry, then it is an "energy device" (like the TESSERACT in the Avengers movies). The goal is to bring the enemy and its group inside a pre-planned location where they would either be all captured or killed via an unexpected ambush.

Quality 3: He keeps on playing even when completely alone

Comment: There are two kinds of gamers; the ordinary and the extraordinary. Most of the gamers in the world are ordinary gamers. They will decide to play only if they become a part of a group and never in a state of singularity. Thus, these people are not courageous at all. They only develop something that is like courage when they are a part of a group. They are like those animals that hunt in a "pack" formation. When they get separated from the pack, they behave just like a pure and timid herbivore that flees at the first sight of an approaching danger. On the other hand, the extraordinary gamer is the true symbol of courage, self-faith and warrior-hood. He believes that the power and the intelligence of his entire group, resides within him. Such a gamer knows the true meaning of the word "honor". The more he honors himself, the more individualistic he would become. He will remain the part of your group only as long as it exists and as long as it brings mental improvement in his life. When the improvement has ceased, he will separate from the group without any hesitation. Most people in the world are the followers of the "herd mentality" and due to this, they are nothing but lions made of paper and according to all the religious books, the blessings of God come only onto the real lions and not the paper ones.

Quality 4: He punishes those group members who lie to him

Comment: The unity of a group implies two goals; that no member will ever misbehave with any of the other members, including the leader, and that no one will ever tell a lie to any of the other members, including the leader. A member can tell lies to his group for two reasons. First, if he is a traitor and second, if he gets pleasure in telling lies. Truth seeking and truth speaking is a pleasurable activity to most people in the world, but there are a minority to whom lie seeking and lie speaking are far more pleasurable. The motive that causes them to tell lies is a strange but not a bizarre one; to observe what happens when their lie is accepted as the truth by all the group members. Just like the scientists do experimentations on the rats, dogs and mice in their laboratories, men also like to do experimentations on each other. The methods are three; injecting a substance into the body of the chosen person without his knowledge, deliberate provocation of the chosen one's anger or sexual energy and deliberate lying. Thus, it is the duty of a gamer to detect the presence of such people in his group either before the gaming begins or during the gaming period.

Quality 5: Before playing, he always does a complete analysis of the size of the "gaming zone"

Comment: The great gamer knows that a great game is always played on a gaming zone of equally great dimensions. He also knows that the bigger the gaming zone, the more is the possibility of "error correction". In a small gaming zone, if he makes an error against an equally powerful enemy, then he will have to face two disasters; the non-possibility of rectification and the sudden increase in the probability of the victory of the enemy. Thus, before the game begins, the great gamer informs his enemy if he wants the gaming zone to be bigger or smaller than it currently is. If the enemy refuses to fulfill his request, he stands down and refuses to play until the enemy changes its mind

Quality 6: If he makes some "new changes" in his game plan, then he makes sure that his enemy never comes to know about it

Comment: As was said before, the great gamer always manages to keep the blueprint of his game plan completely unknown to his enemy. He also knows that he can only bring new changes in the blueprint during the gaming period if and only if they are kept unknown to the enemy. Thus, a gamer who fails to keep his game plan blueprint a secret from his enemy, also cannot bring any new changes into it later. Change cannot survive without secrecy and secrecy cannot survive without change.

Quality 7: He continuously tries to convince his group members that through the playing of the game with the enemy, they are embarking on a "great project".

Comment: The great gamer, before starting to play, knows that he has two goals to fulfill first before reaching the others. The first is to keep everyone in his group as perfect as possible, mentally, and physically and second is to keep the enthusiasm of everyone, including himself, as strong during the entire gaming period as it was during the beginning of the game. In order to accomplish this, all of them must believe that by defeating the enemy they would then embark on a new project of even bigger complexity and beauty. This includes the creation of a "new world" or the extermination of all the evils in the world or the creation of an entirely new sub-species. The favorite one for all the religious people is; the journey to God and the eventual landing up in heaven and living with Him forever. In the real world of today, we see the politicians, the capitalists and the kings of the royal families declare every time they come together in a big conference in a beautiful corner of the planet; we are going to save the planet. We are going to create a better world for our children and grandchildren. We are going to solve the problem of climate change (the truth is that they are all telling lies and they know it. They cannot solve any problem or create a new world because they did not create it in the first place. The priests, who are their puppets, will tell the people that they will succeed because they have the support and the blessings of God, the creator, but they also know fully well that they are lying).

Quality 8: To test the loyalty and the intelligence of his group members, he gives them "puzzles" to solve during the "low phase" of the gaming period.

Comment: The gaming period exists in three phases; the high phase, the mid-phase, and the low phase. During the "high phase", the leader and his group are completely involved in fighting the enemy and its group. They do not get the time to focus on anything else in the world around them. Currently period, the technological and intellectual powers of both the groups are at their maximum display.

During the mid-phase period, both the groups get a small amount of leisure time which they can use to inquire into and improve their wellbeing and to look on the other kinds of games that are being played all over the world. During this phase, they also have the time to make new changes in their game plan blueprints.

During the low-phase period, the leisure magnitude is the highest and in this period the group members indulge in other kinds of activities like having sex and babies, writing personal biographies, or following personal hobbies. It is also in this period, that the leader gives his members some scientifically designed "puzzles" to solve. Some they are told to solve in a fixed amount of time and some in as much time as they need. The former ones are easier than the latter. If the members cannot even solve the "fixed time" puzzles, then the leader comes to know that their intelligence has declined instead of growing. Thus, he soon evicts them from his group. On the other hand, if a member shows impious behavior towards his leader and refuses to solve the puzzles, then he is also evicted.

Chapter 3

Quality 1: He sends only those "signals" to his group members which are undetectable to his enemy

Comment: A great gamer must not let his enemy know about the exact time that he gives new instructions to his group members. Thus, before the game begins, a set of "signals" are created which cannot be detected by any of the various kinds of the "detecting devices" of the enemy. The goal of such a project is to launch unexpected attacks on the enemy, which greatly increase the probability of victory by either destroying the vital infrastructure of the enemy or by sending it and its group members into a great panic attack. However, in most cases, the enemy is also equally intelligent and knows that its rival would create such a project. Thus, it invents its own set of "signals" that are undetectable by the technologies of the other side.

Quality 2: He does not love either life or death

Comment: If a man loves to live, then he would be afraid of death. Thus, he would soon become a pacifist and a stoic. He would go around his nation and the world; why do you play games with each other? What is the point in all of it? Life is so short and meaningless that even if we defeat each other, we would neither become immortal nor would become something significant in the universe. Thus, he would never play any games in his whole life and would convince others to become like him. In such a world, two things would come to an almost frozen state; evolution and scientific progress. It is a truth that the more the number of gamers in a species and the greater the ferocity of the gaming, the faster becomes the speed of evolution and technological progress.

If a gamer has no desire to live, then he would become a nihilist. He would go around saying; everything in this world and the universe is meaningless and has no ultimate purpose. Thus, I do not want to play for the conquest of wealth or power and neither do I care if I live or die. Such a person would soon become a "hippie" and it is a fact of reality that great gamers are the furthest possible deviations from the "hippie" state and are also the destroyers of hippies. In addition to this, if a man has no desire to live, then when he will play a game, he would soon start to make errors and take reckless actions.

Quality 3: He always carries out his "first strike" on the "weakest point" of the enemy

Comment: Before announcing to the enemy; "game on", a gamer has three four duties to complete; the creation of unity between all the members of the group, the secrecy of the game plan blueprint through the creation of security walls, the creation of a set of undetectable signals and to discover the "weakest point" of the enemy. Any enemy has several weak points but one of them is the weakest one because it is the most "fragile". Thus, the gamer must discover the "Achilles heel" of its enemy. In the case of a modern nation like the USA, it is its computer infrastructure (all the essential parts of the three kinds of defense forces are run by computers). If the attack on the weakest point is successful, then it creates a high degree of "instability" in the enemy's infrastructure and a high lowering of its fighting spirit. However, the enemy always knows about all its weak points, including its weakest one and does all it can to make them more and more non-fragile. The best gamer is the one who has no Achilles heel.

Quality 4: In order to deceive and shock the enemy, the great gamer always keeps on transforming his mind by abandoning "old habits" when necessary and taking up "new ones"

Comment: A great gamer always keeps on evolving, both mentally and physically and in ways that are unexpected by its enemy. Those who do not prefer to evolve and abandon those habits and beliefs that they picked up from their childhood and teenage years, are not able to play a difficult game for a long period. There are three kinds of games; the easy, the difficult and the hybrid. The hybrid games are those that are easy in the beginning but become difficult and complex later (the reverse also applies). Thus, those people who desire a static mindset and a fixed way of life are only capable of playing the easy games. Those who have a masochistic mentality coupled with above normal intelligence can play the difficult games only. But in both kinds of games, the laws and the rules remain the same in number and meaning. It is the hybrid games, the ones that are easy at their start and difficult later are the greatest ones in the universe and will give the greatest rewards if victory is achieved. These games "evolve" with time and so must their contestants. Thus, when a gamer plays with an intelligent and evolving enemy, he must also evolve himself/herself, otherwise defeat is certain. If he keeps on evolving "in sync" with his enemy, then the probability of the enemy launching an unexpected attack is very low.

Quality 5: The great gamer takes no account of the "physical beauty" of any of his group members

Comment: A great muscular body or a beautiful face with blonde hair and blue eyes has almost no importance in gaming. The only things that matter are; intelligence, the power of the ego, the ability for decision making and the ability to gather and unite those that will play with you. All scientists say; Nature has no respect for beauty. That is why everyday thousands of beautiful birds, flowers, insects, and fishes die all over the planet and Nature does absolutely nothing to save them. Why? It is because it is a great gamer. Nature plays games with all the species living on the surface of the Earth. Its goal, most probably, is to keep all of them, including the Homo sapiens, loyal to it and to submit their destinies into its hands. They in turn try to prevent this from happening by increasing the power of their reproductive system with each new generation and by increasing the "adaptive power" of every new generation. Thus, a great gamer is also like Nature. He does not admit a member into his group due to his height or muscles or blue eyes. He only admits them based on their intelligence and their ability to endure pain or fear for a long time. In games of very low quality, which will give small rewards, muscle strength is given importance (like what the "bouncers" do in a disco or a nightclub or a fight with some rowdy boys on a street), but in all the high-quality ones which will give big rewards, muscle power is the least important.

Quality 6: The great gamer never harms or kills those that are "unarmed" or those that "drop their weapons" in front of him

Comment: Besides being ruthless and merciless towards the fanatics, the great gamer is equally compassionate towards the powerless and the submissive. It is said that the most coward and idiotic person in the world is the one who either kills or enslaves powerless and submissive people. Such a person does not deserve any kind of honor and the person who gives him honor is as coward and idiotic as him. The tyrants of all the dictatorship nations do exactly this. First, they disarm all the citizens, then they rob them of any kind of political power and then they proceed to enslave them and kill those who refuse to obey their dictatorship (Russia, China and North Korea are the best examples). Thus, all dictators are not real gamers but fake ones. When they will play with a real one, they would soon come to realize the level of their intelligence and their real nature.

Chapter 4

Quality 1: He always tries to maximize the number of "refuge" spots in the gaming zone

Comment: The great gamer never wants to play in a gaming zone where he and his group members have any protection spot from the enemy's attacks. Thus, he will never agree to play in an open desert or open grassland. He will invite the enemy to play in a zone where the number of refuge or shelter spots is the maximum. The enemy will also desire the same. The region where the number of shelter spots is the maximum is a mountain region. Thus, the most difficult and evolving games are played in all the mountain ranges of the world. The games that happen in the mountain ranges have the highest lifespans and the ones that happen in highly open fields have the lowest lifespans. A great gamer always desires to maximize the lifespan of the game that he will play. Thus, the great gamers of the world are the most strongly attracted to the mountain ranges of the world. The goal of the gamer is; to prevent his group members from being killed or captured rapidly by his enemy

Quality 2: He never puts his group members in a spot where the enemy can launch an attack from several sides

Comment: The great gamer always makes sure that his group is always placed in a region where the attack will come from only one side and from the side that is expected by him. If this does not happen, then the rapid death of his group members is inevitable. However, the enemy tries its best to find "multiple attack channels" in the region where the other side's group members are placed

Quality 3: In a game, he uses every instrument and weapon only for its "specific purpose"

Comment: A great gamer is the most rational minded person in the world. Not only does he possesses "practical rationality", but also possesses "theoretical rationality". Theoretical rationality makes him/her create game plans purely out of mathematics, physics, and neuroscience. Through practical rationality, he begins to play only when the proper time has arrived and uses all his resources in the proper manner and the proper amount in each phase of the game. With respect to the resources, the gamer always possesses at least four of them; his group members, an energy creating engine, instruments for various kinds of measurements + detections and weapons. Thus, if he has a telescope, he uses it only for the observation of the enemy's territory and not for observing the planets of the solar system or the distant star clusters. If he has a gun, he uses it only to attack and kill the enemy's partners and not to kill the wildlife in his own territory.

Quality 4: He never allows himself to develop a "prodigal" mentality and tries to prevent the other members in his group from becoming prodigal by training them to imitate him

Comment: A great gamer will always say; no matter how rich you become, use your resources only as much as they are required for any activity and never more than that. After defeating each kind of enemy, the gamer and his group keep getting more and more rich and powerful, but eventually a point comes when they have no one to play with on their home planet. Thus, they become the most powerful beings on their home planet and are regarded as "gods" by all those who are under their rule. From this point on, two situations can develop. First, the leader and his group keep getting more and more conceited and prodigal with the passage of time. There comes a point when they start to believe that there is no species in the entire universe that can defeat them. They come to regard themselves as not only "planetary gods", but also "cosmic gods". Thus, they start to live like gods; consuming in vast quantities and spending in vast quantities. Due to the continuous

Prodigality, their intelligence, and their resources both start to decrease rapidly with each new generation of their group. Eventually, after 200 or 300 years, a gamer with a fanatical and determined mind arises from the population of the ruled people, plays with them, defeats them very soon and takes over their empire.

In the second situation, the leader and his group do not become prodigal, spend and use their powers and resources in an absolutely rational manner. They do this, because they have an immense amount of respect for the cosmos. They believe that although they might be the gods of their home world, they might be absolutely nothing compared to an alien species that is millions of years ahead of them in mathematics, science, and technology. They believe that the cosmos has created gamers which are as intelligent compared to them as humans are compared to cows and goats. Thus, they believe that the only chance of playing with them and gaining some possibility of victory, is to have as much resources as possible and as much intelligence as possible.

Quality 5: Before a game begins and during it, he makes it absolutely clear to his group members that they must focus their minds only on his game plan and his orders

Comment: A great gamer never displays his "entire plan" to his group members. He only shows them half of it and then tells them that they will come to know about the other half if and only if a partial victory has been achieved over the enemy and a road to the final goal is clearly visible. After this, he tells them that a partial victory can only be achieved over an equally powerful enemy if they would have faith in him and would focus only on his orders. This is "absolutely necessary" because, during the game, if the members are also interested in the other things of their territory, like natural scenery, the wild animals, and the activities of the children and the new born babies, then this would not only decrease the power of their gaming mind, but would also give the enemy an opportunity to launch a devastating attack.

The gamer can only extract the absolute loyalty of his members by gaining their respect. Respect is gained by possessing a great "oratorical power" and using it at the proper time and by possessing a beautiful and courageous character.

Quality 6: A great gamer despises "Victorianism" and luxury

Comment: Victorianism is a culture that was present in the royal family of the United Kingdom. It soon spread to all the other royal families of the world and is regarded as the culture that must be followed by every intelligent and civilized man on Earth. It is a combination of two things; living in a palace of a grand size with a huge garden in front of it and spending the leisure time indulging in parties where everyone is talking "very nicely" to each other and is holding a wine or a champagne glass in his hand. In such parties, everyone is dressed in their finest clothes and is behaving in the finest possible manner (although in real life, almost everyone in such a party is the exact opposite of what he displays himself to be).

If a great gamer is taken into a Victorian party, he would soon start to get more and more irritated by the observation of everything that would be occurring around him. He would talk nicely to everyone, but only up to a certain point. He would never agree to do undeserved flattery of anyone in the party (which the people in such a party are expected to do) and would abstain from consuming alcohol. To a great gamer, the undeserved flattery of a person is self-dishonoring and drugs and alcohol are just like poisons. In addition to this, the person who displays the most amounts of "personal luxuries" in a Victorian party gets the highest amount of attention and flattery. A great gamer, however, would never give high attention or flattery to such a person.

The life of a great gamer is a combination of "mild Victorianism" and "mild materialism". He likes to wear fine clothes and eat fine dishes, but only occasionally and not habitually. He likes to drive or sit in limousines and private jets, but only occasionally and not habitually. Thus, a great gamer always maintains a balance in everything in his life.

Quality 7: In the beginning of the game, he sends the "less trained" members of his group first into the gaming zone.

Comment: In the training period, a great gamer always creates a "hierarchy pyramid" with respect to the gaming skills and intelligence of his group members. The individuals that form the "base" of the pyramid are the ones that have least number of skills and have the lowest amount of intelligence. The great gamer always orders the individuals in the upper levels to keep a watch over these members and to keep them in control. He regards them as "expendable" and believes that their deaths would not alter his game plan in even the tiniest manner. The gamer regards them as cattle, but never makes them realize this truth. Thus, in order to know about the nature of the weapons and the detection technologies that the enemy possesses, he sends them first.

Quality 8: The music that is the most preferred by a great gamer is "military music" and "orchestral music"

Comment: The great gamer is only interested in two things; increasing his "playing spirit" and creating harmony and rhythm in his gaming and then amplifying it as much as he can. Military music is for the former and orchestral music is for the latter. The great gamer respects and admires Bach, Mozart, and Beethoven as much as Alexander the great, Napoleon, Patton, and Ho Chi Minh.

Chapter 5

Quality 1: In the gaming zone, a great gamer never "wastes" the ammunition of his weapons and never uses a weapon that cannot give him or his group members any kind of security

Comment: A game should be played with a great amount of pre-planning, rapid adaptation to unexpected situations and a great degree of self-control where it is "absolutely necessary". Self-control is necessary in two spheres; energy production and consumption and the rate of expenditure of the ammunition of the weapons. Only that much quantity of energy must be created and consumed as is necessary for the strong health and continuous progress of the whole "gaming group", and not any more. With respect to the ammunition of the weapons, it should only be used when it is "absolutely necessary" to do so. The great gamer avoids using weapons where he can attain success by other methods. The great gamer views the tendency for "wastage" as a disease that will eventually kill him and his group.

Sometimes it happens that a clever enemy comes to know about this tendency of his rival. Thus, using decoys and fake attacks, it makes its rival expend a huge quantity of its ammunition. Eventually a time comes when its rival has very little ammunition left in its stock and as soon as the enemy comes to know about it, it launches a massive and sudden "real attack".

A great gamer never uses or pays attention to anything that will make no contribution in his journey towards victory. These include the wildlife of his territory, the stars and the planets in the universe, the idiotic and old people in his nation and those weapons that cannot be put to any kind of use. Weapons are of two kinds; those that are used only for personal security and those that are used for killing and destroying. The motto of a great gamer is; what is useless for me does not exist for me.

Quality 2: He punishes a group member if he shows excessive fear or "disregards" his position in the hierarchy pyramid

Comment: The two mottos that a great gamer tries to instill in all his group members is; respect for the "final goal" of the game and respect for the authority. If any group member does not show respect for the final goal, he would soon abandon the group because he will believe that the pursuit of the goal is just a period of insanity that the other members are going through. If he has no respect for authority, then he would soon become rebellious or impious towards his superiors. This would lead to the breakdown of the unity in the group and the increase in the internal disorder. Thus, in order to prevent them, punishments that is created rationally and not out of pure barbaric thinking, must be given.

Quality 3: In the first phase of the gaming, he tries to destroy all the "observation" instruments of the enemy

Comment: As all wise gamers have said; if you become invisible to the enemy then you have already won half the battle. In order to become invisible to the enemy, you must either destroy or permanently disable all the observation technologies that it possesses. This can be done either by launching the "first wave" of attack not on the enemy's soldiers, but on its observation or detection instruments or by sending a "secret agent" inside the enemy's territory whose mission is to sabotage all its observation instruments. A traitor can also be created inside the enemy's territory, but this is far more difficult than sending a secret agent. The agent must be trained brilliantly in the art of hiding and the art of quick movement when his presence has not been discovered. He must also possess the ability to make his own decisions in the enemy's territory in order to complete the mission.

In a game where the two competing sides are "equally intelligent" powerful and complex security systems are created around the observation instruments. They are always a combination of a group of different kinds of weapons and cyber firewalls. However, if the first side manages to either destroy or disable all the observation instruments of the second side, then the second side has the task of re-organizing its gaming group against an invisible enemy. This is almost impossible to do.

Quality 4: He puts his enemy in such a situation that if it does not play, it will perish

Comment: The best game is played when both sides know that they will lose everything that they possess if they either play badly or do not play at all. Nature also creates the same kind of deal with all living organisms on Earth. If an organism does not wrestle with the others for food, water, and mating partners, it will soon die in a very terrible manner. Since a great gamer only shows mercy and compassion towards its enemy after it has invaded each section of its territory and captured everything that it possesses, he would say to his enemy; if you do not play, I will enter your territory and take away everything that you have.

To increase the enemy's resolve and aggression, he tries to take away an object that is of an immense value to the enemy. This object is so dear to the enemy that it believes that it cannot "live on" without it. The best one is to take away either one or two children of the leader of the enemy group.

Quality 5: He creates a security system through which he causes a great amount of damage to the enemy and very little to his own group.

Comment: The great gamer knows that his enemy can be done harm not only by weapons but also by an immensely powerful and complex security system. In addition to creating weapons of great power, he considers the creation of such a system as equally important. The harm that is done to the enemy is the expenditure of a large amount of its personal resources in trying to bypass or break down the security system of its rival. The only kind of security system that comes to mind is a "force field". Such a force field will destroy any kind of missile, radiation, and a complex object (like a fighter jet) that will collide with it. Thus, a great and long-lasting game can never be played unless both sides have created force fields around their ships, tanks, jets, and the other types of military machines.

Quality 6: The great gamer does all that he can in order to prevent the enemy from capturing his weapons

Comment: The successful capture of one or more group members is bad news for the gamer, but the successful capture of either a very powerful weapon (like a cannon or a nuke) is far worse news. Thus, the great gamer not only protects his weapons from being destroyed or disabled by the creation of force fields and cyber firewalls, but always keeps them placed even when they are on the move, in a place where the probability of capture is very low. In order to reduce this probability as much as possible, he places many his group members around the weapons. These members have very sharp sense organs and possess great fighting skills. Observation instruments are also placed around the weapons and measures are also taken to protect them from an attack.

If the gamer is extremely clever, he orders the creation of weapons that can be made to self-destruct through remote control if they get captured by the enemy.

Chapter 6

Quality 1: He increases the anxiety of his enemy by declaring to it that he has some new help arriving from a foreign territory

Comment: Both before and during a game, both sides try to increase each other's anxiety levels. This is done by both sides pretending to be much more powerful and resourceful that they really are. Thus, both sides constantly keep creating delusions. The only way to know about these delusions is to have powerful and wide reach observational instruments. Such instruments can not only see very minute details of the enemy's territory, but also see a very large area of that territory. As was said previously, the great gamer does all that it can to destroy or disable the observation instruments of its enemy. Only after this mission has been accomplished, can it proceed to create delusions with increasing boldness.

However, the declaration of foreign help is not a delusion every time. In some games, the two original gamers are soon joined by new gamers if the latter see that it would be immensely exciting to play with them. Such foreign help can be of two kinds; terrestrial (of the same planet) or extraterrestrial (from another planet). In the case of terrestrial help the original plans of the two gamers undergoes little change, but in the case of extraterrestrial help, they undergo a vast change.

Quality 2: The perfect gamer conquers his enemy on the very first encounter

Comment: In a game, no matter how great the two gamers are, they always require multiple encounters, spaced unequally with respect to time, to attain victory. All these encounters are present within the three phases of a gaming period (the low, the middle and the high). The number of encounters in the middle phase, are the highest while in the high phase, they are the lowest. Why? This is because after the end of the middle phase, the probability of victory always becomes highly asymmetric (one side has a much higher probability than the other). Thus, in most gaming periods, the high phase is of the shortest duration. If the better side has attained a higher probability of victory, it proceeds very rapidly to exterminate all the remaining "attack bases" of its enemy and to kill the leader and capture or kill all the remaining members of his group.

However, for the perfect gamer, there are no low, middle, or high phases in his gaming period. There is only one phase that consists of only one encounter. Such a gamer possesses intelligence, cleverness and technologies that are beyond the imagination of the rival side. When the perfect gamer strikes, the enemy does not even get to realize as what exactly has hit it. There is the strike and it is immediately followed by the victory.

Who is the perfect gamer? According to the laws of mathematics and physics, it is not made up of atoms and does not think "at all" like the atomic beings of the cosmos. Thus, the perfect gamer can only be God or Allah.

Quality 3: The great gamer "transforms" both mentally and physically in response to the transformations in his enemy's environment, terrain, and gaming group.

Comment: Adaptation cannot happen without transformation. This is the foundation of evolution. In the low and the middle part of the mid-phase of the gaming period, the goal of a great gamer is to maintain an equal amount of probability of victory with his enemy. This can only happen through transformations. In the gaming period, a great enemy never remains in a state of stasis, but continuously keeps on changing both its surrounding environment and the biology of itself and its group. Thus, the great gamer must make sure that none of the transformations of his enemy goes undetected (this can be altered by the destruction or disabling of the observation instruments). After successful detection, the next step would be to bring rapid change in his environment and biology. This must be done in such a manner that the new changes must not cause a lowering of the intelligence of the leader and his group and an increase in the biological fragility. Any new transformation should only make the intelligence and the biology of the group more powerful than before. This means that in a "real game", both the sides keep on getting more and more powerful. This leads to a very long middle phase period of gaming, but it finally comes to an end when one side manages to make a transformation that goes undetected by the other side.

Quality 4: When his group members become motionless in the gaming zone, he always places them in a spot which is beyond the range of the weapons of his enemy

Comment: The great gamer does not want his group members to either be injured or killed due to his own folly. Thus, it is an act of pure folly to place your gaming partners in a region of the gaming zone which is well within the range of the enemy's weapons (the range of a weapon is the maximum distance that can be travelled by its fired ammunition). The good enemy possesses multiple kinds of weapons, each having its own unique range. For a successful strike, the target must be nearly motionless. If it is moving, the probability of a successful strike at the first strike decreases. The faster it moves, the more it decreases, but it does so only up to a certain point. Then, it becomes stationary. Why? It is because the target keeps on moving in either a straight line or a ZIG ZAG manner. In order to decrease the probability further, it must be made to move in the Brownian manner (completely haphazard and unpredictable motion). Thus, when his partners have become motionless in the gaming zone, they are ordered by him to stand behind a huge obstacle, like a massive rock or a super thick artificial wall that was created before the gaming began. This is done to avoid suffering any kind of unexpected attack from an unknown weapon of the enemy. When the group finally comes out from behind the obstacle, it is ordered to move in the Brownian manner and to fire very rapidly but carefully at the enemy's group. The enemy, on the other hand, also follows the same procedure.

The great gamer applies Albert Einstein's equation of Brownian motion to the movement pattern of his group.

Quality 5: In the "art of gaming" there are three modes of playing and two modes of the formation of the gaming group

Comment: The three modes of playing are; the stealth mode, the non-stealth mode, and the hybrid mode. In the stealth mode, the gamer is invisible to its enemy for the beginning of the game till its end. However, to do justice to the enemy, the "game designer" gives it a power through which it can locate the approximate position of its rival before an attack. In the non-stealth mode, the gamer is visible to its enemy from the beginning of the game till its end. All the games that are played on the gaming consoles (XBOX, PlayStation and ones that are present in the video game parlors) belong to this kind of gaming.

The hybrid kind of gaming is the most complex kind of gaming and is the most difficult to create according to the "game designer". In it, the player is visible to the enemy at one time period and is then invisible at another time period. Playing and defeating such an opponent is the most difficult and challenging for the enemy. It must create two game plan blueprints; the first one for the stealth mode of its rival and the second one for the non-stealth mode.

In addition to all of this, the first and the third modes can be further sub-divided into two classes. In the second class of the first mode of gaming, both the rivals are invisible to each other from the beginning till the end of the game. In the second class of the third mode, both the rivals are in the hybrid state (visible at one point of time and invisible at another).

The two modes of formation are; the Phalanx and the Battalion. In the former, the gamers are arranged in a "clustered fashion". In the latter, they are arranged in a set of equally spaced rows and columns. In the phalanx formation, the army of the gamer arrives and attack in only a single wave. In the Battalion formation, it arrives and attacks in a series of waves. The Battalion formation is preferred by the intelligent and modern gamer and the Phalanx formation is preferred by the low intelligence and ancient gamer.

The gamers in the gaming zone are of two kinds; the Cavalry are the ones that fly and attack from the skies and the Infantry are the ones that move and attack from the ground. Thus, the Phalanx and the Battalion formations can be further sub-divided into three classes; the Infantry on the ground which is accompanied by a Cavalry group on both its sides, the Infantry accompanied by the Cavalry only on its front side and the Infantry accompanied by the Cavalry on both the sides as well as the front. In the second class, the Infantry is very powerful, but in the third class, it is not very powerful.

If we observe the Milky Way galaxy, we see that the 200 billion of its stars are arranged in the Battalion formation while the M51 star cluster that lies outside its plane, they are arranged in the Phalanx formation.

Chapter 7

Quality 1: The army of a gamer is of three types

Comment: The first type is the one that can battle and defeat the Infantry, but not the Cavalry. This is because it does not possess the weapons through which it can launch surface to air strikes (like the Surface to Air Missiles). Such an army can very easily be exterminated by an even moderately powerful Cavalry.

The second type is the one that can battle and defeat the Cavalry, but not the Infantry. This is because most of the gamers in it are members of the Cavalry and have little skill in killing the Infantry members on the ground. Such an army is far more abnormal in its qualities than the first type.

The third type is the one that can battle and defeat both the Infantry and the Cavalry. In such an army, the gaming group is divided equally amongst the two kinds of forces (the Infantry and the Cavalry). This type can be further divided into two classes; the non-hybrid and the hybrid. In the first class, the gamer on the ground can only fight skillfully as a soldier and not as a pilot and the gamer in the sky can only fight skillfully as a pilot and not as a soldier. Thus, if his fighter jet is shot down by the enemy's jet and he manages to survive when landing on the ground below, he is very soon killed off by a member of the enemy's Infantry. On the other hand, if an infantry member manages to capture a fighter jet of the enemy's Cavalry, he is soon killed off by another member of the enemy's Cavalry during sky warfare.

In the second class, the gamer in the sky is as good in fighting as a pilot as he is in fighting as a soldier on the ground. Thus, if he falls on the ground due to the destruction of his fighter jet, he fights as well as before and if he captures a fighter jet of the enemy, he fights with great skill and power.

Quality 2: A great gamer always provides all his soldiers with "body armor"

Comment: In the gaming zone, it is inevitable for a soldier to make at least one mistake, no matter how intelligent he is and how long and brilliantly trained he is. The less intelligent and the less trained soldiers will commit more than one mistake. The enemy, if it is a great in the art of war, will not miss the opportunity that is given to it through this mistake. It will thus try as best as it can to either kill or capture the mistake ridden soldier. If the soldier displays some escape strategies that are not expected by the enemy, he would be able to save himself from either death or enslavement, but if he does not know of any escape strategy due to the commitment of a mistake, then he is doomed. Besides giving his soldiers the best kind of training and diet, he also makes them learn the various kinds of escape strategies. The strategies are of two kinds; the first kind, are to be employed when you have run out of ammunition and the second kind are to be employed when you have committed a mistake.

The picture is different if every soldier, including their leader wears body armor. Through the armor, long lasting protection can be gained from the physical and weapon attacks of the enemy's soldiers. A soldier wearing armor can commit more than one mistake in the gaming zone, but there is also an upper limit to the number of mistakes that he can commit. The quantity of this upper limit depends upon the nature of the body armor. An armor that is made up of multiple layers of "alloys" will have a greater upper limit than the one that is made up of either a single alloy layer or a single "pure metal" layer. Every soldier in the gaming group or the army must be wise enough to know these two truths about the armor.

In addition to all of this, the great gamer or their leader also knows that if a soldier is given a great armor, his desire to play or fight increases immensely due to the increase in his courage.

Quality 3: The great gamer considers it his duty to smash the age-old truth about gaming or warfare; the more heavily armed and organized an army is, the more slowly it moves.

Comment: The movement velocity of an army or a gaming group depends upon three things: the weather conditions, the health state of the soldiers, and the amount of "luggage" each one of them is carrying. The luggage consists of all the weapons that they are carrying, the body armor and the clothes they are wearing and all the food and medical supplies they possess.

As was said before, a great gamer organizes his army into a series of waves (the Battalion). The first wave contains the least trained and the least armed soldiers while the last wave contains the best trained soldiers and the most heavily armed soldiers. However, in the gaming zone, or before entering it, all the waves move at an "equal velocity". This is done in order to prevent one wave from merging or colliding with another (it would soon destroy the Battalion formation). However, the great gamer considers it his duty to maximize the marching velocity of his Battalion and maintain the greatest possible "order" inside it at the same time.

This is deemed as an impossible task by the ancient gamers or war commanders. They said that the faster an army moves, the more disorganized it becomes due to the increase in the "entropy" of the Battalion. Every Battalion or Phalanx has its own unique "entropy value". If this value goes beyond an upper limit, the formation collapses. In order to prevent this collapse and keep on increasing the marching velocity at the same time, the great gamer uses all the known laws and techniques of mathematics and physics (including the laws of Thermodynamics). Plus, he always commences the march of his soldiers in almost perfect weather conditions and when all of them in all the waves are in almost perfect health.

In addition to all of this, the soldiers, or the gamers in the last and the second last waves of the formation are given "performance enhancing" drugs that are created by the best biochemists in the territory of the leader. In some cases, the soldiers in the last wave are not biologically like those in the other waves. They are either "meta-humans" or "mechanically upgraded" super soldiers (Like the ones in the movies Universal Soldier and Terminator: Dark Fate).

The goal of a great gamer is; the minimization of the entropy of his army and the maximization of its fighting or gaming power.

Quality 4: A great gamer uses his Cavalry for not just one, but various purposes.

Comment: In addition to attacking the enemy, the great gamer also uses it for four other purposes. The first one is for reconnaissance. A fighter jet and its pilots can be used for spying on the enemy's territory either before the game begins or during the game. Such fighter jets are equipped with radars, an infrared camera, and a normal camera. In the case of an advanced gaming force, they are also equipped with multiple tiny drones which are deployed by the pilots when flying over the enemy's territory.

The second one is for harassment. The harassment can be done through the launch of a mock attack on the enemy's soldiers below. The purpose of a mock attack is not to kill or destroy, but only to frighten. If the pilots are flying over a forest, they would deploy several "flares" which would lead to the onset of a forest fire. If they are flying over a river or a lake, they would deploy "depth charges" into them. If they are flying over a military or civilian base, they would activate a "sonic cannon" that would cause temporary deafness or strong headaches in the enemy's soldiers and people.

The third one is for the destruction of a "supply route" of the enemy through a missile attack. Through the supply route, the enemy brings the agricultural products, the factory machines, the medical equipment, and the different kinds of weapon consignments into its military bases and its cities. In the mountains, the supply routes are the narrow roads and the bridges. In the plains, they are the highways, and on the rivers and lakes, they are the bridges. The goal of a great gamer is to minimize the number of resources that they enemy will possess just before the battle or the gaming begins.

The fourth one is for the pursuit of either the enemy's escaping soldiers or of the tanks, the weapons carrying trucks, and the battle and cargo ships.

Quality 5: The great gamer always prefers to play or fight in a gaming zone where his army or group can easily "spread out" if they are ordered to.

Comment: The narrower is the structure of a Battalion, the easier it becomes to destroy it. The great gamer is fully aware of this truth. When playing in the mountain ranges, the great gamer never sends out a Battalion towards its enemy. This is because it would have to go through several mountain passes and valleys where its dimensions would be narrowed down. He would thus send only a small group of soldiers.

The narrowing down of a Battalion increases its entropy and thus its fragility. If a large Battalion is suddenly attacked inside a valley by a very powerful Cavalry of the enemy, the probability that all the soldiers would be killed is very high.

The spreading out of a Battalion decreases its entropy, but only up to a certain point. Beyond this point, it increases because the different waves of soldiers lose proper communication with each other (great communication is necessary for the preservation of low entropy).

The perfect gaming zone, according to a great gamer, is a plain of huge dimensions which is surrounded by mountains on at least three sides.

Quality 6: The great gamer has none of the qualities of a criminal

Comment: People who are not interesting in warfare or gaming and are thus pacifists, believe that there is zero difference between a great gamer and a criminal. The truth is just the opposite. A great gamer is a person of the most beautiful character that can be built in a lifetime. He believes and does all that can be done to create and preserve justice, rational benevolence, and ethics all over his territory.

A criminal tries to improve the quality of his life through two activities; robbery and "ransom demand" after kidnapping someone or sabotaging a very important device. The great gamer, on the other hand, never tries to rob any person in his territory no matter how much he needs wealth. He also never even dreams of kidnapping someone or disabling his nation's communication or electrical infrastructure and then demanding a huge ransom in order to put the situation back to normal again. The great gamer does not hate poverty, but also does everything he can to avoid it. A criminal, on the other hand, hates poverty and is willing to do anything, no matter how horrific, in order to escape from it. The criminal says: money is God. The great gamer says; self-honor is God.

A real criminal hates military training as much as he hates poverty. He dislikes talking to real warriors and sometimes "pretends" to be a pacifist. The opposite is the case for a great gamer. He believes that without properly created military training, a person's character is "incomplete".

The criminal believes in the proverb: high living and low thinking. The higher becomes the life of the criminal with respect to wealth and power, the lower becomes his way of thinking. When he reaches a great peak of wealth and power, his mind becomes almost like a wild animal.

The great gamer does not believe in the truth of the proverb: simple living and high thinking. This is because the goal of high thinking is to make own life as well as that of the others more and more complex with the passage of time. A man of high thinking will tolerate a simple life only up to a maximum time period. Beyond that, he will do all that is possible, to increase the complexity and the grandeur of his life. The great gamer cannot play for long if he is a lover of simple living. The higher you go up in the "gaming universe", the more complex becomes your way of life. If you have contempt for a life that becomes increasingly complex with the passage of time, then you can forget about being a great gamer. What is the point in high thinking if you have no desire to make your life increasingly complex?

The great gamer becomes aware of all these truths early on in his life (in his teenage years). He is also aware of a truth that is above all of these; you must become aware of the laws and rules of the "gaming universe" early in your life. If you become aware of them very late in your life (in your fifties or sixties) then there is no point in becoming a player. A philosopher said; when I understood what life is, life had passed away (this statement was also the main message of a song that was sung by the Indian singer Kishore Kumar).

When a great gamer becomes wealthy and powerful, he does all that is possible to catch and remove all the criminals from his civilization.

Quality 7: The great gamer makes sure that he and all his fellow gamers possess the ability to "run fast".

Comment: In their mental training, the soldiers of a great gamer are given the foundational knowledge of mathematics, physics, and biology and are make experts in the art of deception via cleverness. In their physical training, they are taught about the art of bodybuilding, gymnastics, and running. A soldier who is a great runner has three advantages in the gaming zone. First, he can arrive at the battlefield "before" his enemy. This gives him additional time for last minute preparations. Second, he can attack unexpectedly. An ambush can only be created by a group of soldiers who are very fast on their feet. Third, he can easily pursue an escaping enemy for a long distance. He also gives his enemy a very hard time in its pursuit of him.

Chapter 8

Quality 1: If a large part of his army is killed in the gaming zone, he immediately orders them to come back home and after this process has been completed, tries his best to create a huge army again very rapidly.

Comment: The gamers of the ancient periods, such as Alexander the great and the very first Mughal emperor Babar, went with their army into the gaming zone to fight with them. Today, however, the reality is different. The great gamer sends his army into the gaming zone or the battlefield, but sits in an ultra-secure facility that is very far away from the gaming zone. He does this because he considers the preservation of his or her life as the greatest priority during the gaming period. He will never agree to go into the gaming zone and fight with his soldiers no matter how much they or the civilians urge him.

If the enemy is successful in destroying more than 75% of his armed force, he orders them to come back home and then requests the enemy to hold on till he is again ready to play. If the enemy is also a great gamer, then it agrees to the request, but if it criminal minded, it refuses to obey, pursues, and takes the remaining 25% of the army as hostages or war prisoners and then soon launches a massive attack on the capital of its rival's kingdom or nation.

A great gamer, never tries to kill his enemy if he is requested not to. However, he shows compassion only if he is 100% certain that the enemy is not cooking up anything fishy or is setting up a booby trap through the demand for compassion. As was said before, all acts of compassion, kindness and magnanimity of the great gamer is a product of 100% rationality. The biggest killers of rationality are all the religions of the world.

The re-creation of a huge army is accomplished by two methods; a dramatic increase in the agricultural output and a dramatic increase in the number of mating and reproducing male and female pairs. The great gamers orders all of his "entertainment creating" people to rapidly increase the vulgarity and the quantity of the songs that are created by the music industry. In addition to this, the ease of access to pornography is also ramped up. The priests are ordered to encourage the people to have babies and the doctors are ordered to encourage the people to eat more and more healthy foods and avoid consuming cigarettes and alcoholic drinks. Sexual altruism is discouraged and punishments are given to those young men and women who practice it for too long.

Quality 2: The great gamer is an expert in sign language

Comment: The great gamer tries to make himself an expert in all the four possible ways of communication; through mathematics, through letters and essays, through signaling via flares and fires and through sign language. In addition to these, there is also a fifth method of communication; telepathy.

Sign language consists of a combination of multiple gestures. The complexity and the length of the message that is to be communicated, determines the number of these gestures. The great gamer knows that his enemy will constantly keep sending spies into his territory. They will be around him and would be watching him continuously. Thus, wherever he goes, he always carries with himself a group of people who are expert in the detection of spies in the surrounding environment. If, in a particular environment, a spy is detected by one of these experts, he immediately communicates to his leader through sign language about the presence of the spy. After that, the great gamer communicates this message to the other members of his via sign language and from then on, they communicated only through this kind of language.

In addition to all of this, the great gamer creates his own unique sign language so that the spy is unable to understand as to what he is saying to his group. He does all that is possible to prevent this sign language from being known to the enemy before the battle begins much later.

Quality 3: In order to gain and increase his respect amongst his people, he creates an army and tries his best to make it as huge as possible

Comment: Normal people do not pay any attention to the level of the intelligence of a ruler. Their respect of the ruler is a product of his wealth and the size of his personal army. The person who has a net worth of 2 billion dollars plus 1 million followers on social media but is as idiotic as a caveman, is far more respected than the one who has a net worth of 1 million dollars and 100 followers on social media, but has the same level of intelligence as Albert Einstein. The normal people only have respect for wealth and power and almost none for intelligence and justice. When they talk about God, they only focus on His wealth and power and never on His intelligence and His role as a cosmic judge.

A great gamer knows that the people who he rules over are 50% children and 50% animals. Thus, sometimes he treats them as children and sometimes he treats them as animals. The philosophy of "capitalism" also informs the capitalist to think this way. Thus, the greatest gamers in the world are created in a purely capitalistic nation.

Besides earning the respect of the normal people, a huge army brings two additional benefits on the great gamer. The first is a great degree of personal security and the second is the increased ability to intimidate his enemy.

Quality 4: A great gamer and his soldiers get great delight in the possession and the use of weapons

Comment: It has been said by all the aggressive and ambitious men throughout the various ages; a man is incomplete without the possession of five things, a good physique, a beautiful home, a beautiful and powerful car or bike, a beautiful wife, and a powerful gun. Thus, all that they did in their lives, from their teenage years was to make the efforts in order to build the roads which would eventually lead them to the possession of these 5 entities. However, all their efforts would never have given them anything in return if they were not great gamers.

Weapons are of two kinds; physical and psychological and the wars are also of two kinds; technological and psychological. The temporary goal of the two kinds of wars is different. Their final goal is the same; victory.

The temporary goal of a physical war is to either destroy the vital infrastructure of the enemy or to maim itself and its soldiers. The goals of a psychological war are either to intimidate the enemy or to convince it to submit without any fighting and become a slave or to put it in such a great state of confusion that it becomes almost paralyzed both mentally and physically. The use of the physical weapons is taught in the facilities that are created and run by the army and is purely for the use of the civilians. The use of the psychological weapons is taught in the schools, colleges, and the universities via the formation of "unions" (that of the students and that of the faculty members).

Before the creation of a huge army and a war-loving nation, the great gamer has two goals in his mind; to increase the "bellicose-ness" of all the men in his nation and to arm almost all of them. The first goal is achieved by a rapid increase in the creation of militarist propaganda, by increasing the production of meat and meat related products, by encouraging the population to consume more and more non-veg foods, and by a rapid increase in the production of military music and military songs. The second goal is achieved by the rapid production of various kinds of guns, semi-automatic rifles, and shotguns.

The goal of the creators of the Constitution of the United States of America was to create a nation whose gaming abilities were so great that none of the other nations, including Russia and China, would even think seriously about challenging it. By looking at the present state of the United States, it appears that the founders have failed to achieve their goal. More and more of the young of the nation are losing their health and their minds by an increasing consumption of drugs, cigarettes, alcohol and junk food, economic loss caused by climate change is increasing rapidly every year, Russia and China are getting more and more aggressive economically and in their militaristic threats, thousands of people are dying every month due to various kinds of diseases and an anti-gun lobby is getting more and more powerful due to the frequent occurrence of "mass shootings". However, all these nightmares are only temporary. America's "Golden Age" is yet to come.

The founders of America's Constitution were all great gamers and thus they created the Second Amendment. They desired to create a population that would love the acquisition and the use of weapons as much as it would love its own existence. However, they did not foresee the occurrence of one thing; the mass shootings caused by the psychotic individuals. A great gamer, in the process of arming all his people, also creates a massive infrastructure where the violent and psychotic people are treated in the best manner possible by the best kinds of doctors. He considers the preservation and the maintenance of such facilities as of a far greater importance than the preservation and upgrade of the "space industry".

In the real world, corruption is immense in all the sectors of a nation, including the medical sector. The psychotics, who come into these facilities, are not at all given the kind of care and treatment that they must be given in order to make them as normal as possible.

The greatest products of the Constitution of the United States of America are three; the Supreme Court, NASA, and the National Rifle Association (NRA). The goal of the first is to give justice to every American, the goal of the second is to expand his knowledge and the vision of the universe and the goal of the third is to instill a bellicose mentality, a great love for different kinds of weapons, and to prevent the rise of a dictator. Injustice is the greatest cause of the birth of a psychotic mind. Injustice is of two kinds; economic and genetic. The former is done by humans while the latter is done by God. We cannot undo what God does but we can undo what humans do. Thus, if America's Supreme Court was a perfect organization, it would have done its job perfectly and would have minimized the number of insane people in the nation and the mass shootings caused by them.

In his goal of creating a nation that is a great "war machine", the great gamer considers it his priority to remove all the pacifists and the BIOPHILIA (the love for plants and animals) afflicted people in his nation. You can never become a great gamer if you hate war and if you love animals and plants more than the upgrade and a glorious destiny of the nation that you are a part of.

Quality 5: Before he begins to rule them, a great gamer gives all his soldiers a minimum amount of mental and physical contentment.

Comment: When a man appoints himself as a ruler over a group of willing subjects, they believe that it is his duty to give them the amount of mental and physical contentment that they dream of. The "physical needs jar" of almost every man is far bigger and deeper than his or her "mental needs jar". Thus, if you give a normal person physical pleasure in the form of sex, delicious food, and a comfortable place for sleep, he would not demand anything else from you and would remain loyal and faithful to you for as long as you desire.

The great gamer, however, is aware of a bitter truth of the universe. The more mentally and physically contented a population becomes, the more pacifist minded it becomes. Thus, he soon creates a set of laws and an infrastructure where you can satisfy your mental and physical appetites but never to the degree that you dream of. An upper limit is set and if you try to go beyond this limit, you are given a warning by the law enforcement groups and if you go beyond it, you are punished. If the sexual appetite of every man in the nation was satisfied to the degree that he dreamed of, then all of them would turn into a Buddha. This would be catastrophic for the gamer and his nation in the long-term future.

Chapter 9

Quality 1: In order to unite his soldiers, he first divides them

Comment: There is a paradox in Zen philosophy which says that in order to unite, you must first divide. A great gamer is a combination of Alexander the Great and a great Zen master. He is a follower of Lao Tzu (the inventor of Tao) and Bodhi Dharma (the inventor of Zen). A group of people will never come together in an everlasting unity unless they realize each other's value. The value of another person is only understood during a period of a great crisis. In peacetimes, when everything is going great for us, we believe that we do not need anyone for the preservation of our mental health and our life. During their normal periods of existence, Bill Gates or ELON MUSK would never even say a word to you, you are unimportant in their eyes, no matter how much you try to persuade them, and they will try their best to keep you away from them. But if they are tossed off a ship by a hurricane into the stormy sea, and you are the only person in front of their eyes, they would burst their lungs out by talking and pleading to you for help. If you are successful in saving them, there is a high probability that they would strike a lifelong friendship with you. Such is the nature of all human beings in this world. Give a man an immense amount of wealth and power, and he will behave as a god and treat you like an insect. Throw him into a life- threatening situation where he cannot save himself by his own efforts and you are the only one around, he would treat you as a god.

Thus, when he makes plans to create an army, he executes the first phase of the project. Through a carefully created propaganda, he persuades a significant number of men to come together for a common goal. Then he places them inside a pre-created encampment. Their interactions with each other and their behavior during periods of solitude are observed by the scientists of the great gamer and by the gamer himself, through the video cameras installed in the encampment. It is observed with the passage of time, that the group members start to quarrel with each other over trivial things with increasing frequency and boast to each other that they can survive without each other. This is due to a law of physics; the Entropy of an "open system" always increases with time. With the increase in the entropy follows an increase in the Ego.

In addition to this, the great gamer also tries to increase the entropy of the encampment further by sending instructions, in a mysterious manner, to some of the soldiers to provoke each other and fight aggressively when the war spirit has been fully aroused.

When things become bad beyond the limit that is pre-decided by the great gamer, he commences the second phase of the project. It is to create a new crisis, that comes into the camp from the outside world, and which is unexpected by all the group members. The crisis can be created either by the creation of a Zen KOAN or by the creation of a disease, which is bad, but not fatal, to all members of the encampment.

A Zen KOAN is a puzzle that can never be solved either via mathematics or physics or via the rational thinking that is produced by "practical wisdom". The only way to solve a KOAN is either to ignore its existence or to destroy it. Thus, when the soldiers, in their state of huge disunity and contempt for each other, come face to face with a KOAN, they soon realize the smallness of their own intelligence and ego and thus become aware of their powerlessness in the isolated state. In order to solve the KOAN, they eventually decide to forget all their past quarrels and egoistic assertions to each other and come together to solve the puzzle to save themselves from a great tragedy. It then happens, that even in the state of unity, they are unable to solve the KOAN. It is then, that their leader decides to jump in and inform them about the origin of the KOAN and the purpose of its creation.

When the soldiers get the essential information, they breathe a huge sigh of relief and then the leader takes the responsibility of informing them about the importance of unity. He says to them; when you would be playing with the enemy in the future, situations would arise whose complexity would be almost like a Zen KOAN. The only way to overcome these kinds of situations would be to destroy the KOAN in a state of 100% unity.

When a man gets sick, his ego is chucked out of the window. In this state, he pleads with those people with whom he was fighting with, in the healthy state to stay with him as long as possible and to take great care of him. Initially, his caretakers laugh at him in their minds, but soon they get down to getting him back to normal health again. Thus, after the great gamer creates an epidemic inside the encampment, the soldiers soon forget all their personal feuds and get down to helping each other in the sincerest fashion. The great gamer sends out various kinds of medicines, doctors, and food supplies into the encampment. After a significant time period, all the soldiers in the camp get cured and the internal unity is increased by a great degree. It is then, that their leader jumps in and informs them about the origin of the epidemic and its purpose.

Quality 2: The great gamer always tries his best to increase and preserve "discipline" in his army.

Comment: All the great scientists, politicians, and the capitalists of the past and the present time were men of great discipline. It has been said that if you are ambitious, but have contempt for discipline, you can forget about becoming extraordinary in this world. The products of a non-disciplined life are 4; fear, laziness, a simpleton mind, and a hippie personality.

Who are the people who are the most in fear in today's world? They are those that are the most undisciplined. A man goes into fear if he does not get the things that he desires. The law of economics says that nothing is free in the world. Thus, by living an undisciplined life, the man is unable to earn money and acquire the things that would give him pleasure. Only the disciplined people achieve success in the economic world.

A non-disciplined person keeps getting lazier with the passage of time. This is because, non-discipline amplifies the tendency for idleness and this in turn amplifies the desire for laziness. It is a vicious cycle which keeps on getting more and more powerful and the man who gets caught up in it due to purely his own doing, is never able to get out of it for the rest of his life.

A non-disciplined person soon becomes a simpleton. Who is a simpleton? He is a person who possesses three qualities; First of all, he has no interest and is unable to understand complex mathematics, physics, computer science and the science of economics. Second, he has no ambition for above normal amounts of money, power, and pleasure. The simpleton says that you should earn only as much money as is necessary for day-to day survival, you should not try to extend your power beyond your house and you should marry and have sex and children with only one woman in your life. Third, he has total inability for "cunning" thinking and frequently does acts of great foolishness and thus becomes a source of laughter for all the non-simpletons around him.

A great gamer is aware of all these truths and the dangers obtained by not respecting them. Thus, he amplifies the degree of discipline in his army but not beyond an upper limit. Beyond this limit, the life of the soldiers becomes too hard and too painful. In such a state, they would soon become mutinous towards their leader.

Quality 3: During the training period of the soldiers, he is always on the lookout for those soldiers who display abnormal amounts of courage and vitality.

Comment: The goal of a great gamer is not to create soldiers, but to create super-soldiers. Super soldiers are the ones whose strength, endurance, vitality, and courage are far above that of the ordinary ones. Such soldiers can lift much heavier weights in the gym and in the gaming zone than the ordinary ones, are able to run longer and faster than the ordinary ones, sleep less and have a much more powerful blood circulation system and digestive system than the ordinary soldiers, and display acts of courage that the ordinary ones would never even dream of executing. If the potential super soldiers are discovered in the encampment, the great gamer isolates them from the ordinary ones and places them in a new part of the encampment where they still subjected to the old training blueprint, but are now subjected to a newly created blueprint (which the ordinary soldiers are never subjected to), are given new kinds of foods to consume, and are given some privileges which the ordinary soldiers are not given.

The great gamer is a person of pure justice. He says that everyone should get what he deserves according to his mental and physical merits and the unmerited should never get what they do not deserve.

In the gaming zone or the battlefield, the super-soldiers are placed in the last wave of the Battalion.

Quality 4: Before the real war begins, the great gamer tries his best to maximize the number of "mock wars" inside his encampment.

Comment: A real war or game can never begin without N number of mock wars or games preceding it. The value of N depends on two things; the resources and the mentality of the leader and the period of the stability of the surrounding environment. The higher the resource that a leader possesses, the higher is the value of N, for him. However, his goal is to use the least quantity of resources in each mock war. He along with the scientists, determine the quantity of resources that would be "just sufficient" enough to complete the mock war. The goal of the great gamer is to maximize the value of N in the period before the real war and to preserve "at the same time" as much of his resources as possible for the real war. This is a very challenging project to accomplish, whose success also depends upon the stability of the atmosphere and the geology of the planet and the absence of an extraterrestrial intelligent species.

It is a law of gaming or warfare that those armies, which fight the real war with a very high value of N in their training period, can easily defeat those with a much lower value of N.

Quality 5: He does not allow his soldiers to get united to an "extreme" magnitude

Comment: All the wise men in human history have said repeatedly that a "good thing" must be embraced and preserved, but if its magnitude is taken to an "extreme" point, it would cause the same amount of destruction as it's opposite. Reality gives us innumerable examples of the truth of this theory. Heat is a good thing, but if taken to an extreme, causes the same result as coldness, death.

This theory also applies to the unity of a group of people. If the members are excessively united, then they would care about each other's lives as much as their own and if one of them would die in the gaming zone, the others would feel so sad and regretful that they would be unable to fight any further. Thus, the great gamer creates a social environment inside the encampment where the soldiers are only allowed to become each other's friends and not each other's brothers or sisters or parents. Extreme unity is also the result of a deeply fulfilling sexual encounter and if an encampment contains both male and female soldiers, the frequency, and the longevity of all the sexual encounters between them are monitored and regulated very carefully by the leader and his scientists.

Quality 6: He creates a military infrastructure where his soldiers are always protected from the thoughts and the activities of the idiotic and the immoral citizens of his nation

Comment: In the world of our present times, the strong and the intelligent suffer the consequences of the thoughts and the actions of the weak and the idiotic. The strong and the intelligent desire to reach their goal or their destiny through their own self-created path, but at some point of time during their journey, their leaders, whose bodies are not only riddled with several diseases, but whose minds are unable to understand even the fundamental theories of physics and biology, create either a new law or an economic reform, which not only destroys all the progress that these brave, strong, and intelligent people have made, but also demoralizes them.

The great gamer, if he continues to remain in power, never desires this to happen. Why? It is because he and all the strong, brave, and the intelligent citizens of his nation have a common goal, the increase in the wealth and power of their nation and its rapid expansion

Chapter 10

Quality 1: When a great gamer becomes too old for his job, he willingly abandons his seat of power and replaces it with a much younger gamer.

Comment: In addition to all the goals that have been mentioned before, the great gamer is also aware of the last, but not the least one, to prevent a major accident from taking place in his army either before the gaming begins or during its period. The causes of a major accident can be three; the presence of a traitor in the group, the occurrence of a natural disaster, and the age of the leader. The last cause needs to be given the highest amount of importance if the possibility of the other two is almost zero.

It is known by all the scientists that the older you become, the more powerful become the various kinds of mental disorders like the Alzheimer's, and the Parkinson syndromes. Old people suffer from memory loss, think very slowly even on trivial matters, and become very non-ambitious because death is very near. All these qualities would result in a great catastrophe for a gaming nation sooner or later. The only way to prevent it is to create laws through ethical legislation that would prevent a leader from sitting on his seat of power for as long as he likes. In a great gaming nation, the leader is not the legislator. The task of legislation is in the hands of a small group of people who have a great degree of expertise in physics, neuroscience, and genetics. Thus, they always replace an old leader with a new and much younger one if the former is unwilling to let go of his status.

This, however, is not the case for a real gamer. When the time comes to let go of his status, he lets it go without a trace of unhappiness. In addition to this, he keeps on saying that the future of his nation lies with the young people and not with the old. He hates the proverb; old is gold. He believes that; the young are gold while the old is rusted iron.

Quality 2: If his enemy slanders him, then he, in order to preserve his reputation amongst his army, orders a "low grade" soldier to go and attack one of the border posts of the enemy for the sake of revenge.

Comment: The great gamer divides his army into three sections. The first one contains soldiers that are expendable for him under all the possible kinds of circumstances. The second one contains soldiers that are expendable for him only under a few circumstances. The third one contains those that are never expendable for him under any kind of circumstance that the universe might throw up. The first sector contains the least trained and the most idiotic soldiers, the second sector contains the normal soldiers, and the third sector contains the super soldiers. In all the gaming nations of the world, the first sector contains the highest number of soldiers, while the third sector contains the least number of soldiers.

During peacetimes, the great gamer creates the greatest amount of security around the third sector and the least around the first sector. He also treats the super soldiers as his own children and suffers a great degree of sadness when one or more of them get killed in the gaming zone or the battlefield.

In order to disturb or provoke the enemy via the launch of verbal abuses and mock attacks, the great gamer always uses the soldiers of the first sector. Since he considers them expendable, he sends them into places of great danger without thinking twice. The great gamer considers it as his goal to maintain his image in the mind of his enemy as a "no bullshit taking" player before the war begins. Thus, if his enemy throws bullshit at him, he sends his least important soldiers to clean it up and does not give a damn if they get killed in the process.

Quality 3: The great gamer always wants to reach the peak of power in his nation after passing through a period of great hardship and great military training.

Comment: As was said before, a great gamer is not and will never agree to become a great criminal. A criminal wants to acquire huge wealth and power without enduring hardship and military training. This is because he makes great efforts to run away from them. It is a law of evolution, that given the right set of environmental conditions, all organisms, whether big or small, will take the "shortest route" towards their goal. In most cases, the shortest route is the one that contains the least amount of hardship and training. In its natural environment, no organism wants to suffer pain willingly or transform its mind or body via a high degree of effort. If you go into a forest, you will never see, in your whole lifetime, an elephant reading a book that you have thrown in its path or a tiger trying to lift rocks in order to commence bodybuilding or a deer not eating the grass and just looking up at the sky and contemplating, for a very long time, on the origin of its blue color or the clouds in it. Animals never desire transformation, but will do so, only to a small degree if Nature forces them to.

The same applies to small children. They have no desire to read books, no desire to do mathematics and physics, no desire for knowing the art of war and no desire for bodybuilding or gymnastics or martial arts. As was said before, most of the people in this world are 50% small children and 50% animals. Thus, they want to reach all their goals via the shortest and easiest routes. If this is not possible, they either decide to transform themselves, but never to the magnitude that a great gamer does, or start to get more and more depressed and suicidal.

A criminal is also half child and half animal. The only difference between a criminal and a child is that he violates the human rights of others in the process of living and upgrading his life, while the child never does so. The difference between a criminal and a forest animal is that the former has a much higher degree of intelligence than the latter.

The great gamer is neither a criminal nor a child nor an animal. He appears to be a great wonder and mystery of the universe to the normal people and the criminals. Although his tendencies appear to be animalistic (hunger for food, sexual pleasure, offspring, and hierarchical power), his final goal in life is 100% dissimilar from that of a criminal or a child or an animal.

The great gamer willingly and with a great peace of mind undergoes the most brutal kinds of hardship and training because he is a die-hard follower of the proverb; no pain no gain. He believes that "real progress" is only made after the endurance of great suffering and training. The progress that is made after a small period of suffering and training or after a period of pleasure and idleness is "fake progress" and its nature is shown to its recipient very soon by the universe. The criminal always follows the proverb; great pleasures and great gains.

Quality 4: He can adapt rapidly to any kind of new environment that he unexpectedly finds himself in during the gaming period or the war.

Comment: The great gamer is just like a chameleon. He changes his colors according to the change in the surrounding environment. The colors of a gamer are his behavior patterns. Thus, like the chameleon, he only changes his colors but not his way of thinking. If a chameleon turns itself brown from green, it keeps on thinking like a chameleon and not like an Isaac Newton. Due to this nature, the enemy of low intelligence is fooled into believing that an attack from the great gamer is far off into the future or that the great gamer is a simpleton or that it wants to become its friend.

The great gamer is a perfect product of Darwinian evolution, but his final goal in life is something that Charles Darwin would never understand.

Quality 5: He does all that is possible to make sure that he and everyone else in his nation does his duty till the end of his lifetime,

Comment: All wise men have said; it is purpose that defines us and binds us. Without purpose we are nothing and we would cease to exist. It is very well known by all the practical minded people of the world that if a man does not have a purpose in life, he would soon commit suicide. It is a purpose that makes life worth living. Purpose is as important to us as the blood circulation system that is implanted in our brain and body. If purpose is the circulation system, then its center is God or Allah. Since all the blood cells in the body eventually want to reach the heart, all the people in the world eventually want to reach God or Allah.

What is the difference between purpose and duty? Does a purpose create a duty or does a duty create a purpose? A duty is either natural or unnatural. In the former, you indulge in it with a sense of happiness and pride while in the latter, you indulge with a sense of unhappiness and an injured pride. In the former come the want for food, sex, babies, and sleep. In the latter come; going to the school, doing a job, paying taxes to the government, and being obedient to the laws of the nation. A purpose is also of two kinds; that which you make by yourself and that which is imposed upon you by a superior external power. For the former, we do all that we can in order to attain it, while in the latter, we do all that we can in order to escape it.

For most people in the world, the natural duties are the creators of their purpose in life. They believe that their purpose in life is to eat well, copulate well, reproduce well, and sleep well. They do not do these for the sake of something that is otherworldly. When they have attained all of these, they become purposeless and start sliding very rapidly towards boredom and depression. In order to give them freedom from boredom and depression, an entertainment industry of global proportions has been created which runs non-stop 365 days of the year, every year. They do not, however, allow the unnatural duties to create the purpose of their life. It happens that when the entertainment world is unable to save them from suicide, caused by prolonged boredom and depression, they request an external power to give them a new purpose in their life. From this point on, the Priests step in and convince them that their new purpose is to glorify the prophet and beg to him to return to the world that he forsake and to glorify the creator of the prophet and the holy book by indulging in all the rituals. Thus, they start their lives with a self-created purpose, but end up with an externally imposed one.

The great gamer does not fall prey to such a fate. He creates a self-created purpose and sticks to it till the end of his life. Thus, he has no need for the entertainment world in order to attain peace and happiness and will never become a puppet of the Priests. Does this imply that a great gamer is an atheist? No, he is not. He believes in the existence of a creator of the universe, but does not believe in the contents of any of the various holy books of the world. According to him, religion is like a drug (like Karl Marx said) and as long as he lives, he avoids the consumption of drugs and alcohol.

In his army, he attains success by giving every soldier a purpose through the duties that he has imposed upon them. The soldiers of the great gamer do their imposed duties as cheerfully as they would do their natural duties.

Chapter 11

Quality 1: After a great army has been created, the great gamer considers his prime duty to preserve its hierarchy pyramid

Comment: It is known to every scientist that where "order" exists, it is purely because of the creation of a hierarchy pyramid. Order is the product of a hierarchy pyramid. It is impossible to create and increase the magnitude of the order in a civilization without the construction of a hierarchy pyramid. Thus, a group of people who live and work for a final goal or purpose always live their lives inside a hierarchy pyramid and do everything that they can in order to preserve its existence and its continuous state of growth. If the pyramid exists, they are united and if it is destroyed, they will immediately realize that there is no meaning of them living together.

There are two qualities of a hierarchy pyramid; its size and its lifespan. The size of the pyramid is a product of the size of the population and the number of different kinds of "levels" in it. Each level rules the one that is below it and never allows the inferior one to rule it. A member of a level is known as a "HOLON" and the number of HOLONS in each level decreases as we go up the pyramid. The rate of the increase in the height of the pyramid depends upon the rate of population growth and the rate of the growth of new knowledge. As some new piece of knowledge in either mathematics or physics is added to the civilization, a new level is added to the pyramid and some of the HOLONS of a specific level are transferred into either a higher level or an even lower level. The rate of the population growth depends upon the rate of increase of the agricultural output and the frequency of the occurrence of natural disasters.

The lifespan of the pyramid depends upon its height and the gravity of the planet on which it is created. Taller hierarchy pyramids are always longer lived than the less-taller one because they contain a greater amount of energy due to the presence of a greater number of levels and HOLONS. Thus, the goal of all the mathematics and the other branches of science is to maximize the height of the hierarchy pyramid of the civilization. The more the height increases, the greater becomes the magnitude of the "order" inside the civilization. The continuous increase in the height of the pyramid keeps on decreasing the two disorder creating powers; the criminals and all the religions. Thus, in a civilization that has attained the greatest possible height of its pyramid, all its members are atheists.

A hierarchy pyramid is highly like a mountain. It is known by all the geologists of the world that any mountain on Earth cannot become higher than 35,000 feet. This is purely because of the magnitude of the gravity of the planet. The taller a mountain becomes the more unstable its upper portions become. A mountain can reach a great height only if the diameter of its base also keeps on increasing "in tandem" with the increase in its height. When we apply this fact to the hierarchy pyramid of a big civilization, the lowest level should contain the highest number of HOLONS. The increase in the population of the HOLONS in the lowest level, increases the diameter of the base of the pyramid and in this situation, the upper levels can afford to go even higher than before (they can move to a "higher plane" of existence). The lowest level of the pyramid contains the poorest people of the civilization. This is the reason as to why the government and the capitalist community of every major nation of the world make great efforts to maximize the population of very poor people.

The conclusion that we can draw from this theory is that the gravity of the planet not only determines the rate of growth of the population of the dominant species on it, but also how high the global population can reach. For Earth, the upper limit is around 10 billion people. If the planet was 1.5 more massive than it currently is, this number would be around 7 billion.

The great gamer is aware of all these truths. Thus, after becoming the leader of a nation, he sets forth to rapidly develop further the hierarchy pyramid that was created by his ancestors and to make some new changes in it. He creates three kinds of pyramids; those with respect to intelligence, those with respect to the political power and those with respect to the physical abilities. After creating each of them separately, he proceeds to join them together through a bridge that consists of a set of laws that are created by the best legislators in his nation.

Quality 2: He keeps the greatest degree of observation on the new soldiers that come into his army and the least on the most experienced ones

Comment: One of the greatest fears of a great gamer is the unexpected eruption of a mutiny within his army before the gaming or the war begins. The probability of the eruption is the highest inside the group of soldiers that are the FRESHERS (new students) of the army. Since they hardly know anything about the other "senior" soldiers of the army and the character of their leader, they are the most susceptible to being transformed into traitors by a spy of the enemy and most susceptible to forgetting their proper place in the hierarchy pyramid. Thus, as long as they remain untrained and inexperienced, they are kept under a great degree of observation by their leader and through both the senior soldiers and "specially appointed" trainers.

Quality 3: If one of his soldiers transform into a traitor, he does not kill him, but sends him into his enemy's army.

Comment: For a great gamer, his spirit of compassion is as great as his spirit of playing or fighting. Thus, when he discovers a traitor in his army, he gives it what it desires; to become a part of the enemy's army and to fight with his army. He orders this to be done only if the traitor does not make any attempt to kill him. He is first and foremost a spiritual person and according to spirituality, you have no right to take the life of any human being because you did not give it to him in the first place. However, it also says that if the other person is trying his best to take away your life, then it is righteous to kill him.

By sending the traitor into the enemy's army, he not only foils the plans of his enemy, but also receives a temporary gratitude from it.

Quality 4: After attaining victory, the great gamer never becomes unaware of the remaining parts of the enemy.

Comment: In martial arts, after the end of the battle, the loser always had to make a respect filled "bow-down" to the winner. The winner, on the other hand, also did the same to the loser. According to a law of martial arts, you must show a minimal amount of respect to the loser because he also trained as hard and in the same disciplined manner as you, before the battle. However, the great martial artist, Bruce Lee said that even when you are bowing down to your defeated enemy; never take your eyes away from him. This is because, in his state of boiling anger, he might try to deliver a last second revenge attack on you. If you are not watching him, you would be completely unprepared for this attack. Thus, it is highly probable that the enemy will get what it desires; to give you a life-threatening injury.

Thus, the great gamer follows the Bruce Lee principle. After victory, he remains as alert and careful as he was before and during the battle. After a large part of the enemy has been annihilated and victory is achieved, he orders his best soldiers to immediately pursue and capture the remaining soldiers of the enemy and to kill those who make a final try to kill them.

Quality 5: During the game, he wastes no time and makes an announcement to his army in the loudest possible manner, if someone very important from the enemy's side has been killed.

Comment: The soldiers of the great gamer are always hungry for encouragement, before the war and during the war. Before the war, the great gamer tries to encourage them to fight by informing them about his character, the rewards that they would receive if victory was attained, and by equipping all of them with body armor. Soldiers would willingly "fight to death" in the battlefield if they are convinced that their leader is a person of a character of immense beauty. They would also fight with immense ferocity if they know that the rewards of victory would be immensely pleasurable to them (beautiful women and great treasures).

During the game or the war, it becomes extremely hard to give them encouragement to keep on fighting. The only way this can be done is by appointing a few individuals whose only task is to immediately inform the soldiers if someone very important on the enemy's side has either been captured or killed.

Quality 6: Before or during the war, the great gamer creates "unusual objects" in the gaming zone or the battlefield

Comment: The goal of a great gamer is to temporarily destroy the "mental focus" of his enemy. This he does through two ways; by launching a surprise mock attack in his enemy's territory and by creating an unusual looking object in the battlefield before the war begins. The great gamer makes sure that his enemy possesses no knowledge of the nature of the unusual object and did not foresee its creation. In the art of war or gaming, the creation of surprises is as important as the creation of powerful weapons and new strategies and tactics.

Chapter 12

Quality 1: The great gamer is always aware of the truth; if you believe that you can never win, you will be defeated

Comment: As all the wise men have said; victory only comes to those who believe in its existence. When a great gamer looks at an equally powerful enemy or an even more powerful one, multiple thoughts are created in his mind. The two most important ones are; how long will the war with this enemy last? And, will I attain victory in the end? The answer to the second question is connected to the first. The longer a war lasts, the higher becomes the probability of a "stalemate". This is because there comes a point when the human and the non-human resources of both the sides have reached an equally low level.

In order to maximize the probability of victory, the great gamer always tries to finish the game or the war in the shortest possible time period. His enemy also does the same thing. However, in such a situation, there soon comes a point when the level of the human and the non-human resources of one side is higher that than of the other. When this has occurred, the side with the higher resources wastes no further time and by ordering a sudden acceleration of his army in the warzone, moves inside the enemy's territory and ruthlessly exterminates all its remaining soldiers.

We have all heard the story of the king who, after suffering a temporary defeat, escaped from his army and hid in a cave. As he sat over there, he was completely convinced that he had lost the war and victory was just a fantasy. However, at that point of time, a spider appeared on a wall in front of him. It was going towards its web at the top of the wall, but fell many times to its bottom. Finally, a moment came when it kept on climbing and reached its web. It attained success because its determination to reach its goal was not crushed even by a tiny amount due to the multiple falls. The king took on the mentality of the spider, went back to his army, reorganized it, fought again and eventually won.

Quality 2: In order to maintain the fighting spirit of his soldiers at the same as it was at the beginning of the war, he tries to impress them as much as possible with the beauty of his character

Comment: As was said before, soldiers would willingly fight to their deaths for a leader whom they truly respect and admire and whom they consider as having a greater character than themselves. If a leader wants his soldiers to admire and respect him, then he must not be licentious, talk foolishly, show irrational fear, and anger, and have a great taste for things that have absolutely nothing to do with the art of war. Thus, the leader that is respected the most by his soldiers is the one who displays all the aspects of his "private life" to them. The great leader never maintains any kind of secrecy from his soldiers.

The great leader always tries to minimize the duration of the war because he knows that the longer the war lasts; the more irritated his soldiers become (their longing to return to their homes and families increase with time) and the probability of them forsaking him keeps on increasing. However, these can be prevented by the application of the above-mentioned method.

Quality 3: When a great gamer gives a speech or a lecture, him wants his soldiers to listen to him as carefully as they can and never to interrupt him in the middle.

Comment: A soldier, who does not listen with full mental focus to his leader's speech or lecture and interrupts him during it course, can be either of the two things; a traitor or a potential future mutineer. Thus, the great gamer considers it as his duty to spot such individuals in his army and to scold them for their impious behavior. If they refuse to change after two or three scolding, he immediately removes them from the training encampment and sends them to a psychological evaluation facility where their real intentions are eventually determined and informed to their leader.

Quality 4: The nation's flag acts as a "spirit up-lifter" for the soldiers

Comment: The great gamer knows that there are three things that uplift the fighting spirit of his soldiers; the beauty of his character, the photographs of the enemy nation's women and the national flag of their leader's nation.

Most men in their youth believe that there are only three things on this planet that are worth fighting for; money, power, and beautiful women. The fight or the gaming for money is known as "business". The gaming for power is known as politics, but there is no word that represents the gaming for beautiful women.

This is because if a man acquires great wealth or power, then he automatically becomes attractive to beautiful women, no matter how ugly looking he is, physically. Thus, the gaming for the conquest of beautiful women is 50% business and 50% politics.

After he displays to his army, the beauty of his character, many them would happily fight to death for their leader, but there will always remain plenty of soldiers with a powerful physique, good training and good intelligence who would show reluctance to fight. In this situation, the great gamer knows what should be done to make them as fanatical minded as the rest. In the first phase, he would separate them from the army and subject them to a psychological evaluation. The goal of the psychologists would be to determine the magnitude of the licentiousness of these soldiers. If all of them turn out to be extremely licentious and great lovers of sexual pleasure (which all soldiers are, because they are primarily beings of the "body" and not of the "mind"), then the great gamer would proceed to the second phase. In the next phase, the great gamer would show them photographs of the young women in his enemy's nation. If all these women turn out to be far more beautiful in the eyes of the soldiers, than those of their own nation, then their gaming or fighting spirit would take a "quantum leap" in the upward direction. But at this point, there lies a hidden danger which the great gamer would be aware of. During the war, their mind would be far more focused on the women of their enemy's nation than the enemy soldiers in front of them. During the reloading and the firing of the weapons, they would keep on dreaming about them and this would eventually cause a great accident to occur. Thus, after the photographs have been taken away, the great gamer would send them back to the army and then give them strict orders to keep their minds 100% focused on the warzone and not on one of the rewards of victory.

The display of the nation's flag also uplifts the spirit of the soldiers, but nowhere near as much as the photographs of the young women of the enemy nation. A nation is always represented by two kinds of symbols; the living and the non-living. The living symbol is its leader and the non-living one is its flag. Since all the soldiers in an army are living things, the primary source of their fighting spirit is the physical and character beauty of the nation's leader and the flag is the secondary source. They always give more importance to the beauty of his character than that of his body. A leader with a character of great beauty has no need to build and preserve a beautiful body.

If the character of the nation's leader is very ugly, then he would soon become in charge of an army that would be filled with mutineers and "lady minded" soldiers. If an evil leader creates an extremely beautiful national flag, then he will not acquire an army that loves him and has 100% faith in him. The creation of an extremely beautiful flag should always be accompanied by a leader of a beautiful character. If not, then defeat and invasion are 100% certain. If, however, a leader possesses a beautiful character, then the creation of a beautiful flag is not very important.

The flag of the United States of America is a great example of what has been said above. The beauty of its flag is greater than the character of the president of the nation. The leaders of that nation, which include all the Senators of the Senate, the generals of the Pentagon and the President, wanted an army in which all the soldiers loved them. They knew that if they displayed to them their "real character", then most of the soldiers would abandon the army without giving a second thought, but they tried to solve the problem of loyalty by not letting them know anything about their private lives and by creating a national flag of great beauty.

The flag of USA is a combination of two sectors. In the first sector, there are 50 stars that are embedded in a deep blue medium and in the second sector there is an alternating pattern of red and white stripes. What message do these two sectors give? The first sector informs the enemy that the USA is a combination of 50 "states" and each state is as glorious and powerful as a star of the Milky Way galaxy (this is of course a lie) and that they are emplaced in an ocean that is blue and not black colored.

The message of the second sector is far more serious. The red stripes imply that the USA is a blood drinking and blood spilling nation and the white ones imply that after a period of blood drinking and blood spilling it gives the victimized nation and the other nations, the light of "enlightenment" (which is always white in color).

Before and during the war, the great gamer would place the nation's flag at specific pre-chosen spots outside the war zone and inside the war zone.

Quality 5: The army of a great gamer maintains its original level of organization inside multiple kinds of different environments.

Comment: In the Darwinian evolution theory, the most successful species on a planet is the one that survives and thrives "equally well" inside more than one kind of environment. Thus, for a species that is a great masterpiece of evolution, its members remain as healthy and fertile in a polar climate as they were in a tropical climate. When it comes to the great gamer and his army, he is acts as an "evolution creating force" (just like the Sun or radioactivity) and the army is his product, but unlike the natural evolutionary forces, he evolves his army according to a carefully created plan. The goal is to create an army that would fight with an equal ferocity and magnitude of organization in multiple kinds of climatic zones.

Quality 6: For rare the soldiers who show reluctance to fight even after witnessing the beauty of the character of their leader and the pictures of the women of the enemy's nation, the great gamer says to them; if you do not fight, then you will be punished by God after you die.

Comment: As was said before, the perfect civilization is the one where every individual is an atheist and considers all the religions as diseases or drugs. However, there is a paradox over here. The perfect civilization is not necessarily the most war minded or the best fighting civilization. The perfect civilization is the one which is the most creative in mathematics, physics, genetics, and philosophy. However, it never creates any kind of weapons using all these fields of knowledge. It only uses the knowledge of these various fields to keep on increasing the health and the lifespans of all its members and to keep on increasing its expansion in the Cosmos. Since it possesses no weapons, it stays away from those planets where it would have to fight a much lower, but highly militarized civilization in order to establish a colony.

The situation is different for a civilization whose foundation is based on a single religion. Such a civilization, unlike the prefect civilization, believes in the existence of something known as God or Allah, and believes in the existence of good and evil (unlike the prefect civilization). Thus, a great gamer in such a civilization believes that any person who does not do his duty is an evil person. It is the duty of a soldier to fight in the warzone, but if he does not do his duties, then his leader considers him as an evil person. Since a war hungry leader requires as many people as he can in order to play in the warzone and maximize the probability of victory, he tries to persuade the duty hating soldier to change his mind and fight.

If the soldier keeps his constant, the leader attains failure. From this point on, two situations can arise. In the first case, when the leader threatens to kill the soldier for his behavior, he changes his mind and goes into the warzone to fight.

In the second case, after the death threat from his leader, the soldier keeps an unchanged mind. Over here, the non-clever leader goes ahead and kills the soldier, but the clever leader says to him; you will die one day and when your soul will go up to God, He will immediately insert you into Hell and punish you for an eternity for the non-fulfillment of your duty. Since the soldier is not an atheist and does not know as to what will happen to him after death, the tactic usually gives success to the leader.

In the US, we observe the rapid and ongoing growth of fascism that is in 100% coherence with the rapid growth in the power and spread of Christianity.

Chapter 13

Quality 1: The great gamer will never desire to go to war with his enemy if he does not have an advantage over it.

Comment: There are two kinds of wise people. The first kind, are pacifistic and are usually found in the villages of a nation. The second are militaristic and are always found in all the great cities of the nation. A militaristic person is a complexity loving person and thus prefers the "complex life" over the simple life. A complex life can only be developed and preserved in a city of great dimensions and never in a village. People, who live a simple life in a great city, always end up as insanity ridden individuals. It is a law of economics that in order to live a good life and have a good mental health in a big city, you "must" become militaristic minded if you are pacifistic minded initially. A pacifist will not remain a pacifist if he keeps on increasing the complexity of his life.

The wisdom of a militaristic person is considered as a treasure by those young men who want to live a life of immense complexity and huge challenges and who want to attain honor and glory in it and after death. The wisdom of a pacifist is considered as a treasure only by those men who either want to become farmers in a village for their whole life or want to become "hippies" in a big city.

When a young soldier approaches a militaristic person of great wisdom for advice, the first thing that he tells him is; when you are going to fight with an enemy that is as powerful or even more powerful than you, never start to fight unless you have an advantage over it and make sure that it remains unknown to it till the war begins. The creation or the inheritance (from the universe) of an advantage that is unknown to your enemy increases your probability of victory and if you create or get another new and unknown advantage, it is increased further.

The advantage can be of two kinds; with respect to the physical abilities and with respect to the intelligence. In all the wars or games, both the sides try their best to increase the quantity of both the two kinds of advantages.

Quality 2: In the war, the great gamer will fight till his death if there is no escape route available to him.

Comment: The process of escaping death is also an art. In the animal kingdom, there are two ways of doing it; by the deployment of a single or multiple decoys or by "playing dead" (the gecko lizard and the centipede are the best examples). Some animals also release a bomb that is either made up of a black fluid or an extremely foul-smelling substance (the squid and the skunk are the best examples).

However, this is only the first phase of the entire process of a successful escape from the enemy's clutches. In the second phase, the organism must have knowledge of an escape route on which it can travel without stopping while the enemy is still focused on its decoy. An escape route can either be natural or artificial (built by the organism before its encounter with its enemy).

Based on their nature, an escape route can either be in the sky or on the ground or underground. Underground escape routes offer the highest probability of a successful escape and a ground based one offers the least. When it comes to the expenditure of energy, an underground escape route needs the highest amount of it to get built while the sky based one requires the least.

In the third phase of the escape process, the organism must locate and join up with a large group of the members of its species. The location period must be as short as possible because if the organism is alone, it is still extremely vulnerable. Both its group and it must have a powerful signaling device (a flare or a laser beam emitting torch). Only when it successfully rejoins its group, does a rational brained organism, loses a great amount of fear.

A great gamer always creates multiple escape routes. One of them is through the sky, the other is through the surface of the earth and third one is underground. The best thing about the underground world is that multiple escape routes can be created in it in the form of tunnels. On the surface, multiple escape routes can only be created in a mountainous region, but on a plain, only one can be created. In the sky too, only one can be created.

The great gamer knows about the two truths of any enemy. First, if he creates not one, but multiple escape routes, then his enemy would never pursue him because then it would have to divide its army into several groups. No intelligent enemy wants to do this. Second, if he drops some expensive items in the enemy's path (like a few gold bars or a small pack of diamonds), then it would first go for the expensive items and then for its prey. However, if the enemy does not show greed on the battlefield, it would ignore the expensive items and go straight for its prey. This is almost impossible because only greedy people indulge in gaming and warfare and greedy people show greed everywhere.

If he is unable to discover an escape route or is unable to construct it, he differs from a child and an animal. When a child is caught by its enemy, it just surrenders immediately without any verbal or physical retaliation. When an animal is caught by its predator, it executes physical retaliation, but only to escape from its enemy's mouth or hands. It does not attack its enemy directly.

For the child and the animal, there is no such thing as the preservation of self-honor. When they are convinced that defeat is 100% certain, they just let go. However, the great gamer never does this. Even when he is convinced that his defeat is 100% certain, he delivers an all-out last moment attack on his enemy and does not give a damn about his death. He believes that self-honor is bigger than life.

Quality 3: The goal of the great gamer is to drain away the initial enthusiasm of his enemy and attack when success has been achieved

Comment: Before the game or the war begins, both the sides have a certain magnitude of enthusiasm for the things that are going to happen in the future. However, this enthusiasm is not 100% pure and is adulterated with anxiety. If both the sides contain great leaders, then each tries to increase the quantity of the impurity, which is anxiety, and to decrease the quantity of the base substance, which is enthusiasm. The base ingredient is itself made up of two things; optimism and the fighting spirit. The impurity is also made up of two things; fear and skepticism. The great gamer knows that enthusiasm is like the colligative property of water (the boiling and the freezing points at sea level). The property depends upon the quantity of the solute inside the solvent.

In the case of enthusiasm, the solvent is a compound that is 50% optimism (the firm conviction of victory) and 50% fighting spirit (the desire to kill and destroy). The solute is 50% fear and 50% skepticism (the uncertainty of victory). Thus, the great gamer tries his best to maximize the quantity of the solute in the mind of the enemy's leader. The lowering of the fighting spirit and the increase in the anxiety can be done in two ways; by the secret deployment of a disease-causing pathogen in the enemy's territory or by the distribution, in a cunning manner, of serotonin increasing tablets.

The spread of an epidemic in the enemy's territory causes the destruction of the mental and physical health of most of its soldiers. Thus, they will not desire to fight. A soldier only desires to fight if he is in great health.

The consumption of serotonin enhancing tablets will make the soldiers feel satisfied and happy without indulging in a war and attaining victory. Aristotle said that the goal of all activities is to acquire happiness in the end. This also applies to gaming or war. The pursuit of a victory is for the sake of the attainment of happiness. However, if the mental state post-victory can be artificially created through a drug, then the fighting spirit of the person will almost vanish. If he is told to fight because it is his duty, he will reply; why should I fight when my life is great and I am happy?

Quality 4: The great gamer tells his people that they must look at war just like a hungry lion looks at a piece of meat

Comment: A nation that is a perfect "war machine" can only be created if its every citizen loves to initiate and engage in a war. However, there is a great danger in trying to make every citizen "war hungry". If the hunger for war of each citizen turns towards the other citizens, then the nation will collapse very rapidly. This is exactly what is happening in the United States. The proof of this is the mass shootings and the isolated homicides that are becoming more frequent each year.

The great gamer through his speeches and legislators, tries his best to tell the people that they must direct their hunger for war towards the people of other nations and not on each other. He says that each citizen of the nation, including himself, is a cell in the body of a lion. The enemy nation is the piece of meat. If the cells of the lion's body start to fight against each other, then the lion would die before reaching and grabbing the piece of meat in its mouth and then consuming it. Thus, for the lion to reach its goal, all its cells must be locked up in a symbiotic relationship. The strongest and the longest lasting nation in the world is the one where all its citizens are held together in a symbiotic relationship. The sad news is that such a nation is only a scientific, legislative and a political fantasy. No leader of any nation on Earth in the entire history of the modern world has been able to create such a nation. I believe that such a nation would never be born in the future due to the impossibility of the extermination of Class Warfare. The rich believe that what is good for them must never be given to the middle and the lower classes. The middle class believes that it is the most virtuous and intelligent of the three classes and the lower class believes that it is the most brutalized and that great injustices are done to it regularly by the other two classes. Thus, the contempt between the three classes never goes away and the source of this is the "economic inequality" between them.

As-long-as the phenomenon known as "economics" exists, the population of any nation will be divided into the three classes and class warfare will continue. This implies that in the long-term future, economics becomes the greatest destroyer of a nation.

If the citizens regard the enemy nation as a piece of meat, then they would also get great pleasure when they would witness the great destruction of its civilian and military infrastructure.

Quality 5: The great gamer does not demand perfection from the untalented and the unskilled

Comment: The great gamer always makes great efforts to increase the fighting and the physical abilities of his soldiers, but before he subjects them to their training period, he subjects them to an examination of the genome of their brain cells and that of their body cells. If his geneticist informs him that a particular examined soldier does not have the genetics to become a John Rambo like soldier, then he never makes the soldier do tasks that could be done only by a John Rambo like soldier. In the encampment, each soldier is put into a group that is almost like him genetically. Each soldier is given the kind of training that is the best for his genetics and would maximize the various abilities that are present in it.

The great gamer is a pure materialist when it comes to mental and physical abilities. He believes that the genetic qualities that a man inherits from his ancestors can never be broken down or defied. If a man is genetically programmed to become and remain an idiot for his entire life, then no amount of education or any kind of teacher can change his destiny. The great gamer does not believe in "divine miracles".

Chapter 14

Quality 1: The great gamer makes great efforts to attract and seduce the best soldiers and the best scientists of his enemy

Comment: It has been said that if you are successful in robbing a person of his most precious possessions, then you have turned him to a comatose patient. For a gamer, his most precious possessions are not his children, but his super soldiers and the geniuses of his nation's scientific community. He gives them a greater amount of security and care than he gives to his children. This is because he believes that the future of his nation lies as much as in their hands as it does in his own hands. He spends a great amount of the resources of the nation to keep them happy and to keep them loyal and faithful to him.

It was said by Sun Tzu, that the greatest gamer or fighter is the one who wins a war with a little or zero expenditure of his own resources. The goal of achieving victory through this method can be done in two ways. The first method is; to make the leader of the enemy nation either insane or stupid and second, to seduce and take away all its super soldiers and scientific geniuses. The second method is much easier than the first. It requires a lower expenditure of personal resources and can be accomplished even by spies of low skills.

It is a known fact that the best soldiers and the best scientists of any nation of the world are not moral and self-control loving beings. If you become a super soldier, you reach the peak of all your biological powers, including your reproductive power. Thus, the passion for women and sex of a super soldier are great as his passion for bodybuilding and weapons. The same applies to a genius. Their passion is primarily for wealth, but their passion for sexual pleasure is also greater than that of normal human beings. If we look at world history, two great examples come up. The first is that of Isaac Newton. The primary passion of this genius was for knowledge and creativity. Thus, he acquired all the accumulated knowledge of mathematics and physics very rapidly and then proceeded to create Differential Calculus, the Prism, and the

Reflecting Telescope. However, his greatest achievement was the creation of the immortal book, Principia MATHEMATICA. Initially, he kept all the material of the book with himself, but after he acquired some rich and powerful friends, they urged him to publish his book and he did it, ASAP. This, is because his passion for wealth was nearly as great as his primary passion. The book increased his wealth very rapidly and made him famous all over the United Kingdom and Europe. However, his passion for sexual pleasure was zero and due to it, he died as a virgin, but this does not imply that he was a moral being. He was not a moral being because he was racist (considered the Jews as the most supreme race of Earth), respected the Bible as much as the PRINCIPIA MATHEMATICA and did nothing for the extremely poor people of his nation.

The second one is that of Erwin Schrödinger. This genius invented the Schrödinger Wave Equation and the Affine Field Theory. His passion for knowledge and creativity was as great as his passion for sexual pleasure. Thus, he married twice and in addition to this, also possessed several mistresses and teenage women. It has been said that outside his two marriages, he fathered several illegitimate children.

In the case of Albert Einstein, his passion for knowledge and creativity was much higher than his passion for sexual pleasure, but the latter was not zero either.

In the pre-battle period, the great gamer sends men into his enemy's nation and orders them to talk to all the super soldiers and the science geniuses. When his sent people finally meet up with their target individuals, they ask them the many questions that were created by the best psychologists and the neuroscientists of the great gamer. The goal is to know whether their mind is of the Isaac Newton type or the Erwin Schrödinger type or the Albert Einstein type. When they have collected all the necessary data, they come to their leader, ASAP.

The great gamer tries to seduce the Isaac Newton type super soldiers and scientists through the message that they would be given a far greater amount of salary and privileges than they get in their own nation. For the Erwin Schrodinger types, he tries to seduce them by promising them to give the most beautiful women of his nation and for the Albert Einstein types, he tries to seduce them by promising them both great wealth and beautiful women.

Quality 2: The great gamer says to his soldiers during their training and just before a war begins; if you can conquer something "big" do not waste your time and energy on conquering something "small"

Comment: The great gamer is a "big minded" person and always displays large mindedness in all his speeches. He is not focused on fighting and conquering small things, like his next- door neighbor's house or his teachers at the school or college or the person that he loves. He is focused on conquering a big business corporation of his nation or the government of another nation or the entire planet. Does this mean the best kind of gamer is the one who has an imperialistic mentality? Yes, that is true, but here too there is something new to be said.

Imperialists are of two types; the Nero type and the Julius Caesar type. The first type, are always the inheritors of the creations and the powers of the second type. By themselves, they do not create anything new. They only sit in their grand palaces, keep on living their prodigal and licentious lives and do nothing to inspire their soldiers and their scientists. When they do issue new orders, they are always a product of their whim and their low intelligence. The Nero type imperialists want their scientists and their soldiers to do their job and eventually come back to them and give them a splendid and delicious dish to eat. When his soldiers are in front of him, they remain in a state of fear, loyalty and display fake respect, but when they are inside their encampment, they say to each other; what an asshole he is. What sin did we commit in our previous life in order to inherit such a leader? I will never lay down my life in order to save his ass no matter how much money he gives me beforehand for such an action.

The Julius Caesar type imperialists are the ones who the founders of a great empire, are the role models of their people, their soldiers and, their scientists and shine on like blue supergiant stars in the history books after their death. They are the creators of the standards and the records through which all the future great gamers judge their own abilities. In addition to the creation of a great empire, they also create its very first set of laws. Thus, they are as great in the art of legislation as they are in the art of war.

Since they soon become the idols of their soldiers and their scientists, the latter soon start to imitate them. Only after the Caesar type imperialist observes this happening, does he give them the most important message of their lives; my friends never think small. Always think big and of the creation and the acquisition of the big things of the world. Focus on the small only for the sake of attaining the big. Never focus on the small for its own sake.

Quality 3: When surrounded by his enemy's soldiers, the great gamer orders his own to attack them and uses the fighting period to escape from the scene

Comment: When fighting or playing with an enemy that is equally intelligent, equally resourceful, and equally powerful, unexpected things are bound to occur. The great gamer knows that no matter how great his plans are the enemy would eventually find a "crack" (weak point) in it and immediately slip in a group of its own soldiers. They eventually reach the spot where the great gamer is seated and surround him from all sides. If this does happen, the great gamer always keeps ready an escape plan. There are three kinds of escape plans; first, to activate a device whose existence was completely unknown to the enemy and use it to either kill all the soldiers or to escape them (an invisibility cloak is a great example). Second, to self-destruct using a bomb and third, to surround oneself by your own soldiers before the enemy's soldiers arrive and order them to fight till their deaths in order to save your life.

The second strategy is followed by a gamer which puts his self-honor above his own existence. This mentality was seen by the alien in the Hollywood movie Predator.

Quality 4: In a dangerous situation, he looks at "all" the abilities of his soldiers.

Comment: During peacetimes, a great gamer only pays attention to the biggest qualities of his soldiers. They are; courage, patriotism, intelligence, and physical health. He remains ignorant of their minor qualities. These are; the amount of interest in philosophy, the magnitude of licentiousness, the degree of attachment to their wife and children, and their level of interest in forests and animals. However, just before the beginning of a major war and during its running period, the minor qualities are given as much importance by the great gamer as the major qualities. It always happens that the great gamer orders his soldiers to sacrifice the minor qualities for the sake of the preservation and the amplification of the major. Thus, the soldiers are ordered to stop taking interest in philosophy, eliminate their licentiousness, stop taking interest in their wives and children, and pay no attention and importance to the natural world of their nation. The great gamer knows that if the minor qualities are not fully exterminated, then the probability of victory is low.

Chapter 15

Quality 1: During the war, he stops his good soldiers from rescuing the bad ones

Comment: As was said before, a great gamer considers his/her best trained and the most intelligent soldiers as his greatest asset (even more than his/her own children). According to him they are expendable, but they should die either in a glorious manner or in trying to save his life. They should not die in a wretched manner.

According to a great gamer, a great soldier dies a wretched death if he is; killed by a natural disaster or killed by a disease or killed by an insane civilian or killed in a road accident or killed in the warzone by trying to rescue a defect ridden soldier. The great gamer knows that he can do nothing to prevent the occurrence of natural disasters in his nation. That lies in the hands of God or Allah. However, he tries his best to make his nation as free of all kinds of parasites, viruses, and bacteria as possible through the creation of a disease monitoring and eliminating organization. In the United Sates, such an organization is known as the Center for Disease Control (CDC).

To exterminate the population of insane people in the civilian population, he tries his best to maximize the speed of the economic growth of the nation so that every citizen would not be deprived of the four necessities of life; food, water, house, and a mating partner. In addition to this, he creates many hospitals which contain highly trained psychiatrists and psychoanalysts. However, he gives the greatest importance to the creation and the growth of pharmaceutical organizations. This is where new kinds of medicines for the preservation and the uplift of mental health are created. The psychiatrists are a bridge between these organizations and the civilian population.

To minimize the occurrence of road accidents, he creates carefully designed traffic movement laws and a semi-militaristic organization, less powerful than the army but more powerful than the police, to implement them all over the nation and to punish those who try to violate them. In addition to this, he also makes great efforts to renovate all the roads in a city and all the highways in the nation by the elimination of the cracks and the potholes in them. Since the desire for speed is one of the major causes of road accidents, he spends a huge amount of money on the creation of "bumpers" on all the major city roads and the national highways. In addition to all of this, he also tries to minimize, in the civilian population, the consumption of alcohol and other intoxication causing drugs.

When it comes to the last cause of a wretched death, he orders the defect ridden soldiers to pay as much attention to their own defects as they do to the enemy's soldiers. He knows that no matter how much training is given to a big army, there will still be plenty of soldiers in it who will possess defects that can never be eradicated by any human organization. This truth will deliver a high degree of sadness to a great gamer with a Julius Caesar type mind. However, he will try to reduce its magnitude by informing the strong and the super soldiers to stay away from the defective soldiers if they get caught up in a "no escape" situation entirely due to their own defects. He says to the super soldiers; do not consent to pay a price for the mistakes of your inferiors. If they get into deep trouble and are unable to discover an escape route, then they are on their own. Give them this message during your training inside the encampment. Stay united with them inside the encampment, but in the warzone, only stay united with each other and give them only that much help as they deserve to. If you die and they keep on living due to your sacrifice, then there is no point in continuing to fight.

Quality 2: The perfect game plan for a great gamer is the one where he and his army move very carefully, but with a speed that takes the enemy's breath away.

Comment: It has been said by all great martial artists; in the world of Kung Fu, speed determines the winner. This also applies to warfare. A war is a Kung Fu match that is fought with weapons. The great gamer desires two things; to maximize the probability of unexpected attacks and ambushes and not to allow the enemy to think too long. If he allows his enemy enough thinking time, then there is a high probability that it would create a new attack strategy. Thus, the goal of extremely rapid movement is to prevent the enemy from increasing the total number of strategies beyond its original plan.

There is also another reason as to why the great gamer prefers an enormous forward movement speed in the gaming zone. This is done in order to prevent the enemy from discovering his "weak point". You can never discover the weak point of an army that is moving with an incredible speed towards you only because it would not give you enough time to conduct research on it.

Quality 3: If he comes to know that his enemy is in a state of non-awareness and is not ready to fight, he takes the full advantage of this opportunity

Comment: The great gamer considers it as one of his highest goals to get a great degree of knowledge about the private life of his enemy. This implies the quest for two things; when does the enemy leader sleep and for how long and when is he busy in sexual activities and big parties. In order to get the necessary data, he sends either diplomats or scientists into its territory and its place of residence. These diplomats and scientists not only give something new to the leader of the enemy's army, but also act as spies and carry strange types of cameras (hidden inside pens or the tie around their neck or the spectacles or the eyes themselves) and other recording devices whose existence remains unknown to the leader. Before leaving their home nation, they are ordered to do everything that is written in an instruction manual (a small part of the game plan of their leader) which they read up and memorize before departing on their mission. If the mission becomes a complete success, and the spies come back to their leader and give him the necessary data, then he acquires a great advantage over his enemy and this not only gives an immense boost to his aggression, but also increases the probability of victory.

The great gamer, however, only plans and executes such a mission if his scientists have created new kinds of spying technologies whose existence remains unknown to his enemy.

Quality 4: The great gamer is always willing to suffer small misfortunes in order to avoid suffering the big ones

Comment: All the wise men of history have said; those who willingly endure small accidents in the present will always manage to escape the big ones in the future. The proof of the truth of this assertion lies in the issue of climate change. If the whole world, 50 years ago, had closed all the fossil fuel burning power stations in the world, replaced them with alternative sources of energy, and had taken away a large number of fossil fuel burning vehicles from both the land and the sky, and had replaced them with battery powered ones, then the accidents that it would have suffered would have been small compared to what it is suffering now and will suffer in the future if global warming keeps on intensifying rapidly. This however, could only have been achieved if the global population was kept below 3 billion people. The global population was made to explode by three kinds of people; the politicians, the capitalists, and the priests. The more the number of people that gather to listen to his election speech, the more powerful and "cosmically meaningful" does a politician feel. The more are the number of consumers of his/her products, the richer the capitalist becomes. The more are the followers of a religion, the more powerful and "apparently true" it becomes and the richer become the priests in it. Thus, if the great gamer suffers the misfortune of celibacy due to the non-availability of women, he remains celibate in order to avoid an even bigger misfortune, that of not enduring it, going to a prostitute, and contracting a sexual disease.

Quality 5: The great gamer never lets his enemy know about his exact location and, during war, hides in the most hostile places in his nation

Comment: Secrecy is as important before and during a war as is a great army, a great air force, and a great population of "well armed" citizens. The great gamer creates two kinds of secrecies; with respect to his gaming blueprint and with respect to his exact place of residence. Both kids of secrecies are equally important because the enemy knows that if it kills the leader of its rival, then the gaming blueprint would not be executed as well as by his successor as it would have been by its creator, and the inspiration and motivation enhancing idol of the soldiers would be gone.

In order to kill the leader, the enemy leader does all it can to know about the exact location of his rival both before and during the war. The great gamer can escape detection by his enemy through the construction of multiple residences in his own nation and in those nations that are his true friends (not potential traitors). One or more of these residences always lies in a major mountain range of his nation and one or more is constructed underground in a huge desert. All the communication that is done by the great gamer is only using transportation vehicles and never using radio waves or the other kinds of electromagnetic radiations.

Chapter 16

Quality 1: The great gamer always plans to attack from those places that are beyond the "strike back" range of his/her enemy

Comment: In the art of war or gaming, the winner is always the one who possesses three qualities; he moves with a speed that overwhelms his enemy, he known far more about his enemy's mind that it knows about his, and he launches his greatest attacks from those places which cannot be struck back by his enemy. With respect to the last quality, there is something extremely important to be said.

In 2022, we saw the eruption of a war that shook the whole world, temporarily. This was the attack and the invasion of Russia on Ukraine. At the beginning of the war, the smaller cities of Ukraine were bombed and this led to a mass exodus of its civilian population and the students who had come there to study from foreign nations. As the war proceeded further, tens of thousands of Russian soldiers entered the smaller cities, fought with the Ukrainian soldiers, and executed mass massacres on those civilians who chose to stay behind. Its leader, Volodymyr Zelensky, told the whole world about how terrible a nation Russia was and how even more terrible was its leader, Vladimir Putin. He said that he was enraged beyond words at the actions of Russia and retaliated with weapons that were given to his army by other nations.

Now, in 2023, another war has broken out and it is just starting to become more and more ferocious. This is the war between Israel and Palestine. A terrorist group known as Hamas attacked first, through rockets, and killed more than 1200 Israeli civilians and then Israel retaliated in return by firing rockets into the capital of Palestine, Gaza, killing more than 1000 Palestinians. In retaliation, the Hamas terrorists, invaded and attacked a music festival gathering, shot dead more than 250 young people, raped young women, and have taken hostage more than 150 people.

All the news channels are informing their audience that both the wars are a result of the insanity of evil people and are a fight between the good and the evil. However, they would never give their audience the real cause behind the eruption of these two wars. Why? It is because they are ordered not to by the leaders of the organizations that initiated these wars for the fulfillment of their own goals.

It is a fact of war science, that every military organization, after creating a vast army, air force, naval force, and a global cyber infrastructure to protect and run them, starts to manufacture weapons on an increasingly massive scale. They are of three kinds; physical, chemical, and biological. After creating them, it starts to store them inside vast facilities. However, the goal of the organization is not to store them for as long as possible, but to take them out and use them, ASAP. This must be done, because a new stock is constantly being created and in order to insert it into the facility of a finite size, the old stock must be removed. In order to remove the old stock, it must be sent to a location where it will be used up by the population of that location. Thus, the organization creates special people for the job of the sale of its weapons all over the world. They are known as the "arms dealers" and they sell the manufactured stock of the organization through aero planes, huge care ships and huge container carrying trucks (Nicholas cage was such a person in the Hollywood movie, Lord of War). These dealers are highly skilled in the art of talking, and in the art of escaping the "anti-weapons" agencies. They visit the two nations which are locked up in a war and sell their cargo to the leaders of both. When the buying period is completed, they inform their organization about their success.

In the United States, the biggest military organization is known as the Pentagon. Its leader is the defense secretary of the nation. The Pentagon creates all kinds of physical weapons in huge quantities every year and not only distributes them throughout the nation through another organization knows as the National Rifle Association (NRA), but also throughout the world either through the Central Intelligence Agency (CIA) or through its own "arms dealers".

In Europe, the biggest military organization is known as the North Atlantic Treaty Organization (NATO). Its leader is known as Jens Stoltenberg. The names of the ones in Russia and China are unknown.

In addition to all the above-mentioned goals, the two other goals of a military organization are; to rapidly expand its empire on Earth and eventually beyond it and to amplify fascism in every nation under its rule. So, what exactly happened before the war in Ukraine?

A meeting between the defense secretary of the United States, the leader of the European Union (EU), the leaders of NATO and the military organizations of Russia and China and the leader of Ukraine was held in a top-secret location. During this meeting, the leaders the EU and that of NATO told the leaders of Russia and China that they desired rapid amplification of military dictatorship (fascism) of all the EU nations. Then, the Pentagon replied that it desired to sell a part of the massive stockpile of weapons that it had created in the last 30 years. Then, the leader of Russia said that the only way this could be done was to attack and invade a nation that was not a part of both EU and NATO. The leaders of the Pentagon, the EU and NATO then told him to go ahead and attack Ukraine. After hearing from all these people, who were like the Gods of Olympus compared to him, Volodymyr Zelensky agreed with everyone.

After the war had reached a certain stage, the United States and Germany (an EU nation) began to sell weapons to the army of Ukraine through the EU and NATO. By the distribution of their production, the Pentagon amassed an immense amount of wealth. Then there came good news for NATO. The people of all the remaining nations of Europe were sent into a state of great fear from Russia. Initially, before the war, most of them had an anti-fascism mind, but soon it was transformed into a pro-fascism one. Now, NATO, without much worry, will rapidly develop the military infrastructure of every European nation and this would not only give an immense uplift to its power, but also to its wealth. Since the EU and NATO are locked up in a symbiotic relationship, the power and wealth of EU will also rise to the same magnitude as that of NATO.

The leader of Ukraine was not at all upset by the invasion of Russia on his nation. This is because of two reasons; first, he was given a great amount of wealth by both EU and NATO before the war began and second, that he was now a global celebrity instead of a national one. In his own nation, he was a comedian and a film actor before his life as the leader of that nation. Ukraine is a nation of CELEBRITOCRACY, which means that the icons of its film industry become its leaders. Thus, the war amplified his professional state of existence, that of a celebrity. He travelled to various nations of the world and gave speeches which were given a great applause by all the people who sat in front of him. From a national celebrity, he became a global one through the war and the news channels.

In the present war between Palestine and Israel, the group Hamas consists of the surviving leaders of the ISIS organization, the Islamic fanatics of Gaza city and others who are the descendants of the leaders of the Nazi party of Germany. The leaders of Hamas get their money from the nations on the Arabian Peninsula. Before the war, the arm's dealers of the Pentagon, NATO, Russia, and China met the leader of Hamas and took an assessment of the wealth of his group. Then they arrived in Israel and met with its leader, Benjamin Netanyahu, the leader of the armed forces and the leader of the secret service of the nation, the MOSSAD. They told them everything that had been discussed between them and the leader of Hamas. They told Netanyahu that they had told the Hamas leader that they would sell their weapons to him only if they would attack Israel with them (and they had an obligation to buy the weapons because the Arab nations had given them their bag of money for this purpose and to keep 10%-20% of it with them). The "weapons deal" between them was signed only after the leaders agreed to their assertion. After hearing this, Netanyahu and his companions also went ahead and signed a weapons deal. Thus, after the Pentagon, NATO and the military organizations of Russia and China had given them the stock that was agreed upon in the deal, Hamas attacked Israel. The leader of Israel knew that this would happen and he began his own attacks in return.

In addition to this, the two nations are also fighting with each other for the conquest of the Al-Aqsa Mosque. The Rabbis of Israel believe that before the mosque was created, there was a Synagogue over there (The Temple Mount). The people of Palestine say that this is a lie. The mosque was built by their prophet, and he gave the very first AZAAN, from this place and he said to all his followers before he departed from the world that when he would come back again to Earth, he would want that mosque to be as beautiful as it was when he left it. The Jews, on the other hand, say that before the mosque, there was a Synagogue and Moses would only come back if the mosque is destroyed and replaced by that Synagogue.

Thus, the elite Rabbi priesthood of Israel told an extremely superstitious Benjamin Netanyahu; you are close to death and the only way that you can please Jehovah and his prophet, Moses, is to destroy Palestine and Hamas, send your army to conquer the Temple Mount, destroy the mosque, and create the Synagogue. If you succeed, you will not only ensure the return of Moses, who will save and give salvation to all the Jews in the world, but will also secure a place in Heaven for yourself and your wife.

The leader of Hamas has also been given a similar incentive by his own elite group of priests. Since all the rich and powerful men of the world become extremely superstitious only in their old age, they would do anything to please the god and the prophet of their religion and then live happily ever after with their favorite wife inside Heaven.

Thus, we see that the two world wars of the past, the war in Ukraine and the war between Israel and Hamas are nothing but "orchestrated circus shows" of the big military organizations of the world. These organizations also create and then destroy a terrorist organization. Why did the ISIS organization eventually fizzle out? It is because all the major military organizations of the world stopped their supply of weapons to it.

Why and how was Osama Bin Laden killed? The 9/11 attacks on the World Trade Towers and the Pentagon were pre-planned circus shows by the Pentagon. They wanted to send their army into Afghanistan in order to create a huge military infrastructure from which they would battle their old enemy, Russia. The terrorist organization, Al Qaeda, with Bin Laden as its leader was given all its weapons by Russia. They were the first to create their military infrastructure in Afghanistan and in order to prevent the United States from creating its own, rapidly armed up the biggest terrorist group over there and the native war-loving men known as the Taliban.

In order to penetrate Afghanistan and create its own infrastructure, the generals of the Pentagon sent their arm's dealers to the nation and create a new weapons deal with themselves and Al Qaeda. Bin Laden accepted the deal of the arm's dealers of the Pentagon because the officers and soldiers of the Russian bases were committing war crimes in Afghanistan (raping the native women, killing, or enslaving the male children of the Taliban and making the peaceful native adult men do extremely terrible jobs at their military bases).

After the deal was successfully completed, Bin Laden gave the green light to America. After they saw the green light, the generals of the Pentagon, including the defense secretary, made president George W Bush sign the 9/11 attack approval document. When this was done, a group of people were sent into the two world trade towers for the implantation of "demolition explosives". Similar explosives were also implanted inside a section of the Pentagon. After the completion of these two tasks, two passenger planes were slammed into each of the two towers. The planes were remotely controlled by a pilot who was sitting in a location that was very far away from New York. 30-45 minutes after the impact moment, the demolition explosives were activated via remote control and the two buildings were brought down.

The sheer scale and horror of this act by the Pentagon sent the pro-war mentality of most Americans to record high levels. After gaining the invasion approval of most of the population, the United States invaded Afghanistan and Iraq. In Iraq, they wanted to exterminate Saddam Hussein because his private army had also received all its weapons from Russia. In addition to this, they wanted to fight Russia over there for the huge oil fields.

Just like in the Cuban Missile Crisis, the Pentagon was told by the CIA, that Russia had made plans to establish a base in Iraq and Afghanistan which would house multiple ICBM's. It then told the leaders of the Pentagon that if they did not act soon and invade these two nations, then Russia would succeed in its mission and soon it would drop its first ICBM on Israel. Since Iran is sandwiched between Iraq and Afghanistan, they would also give nuclear weapons to that nation (which might deploy them either on India or Turkey). Thus, for the future survival of its own citizens and the prevention of the deaths of millions of Jews in Israel, the leaders of the Pentagon killed more than 2600 people in the 9/11 attacks. This, according to the Pentagon, was a very small price to pay for the security of many millions of Jews and Christians.

When Saddam Hussein was killed (because Russia denied his plea of a refuge spot inside it) and America had completed its creation of a huge military infrastructure in Afghanistan, it had no further use for Bin Laden. He, however, was not given this news because after knowing it, he would have run away from the location that was known to the Pentagon and the CIA and taken refuge in a mountain cave. The soldiers that were posted over there were sent to the location and they eventually completed their mission.

Due to the continued decline in its economic growth and the rising costs of natural disasters and public health care back on its homeland, the Pentagon eventually made the decision to pull out most of its soldiers from its military infrastructure in Afghanistan. However, this decision was made only after the entire infrastructure could be run smoothly by all computer infrastructures back home and a very small number of soldiers over there.

For the leaders of the military organizations, money and power come first and then comes human life. They are willing to kill millions of people in order to maximize their wealth and power. The newspaper and television news organizations are nothing but their puppets or their pet dogs. They will fight to their death with those who come out and try to wipe out the Pentagon or NATO.

But why do they desire to maximize their wealth? This is because their leader wants to become the "ultimate gamer". Who is such a person? He is a person who strikes from a place which is so far away that his enemy can never carry out a retaliatory attack. This place can only be; the space surrounding the planet or another planet in the solar system.

The leaders of the Pentagon, NATO and the military organizations of Russia and China have already made plans in collaboration with their top scientists to create rotating military bases between the Earth and the Moon, on the Moon and even on Mars. The cost of these projects would be as vast as their technical complexities. Thus, by regularly creating wars on Earth, and selling their weapons to the fighting governments, the leaders of these organizations move closer and closer to the realization of their science fiction dreams.

In the future, the superpower nations would not only strike at each other from the Earth's surface, but also from the other celestial bodies in the solar system. However, a ferocious race is going on between them as to who will be the first to create a military base on the Moon or Mars that would launch missiles or nukes that would be able to reach Earth easily. Whoever does it first, will acquire a massive advantage over the rest and put them under its mercy, temporarily.

Quality 2: The great gamer always attacks his enemy at a place after which it will be forced to come out of its hiding place

Comment: It has been said by all the wise men of history that a person gets the angriest if you attack him at his Ego. People tolerate living in a polluted environment, disease causing pests, poverty, and even government corruption, but no one tolerates an attack on his Ego for long.

If the soldiers of the great gamer are successful in reaching and surrounding the hiding place of the leader of the enemy army, but are unsuccessful in breaching its outer gates and entering inside, then the great gamer delivers his last attack. He orders one of the soldiers to take out the radio that he is carrying and attach it to a small loudspeaker. When this has been done, the great gamer delivers a deluge of insults and abuses at the enemy leader and his parents and ancestors. This tactic, however, would only work if the enemy has put on a fake identity and is sexually frustrated on top of that. A person, who is sexually depraved, is always boiling inside his mind and is extremely eager to lash out at anyone who either insults him or throws an abusive word. Thus, before he plans to use this tactic, he tries to find out everything about his enemy's sex life.

Quality 3: The great gamer keeps on altering his plans during the war

Comment: There are two kinds of gamers; those who create a gaming blueprint and never make any changes in it during the entire war period and those who keep on making changes in their gaming blueprint. The first are people of either low or moderate intelligence, and the second are those who possess either high or very high intelligence. If the enemy is the first kind of gamer, then its probability of victory against a second kind of gamer is either low (if it gets, time to time, some help from God) or very low.

The second kind of gamer brings Evolution not only in his gaming blueprint, but also in his own mind. As the war progresses, he drops his old habits and takes on new ones, drops his old and useless knowledge and takes up new and useful knowledge, and creates new laws within his army and the civilian population of his nation.

The second kind of gamer is a mirror of the actual nature of the Cosmos.

Chapter 17

Quality 1: If the great gamer does not want to fight or play, he starts talking about something that has absolutely no relation to war

Comment: A gamer in a state of either peacefulness or deception says to his enemy; let us talk about the philosophy of Immanuel Kant or let's talk about Copernican astronomy or let's talk about the prophecy of Jesus Christ in the Bible or let's talk about the continental drift theory, and the geologic time scale. He does this in order to ease off some of his pre-war stress and to create a fake friendship with his enemy. However, if the enemy is as clever and intelligent as him, it knows about his real intentions behind all of this "high flown" and non-practical talk. A highly clever and intelligent enemy can only be deceived by new kinds of "decoy" creating weapons.

Quality 2: The great gamer endeavors to keep his/her gaming blueprint completely unknown to his/her enemy so that it would be forced to divide its army

Comment: Your 120 soldiers arrive at the battlefield at the proper time but neither any of them nor you know anything about from where exactly your enemy would attack you. You split your group into 4 or 5 sets, each containing an equal number of soldiers. If you are an expert in the art of war, you would insert your best soldiers in the place where you would expect the lowest probability of an attack and the worst soldiers in the place where you expect it to be the highest. The great gamer always sacrifices the idiots to the geniuses.

Your enemy, however, would only prefer to attack from multiple locations, if you have failed to know much about its gaming blueprint and if it has destroyed or disabled all your sky based and space based observational instruments.

Quality 3: The great gamer knows that the fighting spirit of his soldiers is the highest after breakfast and the lowest after dinner

Comment: We are always told by our elders from our childhood; breakfast like a king, lunch like a prince and dinner like a hermit. A soldier, due to his daily lifestyle, requires more calories per day than a civilian. This is because in addition to his training, he also does bodybuilding and swimming. Thus, in order to start his training at any day, he must consume a large amount of carbohydrates and protein at breakfast. This, after digestion, gives a big boost to his testosterone levels (which is the hormone that is necessary for fighting). This boost increases the strength and the power of his muscles and the speed of the flow of blood in his veins and arteries. These two things are exactly what are needed for long period of training and fighting in the battlefield. Thus, two great gamers will always prefer to fight after all their soldiers have eaten their breakfast and are exploding with testosterone.

A soldier never eats his dinner like a hermit. This is because a hermit has no responsibilities in his life. He just sits in a temple or under a tree and keeps on meditating on those things that have absolutely nothing to do with war. A soldier, however, has two great responsibilities; first to serve his leader and the nation and second, to ensure the safety of his friends in the encampment. Thus, a soldier, in his dinner eats more than a hermit, but less than what he ate at breakfast. However, since he is focused on going to sleep, his testosterone levels do not increase to the same magnitude as after breakfast. Thus, the fighting spirit of most of the soldiers in an encampment is low after dinner (the magnitude of the fighting spirit of a soldier is also deeply connected to the presence of the Sun in the sky).

Here, there is something important to be said. The great gamer always prefers to attack his enemy's army at night, but he will only do this if; he is successful in keeping his gaming plans secret and if he has managed to discover a way of keeping the fighting spirit of his soldiers as powerful after dinner as it was after breakfast.

Quality 4: The great gamer knows that the fighting spirit and the unity of his army is proportional to the magnitude of its penetration into the enemy's territory

Comment: It has been said by all the wise men of history; the richer a man becomes, the greedier he becomes. The same applies to power and sex. The more success a person attains in the sexual world, the more licentious he becomes. This ever-increasing hunger for sexual pleasure is only brought down by the process of aging. Thus, it is an irony to know that the greediest man in the world is not the poorest man in the world, but the richest man in the world. The man who is the most-hungry for power is the one who is the most-powerful in the world.

The amount of wealth that a man amasses depends upon his magnitude of penetration inside the "economic world" (stock markets, banks, etc.). The deeper he penetrates this world, the richer he becomes. Bill Gates has penetrated this world far more deeply than Tom Cruise. The case for power is also the same. The deeper you penetrate the world of politics, the more powerful you get. However, the deeper you get, the hungrier you become to go even deeper. You never desire to say to yourself; Stop! This is enough.

If this Cosmic Law did not exist, then no one in the world would amass more than 100 million dollars of wealth. When we see the total net worth of the technocrats of the United States, we get shocked, temporarily. If we are wise, we ask ourselves; why the hell has Elon Musk amassed 230 billion dollars? Even if he possessed twice that amount, he could not even build a self-sufficient and comfortable home on the Moon or Mars, and even if he possessed 1 trillion dollars, he could not stop, forever, his own old age and death. He is fully aware of the fact that his global business empire would not even last 2 seconds on the geologic timescale.

The practical answer to Elon Musk's massive wealth (only with respect to the human world, with respect to the Cosmic Viewpoint, he is as poor as an old and diseased beggar sitting and begging on a dirty footpath in Mumbai) is that money brings power and respect. When he arrives in front of a large group of people who have the same mentality as him, he is treated as a god and everyone believes that he would eventually solve all the problems of the world. He also knows that the magnitude of sexual freedom is proportional to the magnitude of wealth. Career minded women are always attracted to the super rich men. If such men treat them nicely and with the amount of respect that they desire, they would happily have sex with them. If the wife of a super-rich man discovers that her husband is having sex with other women, she does not divorce him or do "character assassination". She does not disturb him and even feels proud by thinking; I am married to a real man. Women only show their Ego and their nagging tendency towards men whom they consider as inferior to them, intellectually.

Another reason as to why Elon Musk has amassed more than 230 billion dollars is because he will use it to complete his three personal projects;

1. A large human colony on the Moon and Mars.

2. The creation of a "cosmic highway" that will connect the Earth to its moon, Mars, and the 4 gas giant planets. The interplanetary ships that will carry the colonists and the fresh supplies to the pre-made colonies would travel on this highway.

3. To live, die and have his funeral on Mars (he has said that although he was born on Earth, he would not die here).

Men, who have an undying passion for wealth, power, and sex, invent many kinds of fantastic theories to pursue and justify their fortunes and their way of life. However, deep in their minds, they themselves believe that whatever they have told the world is complete bullshit.

When it comes to speaking bullshit, no one does it better than a politician. The paradox of political science is; the more bullshit you speak, the more successful you would become on the political landscape. This brings me to a question; what are the 3 qualities that you must possess in order to become the prime minister or the president of a nation?

The three required qualities are;

1. Feeling pleasure and not pain when telling one lie after another.

2. Living an extremely social life and connecting with only those people who are useful in your mission.

3. Possessing a passion to dominate those who are inferior to you either in intelligence or in cleverness and who are superior to you in character and morality.

There are two kinds of people in the world; the practical minded and the non-practical minded. The former believes that there are only three good things in this world; money, power, and sexual pleasure. Thus, they say to their children that they must plan and make all kinds of efforts to acquire and maximize the quantity of these three things in the "career life" before old age and senility sets in. Thus, these people only admire, respect and are extremely eager to meet those who have excelled in the economic, the political, and the sexual world. Most of the people in the so called "western world" are practical people and are thus, non-simpletons. When they are in the pursuit of these three things; they never display foolish behaviour and always act in a clever manner. In addition to this, they hate rational wisdom and the often-heard terms; our planet, our sun, our solar system, and our galaxy, are created by them.

The non-practical minded people say that the worst things in this world are; money, power, and sexual pleasure. They say that the best things in the world are; morality, character, and wisdom. They say to their children that they must not become greedy for the worst things, because such a life would soon destroy their morality, character, wisdom. They say to their children; go after money and sexual pleasure, but only till the amount at which you can live highly peacefully. Such people are powerfully attracted to the philosophies of Buddha, Seneca, and Epictetus and in order to preserve their wisdom, increase their level of interest in astronomy. When they see as to how small a place planet Earth is in the Cosmos, and all the vast processes that are going on out there, they feel satisfied with whatever they have. Such people are always simpletons and show foolish behaviour in the industrial world and dislike cleverness and deception. They have a powerful desire to live in a village and not in a big city.

Coming back to warfare, the great gamer creates his plans in order to maximize the penetrating power of his army. This power depends upon; the speed of movement, the quality of the soldiers and the total amount of "weapon load" of the army. On the other hand, the enemy creates his plans in order to maximize the "hardness" level of his territory.

The parts of a territory are of three kinds; soft, semi-soft, and hard. Since a soft object can be penetrated the most easily, the soft parts of a territory are the easiest to enter and go even deeper rapidly. The semi-soft ones are easy to penetrate, but the going ahead becomes more difficult. The hard ones are very difficult to penetrate and even more difficult to be penetrated further after entering. Thus, before the war begins, both the gamers try their best to convert the soft and the semi-soft parts of their respective nations into the hard parts. This is a very difficult process, and requires the expenditure of a large amount of resources, but the results of the success are always worth the cost.

The goal of both the gamers is to prevent the fighting spirit and the unity of the soldiers of the opposite army from increasing beyond the level that was set by their leader.

Quality 5: The great gamer, in addition to all his physical, chemical, and biological weapons, also uses water as a weapon

Comment: A pound of water moving at a velocity of 50 km/hr. will hit you with a force that is 100 times greater than a pound of air moving at the same velocity. Water can be used for both military and non-military purposes. In the military it is used in water cannons.

Water acquires its greatest destructive power in a tsunami or a tidal wave. We saw the best example of this in the 20011 Earthquake in Japan. The tsunamis that were generated, not only destroyed many small towns, but also severely damaged a nuclear reactor.

One of the goals of the great gamer is to create an artificial tsunami either in his enemy's territory or in the battlefield. Since none of the gamers on Earth possess the kind of technology that the aliens in the Hollywood movie, The Abyss, possessed, they only way that they can generate an artificial tsunami is to destroy a dam that has a huge reservoir of water behind it. The dam must be broken down at the period when the enemy's army is marching towards it and has reached close to it. The magnitude of the escape time must be minimized.

When it comes to the creation of the water reservoir behind the dam, the great gamer either allows it to be built up by the natural rainfall in the region or tries to increase the amount of rainfall by artificial methods (cloud seeding). If the dam is in his enemy's nation, then the artificial enhancement of the water reservoir is difficult, but if it is in his own nation, then it is easy.

Since the goal of the great gamer is to break down the dam only after a vast amount of water has been collected behind it, he is the most eager to create an artificial tsunami at the peak of the rainy season in his nation and thus makes great efforts to provoke his enemy to send its army to attack him during this period.

Chapter 18

Quality 1: Before attacking his enemy's nation, the great gamer makes a lot of effort to make many friends with the natives of that nation

Comment: The hidden wealth of a great gamer is of two kinds; the inorganic and the organic. The inorganic are the new weapons whose existence is unknown to the enemy and the organic are the citizens of the enemy's nation.

Traitors are of two kinds; the totalitarian and the hybrid. The former, after their conversion, only work for their chosen side till their death. The latter, after their conversion, sometimes work for their own nation and sometimes for the enemy nation. Their state depends completely upon the external circumstances. If, working for their enemy nation in the prevailing circumstance is more beneficial for them than working for their own nation, then they would choose the former. The hybrid traitors are not faithful to both sides. They do not believe in the ideology of their own nation's leader and the ideology of the leader of the enemy nation. They do not have any firm belief in the victory of their own nation nor that of the enemy nation. They do not have any respect for the culture of their own nation and the culture of the enemy nation. Thus, these people are always the nihilists (they do not believe in any ideology, culture, and propaganda).

The hybrid traitors of his enemy's nation also become the friends and the spies of the great gamer. The great gamer considers it as his duty to send his spies, who are pure patriots, into his enemy's territory in a secret fashion. Their orders are specific; go into the cities, talk to as many people as you can, discover the nihilists, ask them to allow you into their homes, have dinner with them and then discuss with them about your real intentions, if they refuse, give them more money that they get per month from their job and tell them about the future benefits that they would receive if they worked for their leader's enemy.

The patriotic spies go with great enthusiasm into their mission and when they complete it, they return, ASAP, to their home nation. They also create a "communication line" between the hybrid traitors and their leader. Through this line, the great gamer regularly keeps telling them what to do. The duration and the frequency of communication, reaches its peak just a few days before the beginning of the war.

The great gamer, is also aware of the fact that since these are hybrid traitors, they are also working with an equal intensity for the leader of their own nation. Thus, he remains as alert as he would be if these people were the totalitarian traitors.

If the enemy is an equally great gamer, he considers it as his duty to discover all the nihilists in his nation, capture them, and to discover whether they are working as spies for the other side. If a hybrid traitor is discovered, he is ordered by the leader of the nation to either abandon his job or to face the death penalty.

Quality 2: When the great gamer is observing his enemy with the greatest degree of intensity, he pretends indifference towards it

Comment: Indifference is either real or fake. Real indifference is shown by people towards those who are real strangers in their minds. In such indifference, you have no desire to talk to the stranger or even look at him if no one tells you to. In fake indifference, you pretend to not be interested in the other person, but take a great degree of observation of his body and behaviour when you think that he is not looking at you. However, the moment he starts to observe you, you turn your head away from him. However, when he again turns his head away from you, you go back to your observation period.

The phenomenon of fake indifference is always practiced by the great gamer. He only observes the state and the activities of his enemy, through the various kinds of surveillance technologies at his disposal when he knows with full certainty that the enemy is not surveying him. When he comes to know that his enemy has started its surveillance of him, he immediately stops his own.

Quality 3: During the war, the great gamer always prepares "multiple baits" and makes all of them easily accessible to his enemy

Comment: Baits can be organic and inorganic. Organic baits include soldiers and animals and inorganic baits include diamonds and gold. The great gamer is aware of the truth that, before a war, his enemy would be more powerfully attracted to the inorganic baits and during the war would be more powerfully attracted to the organic baits.

Quality 4: If the great gamer discovers that he has a short-tempered nature, he does all that is possible to exterminate it ASAP

Comment: The two greatest killers of a great gamer are; low intelligence and short-temperament. The former creates and fuels the latter. Since the great gamer is aware of this truth, he does his best to increase the magnitude of his intelligence. However, a high intelligence must also be coupled up with a good life. The good life is a life in which you have acquired as much wealth, power, and sexual pleasure and reproduction as you desired. There is, however, a problem over here.

As was said before; if a person acquires as much sexual pleasure as he dreamed of then he would turn into a Buddha and a pacifist. A Buddha can never become a great gamer and he does not have any interest in the gaming world. Thus, the great gamer resolves to walk on a narrow road. He makes efforts to acquire sexual pleasure, but not so much that he would turn into a Buddha. If on the other hand, he practises unwilling celibacy, then he eventually becomes a walking volcano. If his enemy comes to know about this, it takes the full advantage of his weakness and provokes him through the deliverance of abusive language. This makes him lose all his rationality and take insane actions thereafter which bring great and irreparable ruin to only his army.

Quality 5: The great gamer is not greedy for public honour and public opinions

Comment: When it comes to honour and opinions, the great gamer primary focus is on his army and the secondary focus is on the civilian population of his nation. This is because his biggest goal in life is to win wars, both inside his own mind and those that occur with another being, either terrestrial or extra-terrestrial.

He wins his inner conflicts via the process of total self-knowledge and character building. Regarding the external ones, he wins them via the creation of a big and powerful army and in which all the soldiers are dead loyal to him due to faith. The faith of the soldiers is estimated by their eagerness to give gifts to him and their eagerness to do real flattery. A soldier can honour his leader by giving him a gift through his own hard-earned money. A soldier is always eager to flatter his leader if the leader transforms his life through his teachings, and gives him a lifelong economic and military security. Thus, the great gamer does nearly as much for all his soldiers as he does for his own children. If he is very depressed and shows scepticism regarding the faith of his soldiers in him, a great number of soldiers come to him very soon and say; you are more than a leader to us. You are our second father. We will love you forever.

The goal to 100% victory over the enemy is divided into four parts; a mind of great intelligence and fighting spirit (33%), a complex and secret gaming blueprint (33%), a huge, powerful, and loyal army (33%), and the goodwill and help of God (1%).

When it comes to the civilian population, the great gamer sometimes treats them exactly the way he treats his soldiers and sometimes as livestock animals. The great gamer regards his own nation as his private property and a farm land. He views himself as a farmer who is nurturing the growth and the proper development of the crops whose seeds were implanted by Nature into the soil that was created by God. Thus, he believes that the plans and the efforts of God and Nature would never succeed if he was not there to help them. The best crops become the top scientists, the top capitalists, and the super soldiers. The second best become the entertainers of the film and the sports industries, the third best become the proletarians of the nation and the fourth best or the worst (in the eyes of the great gamer) become all the people that are locked up in the mental hospitals of the nation and all the idlers in their homes, and the hippies.

When the great gamer treats the civilians the way he treats his own soldiers, they become immensely patriotic and shower praises and goodwill on him. During this period, they feel that their life is not meaningless, but has a purpose. However, when he treats them as farm animals, he only uses them to increase his own power and the size and the power of his army. He however, uses them in such a way that very few of them feel that they are slaves and are being ruthlessly exploited. Thus, during this period, their opinions, goodwill, and praises take a deep downward dive.

Quality 6: The great gamer does not think excessively about the welfare of his soldiers

Comment: The great gamer regards his soldiers as his children, but not children in the actual sense. He tries his best to make all of them as mature and intelligent as possible according to their genetics. Thus, he takes great care of them, but not to the level that is given to the new born babies or the small infants. This is because he knows if he did so, then all of them would eventually turn into babies or infants. Instead of going through "forward" evolution, they would go through "retrograde" evolution.

Quality 7: He shocks his enemy via false and unexpected appearances

Comment: In the Mission Impossible movies of Hollywood, one of the ways in which Ethan Hunt and his friends, completed their task, is by wearing an artificially created face mask. The mask completely concealed their real identity and created a fake identity that was so good, that even their highly experienced enemies failed to detect them. When they got what they wanted from their enemy, they took off the mask and revealed their real identity to them.

The great gamer also plays in the same way with his enemy. He creates identity concealing face masks and by using them, either goes himself to meet his enemy or send one of his super soldiers to do the work. When the work has been completed, he either reveals his real identity to the enemy or decides not to and let the enemy figure it out by itself.

Quality 8: He tries to minimize the difference between the super soldiers and the normal soldiers

Comment: A great nation and a great army is a product of a hierarchy pyramid of a great size and complexity. There is a difference of the total energy content between the various levels. This is because of the abilities of the HOLONS in each of those levels. The HOLONS of superior abilities can gather up more energy than their inferior counterparts. However, the great gamer is aware of a big truth. The most stable and long-lasting pyramid is the one in which the difference of the total energy between the various levels is low.

A hierarchy pyramid has two kinds of symmetries; the geometrical and the energy. To preserve the former, while the growth of the pyramid is continuous, the number of HOLONS in each level must be kept on increasing in a gradual manner. If the number of HOLONS in any single level starts to increase rapidly, then the geometrical symmetry will start to wither away and the pyramid will become more and more unstable.

The same applies to the energy symmetry. If the total energy content of any single level starts to increase rapidly, then the pyramid would become more and more unstable. Thus, in order to prevent this, the great gamer tries to minimize the difference between the abilities of the HOLONS at all the levels.

The greatest army is one in which the normal soldiers are nearly as good as the super soldiers.

Chapter 19

Quality 1: The great gamer keeps on increasing the power of the secret service of his nation

Comment: The goal of the great gamer is to win the war against his enemy with the minimal expenditure of personal resources and this can only be achieved by the secret service of his nation. The secret service excels in the art of fighting without fighting; that is, fighting without the use of the army, air force, and the navy. The secret service of all the so-called superpowers of the world, have three goals; to discover the gaming blueprint of the enemy, to kill the commander in chief of the defence forces, and to create and amplify the instability and the disunity amongst the soldiers of the defence forces and the civilian population. It accomplishes the first two goals, by the deployment of its own highly trained "secret agents" and the last goal is reached by the creation and the preservation of loyal traitors in the enemy's nation.

The secret service has access to and can use, for as long as it likes, all the top mathematicians, physicists, chemists, geneticists, biochemists, computer hackers and scientists and psychologists of the nation. In addition to this, the leader of the nation also gives the secret service the power to extract as much wealth as it desires from the nation's "reserve bank" in order to complete its missions.

Quality 2: The great gamer shows his mysterious and unknown power midway in a war

Comment: Since a great gamer wants to minimize the duration of war, he makes the decision to deploy his new and unknown power when the battle has reached its peak. This is because at this period, the fighting spirit of his soldiers is at its peak and the soldiers of his enemy are in their most restless and anxious state. Thus, for the new power to have the maximum impact on the enemy, it must be coupled up with the maximum fighting spirit of the soldiers.

Quality 3: The great gamer shows kind treatment to the people of his enemy's nation and thus converts them into spies

Comment: It has been said by all the clever and ambitious people of the world; treat the people of your enemy with a greater amount of kindness that their leader shows them and with the same amount of benevolence. These people are the ones who are the closest to the enemy and in whom the enemy has a high degree of trust. Thus, before embarking on this risky project, you must make your choices very carefully. The project is risky because if the enemy discovers your activities and your intentions, it would either kill all your chosen people or will decide to attack you very soon.

Regarding the treatment, the kindness part consists of two things; talking to them in such a nice manner that they forget their real identity and feel honoured, and forgiving or ignoring their bad behaviours or mistakes in your house or nation. The benevolence part consists of two things; giving them as much gifts and money as their own leader gives them, and giving them physical pleasure by inserting them in a place where there are a high number of women and ordering the women to behave nicely towards the guests and not to offend them.

Most people in the world desire undeserved kindness and benevolence from their superiors because it makes them forget their real identity.

Quality 4: The great gamer does not listen to more than 1 negotiator from his enemy's territory

Comment: Before the beginning of the war, the enemy has three goals in its mind; to know about the gaming blueprint of its rival, to create and amplify disunity amongst the soldiers of its army, and to create and amplify the magnitude of confusion in its rival's mind. The first goal can be reached by the deployment of secret agents, the second can be reached by the intensification of the propaganda of the superiority of its own culture and future vision and the third can be reached by the deployment of negotiators.

The negotiator has two goals in his mind; to persuade the great gamer to alter his decision regarding the date at which the war would begin and to persuade him to make peace and an alliance with his target nation and then fight together with the other enemy nations. Since a great gamer is always a person of immense patience and tolerance, he listens to all that the negotiator has to say and then sends it off back to its home nation after saying; I will consider as deeply as I can about everything that you have told me, but in the end, the final decisions will come purely from my own intelligence and ego.

The great gamer knows as to why his enemy send out a negotiator. Thus, when it calls him again and proposes to send another negotiator, he refuses its decision. This is because he knows that by increasing the magnitude of confusion in his mind the enemy would not only be increasing the instability of his army, but would also be increasing its own probability of a successful surprise attack.

Quality 5: The great gamer always plans to launch his first strike at the heart of his enemy

Comment: In the art of war, if you are successful in destroying the heart of your enemy, then you have already won 80% of the war. If the enemy nation is regarded as a living organism, then its heart is where all the energy of the nation (its blood) comes into and is then pumped out again towards the various organs and the brain. The leader of the nation, however, does not sit or live inside the heart, but inside the brain, but he visits the heart from time to time. There is some truth in the scientifically nonsense saying of humanitarians; think with your heart and not with your head. Our consciousness sometimes abandons our brain and migrates down towards the heart. When this happens, we view the universe around us in a purely subjective manner and when it comes back again to the brain, we view it in an objective manner.

Before our consciousness abandons our brain, it reproduces asexually and created an imperfect copy of itself (like what the machine that was sent from the future to kill Dani Ramos in the Hollywood movie Terminator: Dark fate; did). Only after this reproduction has taken place, does it make the decision to go to the heart.

The heart of the enemy is the second most important region of its nation. Since a functioning brain cannot exist without a functioning heart and vice versa, if the heart is destroyed, the brain is also condemned to death.

For the United States, its heart is the Pentagon. Regarding its brain, the left cerebral hemisphere is the Senate house and the right cerebral hemisphere is the Supreme Court. For Europe, its heart is the headquarters of the European Union and its brain is the headquarters of NATO.

Since every intelligent enemy is aware of the above-mentioned truths, it places its greatest amount of army and air force security around its brain and its heart. Thus, delivering a successful strike at the heart or the brain of the enemy is an extremely difficult task to accomplish and the great gamer only undertakes it if no major accident occurs at his home in the process of completing it.

Quality 6: The great gamer makes a big move on his enemy only when there is a big advantage to be gained from it

Comment: During the game or the war, the gamer's mind is always focused on two things; the rate of expenditure of his personal resources and the projected period of the war. The former depends upon two things; the intelligence of the soldier and the ferocity of the war. Every gamer knows that soldiers of low intelligence have the tendency to waste ammunition and their personal food and water supplies. Thus, in order to avoid this, their intelligence is increased as much as possible during their training before the war. This requires two things; a group of great trainers and a nationwide project of "selective breeding" inside the civilian population.

The ferocity of the war depends upon the surrounding environmental conditions (the more ideal the environment is for fighting, the more ferociously the two sides fight), the nature of the weapons of the two sides, and the fighting spirit of the two armies.

Advantages are of two kinds; those that are inherent in the gamer and his army and those that are supplied by his enemy. The latter is as important as the former. However, the latter is of two kinds; small and big. An intelligent gamer always ignores the small advantage and makes maximum use of the big. The maximum use of a big advantage is done either by making a powerful attack on the "core" of the enemy's military infrastructure or ordering the army to accelerate its motion into the enemy's nation.

The great gamer does this in order to stick to his biggest goal; to minimize the duration of the war or the game.

Chapter 20

Quality 1: When the great gamer sees that his enemy is ready to receive him, he does not attack and waits for the enemy to make the first move

Comment: Since the goal of a great gamer is to minimize the duration of the war, it can only do so if it is successful in understanding the nature of his enemy both off the battlefield and on the battlefield. Off the warzone, he tries to do his research on his enemy via the use of spies, diplomats, and the sending of luxurious gifts and beautiful women. The information that is gathered is then applied by him just before the war begins and during the war.

If he discovers that his enemy is very licentious, then he immediately draws the conclusion that it must be impatient natured too. Only evil people are licentious and all evil people do not possess the virtue known as "patience". They ridicule and despise those who possess this virtue and always say to them; why are you showing patience? Don't you know that life is too short? Let it go and enjoy life to its fullest because who knows, "KAL HO NA HO" (a phrase from the Hindi language of India). Such kind of people have no place in gaming or warfare and will soon be destroyed by even a moderately skilled gamer.

When a licentious person makes his first move, it will always be an erroneous one and will give far more benefits to his enemy than it will give to himself. Thus, the great gamer forces his enemy to make the first move only if he comes to know that it is evil and licentious natured.

There is also another reason for the display of this quality by the great gamer. When his enemy arrives at the battlefield, its enthusiasm and fighting spirit are at their peak. However, if the enemy also displays this same quality and waits for its rival to make the first move, then there arises a "deadlock" situation. This situation leads to the gradual decrease in the enthusiasm and the fighting spirit of both the sides. However, it is eventually broken down by one of the sides (due to the greed for victory) and the great gamer makes sure that it is always his enemy.

Quality 2: The great gamer tries to discover the weak points of his enemy by "forcing" it to reveal itself

Comment: Weak points are of two kinds; non-psychological and psychological. The former lies outside the body of the enemy whereas the latter lies inside its brain and body. The former is discovered via the use of spies and air reconnaissance technology, which includes satellites. The latter are discovered via the operation of mind experiments on the enemy without it being aware of it and via the deliverance of verbal abuses and mockery at the proper opportunities.

It is found, that the number of non-psychological weak points are always greater than the number of the psychological ones. This is because the territory of the enemy is vastly bigger than the dimensions of its own brain and body. However, the great gamer knows that discovering the psychological weak points is more important than discovering the non-psychological ones. This is because if you are successful in delivering a direct hit on a psychological weak point of the enemy, then there can be two possible outcomes; uncontrolled anger and loss of rationality or total paralysis due to fear. If either of them occurs, then the great gamer rapidly accelerates the movement of his infantry and cavalry into his enemy's territory.

Quality 3: The great gamer always shows the same degree of hostility towards the two types of rebellious soldiers

Comment: The two kinds of rebellious soldiers are; those who attack without receiving orders and those who retreat against orders. The former show impatience, disrespect for the authority, and display individualism. They display an attitude that is known as the John Wayne attitude. The latter, are cowards, show lack of faith in authority, and display individualism.

Individualism is the quality that is the most rapidly crushed in a soldier during his training. Inwardly, every man and woman keep's on saying; it is my life, my body, and my mind. I am a child of God and thus I am not bound to any Earth based authority. Freedom and free thinking are my rights and will fight as long and as hard as I can to preserve them.

The goal of the great gamer and his group of equally great military trainers is to destroy all these beliefs in their soldiers in a scientifically planned and gradual manner. These beliefs destroy a virtue that is the most important and the most admired in a soldier; discipline. The more powerful these beliefs become, the more undisciplined and "hippie minded" a soldier becomes. Thus, the trainer makes them live together in a single location, eat together, bathe together, sleep together. In this way, those soldiers who willingly embrace the "disciplined life", pass on or infect those who embrace it unwillingly. They are kept together for several years and the result is a loyal, powerful, and a disciplined army.

Before he sends them to the warzone, the great gamer tells to all his soldiers; you should never exhibit the desire for freedom and free thinking on the battlefield. You must do what you will be told to do and stick to collectivism till the day of victory. Those who show the John Wayne behaviour and those who show "mouse like" behaviour, will be punished with equal duration and severity.

Quality 4: The great gamer uses war as a tool to clean up the "human garbage" in his nation

Comment: In any nation of the world, the population can be divided into two kinds; the non-garbage and the garbage. The former are all those people who have made the decision to serve their nation as long as they can and keep on making it more powerful, bigger, and richer. The latter are those who have no desire to serve their nation and only want to either harm it or stay indifferent towards it. Those who decide to harm their nation are known as the "criminals" and those who remain indifferent towards it are known as the "idlers".

Both the criminals and the idlers are deeply connected to each other. They are the two sides of a coin that, if not destroyed, will destroy the nation instead of upgrading it and bringing it the respect of the other nations. All criminals decide to spend an idle life when they are not indulging in their criminal activities and all the idle people, resort to criminal actions occasionally and at the right opportunity. They live their life in such a manner because both possess the inability to earn money via hard work and by serving the central authority of their nation.

Why did Vladimir Putin invade Ukraine? Besides the two goals of reducing the "weapon's load" inside his nation's storage facilities and rapidly increasing the magnitude of fascism in Russia, he also had a plan to exterminate a large portion of the prisoner population inside his nation's many prisons. A military organisation known as the Wagner Group was responsible for persuading and transforming an immense number of Russian criminals into soldiers. The leader of this group was Yevgeny Prigozhin, who was one of the closest friends of Putin. Thus, after the war began, many thousands of Russian prisoners, who were known as the Wagner mercenaries, were deployed by Putin into Ukraine. They fought, killed, plundered, massacred, and raped the civilian population of the nation. Eventually, they were all killed by the soldiers of Ukrainian army who were supplied various kinds of weapons by the Pentagon, NATO and maybe even China.

After Putin had exterminated the pre-planned number of prisoners from the various prisons in his nation, he made the decision to exterminate Prigozhin. This was necessary because he knew several secrets of Putin's own mind, the core of his military infrastructure, and the secret service of his nation, the KGB. The decision to exterminate Prigozhin was made by Putin only after he came to know, through the KGB, that both NATO and the Pentagon had offered him an immense amount of money and a citizenship of both the United States and the European Union in exchange for all that he knew about Vladimir Putin, the Kremlin, and the KGB.

After he had struck a deal with the two western military organizations, he launched a "coup" against Putin and this put Russia into a state of high internal instability. Putin, being a great gamer and a man of immense practical wisdom, knew what had to be done in order to exterminate any kind of future threat to his own life and those in his political party and to restore stability in his nation, ASAP. He ordered the best computer scientists in his nation to hack the autopilot of the plane in which Prigozhin was travelling towards the headquarters of NATO and then send it straight down towards the ground. They got down to their given task, ASAP, and achieved success.

Russia is a nation where crime and the criminals are as abundant as its wealth. This is due to the rampant and the nationwide over consumption of high alcohol drinks (vodka and whisky), drugs in their pure form (cocaine, heroin, opium, etc.) and a large meat-eating population. All the nation's prisons, before the war in Ukraine, were overflowing with prisoners. The government officials, who oversaw all these prisons, informed their leader about the seriousness of the situation and the need to do something urgently in order to reduce the size of the population in each of the prisons. They also informed him about the catastrophe that would befall on the ordinary, innocent, patriotic, and hard-working Russians if one of these prisons was destroyed in an earthquake or a climate change related natural disaster.

In addition to the prisoners, there are also many Russians who decided to live an idle life till their death and keep on surviving either through robbery or through the wealth that they inherited from their ancestors. Since Vladimir Putin is a great leader, every great leader believes that those who refuse to serve the nation through their mind and body should not remain a part of it. They must either be gradually inserted into such a state where all their wealth is gone or they must be deported to another nation. Since deportation is a very costly and time-consuming project (the other nation would refuse to accept the deportees), Putin chose the first option.

In the war on Ukraine, a large part of the wealth of the Reserve Bank of Russia was drained off and the only way to refill it back again was to force the civilians to pay more for the essential things in their lives. Thus, the war caused a large increase in the prices of fruits, vegetables, meat and dairy products, and the packaged foods. This caused a blow to all the proletarians, but gave a far bigger blow to all the idle Russians, since they were not earning any money.

When the war in Ukraine would be over, Vladimir Putin would have done a great detoxification project on his nation. The quantity of the two organic toxins, the prisoners, and the idlers, would have been almost wiped out.

Quality 5: The great gamer always tries his best to prevent one of his super soldiers from dying a shameful death

Comment: The great gamer believes; a super soldier must die in a manner that must be as glorious as the way in which I would die. Thus, during their training, he takes far greater care of their mental and physical well-being than the ordinary soldiers, and in the battlefield, equips them with a far greater amount of security than the ordinary soldiers. In the former case, it includes the allocation of the best quality food, water, and living environment to them. It also includes a greater allocation of food, and water during times of scarcity. In the latter case, it includes the handing out of a special kind of body armour (which is never given to the ordinary soldiers), weapons of immense power and accuracy, and ordering the ordinary soldiers to stand in front of them and sacrifice their lives if the enemy's army manages to launch a surprise attack.

A super soldier can die shamefully in three ways; committing suicide or getting killed by an ordinary soldier or a civilian or getting killed by a natural disaster.

Chapter 21

Quality 1: The great gamer hates and remains careful of "actors" as much as he hates and remains careful of disobedient soldiers and traitors

Comment: All the news channels and the newspaper organizations of the world constantly keep calling the actors of the various film industries of the various nations as "stars". They do this so that the people would eventually come to regard them as cosmic and not terrestrial entities. They also do this in order to make the film organizations of their nation, richer and more powerful, year after year. Thus, through their lies, the endless cycle of work and entertainment is preserved and amplified in its power.

The great gamer, however, is always a person of vast practical wisdom and rationality. He sees things as they "actually are" from the mathematical and physics viewpoint and not from either a religious or delusional point of view. Thus, according to him, the movie actors are nothing but tiny bags of flesh, blood, and bone whose duration of existence on the geological and the cosmic timescales is infinitesimal in size. He regards them as products of the 4-billion-year history of biological evolution and only marginally more intelligent than an earthworm crawling in a mud pit in the Amazon rainforest.

When a great gamer goes into a film festival or the Oscar ceremony, he behaves with all the actors and the other fake identity lovers, exactly according to the way in which they should be treated. Thus, when an actor displays his humanitarian side to him and talks with great enthusiasm and concern for all those people who are suffering in the warzones and the poorest nations of the world, he just stays quiet and talks the bare minimum in return. He knows that when this actor would go back to his luxury room in the super luxury hotel where he is staying, he would either start to consume alcohol or drugs or would pick up the phone and start doing the most vulgar conversation with his new friend or would start to watch pornography on his mobile phone. He behaves in the same manner to politicians, the priests, and the capitalists.

In the warzone, he never orders his soldiers to pursue an enemy who is only pretending to run away. He knows that such an enemy might be leading his soldiers into a trap which could either be an ambush by a large magnitude of its heavily armed and the best soldiers or could be a place where a huge bomb has been planted before the war began. Thus, with a great gamer, the best kind of acting by his enemy does not produce any good results for it.

Quality 2: The great gamer allows a partial degree of individualism to his super soldiers in the battlefield

Comment: The mind of a super soldier is nearly as intelligent as his leader. The great gamer knows that a situation might arise when he would order or by mistake lead his army into a region inside the enemy's territory which has hardly been studied before the war by his scientists. Thus, for the gamer, all such regions are extremely dangerous to his army. In such a case, he tells all the super soldiers that it is their responsibility to analyse the uncharted regions of the enemy's nation from a safe distance and to make their own judgement whether it is safe for the penetration of the rest of the army or not. If the super soldiers declare that it is not safe, then the great gamer respects their decision and proceeds to enter or attack his enemy through other methods. If 4 new methods are created, then the great gamer asks his scientists to create 2 of them and his super soldiers to create the other 2.

Quality 3: The great gamer regards his best spies as precious as his best soldiers

Comment: Spies are of four kinds; local, converted, doomed, and surviving. The first are those that are recruited from a very young age by the secret service of the nation. These are the best and are nearly as good in martial arts and camouflage techniques as the super soldiers. The second kind are those that originally were trained and worked for the secret service of the enemy's nation, but now have become traitors. They live in the enemy's nation and always manage to hide their secret activities from their leader or migrate and become the citizen and a servant of the leader who converted them into a traitor.

The third are the native and the ordinary citizens of the enemy's nation. When they are transformed into traitors, the great gamer tells them: your safety and security is in your own hands and in the hands of your friends. If your real identity is discovered by your leader and you get caught, then I will do nothing to save your life. You are completely on your own. The spies agree to this statement of their new leader only because they are regularly paid large sums of money for their work.

The fourth kind, are those that have served the secret service of either the great gamer's nation for many decades or initially served the secret service of his enemy, but after becoming traitors and successfully migrating into their new leader's nation, served his secret service for many decades.

For the great gamer, the first kind are the most precious, the fourth kind the second most precious, the second kind the third most and the third kind the least.

Quality 4: When it comes to the creation of spies in his enemy's nation, the first target of the great gamer is the population of the criminals in it

Comment: It has been said by all the great legislators, judges, and the political scientists; the more criminals that a nation's ruler creates, the more fragile he makes the nation. The fragility of a nation depends upon three things; the size of its young population, the size and power of its defence forces, and the size of its population of civilian criminals.

Today, we see the unfolding of a great crisis in all the 5 super powers of the world. In all these nations, the population of the middle and senior citizens is growing far more rapidly than the population of children and the young people. There are two reasons for this; access to very good medical care for the middle aged and the old people and the lack of interest of the young to marry and produce at least three children before the age of 45. The young in all the developed nations of the world are marrying late and after marriage produce a maximum of two children. Many of them have so much sex before marriage that they are not even interested in producing 1 child. They view sex as an enjoyment producing and stress busting activity only. In addition to this, the fear of the incoming catastrophes caused by climate change and new pandemics are also dominant on their minds. When a young man in the United States was asked; do you want to have your own family after you get a job, he answered; what is the point in it when 25% of my country would be underwater, 25% would be under a prolonged drought, 25% would be constantly ravaged by wildfires, and the remaining 25% would be regularly ravaged by hurricanes and tornadoes?

The power of a defence force depends upon the number of young soldiers in it. The greater their number, the more powerful is the force. Thus, a great military leader always encourages the young men and women of his nation to have at least 3 children in their reproductive lives. To increase their interest in sex, he ramps up the manufacture and the distribution of pornography in his nation and the creation of comedy shows where a large magnitude of vulgar jokes are cracked regularly by the comedians (the WHOSE LINE IS IT ANYWAY show in the United States is a great example).

The size of the population of criminals is a product of the economic state of the nation. The more poverty stricken a nation is the greater is the population of criminals in it. According to the legislators, a criminal is a person who violates the constitutional rights of the ordinary and the law aboding citizens and on top of that, he is poor. The big politicians and the big capitalists of the nation also violate the rights of the citizens, but they are not considered as criminals only because they are rich. In fact, they are declared to be the people who should be honoured and respected by the population. Thus, the saying "kill a few and you are a criminal. Kill a million and you are great man", is absolutely correct.

Every nation aims for economic growth in order to reduce the population size of its criminals. However, the continuous economic growth intensifies the criminal minds of its politicians and its capitalists. Since all the criminals are unhappy with their government due to ill treatment by it, they are very eager to become the spies of a foreign nation.

Quality 5: A great spy can only be deceived or killed by a super soldier and the great gamer is aware of this truth

Comment: The great gamer never tells his spy to challenge a super soldier of the enemy's army for a duel. This is because he is 99% certain that his spy would be eventually exterminated. In addition to this, before he launches his spies into the enemy's nation, he does a thorough investigation on the locations of the various super soldiers in the enemy's army. If he fails to discover the locations of all the super soldiers, then he tells his spy to travel with the greatest possible care in the foreign nation and if caught by one of the super soldiers, then know that it is totally on its own and no help will come.

Quality 6: The great gamer tells all his best spies; never let your real identity be known to either the people of my own nation or those of the enemy's nation

Comment: A spy has three goals; to discover the structure of the gaming blueprint of the enemy, to kill the commander in chief of the enemy's army and to keep on hiding his real identity from those who are not important to him or from those whom he wants to kill. He manages to keep his real identity hidden from the person whom he has planned to kill by either putting on various kinds of camouflages (face masks or invisibility cloaks). After putting on this fake identity, he acts in a gentle + shy + affectionate manner towards his enemy and when the enemy has finally been deceived and has let its guard down, delivers a powerful and merciless attack.

Quality 7: Despite regarding them as his most precious possession, the great gamer does not have 100% faiths in any of the trained spies of his nation's secret service

Comment: The great gamer knows that all the trained spies of his nation contain a mind that is a product not only of the secret service and the culture of the nation where they were born, but also of the entire universe that is outside planet Earth. Variability and not Uniformity is the one of the biggest laws of the universe. Thus, the great gamer knows that each one of his trained spies is a potential traitor because the law of the universe also applies to their brains. Thus, before the war and during it, he only tell them what they "must know" in order to complete their missions and nothing more.

Chapter 22

A country is just like a 747-passenger aeroplane. Its goal is not to stand still, but to approach the runway carefully and when on it, to accelerate rapidly and take off into the sky above.

When it comes to classifying the airport, the origin of the plane and the different parts of the plane, this is how it goes; the factory where the various parts of the plane are created is the Universe, the airport from which the passengers, the pilots and the cabin crew come from, including the runway, is the planet, the fuel in the two wings, and in the tail, are the natural resources of the nation, the two engines on the left wing represents all the mathematicians and the physicists of the nation, the right wing represents all the politicians and the priests of the nation, the two engines on the right wing represent all the geneticists and the biochemists of the nation, the inside of the central body of the plane represents all the civilians of the nation, the cabin crew represents the police force and all the judges of the nation, and the 2 pilots represent all the capitalists.

What about the right wing? What does that represent? The right wing, including the outer body of the plane represents all the generals of the 3 kinds of defence forces and all the soldiers in the three forces.

What is fascism? It is known as an extreme left-wing dictatorship or a military dictatorship. Unlike a real passenger plane, a nation is like the ship Event Horizon, shown in the Hollywood science fiction movie of the same name. When the crew of a rescue ship reached the Event Horizon, which was floating in the outer atmosphere of the planet Neptune, they were struck by several strange events and accidents. Eventually, the crew of the rescue ship discovered that the entire ship had turned into a living organism after travelling to and coming back from another universe. Thus, the different parts of the plane that represent the different parts of a nation are also the different parts of a living organism.

The four engines plus the two pilots represent its brain whereas, the muscular system plus the skeletal system represents the 3 kinds of defence forces.

In fascism, a nation is ruled by two communities, the capitalists, and the generals of the three forces. The capitalists consider it their duty to supply organic and inorganic resources to the generals, so that the latter can keep on making the nation more and more powerful, secure, and a fighting monster. The generals consider it their duty to give the highest degree of security to the capitalists in return for their services to them. The remainder of the population, including the politicians and the priests, are only the puppets of these two communities.

Before and during World War 2, Germany was the most powerful fascist nation in the world due to the dictatorship of Adolf Hitler. Today, it exists in the United States, Russia, China, India, Pakistan, and Burma. In the United States, the biggest technocrats, also known as the "tech titans", rule the nation in combination with the generals of the Pentagon.

In these nations, the capitalist and the militarist communities have an immense degree of freedom from the parliament and the supreme court of the nation. The members of these 2 communities regard themselves as farmers and the nation as their farmland. They regard all the citizens of the nation as their crops. Thus, sometimes they treat the citizens as cattle, sometimes as their children and sometimes as plants. Due to this, they never show any moral conscience or sympathy for them and use them only to fulfil their own goals.

What are the qualities of a fascist nation? They must be discussed now.

Quality 1: The children and the youth in the schools, the colleges and the universities are taught discipline and loyalty towards their superiors and brutality towards their inferiors

Comment: The students in a school observe that its faculty always keeps on doing two things; to prevent the students from talking to each other in the class "without its permission" and to check whether every student has completed the homework that he was given to do. A student is punished by the teacher who is taking the class if he is caught talking to one of his classmates without the teacher's permission. He also faces punishment when he is caught for not doing his homework. The kind of punishment depends upon the nature of the teacher. There is no rulebook that is given to them, which instructs them to deliver the punishments that are created by the education planners for talking without permission and not doing the homework. The teachers are free to do whatever they like, except murder, eat up or rape the student. The goal of such behaviour of the teachers is to make the students respect them out of fear. Since all the teachers in a school are immoral beings, they do not care whether the students respect them due to their character or due to the fear that they create in them.

The motto of every fascist nation is; when the master has entered remain silent as long as the master wants.

In a school, the outer gates open at a fixed time in the morning and then close after an hour. In this period, the principal, all the teachers, the peons, and the students enter the institution. If any student arrives after the outer gates have closed, then he is not allowed to enter the school. Thus, the next time, he arrives "on time". In addition to this, the outer gates do not open after the duration of the school period has ended. If any student wants to go out of the school for a short while and then come back inside it again, his demand is refused. This is done to transform all the students into "disciplined" human beings, the first step towards being a soldier.

In the colleges and the universities, such a rule is broken down by an organization known as the "student union". Every college and university is a warzone, where a continuous battle is being fought between the faculty members of all its various departments and the students in all the various subjects that are offered by the institution. The union members keep fighting for the right to freedom of the students while faculty members want to transform the college or the university into a school.

The leader of the student union of every good college or university in a nation have the support and the security of all the communist politicians of the nation, while the faculty members have the support of all the capitalists of the nation. Thus, a college or a university is one of the various battlefields on which communism and capitalism are fighting.

The best example of the brutality of the senior students towards the new students is a phenomenon known as "ragging". It either occurs in a hostel or the college itself. In it, many students who are in the second or the third year of their study, ambush the FRESHERS after one of the first-year classes, and then order them to go onto the platform on which the teacher had delivered his lecture and do whatever they will be ordered to. When he stands on the platform, they treat him in a 3-fold manner; a child, a talking animal, and a slave.

After their ragging session is over, every fresher student feels humiliated and extremely angry. However, he keeps all his negative feeling to himself. The senior students do not even bother to inquire the ragged student whether he is feeling fine or not. They just ignore him and quickly move on to their next victim.

After ragging was discovered to be the biggest cause of student suicide in all the hostels in the nation by the social scientists, the government created a set of laws against it.

Quality 2: The young people are educated to be good citizens and not good human beings

Comment: A fascist leader only desires a good citizen and not a good human being. This is because the existence of the former is necessary for the attainment of all his short and long-term goals while the existence of the latter is destructive to them. A fascist leader always says in all of his speeches, that a only a good citizen is a good human being and a good human being who is not a good citizen is an evil person and a traitor towards his nation.

Who is a good citizen? He is a person who; remains obedient towards all the constitutional laws of his nation throughout his lifetime, pays all the various kinds of taxes without any hesitation, serves, and empowers the central government, the capitalist community, and the military organization of the nation, and obeys any new law or reform created by the legislators without indulging in a mass protest and fighting with the police. According to Thomas Hobbes, the founder of modern political science, when compared to an ordinary citizen, a nation is as mighty and as immense as God. Thus, to serve the nation is to serve God and those who serve God will go to Heaven after death.

A citizen serves the nation in three ways; by acquiring and doing a job, by spending his salary for all kinds of survival requirement, and by marrying and producing children. Thus, in order to maximize the number of good citizens in his nation, the fascist leader always creates a national infrastructure where the people can easily get a job and a satisfying salary, have access to a great number of ways in which they can spend their money and keep away the evil known as "boredom", and marry as many times as they want and produce as many children as they want. Since these are the things that the ordinary man and woman most deeply desire, they remain in a state of pure ecstasy in a powerful fascist nation and pay no regard to their character or their level or morality, until a natural calamity strikes them.

A good human being can never become a good citizen and he has no interest in becoming so. People think that all the pacifism loving persons in the world are good human beings. This is wrong. A pacifist is just like a good citizen. He only believes that there should be peace in the world, and that we should find some way of tolerating each other's creeds and walk towards a grand common goal. He, in all his speeches never talks about fighting with and exterminating the big evil men of the world. He asks us to tolerate them too and just observe their activities. He asks us to take on the Buddha mind; just observe and do not interfere.

J. Krishnamurti was such a person. Despite his global popularity and wealth, he never launched any revolution against the capitalists and the military leaders of the world. He only taught pacifism and passive resistance. OSHO or Rajneesh was also a hypocrite. He only blamed the politicians and the priests for all the great problems of the world and never the capitalists. This was because his own Ashrams in India, the United States, and Europe received an immense amount of money from the European and the American capitalists, every year, and that he taught about "erotic spirituality" (to reach God via the complete satisfaction of all your sexual fantasies). Erotic spirituality is making a massive rise in the United States today. Many Bible preachers are arising who are telling the people that you cannot get in touch and in a relationship with God and Jesus if your mind is in a state of "sexual chaos". Thus, before you come to the church, make sure that your mind and the reproductive system are fully satisfied (this teaching is followed by a sect known as the Latter-Day Saints).

The good human being says; do all that is possible to exterminate those people who get enjoyment by torturing, starving, and killing those that are helpless and defenceless, show morality, magnanimity, and compassion only when it is necessary and only to those who deserve it, and keep on increasing your intelligence via the acquisition of new knowledge of the universe and apply it to expand the empire of the human species in the galaxy.

When it comes to mental fragility, a good citizen goes into insanity as soon as the environmental conditions are not according to his wishes (look at what happened in the Superdome of New Orleans in the aftermath of Hurricane Katrina. They were all good citizens). The good human being; however, remains calm and fully functional, mentally, and physically in the worst of the natural disasters.

Who is the prefect citizen in a fascist nation? It is he who will never desire to become a good human being no matter how much he is persuaded.

Quality 3: The young are taught lies about the achievements of their nation and the other nations

Comment: Deliberate falsification of the history of their own nation and the other nations is one of the biggest qualities of a developing fascist nation. The young students are taught that the freedom fighters and the creators of the constitution of the nation were men of great intelligence and character. This is totally false. They only fought against their enemies because man is by nature a hunter and a game player (that is why all the so-called freedom fighters were men). If he is not allowed to hunt or play during his youth, he will soon go insane and his physical health will worsen rapidly. During their freedom wars, they knew very well, in their subconscious minds, that whatever they were doing had no meaning in the long-term future. They knew that after their death, the nation would again be conquered back by the enemy foreign nation in about 50 to 75 years. Still, despite being aware of this truth, they continued to fight on because in that kind of a life they were always in a state of ecstasy, were completely unaware of the real nature of the universe, and received a massive amount of attention, flattery, and respect from millions of people. All psychologists know today that men cannot live without attention, flattery, respect. When they continuously receive these three things, they start to believe that they are meaningful entities in the infinite cosmos that is all around them and that they have a purpose. Thus, the freedom fighters indulged in their activities only because of the two qualities of man; hunting and gaming, and the infinite hunger for attention, flattery, and respect. If these two qualities were removed from their minds, they would not give a shit about the suffering of the people of their native nation at the hands of the foreigners, and its future.

A man declares war on another man or a nation if he is ill-treated by him or it. Why did Mahatma Gandhi decide to become a freedom fighter? It was because he was ill-treated by a British citizen on a train in South Africa. If, he had been invited by the British royal family to London, given a long stay in the Buckingham palace by the queen herself, given wonderful food to eat, and had also been given a large paying job in London by the queen, then most probably he would not have bothered about becoming a freedom fighter. It is even possible that he might have even gone back to India, at the orders of the queen, and launched a mission to persuade its poor and the enslaved people, that what the British empire was doing to them was good and would lead to a wonderful future for their children and grandchildren.

Quality 4: New laws are created when the circumstances are favourable for their successful application and growth and are soon destroyed if the circumstances suddenly change

Comment: In a fascist nation, nothing is permanent. Everything is transient and in a state of continuous evolution. This includes the culture of the dominant religion of the nation, the economic structure, the sizes of the various states or the provinces, the population densities in each of them, the tourism policies, the education infrastructure, and the laws that apply to its farmers and the manual labourers, who are the poorest citizens.

India is a rapidly developing fascist nation. In the early part of 2023 its prime minister, Narendra Modi, created, in a secret meeting with the top lawmakers, economists, and the capitalists of the nation, a set of "farm laws" for the farmers in Punjab. These laws were made and executed on them, without their approval. Why? It is because in a fascist nation, large scale social and economic reforms or laws are executed by its rulers on the common citizens without their approval. Since the rulers regard their subjects sometimes as children and sometimes as cows and goats, they believe that their subjects are totally incapable of giving them any intelligent advice or opinion on the matter. This belief is not a product of their intelligence, but a product of something known as the "class consciousness".

What happened after the farm laws were executed on the farmers in Punjab? They protested in huge groups in the capital of the nation and all the cities of Punjab. Soon, these protests started to become more and more violent and eventually clashes began to erupt between the farmers and the police forces of the various cities which turned bloody and fatalistic for many of them. The prime minister, on the other hand, was celebrating the Republic Day of the nation in New Delhi. After the intoxication of the celebrations subsided in him and his party's people, he soon received a full report about the seriousness of the mess that the farm laws had created. Since, Punjab is regarded as the "wheat basket" of the nation, and the on-going protest would lead to a drop in the production of wheat, he decided to drop all the laws and make peace with the farmers.

A fascist nation is the most beautiful creation of Nature. It has the qualities of all those species which survive the longest on the geological time scale. All those species which keep on changing their behavioural genes in a positive direction, by selective breeding, and which keep on increasing their intelligence in 100% accordance with the changing world around them, survive the longest.

Quality 5: Terrorism is legalised and all kinds of sensual enjoyments are encouraged in the civilian population

Comment: The great gamer of a developed or a rapidly developing fascist nation, considers as his duty to supply the small terrorist organizations in his own nation with money and weapons, and to supply the terrorist organizations in the other nations with even greater amounts of money and weapons. After they have received a large amount of military cargo, they are ordered by the leader, the army, and the air force generals to launch a terrorist attack on the civilians in the region that is pre-chosen by them. They help the terrorists by ordering the police force of that region to back off and do no kind of survey of the area. The terrorists, then move into the area, carefully and heavily armed and when the stage is set, their leader is told to order his people to attack the unaware civilians.

When the terrorists have killed dozens of civilians in the area, they are ordered by their leader to return to the base from where they started. He also, in addition to this, informs the generals about the end of the attack. They, after receiving this, immediately order the police force of the area to go, ASAP, into the affected area and kill all the escaping terrorists. This is done for two reasons; first, to make the survivors in the area believe that the attack was not an orchestrated act by the government of the nation and second, to turn the police officers as heroes in the eyes of the survivors.

A great gamer is always a dictator and no dictator can remain extremely powerful over his people for a long time without the presence of an extremely powerful police force. A police force can be made more and more powerful by two methods; by supplying it with newer and newer and more and more powerful weapons, communication technology, transportation vehicles, and by magnifying its image in the minds of the citizens. The first method is completed by creating rapid economic growth of the entire nation and increasing the annual funding for the nation's weapons research and development organizations. The second method is completed by the creation of pre-planned terrorist attacks by self-created terrorist organizations and then killing some of the terrorists after an attack through one or more of the officers of a police station.

After the shootout between the police and the terrorists ends, the reporters of the various news channels of the nation soon descend on the affected area like locusts falling on a wheat field. They immediately move to interview the officers who killed the terrorists, and then narrate back to their respective channels about the heroism of these officers. The news channels then proceed to glorify the officers in the minds of the population.

The terrorist organization of Al-Qaeda and ISIS were the creations of the Pentagon, NATO, Russia, and China. The 9/11 attacks, as has been said earlier, was a pre-planned project of the Pentagon. The terrorist attacks in Paris in 2012, 2015, 2017, and 2023 were the pre-planned projects of NATO and the 2017 terror attack in St. Petersburg was pre-planned by the Kremlin. Now, all these organizations have created a brand-new terrorist organization, Hamas. The empowerment of Hamas would rapidly amplify fascism in Israel and this would make its military leaders immensely rich and powerful in the future, if and only if climate change does not pick up "warp speed" in its magnitude.

When they are not pursuing the conquest of wealth or power, the rulers, and the citizens of a fascist nation, pursue the third best thing in the universe, pleasure. Each sense organ is a portal to the pleasure lobes in the brain. In the United States, which was the most powerful fascist nation in the world for a long time and now is surpassed by China, the entire population only believes in the existence of four things; wealth, power, pleasure, and the cosmos. Every American is sceptical of the existence of God (although they pretend not to and call themselves as proper Christians), the beneficial effects of morality and compassion in the long-term and truthfulness of the theory of evolution by Charles Darwin.

For visual pleasure, the Americans create all kinds of movies, pornography on both the visible and the dark internet, create huge steroid filled bodybuilders and wrestlers, encourage young women to wear bikinis and walk on the various sea beaches of the nation, encourage the young to do long lasting lip lock kisses anywhere they desire, and create super cars and Harley Davidson bikes. For audial pleasure, they create all kinds of rock music bands (ACDC, AIRBOURNE, BON JOVI, etc.), techno music artists (TIESTO, WARP BROTHERS, etc.) and country music singers (JOHN DENVER). For nasal pleasure, they create all kinds of perfumes and deodorants (the French, however, surpass them in this art). For the pleasures of the tongue, they go to restaurants where beef and pork burgers are made in new kinds of ways (the TV show; DINERS, DRIVE-INS AND DIVES by GUY FIERI is a great example) or to restaurants where the food is created by Gordon Ramsay class master chefs. For the pleasures of the skin, they start to have sex whenever they get leisure from the conquests for wealth and power and after their bellies are fully satisfied.

The perfect fascist nation is created by a gamer or a leader who makes his subjects alternate between period of intense sensual enjoyments and ecstasy and periods of anxiety when they are over. The "anxiety creators" are the various news channels of his nation. They repeatedly keep on informing the population about the various kinds of epidemics, natural disasters, and small-scale wars that are taking place all over the planet.

The more anxiety a news channel creates in the population of the nation, the larger becomes the size of its audience and the more successful it becomes in crushing the influence and the power of its competitors. When people are not getting pleasure, they want themselves to be filled up with anxiety. Why? It is because both pleasure and anxiety keep away the second greatest evil in the universe after death; boredom.

In order to create a population that is equally hungry for pleasure and for anxiety, the great gamer, tries to supress the importance of serious and high-level philosophy in the minds of the people. Such kind of philosophy is of two kinds; Transcendentalism (by Immanuel Kant) and Existentialism (by Jean Paul Sartre). Thus, in a great fascist nation, no one is interested in philosophy and everyone avoids it like a viral plague.

Quality 6: Justice is always done in a delayed and unfair manner

Comment: Since morality and compassion are almost non-existent in a fascist nation, even the high courts and the supreme court of the nation are fully in the grip of immorality and non-righteousness. The judges are nothing but the servants of the dictator of the nation and have no regard for the mental health of the victims of a crime or an injustice. When they enter the court, they walk just like a robot and when they sit and listen to the proceedings, they also behave in the same fashion. They watch the war that takes place between the lawyers on the two sides, the one that contains the assumed criminal and the one that contains the assumed victim. If the lawyer on the criminal's side, and outsmarts his rival, he wins the war and the judge gives his verdict in favour of the criminal and sends the victim to prison. He gets up and leaves the courtroom. He does not even bother to ask the victim whether the verdict is correct or not and if not, then why.

The judge is a good citizen, but not a good human being.

The students of law would say that all of this is done in complete accordance with the law books, but the truth is that justice in a fascist nation is partially a product of the law books and partially a product of a battle of the minds of the two lawyers.

Quality 7: Spying, is the biggest activity in a developing and a developed fascist nation

Comment: In a fascist nation, the second most powerful organization after the "core" of the defence forces is the secret service. However, the more a nation moves towards pure fascism, the tendency for spying becomes stronger and stronger in only the workers of its secret service, but also in its police forces, its news channels, and even in its citizens.

On the orders of the leader of a state or the servants of the dictator of the nation, the police secretly "tap" the phone of the person whom they are told might be a possible criminal. If they do not find anything strange in the multiple conversations that the person has on his phone, they send a small group of policemen, including an officer, to his home with a search warrant and order the man or woman to step aside and let them search his home for the weapons, or the drugs or the bribe money or the self-recorded sex videos created via the sexual exploitation of either children or vulnerable women. Even if they fail to find anything in this search, they continue to keep a continuous watch over the person and his family. This espionage sometimes leads to beneficial results for the rest of the society as many criminals do get caught by it. At other times, however, it puts an entire innocent family in a state of continuous great fear and the worst part of it is that they cannot attain salvation from this fear by their own actions. They attain salvation only when the officer who oversees the investigation, calls them, and declares them to be innocent. Thus, in a fascist nation, the police make life hell for many innocent citizens of the nation.

The citizens also start to spy on each other. Your phone rings, you pick it up, and you hear the voice of either one of your friends or one of the elders in your big family or your brother or sister who is living with his family in another part of the nation. When they talk, they first greet you in a nice manner and then ask about your state of mental and physical health. Then they inquire about the health of your wife and children and after that they move on to talk about the bad events that are taking place in the world and how will it affect the nation in the future.

If there were good human beings, and not good citizens, they would immediately offer their money or one of their possessions if you told them that your mental and physical health were in a bad state and the cause of it was the lack of wealth. However, if you tell them that you are in a bad condition, they would soon start to give you advice on how to eliminate the condition. That is the strangest quality of a fascist nation. Everyone is super-ready to give advice, but no one is ready to give even a small part of his bank money or a small part of his property. Even if you ask them that they should give you money and not advice, they would pretend as if they did not hear what you told them and after a brief period of silence, would continue to give their advice. If you refuse to listen to their advice and continue to say that it is money that you need, then they would soon put down the phone and never talk to you again for a long time. During the boycott period, they would tell their own family members that you have gone mad.

Why does all of this happen? It is because in a fascist nation, everyone is living in a state of fear, although they try their best to pretend that they are happy and optimistic with respect to the future. This fear would only be made greater if they suffered the loss of either their money or one of their materialistic possessions. When they give advice, they do not suffer any loss, and get an "Ego boost" if their recipient accepts (even falsely) their advice.

In a fascist nation, every good citizen is always on the lookout for an opportunity which if not let go, will give a boost to his Ego. When the opportunity is not supplied to them by Nature, they try to create it on their own (like the phone call to a known person).

Quality 8: War movies and war stories get an immense support from the leader of the nation and an immense viewership from its population

Comment: All war movies have two goals; to convince the nation's citizens that although war is a great evil, it is necessary for the uplift of the strength of the nation and its future glory and to display to them the various kinds of weapons, both simple and easy to comprehend (guns, swords, spears, grenades, and rocket launchers) and the exotic and the incomprehensible (laser cannons, sonic cannons, electric field generating grenades, and portable nukes) that have been manufactured by the nation's top weapon's research facilities.

In war movies that are a combination of old-style warfare and science fiction, the weapons that are created by an advanced alien species are also shown (the best examples are Alien VS Predator, The Predator [2018], and the Men in Black movies).

In every war movie, there is a hero who leads a group of other men and women who possess the same ideology as his. War movies are of two kinds; first in which the hero and his group fight with an enemy who has a small group of loyal soldiers, and second in which he oversees a huge army and proceeds to fight with an enemy who also possesses an army of similar size. The first are known as the "action movies" and the second kind are known as the "epic movies". An example of the first are; the 5 Die Hard movies and an example of the second kind are the 3 Lord of the Rings movies.

The faster a nation moves towards 100% fascism, the greater becomes the frequency of the creation of war movies by its biggest film organization. The various Avengers movies of Hollywood are the best example of this. The United States is a nation that only has the greatest passion for the exploration of the Cosmos and indulging in various kinds of adventures in it, but also has an equal magnitude of passion for beings which possess a set of super powers. Since the United States is known as the greatest super power on Earth, they proceeded to display this status by the "digital creation" of beings that were only found in the comics that were created by innovative American citizens and in the religion of the Scandinavian nations of Europe.

After creating all the super beings in the digital cyberspace, they portioned them into two sides, the good and the evil, and then made them clash with each other for the conquest of the Infinity Stones (through which you can control the whole Universe). Thus, there occurs a long succession of planning, plotting, spying, strategy creation, and threatening from the owner of the stones, THANOS, and his group, and from the group containing the "good guys" who were trying to save Earth and its dominant species, the Homo sapiens, from being consumed by THANOS if he acquired back all his Infinity Stones. All the 4 Avengers movies are nothing but a massive and "cosmos wide" struggle for the 4 things that all Americans desire; wealth, power, pleasure, and glory. There is hardly any serious philosophy in it or a scene where true morality is taught to the audience.

However, the Avengers movies were the greatest success of Hollywood and gave an immense boost to the fascist mentality of people in the US, and many other nations of the world, including India.

In India, its biggest film organization, Bollywood is also ramping up its production of war movies. The examples are; LAKSHYA, BAHUBALI, PATHAN, and GADAR 2.

Storytelling of the various wars in the history of the nation becomes the passion of the historians who are given the task of communicating the historical achievements of the nation to the young people in the schools and the colleges. Stories of India's greatest freedom fighter, Netaji Subhas Chandra Bose and the adventures and achievements of his private army are regularly narrated to the history students of all the colleges of the nation, and they are persuaded to narrate them to the students of the other departments of the college.

Quality 9: All the non-militaristic activities begin to be pursued in a militaristic fashion

Comment: In a fascist nation, when people go out of their homes do indulge in their routine activities, they pretend as if they are going into a warzone. When the men are preparing to go to their offices, their wives treat them in such a way as if they are going to a battlefield and would not come back in the same state as they were before leaving. This also includes going to a school or college or even going to the gym. All the athletes in the gym say; when you enter the gym realise that you have come into a warzone and your enemies are the free weights and the machines. Before they begin their workout, they say to each other; let us hit the weights!

The fascist mentality even penetrates the various "reality TV" shows made for the civilian population. The contestants of such shows are given instructions before an episode begins on how and with whom to pick a fight or a quarrel during the episode and how to behave afterwards. Thus, these shows are not reality-based shows. They are run according to a series of scripts that are created by the people who are the employees of the sponsors of the programme. These script writers have a good amount of knowledge in the art of war and the game theory of statistics. The magnitude of the profit that the sponsors make on their investment in the show is proportional to the size of its audience.

In India, there is a famous reality show known as ROADIES. The show is divided into three parts; the audition round, the culling round, and the journey round.

In the first round, people from all over the nation are brought into a place, after they have filled up the entry form, where they await their interview with the so-called judges of the show. When their call comes, they enter a large room where they face 3 kinds of tests; a physical fitness test, a general knowledge test, and a morality test. They must pass the general knowledge test and the morality test, whereas passing for the fitness test is non-essential. During the audition, the judges take a check of the questionnaire form they were given to fill up before the interview. If the judges come across a weird and an immoral reply to a morality-based question (example; Question: what is your deepest secret? The Contestant: I took off my sister's bra when she was sleeping one night, created a video of her naked breasts on my phone and then uploaded it on INSTAGRAM and What's app and shared it with all my friends), they begin to attack the contestant with threats, abuses, and character assassination. They eventually order the contestant to get out of the room. If the contestant refuses to leave and pleads to them to reconsider their decision, one of them gets up, walks rapidly towards him, and threatens physical assault.

After the audition round is over, all the selected contestants are grouped into three grades; grade 1 contains those that passed all the 3 kinds of tests, grade 2 contains those that passed the morality and the fitness tests, and grade 3 contains those that passed the general knowledge and the morality tests. In the culling round, some of the contestants in grade 2 and 3 are chosen for elimination. None of the contestants of grade 1 get eliminated. The word "culling" is used for a flock of chickens or ducks or cows or pigs. Thus, the second part of ROADIES shows that in a fascist nation, the civilians are regarded as animals by its economic and military rulers, who are being prepared for slaughter.

In the journey round, all the final contestants are portioned into three or four groups and each group is known as a "gang" and has a "gang leader". This is in exact coherence with the political structure of the nation and the world. A political party and a nation are a gang and they have their own gang leader.

In the journey round, all the created gangs and their leaders, fight with each other based on their victory or defeat in each of the many tasks that their members are given to do during the entire show. These tasks are of two kinds; those that are based on general knowledge and memory power and those that are based on the strength, endurance, and the gymnastic power of the contestants. The contestants, in the process of executing these tasks one by one, travel to a specific region of India and then move around to the multiple pre-planned locations in it. At each location, they are housed in a series of tents which represents an army encampment.

The journey round also contains another part known as the "vote out session". In this period, the contestants of each gang are given a card on which they must write the name of the person in another gang whom they want to eliminate from the show. This is like a war in which the soldiers of one nation eliminate those of another nation via weapons.

The ROADIES show is not a reality show, but an engineered show. The proof of this is seen in its audition round. All the contestants before appearing for their interview would know how to fill up the questionnaire form given to them. They would never write something that would lower their probability of getting selected for the next round.

Thus, in reply to the question; what is the wildest thing that you have done? Every contestant would write; I went on a long bike drive with my girlfriend and then asked her to sit on my shoulders while I was driving. No one would write; I and my girlfriend's lady friend decided to get drunk after a party and when she passed out on the bed in front of me, I had sex with her.

The contestants who get hammered by the so-called judges are either paid money for writing the weird answers or are a part of the large crew force behind the cameras and the stage.

Quality 10: A fascist nation has none of the qualities of a "real nation"

Comment: The leader of a fascist nation is always an autocrat and when a nation transforms into an autocracy, it never remains a real nation according to political science. A real nation has four qualities; non-rigged elections, job availability for anyone who wants one, a choice whether to obey your superiors or not, and the freedom to ask questions to your chosen leaders.

During his tenure, a politician who desires to be an autocrat, gradually changes the economic, the news channel, the military, and the social structure in such a manner that he will almost guarantee his victory in the next election and reduce the probability of success of his rival to almost zero. After the end of the next election, those who protest are rapidly silenced down by the autocrat via police arrests and brutality in the detention facilities. The best examples are; Russia, China, and Belarus.

In a fascist nation, the population of the unemployed gets bigger and bigger with each passing year. All the unemployed ones are those that have just studied till primary school or have not gone to school at all. Two possible fates await such people; rapidly increasing poverty which eventually turns them into criminals or they kill themselves either via self-hanging or drug overuse. In the United States, in every major city, more and more people are now being seen lying unconscious on the footpaths due to drug overuse or sleeping in tents on the footpaths and the narrow alleys between the big buildings. The same situation exists for the cities in Russia and China. In India, the population of such "stray" people will increase dramatically in the coming years.

In a fascist nation, the result for showing disobedience to your superiors is either expulsion from the organization of which you are a part of or punishment.

In a fascist nation, people know almost nothing about the private lives of their chosen leaders and the leaders themselves do all that they can in order to prevent their people from spying into their private lives. Decisions which will have a big effect on the people and their future generations are taken by their leaders, without asking for their approval. If they have questions, they are not given a cyber-based platform where they can do it and even if such a platform does get created, no one from the leader's side bothers to reply to them. Due to this, the bellicose natured citizens come out of their homes to become a part of huge protests, but they are soon chased back to wherever they came from by the police.

Quality 11: The ruling regime in a fascist nation declares itself to be an aristocracy

Comment: The good citizen of a fascist nation, in his old age becomes something known as an aristocrat. There is hardly any difference between an aristocrat and a film industry actor. Whatever the aristocrat says on-stage, he does its opposite off-stage. The desire to put on a fake identity is as great in an aristocrat as it is in the capitalists and the priests of the nation.

In all his speeches, an aristocrat says that his biggest goal is to free his people from poverty, fear of natural disasters, boredom, and the aggression of the other nations. However, he believes that his goal is only to free himself from the four problems by the gradual and cunning enslavement of the citizens of his nation.

In a nation where all the aristocrats are its military leaders, racism arises and keeps on getting more and more powerful with time. Why? It is because all the aristocrats believe that people of dark or brown skin colour are mentally inferior to the white skinned ones, but physically and reproductively superior. If they are not kept under control via the creation of "racist organizations", unemployment, and harsh economic sanctions, then they would soon take over the complex societies of the white people, destroy them rapidly, and marry and have children with white women. The killing of George Floyd in the United States is the best example.

Which quality do the aristocrats most admire in a person? It is the courage he shows on the battlefield in a war.

Quality 12: In a fascist nation, the rulers create a new organization for a either an intellectual purpose or a peace purpose, but then transform it into a military organization

Comment: The schools, colleges and the universities of a nation were created for an intellectual purpose. They were supposed to be the places where geniuses would arise and would transform the world with the inventions and discoveries and would bring Zionism to it. When Zionism would be born, all the nations of the world would unite into one single nation (its geologic equivalent is the creation of the supercontinent Pangaea). Zionism has already come into existence on the internet, but in the non-cyber reality, it is still a long way off. According to Albert Einstein, Zionism must be brought into existence by all the people of the world in order to permanently prevent the occurrence of World War 3.

Instead of creating and amplifying the Zionistic mentality, the rulers of the nation in combination of the faculties of the various educational institutions across the nation, create and amplify its killers; patriotism and nationalism. They tell the students to love their nation as much as they love their own parents and to glorify it when they go to either study or work in the other ones. They tell the students to view the citizens of the foreign nations as both their potential friends and their potential enemies and not to trust any of them. However, they say that the citizens of their own nation are 100% their friends.

In addition to all this, the students in every school, during their PT class, are made to do army marches, jogging in the school field, and display total obedience to their teacher. In the colleges and the universities, all of this is replaced by the warfare between the student union and the faculty of each department.

The organizations that are created for the rapid restoration of peace if a war breaks out are the religious organizations. However, all the religious organizations in every fascist nation of the world display full support and encouragement to the bellicose mentality of its military rulers. Before the onset of a war, they tell the people to respect and admire their military rulers and during the war they tell them what whatever the rulers are doing is completely right and to have full faith in them.

A good example of this irony was seen in India. SADGURU, who is the leader of a religious organization known as the ISHA FOUNDATION, was sitting in a big hall in a university in south India. Around him sat the officers of the army, the navy, and the air force of the nation. He told many times to the audience that the people who were sitting around him were the guardians, the heroes, and the great luminaries of the nation. He said this despite knowing the fact that the job of an officer of a defence force is to create wars and to minimize the duration of the peace time between them.

Quality 13: The goal of a fascist leader is to make every citizen of his nation "war ready"

Comment: How to keep a person in a continuous "ready to fight" state? It is done by keeping him in a continuous state of anxiety. This is achieved by regularly informing him that there are multiple crises in the world which are most likely to get even worse in the future. The information is given by the all the news channels of the world. Their goal is to keep making themselves richer and more powerful by keeping you in a state of continuous high anxiety. Thus, besides themselves, they do an equally immense amount of good to four kinds of organizations in the world; the military, the cigarette making, the alcohol making, and the pharmaceutical. In all the developed and the developing nations of the world, more and more young people are consuming greater and greater amounts of cigarettes, alcohol, pure drugs, and serotonin enhancing medicines. The news organizations and the 4 kinds of organizations are in a symbiotic relationship.

According to the news channels, there are 3 major crises in the world today; the climate crisis, the crisis of the wars in Ukraine and in the Middle East, and the species extinction crisis. Each day they throw out anxiety amplifying information on the TV and the internet. Before they begin to disseminate their information, they tell the people to trust in them and believe that everything that they tell them is 100% true. Fortunately for them, most of their viewers show trust and after absorbing their information into their brains, soon go into a state of high anxiety.

A person in a state of high anxiety will be unable to show either love or kindness or sympathy to anyone. They will not value each other's mental health and think far more about the information that the news channels have given them than their own well-being. Thus, a fascism amplifying government produce a population of "hippie minded" fighting robots. The citizens take little care of their hygiene and their eating habits and behave like a stoic philosopher. The news channels keep up the high anxiety state of the citizens, 24 hours a day, by showing a news story that is related to one of the 3 crises of the world, many times.

The best example of the hippie and robot-like mentality of the people in a fascist nation is seen in a road accident. A person driving his bike on a road in the city or a flyover suddenly gets hit by a car or a truck and falls on the road. He breaks one of his legs or his arms, is unable to get up, and bleeds profusely. He calls for help to all the cars that pass by him. None of them stop and race past him as if he is invisible to them. The people in all those cars are in a state of high anxiety and care only about themselves. The anxiety eliminates all the qualities of a civilized and a moral person in them. Ironically, if you stop one of them forcefully, they would soon come out of their vehicle to fight with you.

Who are the creators of such a population? They are the military and the news organizations. They believe that a powerful nation is the one in which most of the citizens are in a state of continuous high anxiety.

In the high anxiety nation, two other groups of people also keep getting richer and richer every year. They are the capitalists and the comedians. When people are anxious, they do three things; have sex or go shopping or watch a comedy show. The more anxiety loaded a person is, the more he spends on shopping and even tries to buy those things that are completely useless to him. They also have a powerful desire to indulge in laughing and either travel to the places where talented comedians throw out many jokes, metaphors, and satires on all the world's problems and normal life activities. When the cameras focus on the faces of the people in the audience, we see that in addition to the laughter on their faces, there is also an equal amount of dullness. It seems as if they are doing a duty in order to save themselves from either suicide or insanity.

The more fascistic a nation becomes, the richer the capitalists and the comedians in it become. The best example is the United States. The technocrats are almost

God-like rich in comparison to the common citizens. Comedians like Jay Leno, Jimmy Fallon, and Trevor Noah are also immensely rich.

The outcome of such a system of society creation, many hundreds of years from now, is the world that is shown in the novel The Time Machine by H.G. WELLS. The hippies and the robot mentalities would fission. Each of them would produce their own species. The hippie mentality would produce the ELOIS and the robot mentality would produce the MORLOCKS.

Quality 14: In a fascist nation, the class consciousness of the military leaders, the capitalists, the big priests, and the scientists keeps getting bigger and bigger with time

Comment: The military leaders of every fascist nation say that they are the guardians of its people and without them and their soldiers, the army and the people of the enemy nation would invade their nation in the most merciless and rapid manner and they would lose everything that they have acquired in their lifetime. They would not even be able to sleep after being robbed in a decent shelter. Thus, the military behave as if they are not natural, but supernatural beings.

The capitalists say that with their gigantic wealth and their great administrative intelligence, they would eventually solve all the problems of the nation and the rest of the world. They say that God's help is not needed and the citizens should stop praying to Him.

The big priests say that they are the loved and the chosen ones of God and they would soon bring all the beauty and the pleasures of Heaven to the citizens after the destruction of the Hell like atmosphere of the nation.

The scientists talk about the Cosmos in such a manner as if they had created it and are in control of its evolution. They talk about the way in which the Cosmos began and the way in which it will end. They also talk about the Earth's atmosphere in such a manner as it they know as much about it as God does. Through the computer simulations on the future climate patterns and their own minds, they tell the people all those things that will take place due to climate change in the coming 100 to 150 years. They talk as if they belong to a Type 3 or a Type 4 alien species.

Quality 15: The fascist nation creates men who are like the "knights" of the medieval ages of Europe

Comment: The knights of Europe, who fought in the crusades, had two beliefs; do all you can to preserve your self-image and do all you can to keep your women happy.

For the first case, their image of themselves is always the opposite of what they really are. Thus, all the men in a fascist nation take on fake identities in their youth and their working lives. In order to preserve their fake identity, they behave juts like film industry actors. They talk with an engineered accent, dress up in a suit with tie and trousers and polished shoes, and are ready to talk on any topic that they are asked to in a conversation (this includes the formation process of galaxies, the standard model of particle physics, the purpose of super massive black holes and quasars in the Cosmos, and the deepest secrets of the DNA molecule). All of them are glib-tongued. When they walk, they walk like lions and not like sheep. Thus, they always dress well because it makes them appear "more virtuous" than they really are.

For the second case, they know or learn soon, what women seek in a man. The qualities that they seek are; dressing well, speaking well with no tendency for hurling out abusive language even when immensely angry, flattering and amusing them at the right moments, having far more practical wisdom than theoretical, no interest in philosophy, and an intelligence that works far more in the creation of cunning behaviours than the creation of mathematics and physics.

In addition to all of this, they desire two more qualities; the power to give them great pleasure via a great sexual performance at the period that they demand and the will to sacrifice own life for the sake of saving theirs. Thus, in a fascist nation, the young and the married men pay as much attention to their sexual performance with their women in their bedrooms as they give to the acquisition of wealth and power. For the maximisation of their performance, they eat lots of beef, eggs, and pork and take all kinds of testosterone increasing products and those which keep the penis erect for a very long time and delay premature ejaculation.

An example of the second quality was seen in the movie Titanic. After the ship sank, Jack Dawson sacrificed his life to save the life of his beloved, Rose Dawson. He did this because he was a knight and this is the sole reason as to why Rose got attracted to him in the first place.

Quality 16: No fascist nation on Earth desires to create the "real soldier"

Comment: All the soldiers in the fascist nations of the world are knights and not real soldiers. What is a real soldier? The concept of the real soldier was shown in the movie Soldier, starring Kurt Russell.

The real soldier has four qualities: in order to release his sexual energy, he will either masturbate or indulge in homosexual sex with another soldier, he will never smoke or drink alcohol or consume junk food, he will never go to a prostitute even if they are available to him, and he would show no interest in economics or politics. Through the first quality, he will preserve his war loving nature and not allow his pacifist nature to grow. Through the second one, he would preserve his health and power. Through the third one, he would preserve his self-respect and through the fourth one he would preserve the "purity" of his warrior mind.

In a duel between a knight and a real soldier, the former has 0% probability of victory.

In the future, an organization would be created on another planet of this solar system where the first army of real soldiers would be created and they would be kept forever isolated from the normal human beings of Earth. They would be created for a purpose that the knights can never comprehend.

Quality 17: After a certain point of development, a fascist nation becomes imperialistic

Comment: In order to become imperialistic, a nation must possess two qualities; a high population and a powerful army, air force, and navy. However, this rule is violated today by the five super powers of the world. Except for China, none of the highly populated nations have made plans to attack and invade the United States, Great Britain, France, and Russia. India is the best example. Its population is nearly four times that of the US and seven times that of Russia, but no matter how much it can try, it can never launch a Ukraine like invasion on these two super power nations. Why? It is because there is an immense degree of asymmetry between its population size and the power of its defence forces.

The goal of a great gamer, who is the leader of a powerful fascist nation, is to create and then preserve the symmetry between the population size of his nation and the power of his defence forces. For the great gamer, balance is as important as the empowerment of the defence forces and victory in war. However, none of the generals in the Pentagon or the Kremlin or the military cores of Great Britain and France are great gamers in the real sense. The power of the defence forces of all these nations is far greater than the sizes of their population. Thus, in order to create balance or symmetry, they must do all that they can to increase the population of their nation rapidly while keeping the power of the defence forces "constant". This, however, cannot be done easily because it would require a rapid increase in the amount of annual agricultural production and a large increase in the amount of imported food from the other nations, which would lead to a shortage of food in those nations and result in a large increase in the infant mortality and starvation death rates. A rapidly increasing population would also mean a rapid increase in the amount of carbon dioxide production.

It has now been discovered that the great asymmetry between the population size and the power of the defence forces would lead to a rapid increase in the internal instability of the US, Great Britain, Russia, and France. The products of the rising instability would be a rapid increase in the frequency of violent civic protests which would result in riots, mass shootings, gun, and knife homicides, rapes of women and children and insanity in the young population due to drug overuse.

China, however, will most likely escape the dark fates of the other super power nations because its military leaders, capitalists, and politicians have done a great amount of hard work to bring up the power of the defence forces to the level of the population of their nation. In order to create this symmetry, they have burned as much coal and oil in the last 50 years as the United States did in the last 200 years. This has led to the worsening of the so-called "climate crisis".

India is also planning to walk on the same path as China did, but the other super power nations would not allow it. Why? It is because of their mission to prevent the global temperature from reaching 2 degrees centigrade which would lead to unstoppable climate catastrophes.

Since China has now become immensely powerful, it is making imperialistic plans to attack and invade Taiwan, the Himalayan regions of India, the Philippines, South Korea, and even the United States in the distant future.

Quality 18: The leader of a fascist nation tries to make more and more young people of his nation adventurous and combat loving

Comment: When it comes to the nature of the mind, a young man or a woman is any of the four possible types; adventurous and combative, adventurous, and non-combative, non-adventurous and combative, and non-adventurous and non-combative.

To the first type belong all the teenagers and the young college and university students of the nation. They have a great eagerness to indulge in the two kinds of adventures; sexual and non-sexual. The sexual adventures include going on dates that are created via the dating websites on the internet, persuading the person to get himself crazy about you, and indulging in games where the punishment for loss is the execution of a sexual act like prolonged lip to lip kissing or the fondling of the private parts of the victor. Trekking in the mountain ranges of the nation, sea-diving and wave surfing, driving across the nation on its highways in an SUV or a bike, are the non-sexual ones.

It is a law of nature that if a person is young and loves adventure, he would also be combat or war loving. Those that are adventurous, but pacifistic minded are the middle-aged men and women. Those that are non-adventurous, but combative are the scientists of the nation. They desire to keep their brain buried in their books and their laboratories and remain unaware of the surrounding world. Those that belong to the last type are the old people in the various old age homes in the nation.

Quality 19: The most important declaration of the philosophy of the stoics, life is short, is given maximum amplification in a highly develop and a rapidly developing fascist nation

Comment: In a fascist nation, all the scientists, the movie makers, and the so-called motivational speakers, who are believed to be men or women of great wisdom, regularly keep telling their audience; Life is short. We are only here for an extremely brief period. So, live every day of your life as if it was your last day on Earth. Make each day count! (This is what Jack Dawson, in the movie Titanic, told to the people at the dinner party to which he was invited).

Bertrand Russell said; human life is nothing but a brief episode in the life of a small planet in a small corner of the universe. Carl Sagan would also say the same thing, but instead of calling Earth a small planet, he would call it a "pale blue dot".

This way of thinking produces a good result and a bad result. The good one is the amplification of the power of the defence forces of the nation. The bad one is the production of two evils; greed and impatience. The former is far more destructive to the survival and the growth of the species in the long-run than the latter.

The philosophers of all the human ages, including Buddha, wondered about the origin of the greatest evil in the world and the prime cause of the sorrow and suffering in it; greed. The Indian spiritual teacher, SADGURU, told a young audience in a university in the United States that cause of all the horrors of the world was that no one is willing to share his possessions with another person "for free" (the philosophy of "free sharing" is destructive to the science known as Economics). He had a glass of water on a table beside him and he told everyone (in a shameless manner) that he would not share his water with anyone in the hall. The reason that he gave was; it is because I believe that I do not have enough water with me. Thus, he said that the billionaire or the multi billionaire also possessed the same mentality. All the richest people in the world, including ELON MUSK, believe that they do not have as much wealth as they need.

Why do they believe this? Their never-ending greed is a product of the images of the Hubble and the James Webb telescopes. During the night, after they have completed all their daily tasks and have finished their dinner and making love to their woman, they sit in front of their computer and pour over the various images of the Cosmos that have been taken by the two telescopes. After peering at the photographs of the distant nebulas, the star clusters, the giant planets of this solar system and the scenes outside the Milky Way galaxy, they temporarily go into a state of brain freeze. After this freeze ends, they realise that whatever they have acquired is almost infinitesimal. This realisation, gives an immense boost to their already super powerful greedy mind.

The Cosmos is the greatest "injury causing object" to the Ego of a great capitalist or a great politician or a great priest of the human species. In some people, it leads to an amplification of wisdom and non-ambition for wealth and power, while in the ambitious and the greedy, it leads to an even greater amplification of their greed and their Ego.

Since every citizen in a fascist nation believes that life is short, it produces a massive ambition in them for money, power, and pleasure and this leads to a rapid growth in the economy of the nation. In such a nation, people not only try to enjoy their lives to the fullest each day, but are also immensely impatient by nature. A person, who is impatient by nature, will be extremely greedy and will have no interest in philosophy or morality because these two things can only be pursued by a patience loving person.

The best example of the impatient nature of the citizens of a fascist nation is seen on a road in one of its cities. The drivers in the cars constantly keep blowing their car's horn at the other cars, even when they know that doing it would not give them what they want; a faster movement towards their destination. After the light turns green at a crossing, if you do not move your car, they start to blow their car horn with greater and greater frequency and when you refuse to move your car even after this, they put their head out of their car's window and start to hurl abuses at you. They do not get out of their car in a gentle manner, come to you, and ask you in the politest manner; my friend, why aren't you moving? Is there something wrong with your car or something wrong with you?

Although they are just going to a restaurant to eat or to meet their friend or to an entertainment zone or a public park, by continuously blowing their car horn they pretend as if they are either escaping a police car or are going to save the life of someone who must be saved within 1 or 2 hours. This phenomenon is most powerfully seen in the cities of India.

Quality 20: In a fascist nation, the more powerful the police forces of the various cities become, the worse they become towards the citizens

Comment: In a powerful fascist nation, the police officers, the commissioners, and the superintendents regard themselves as the servants of the politicians of the party that is ruling the nation and the servants of the big capitalists. When it comes to the middle and the lower-class citizens, they are regarded as cattle which are to be exploited whenever the opportunity arrives. During wartime, the police show far more authoritarianism towards the proletarians than during peacetimes. Why? It is because they are given the license by the top politicians and the capitalists to treat the ordinary citizens as either animals or slaves.

Here is a paradox; the more fascist a nation becomes, the more scared become its citizens of the police. Why? It is because the degree of the WEAPONIZATION and freedom of the police is directly proportional to the degree of the military development of the nation. However, a great gamer of a great fascist nation, tries to achieve the opposite; make his police forces immensely friendly and helpful towards the good citizens and make the good citizens more faithful to them than they are to either God or their own family members.

There are five qualities of a good police force; reaching the place where a crime is being committed on a good citizen very quickly, if failing to prevent the good citizen from being killed or robbed by the criminals then analysing all the facts of the "crime scene" as accurately as possible, knowledge of all the places in a city where big crimes are being committed and even bigger ones will be committed in the future, expertise in the prevention of riots, creating great unity between the various members of the hierarchy pyramid of a police station, and developing a symbiotic relationship between the force and the common citizens.

In a highly developed fascist nation, the police are not bothered to attain these five qualities. When a good citizen gets into trouble and calls for help, the police reach the scene far later than the ending of the crime. When they reach there, they only do a superficial and irrational survey of the various facts. In addition, the officers of a big city are busy enjoying themselves in big, pre-planned alcohol drinking parties in the luxury hotels. They do not have a clue and are not bothered about the discovery of those places where serious crimes are being committed by resourceful and hardened criminals.

Lastly, the members of all the police stations only stay united and cooperative towards each other due to the fear of losing their job and not due to respect (they have no respect for each other and the lowest level members of the pyramid, throw out a train of verbal abuses towards their superiors when they are alone with their friends). Since the officers get very high salaries from the dictators of the ruling party of the nation, they are not bothered about their relations with the common citizens.

The best example of this is the United States. Despite the presence of a powerful police force with big fast cars and bikes, crime is exploding in cities like Chicago, New York, Los Angeles, Houston, Phoenix, and Las Vegas. Why? It is because of the increasing military development of the nation. The police forces in all the cities are becoming more and more corrupt each year due to it.

Quality 21: In a fascist nation, the ruler or the dictator does everything that he can to "deify" himself in the eyes of the citizens

Comment: The ruler of a pure fascist nation wants the citizens of his nation to regard him as a "mortal god". Through continuous propaganda, the persecution, and the execution of the rebels, he manages to convince the rest of the submissive population that he is a god who has come down to Earth for a brief period in order to transform the nation and then the world. Since political science regards a political party as a mortal god, and the leader of the party "is" the party, the nation is a battleground where multiple gods are fighting against each other for eternal existence. They have two weapons; the scientists and the common good citizens. A nation is just like the battlefields where the Trojan War and the Mahabharata were fought.

Winning the election is just 50% of the journey of a ruler who desires deification. In order to complete the rest 50%, he must accomplish three goals; create record economic growth and employment, give the people a great degree of security from all the possible "natural hazards" that the nation is affected by, and create an entertainment infrastructure where boredom never touches them even for 1 second. All these 3 goals are extremely difficult to reach, and the only way to attain them is by creating a large pool of scientific geniuses. This is also extremely difficult because the brain of a young man or woman can only develop properly if he is constantly kept anxiety free, kept away from cigarettes, alcohol, fast food, and drugs, and is kept in a zero-pollution environment. This is impossible even for the United States.

The ruler must complete the remaining 50% of the journey, in a state of coexistence with the natural hazards, slow economic growth, and a large degree of unemployment. Success has been achieved and the best examples are; Adolf Hitler ruled Germany, Vladimir Putin ruled Russia, Xi Jing Ping ruled China, and Kim Jong ruled North Korea. The ruler of India, Narendra Modi, is also pursuing deification with great confidence and planning.

In the United States, there is a "deification war" that is taking place between two groups, the so-called Tech Titans, and the Senators of the US Senate. Every Senator wants the ordinary proletarian American to regard him as a god and the proof of this were the church funerals of Senator George Bush Senior and John McCain.

Quality 22: In a fascist nation, the festival of the dominant religion of the nation is celebrated in an immense fashion

Comment: In the United States, the dominant religion is Christianity and the dominant festival is Christmas. What happen during Christmas in the nation is seen by every American and every tourist who visits the nation during that period.

Why is Christmas celebrated in such a great manner? It is because, religious festivals make men more masculine natured than they were "off season" and the women more feminine than they were "off season". When a man becomes highly masculine, he desires to have sex and impregnate a woman and when a woman becomes more feminine, she desires to receive a man via sexual intercourse and get pregnant. Thus, during the Christmas period, a very large number of women get pregnant across the United States which eventually results in the production of new slaves for the generals at the Pentagon and many abortions which lead to a great inflow of money for many public hospitals across the nation, and the corporations that create the "abortion pills".

Quality 23: In a fascist nation, partying and having sex in excessive amounts are always crushed by the rulers

Comment: This is done because excessive partying makes young men and women lawless and idiotic; whereas excessive sexual activity makes them idiotic and pacifist minded (this explains as to why the officers who entered the school in Uvalde, Texas, did not move into the room where the shooter was gunning down the students. They possessed a pacifist and non-fatalistic mind, and thus cared for their own safety. They were pacifistic because they all had a good sex life)

Quality 24: In a non-perfect fascist nation, both the inner and external conflicts keep on increasing amongst the citizens

Comment: The goal of a fascist nation is to create and amplify anxiety in its citizens. This is done primarily through all the news channels and secondarily through the film industry and the educational institutions. Anxiety creates something known as the "inner conflict". What is it and how to decrease it?

The human brain is divided into three parts; the cosmic brain, the mammalian brain, and the reptilian brain. The function of the cosmic brain is to do objective thinking and create concepts via the creation of ideas. The function of the mammalian brain is to do subjective thinking and to create and amplify "unity" between the three brains and the ideas created by the cosmic brain. The function of the reptilian brain is to display or attain a higher hierarchy in the social pyramid of the nation and to create war. As long as these three brains keep working in 100% harmony, there is 0% inner conflict in the person who possesses them. The conflict begins when this harmony is disturbed and gets more and more dismantled. What causes this? It is anxiety and it can either be caused by another person or by an organisation. The greater the anxiety, the greater is the inner conflict. There eventually comes a point where the conflict between the mammalian and the reptilian brain becomes so terrible that it totally shuts off the function of the cosmic brain. Beyond this point, all logic and rationality end, and the state that is attained is known as "insanity".

The magnitude of the external conflict between the citizens of a nation and between the citizens of different nations is proportional to the magnitude of the inner conflict in their brain. In a fascist nation that is badly engineered by its ruler, the magnitude of the inner conflict keeps getting bigger rapidly in the brains of the citizens. This results in rapidly rising internal instability which eventually results in either a war between the citizens and the government or large scale and unmanageable riots. The examples of this have been seen United States (over the war between Israel and Palestine), Russia (over the war in Ukraine), China (over the governments "anti-COVID" measures), and France (over the pension reforms).

The goal of a fascist leader is to make every citizen of his nation bellicose natured. This can only be accomplished if they are kept in a state of anxiety, continuously. However, this is a dangerous project and is like walking on a rope that is fixed between two mountains with an abyss beneath. All wise people have said; beware! What you create to destroy your enemy can destroy you if you are not careful! In a bad fascist nation, the bellicose mind of the citizens turns on each other. Thus, in order to prevent this and bring down the anxiety of the citizens at regular time periods, alcohol bars, sports stadiums, shopping malls, discotheques, restaurants, and legalised prostitutes are created.

The great gamer of a perfect fascist nation creates a population that is as bellicose natured towards the foreign nations as is possible through propaganda and science, but is at 100% "Buddha like" peace with its own members. Towards the citizens of the enemy nations, they behave like Adolf Hitler and towards their own members, they behave like Jesus Christ.

Quality 25: In a fascist nation, the young citizens are taught to observe the sights of the greatest level of bloody battles and mass butchery with a calm and focused mind

Comment: The ruler regards all the children of his nation as the future soldiers and the young people as the potential soldiers of a future war. During his training, a soldier is taught 5 things; to endure long periods of hardship, to eat anything that the enemy's territory has to offer if either stuck in it or moving through it, to never allow obesity to take hold, to help his companions if they are in trouble, and to see all the scenes of blood baths, butchery and the fragmented bodies of his companions and the enemy's soldiers with 100% calm and serenity, and to keep on fighting as if nothing has happened.

A great example of this was the Hollywood movie, Soldier. The students of the military facility that was inside an interstellar travel spaceship, were genetically engineered, and after being nurtured in an environment where there were no girls, cars, bikes, discos, and music artists, they were made to undergo the final part of their training. They were made to sit together around a circular cage and to watch without any guilt or disgust the events that were about to occur in it. After a brief time period, new born babies were brought and put on the floor of the cage. Then, a group of hungry Doberman dogs were released into the cage and they pounced on the babies, ripped them to pieces with their teeth and started to eat them. The floor of the cage was soon covered with the blood, flesh, and the bones of the dismantled babies. The heads of most of the young soldiers did not move even by an inch, but those that did turn away their eyes, were grabbed by their chins by the trainers, who put them back to the original position.

A WEAPONIZED war cannot be fought without blood spilling, mass slaughter, and blowing up of the bodies of children, women, and soldiers.

In the United States, the generals of the Pentagon gave orders to Hollywood, to create movies which contain scenes of great blood spills, loss of body parts, torture, and butcher shop like slaughter. Thus, Hollywood soon created movies like WRONG TURN 1, 2, 3, 4, 5, and 6, SAW 1,2,3, and 4, SAVING PRIVATE RYAN, EVIL DEAD and FINAL DESTINATION 1,2,3,4, and 5. In addition to this, the generals also gave orders to Microsoft, and SONY to create blood and gore filled video games.

This project has produced a horrific result in the United States. This is known as a "mass shooting". A person who is totally immune to the sight of blood and butchery, has no moral conscience (the quality of a good citizen), and possesses weapons, will show no hesitation in killing children or many civilians whenever he desires to.

Quality 26: The great gamer of a fascist nation stirs up and amplifies his rivalry with another fascist nation by ordering a third nation to attack it

Comment: The great gamer achieves his results by creating a fight between 2 people and then using that period to grab all those things that are become ignorant towards because of their fighting. This is also seen between nations.

Russia creates and sells weapons to a poor nation or a terrorist organization and then orders it to attack the United States. After the attack, the United States discovers its cause and then sells its own weapons to the poor nation or the terrorist organization and orders it to attack Russia. If successful, then this leads to an amplification of the war between the two nations. However, after the first attack on the United States, there comes a brief period in which the nation's cyber infrastructure becomes vulnerable to a cyber-attack. The hackers working for the Russian government are ordered to try their best to breach the firewalls of the US's super computers and the topological networks in its military infrastructure in order to paralyse to take control of all its weapon systems and nuclear weapons.

Quality 27: A perfect fascist nation is like a Zen warrior

Comment: The more other nations fight the perfect fascist nation, the more they get hurt themselves and the stronger they make that nation. In addition to this, the more they try to take control of its population or its cyber infrastructure, the more they realise their own insignificance compared to it and the greatness of their superior.

The ruler of the perfect fascist nation is a Zen master and a warrior and he regularly create KOAN puzzles for his enemies.

Quality 28: The leader of a perfect fascist nation is not a barking dog, but is a sleeping lion

Comment: It is known by every psychologist in the world that the more powerful the Ego of a person becomes, the bigger becomes his desire for "attention seeking". A person who has a massive Ego that is coupled up with a low degree of intelligence, does all that he can to divert the minds of the people around him from whatever they are doing to his own face and his speech. He does this by either deliberately breaking something at the place or suddenly shouting out; May I have your attention please? I have something important to tell you.

For the leader of a perfect fascist nation, his great Ego is coupled up with an equally great intelligence. Thus, he only seeks the attention of the others if it is necessary for him or if their lives are in danger. This is because he does not want to bring himself dishonour by turning the people around him away from their own work and pay attention to his trivial statements.

The person with a great Ego and small intelligence is just like a dog. He desires to seek attention by just barking aimlessly. The leader of a perfect fascist nation is like a lion. When he wants something, he gets up and via the art of war, attains it and acquires the attention of the whole world. When he has accomplished his mission, he soon goes back to his private life.

Quality 29: The leader of the perfect fascist nation is a magnanimous man, while that of an imperfect fascist nation is pusillanimous

Comment: What are the qualities of a magnanimous person? They are;

1. He does not care to give compliments to those who are of no use to him. He only gives his compliments to those who bring him more wealth or more respect in the eyes of the rest of the world.
2. When an emergency strikes his nation, he is the last person to ask for help from his soldiers and scientists. He orders them to help the others first and come to help him only when every person in his group is out of danger.
3. He is outspoken and frank towards everyone.
4. He undertakes the biggest problems of his nation and the world with 100% determinism and courage.
5. He maintains his rationality and morality in the company of the most vulgar and insane people of his nation.
6. Treats the poor people of his nation with compassion and desires to be their benefactor.
7. Only runs after danger when it is necessary.
8. Considers Honour and not money or pleasure as the greatest good in the world.

The qualities of a pusillanimous man are;

1. He is ignorant of his own real nature and thus creates a fake identity of himself in the minds of his people.
2. Deprives his citizens of the things that they deserve.

3. Carries out all his activities in a vulgar and showy manner and does them at the wrong times.
4. He takes great risks for the sake of robbing the people of his own nation.
5. He has an immense fear of poverty.

Quality 30: The leader of the perfect fascist nation does that he can to prevent his nation from becoming like the kingdom of Sparta

Comment: The kingdom of Sparta was the most powerful fascist organization of its time. However, despite being so, it did not last long. Why? This is because in it, everyone knew a great deal about the art of war, but very little about the art of living. In it, it was compulsory for all the male citizens to eat together. Those who refused to were imprisoned. The goal of the lawmakers was to transform every young man into a soldier with very little morality.

The Spartans believed that money, power, and pleasure are acquired only via war and not via scientific discoveries and inventions. Plus, a soldier who refused to fight due to a rational reason was soon put to death without any trial.

The Spartan women lived a polygamous and intemperate life, enjoyed more freedom than the men, and indulged in luxurious parties and made the men from the poor families their slaves.

The United States is transforming into the kingdom of Sparta very rapidly. The Hollywood moguls know this and they displayed their belief by creating the movie, 300.

For the leader of the perfect fascist nation, there are two nightmares that he wishes should never come true; defeat in an expected war and the nation turning into the kingdom of Sparta

Quality 31: The leader of an imperfect fascist nation is a slave to his own Ego and so are all his people

Comment: A person, who is not the slave of his own Ego, spends his money or his energy only at the right opportunity. However, a person who is a slave to his Ego spends his money and energy in a whimsical manner. He spends 100 dollars where he should spend only 10 dollars and spends 10 dollars where he should spend 100 dollars. Such a person is a mixture of pusillanimity and prodigality and is an easy prey for robbers of all kinds.

People who are the slaves of their own Ego, become more and more insane minded with time and in order to prevent suicide, they keep on increasing their consumption of cigarettes, alcohol, and drugs. In addition to this, there is another irony associated with them; when a person whose intelligence has conquered his Ego, tells them about their real nature, they just turn around and go away. Afterwards, they either develop contempt or an indifferent attitude towards such a person.

It was said by Jesus Christ; Self-control is the greatest guardian of all our other virtues.

Quality 32: The mind of the leader of the perfect fascist nation is 50% industrial and 50% anti-industrial

Comment: A nation is destined to perish soon if the mind of its ruler becomes either 100% industrial or 100% anti-industrial. The qualities of an industrial mind are; amass wealth via knowledge, skills, immorality, and the art of war, store it in high safety zones, and keep on destroying the natural ecosystems of the nation for the sake of the development and the expansion of the cities, agricultural lands, and factories.

The qualities of an anti-industrial mind are; create and preserve peace and harmony in the region of residence, create and preserve a high degree of morality, regard the pursuit of wealth and power as evil, and stay in complete friendship with Mother Nature by not interfering with her creations.

The industrial mind cannot survive in an anti-industrial society and the anti-industrial mind cannot survive in an industrial society. Both kinds of minds despise each other and try to wipe out each other's existence.

The leader of the prefect fascist nation is equally industrial and anti-industrial at the same time. He only helps, and motivates all the capitalists and the industry empowering scientists to attain their maximum potential, but also gives the same magnitude of help, security, and motivation to all the environmentalists, biologists, and the farmers of his nation.

He knows that his nation cannot become more and more advanced and powerful, if all the natural ecosystems in it were almost destroyed. At the same time, he is also aware of the fact that his nation will never progress rapidly in science and technology if the environmental problems are given too much attention. He never allows the environmentalists and the farmers to become so powerful that they start to tell him and the scientists as to what they should do for the future of the nation.

Quality 33: The relation between the leader of the perfect fascist nation and his people is just like that between a real master and a real servant

Comment: The qualities of a real master and a real servant are;

1. Self-control, courage, and justice are present in equal quantities in both.
2. The master never desires admiration from his servant, but only desires respect. This is also the situation of the servant.
3. The master never says to his servant; you work under me. He always tells his servant; you work with me. The servant also believes in the same thing.
4. The master never tries to take control of the Ego and the intelligence of his servant. The same rule is followed by the servant.
5. The master never shows irresponsibility and incompetence towards his servant and so does the servant towards his master.
6. The master can survive without the servant and the servant can survive without the master.

Quality 34: The leader of the prefect fascist nation believes in the "alpha" theory of life and not the "omega" theory

Comment: The "alpha" theory of life is a product of the Bible and the Koran, while the "omega" theory of life is a product of the philosophy of Epicurus.

The "alpha" theory states that God has created the Cosmos and all the infinite number of species in it. He keeps a constant watch over all of them. The theory is further divided into two types.

Type 1 says that although God keeps a constant watch over all His creations, He never interferes in whatever they do in their lives. This type gives rise to the belief in "free will". However, He might do something if they ask Him for help. Thus, although your destiny is in your own hands, God can change it if you deserve His help and proceed to ask Him via praying. All the Christians in the world believe in the alpha-type 1 theory of creation.

Type 2 says that although God keeps a constant watch over all His creations, He interferes in their lives at His own whim driven thinking. This type destroys the belief in "free will". However, this also produces a result that is immensely more beautiful than what type 1 produces. The followers of alpha-type 1 believe that God will help you if you ask Him even if you have committed 1000 sins in your life. They believe that since you are His creation, He becomes obliged to help you if you ask Him in humble manner. They believe that for God, injustice, robbery, and the murder of the innocent are unimportant. Since God created you, he knew that you would commit many sins before you asked Him for help and guidance. Thus, the alpha-type 1 theory has the greatest number of religious minded followers in the United States, Europe, and Australia. All the leaders of the so-called church Ministries (Joyce Meyer, David Jeremiah, etc.) preach the truth of this theory.

The alpha-type 2 theory says that your life and your destiny are not in your hands. It is in the hands of an all-powerful creator who is engaged in a possibly eternal war with an angel who rebelled against Him and became not only His enemy but also of His other loyal and loving angels. God never tolerates the existence of injustice, robbery, exploitation, and murder of the innocent for long. These qualities are possessed by Satan (IBLIS in the Koran) and it transferred them to many of his master's creations. Thus, if you commit even one sin, you have already lost your "deservedness" for help from God. The theory says that the nations where Satan is the strongest, will soon be destroyed by massive earthquakes and wildfires, category 5 hurricanes, epic drought and heat waves, and floods like the Noah's flood in the Bible. The theory says that the sinners and the followers of Satan have no right to ask God for help if they become miserable.

The followers of the alpha-type 2 theory are the Protestant Christians. They believe that God is not only a warrior, but is also a judge. The entire Cosmos is His court and every species in it is being put on trial by the lawyers, which are the stars. Thus, the Sun is the lawyer of the Homo sapiens species. The Protestants believe that climate change is not a product of the burning of fossil fuels for more than 150 years. It is a product of the on-going fight between God and Satan. The places where the population of the sinners is the greatest will be wiped out first by great natural disasters and pathogenic plagues. Taking into consideration all the disasters that have occurred in California, the EU nations, China, Mumbai (India), Canada, and Australia, there is a high possibility that this theory is true.

The omega theory was created by Epicurus and is also followed by scientists who have the mentality of Copernicus. It says that although God has created this Cosmos and all the species in it, He is not bothered to observe them because He is busy creating new Cosmoses. If God is immortal, then He has an infinite amount of time at His disposal. In such a situation why would He create only one Cosmos and stop making new ones? According to this theory, there are an infinite number of Cosmoses and many of them have laws and forces that are completely different from the one that we live in. These Cosmoses are so distant from the one that we live in, that we would never be able to reach them, no matter how much advanced we became in this Cosmos. Even if we did reach them, we would never be able to survive inside them, because our mind would be a product of the laws and the forces of this Cosmos.

According to the omega theory, we are nothing but a minute pack of organic molecules, assembled purely via the laws of statistical probability and not due to some divine plan, sitting on a dust particle known as Earth, that was assembled by the same method, which is moving without any purpose around a tiny ball of gas and plasma known as the Sun.

The omega theory is anti-religious and pro-science. It gives total support to the idea of free will, the irrelevance of doing prayers and indulging in the rituals of your religion, and the unimportance of living either a moral or an immoral life. It says that if you remain happy by the execution of great immoral acts and not suffer any consequences, then go ahead and do them. Happiness is the greatest priority and you can attain it either via morality or immorality. It also denies the existence of anything happening to you after you die. Thus, it denies the existence of Heaven and Hell and the existence of invisible angels sitting on your shoulders and making a record of every good deed and every sin that you commit in your lifetime.

The leader of the perfect fascist nation is a believer in the alpha-type 2 theory. The leader of an imperfect fascist nation believes in either the alpha-type 1 or the omega theory.

Quality 35: The leader of the perfect fascist nation believes that the greatest protection against weakness and cowardice is "war"

Comment: A person who has been created weak and timid by Nature dislikes war and is pacifist minded. With the passage of time, such a person becomes even more weak, physically, and mentally, and even more timid. He in the prime of his youth behaves like an old person and is unable to carry out even the ordinary daily tasks of his life. His muscles becomes thinner and thinner, the appetite goes below normal, and the degree of fatigue keeps on increasing due to which he prefers to lie on the bed far longer than normal people. He makes his life increasingly sedentary and the magnitude of despise for the industrial world keeps on getting higher. In addition to this, he starts fearing those things that must never be feared, becomes paranoid, and due to it gets highly startled even by a small noise around him, starts to believe in the doomsday prophecies of others and creates a few by himself, and is easily put into a submissive state even by a petty criminal or robber.

War and an ambitious and bellicose mind are the only way to avoid such a fate.

Quality 36: The leader of the prefect fascist nation never feels the thoughts that all the power holders of an imperfect fascist nation feel

Comment: The three thoughts that all the generals, politicians, capitalists, and the priests of an imperfect fascist nation feel are;

1. A shipwrecked sailor floating in a raft on a stormy ocean.
2. Standing alone on a sea shore with no hope of any one coming to relieve them of their loneliness.
3. Doing continuous self-mockery.

The leader of the perfect fascist nation believes that he is an eagle who is flying majestically and serenely over a stormy ocean with zero probability of falling into it. He believes that he is standing in a place that is beyond this Cosmos and is surrounded by gods who are looking at him with loving eyes.

Quality 37: Of the four types of people that are found in the world, the leader of the perfect fascist nation tries his best to amplify the population of type 2 and type 3

Comment: The four types of people that are created by the Cosmos are;

1. They desire only their own happiness.
2. They desire the happiness of their children more than their own.
3. They desire the happiness of their nation more than their own happiness and that of their children.
4. They desire not only their own happiness, but that of their children and all the nations of the world.

In type 1, comes a real tyrant king or a dictator. In type 2 come those parents who are neither communistic minded nor capitalist minded, but are spiritual minded. The former regard and treat their children as their servants and the latter regard their children as their farm cattle.

In type 3, come those people who are known by the constitutions of the nation as the "true patriots". In type 4, come those people who are as humanitarian minded as they are scientific minded. They want all the nations of the world to unite into one single "super nation" so that the occurrence of World War 3 can be permanently prevented. The best examples are; Albert Einstein and Carl Sagan.

Both Type 1 and Type 4 are destructive to the development of a great fascist nation.

Quality 38: The leader of the perfect fascist nation tries his best to minimize the population of "wailers" in his nation

Comment: When a person experiences severe depression for a long period of time, he becomes a wailer. The great gamer of the perfect fascist nation knows about all the causes that transform a normal man or woman into a wailer. These are;

1. Doing exhaustive work without any payment at the end of it.
2. No thanks from those for whom the work has been done.
3. The non-availability of any kind of medical help for the after-effects of non-paid work.
4. Subjection to intimidation from childhood and during the non-paid working life by either the superiors in the workplace or by the impious and malicious individuals.

The leader of the perfect fascist nation always seeks out those citizens who are engaged in work that is essential for the survival and the growth of his nation, but are not paid even a small salary for it. The best example of such a citizen is a "housewife". Thus, the leader will create a law due to which every housewife in the nation can come to a government facility and apply for a salary after giving an irrefutable proof to the authorities placed there that she is only a housewife and does not indulge in any kind of economic activity outside her home.

The leader will also order all the children and the young people of his nation to give gratitude to their parents, at least twice every day, for what they do for them. To encourage them to do this, he will create a facility in every major city where the children and the youngsters can come and play war video games on the best gaming consoles, and eat delicious food for free for at least 3 hours. However, he will also tell them that they would only be allowed inside the facility after their parents contact its authorities and tell them that they are doing what they were told to do.

The leader will also create a law which will order the authorities of all the schools and colleges of the nation, that they will never intimidate or humiliate a student who has not done something that is harmful either to his school or college or to the nation. If a teacher does this, even after the law has been passed, then the student will have the option to come to a facility where he will give proof to its authorities of the teacher's illegal act. If the authorities accept the proof, then punishment would be given to the teacher.

None of these qualities are found in the fascist nations of the real world.

Quality 39: The leader of the perfect fascist nation has all the qualities of the Chief Executive Officer (CEO) of a great capitalistic organization

Comment: The qualities of the CEO of a great capitalist organization are;

1. Ability to decide rapidly after the analysis of the facts with the deepest rationality and consultation with the others in the organization.
2. A will that is as strong and unshakable as a mountain with respect to the enemies.
3. Giving speeches that are brief but possess a great intellectual depth.
4. Ordering the equals in his organization to respect each other.
5. Giving motivation to the talented inferiors in his organization.
6. Great skill in negotiating, and diplomacy.
7. 100% ruthlessness towards the enemy.

Quality 40: In the perfect fascist nation, no man possesses the qualities of a person who lives a solitary life

Comment: The qualities of a solitary person are;

1. He is a either a pessimist or a nihilist.
2. He has a sullen face.
3. He is a patient of ANHEDONIA and dislikes meeting and talking to people, but if he does talk to them, he soon starts to talk in an angry manner.
4. He has a paranoiac mind.

All the citizens who are young, but are living a solitary life by their own will, will eventually become criminals. The leader of the perfect fascist nation is aware of this truth and orders his create a project whose goal is to locate and isolate all such abnormal individuals, in the various cities, from the rest of the population and bring them to a new facility that is specially created for them. Once here, they are given treatment by the best neuroscientists of the nation who try their best to transform them into normal humans. The successful cases are inserted back into the civilization of the nation and the unsuccessful ones are kept inside the facility for their entire lives.

Quality 41: The leader of the perfect fascist nation believes that creating a great nation is just like creating a great movie

Comment: Any movie made by Hollywood contains two kinds of incidents; the hypothetical and the non-hypothetical. The former, are those that cannot be explained via rationality while the latter are those that are a pure product of rationality. A movie that contains only non-hypothetical incidents becomes very boring, very soon, to its audience whereas a movie that contains only hypothetical incidents is impossible to create.

All the great movies of Hollywood contain an equal number of hypothetical and non-hypothetical incidents which are combined in a perfect harmony by the best script writers and computer experts and a large crew that consists of all the actors, the make-up artists, and the director of the movie. At the Oscar awards, the judges give either one or multiple Oscars to those movies in which the hypothetical and the non-hypothetical incidents have been so beautifully combined with each other that they cannot exist without each other.

In a fascist nation, the audience at a movie hall, get far more pleasure and excitement from the hypothetical incidents than from the non-hypothetical ones. This is because in a fascist nation, all the ordinary citizens think and behave irrationally most of the time during any day. Their rulers, however, behave in the opposite manner.

In order to increase the pleasure and excitement that the audience feels when they view a non-hypothetical incident, the script writer, and the director, shows the incident in a "new way". Movies in which all the non-hypothetical incidents are shown in a new way and the hypothetical ones are created in an immensely beautiful manner by computer engineering, become the biggest blockbusters and wealth earners in not only their own nation, but in many other nations.

When developing his nation, the ruler, or the great gamer, regularly keeps creating rational and irrational incidents in all the parts of it. The rational incidents are; the creation of science or business conferences, the creation of buildings, highways, flyovers, urban roads, factories, and housing colonies, and the creation of airports, shopping malls, restaurants, hospitals, education institutions, and public parks. The irrational incidents are; terrorist attacks, the creation of wars at the borders of the nation, and the invasion of a smaller and weaker nation.

In order to preserve or increase the greatness of his nation, the ruler makes sure that the number of the military activities of his nation is always equal to the number of civic activities. Thus, a nation whose civic infrastructure develops with immense speed and complexity, its military infrastructure also develops with the same speed and complexity. The best example of this is China.

Quality 42: The great gamer always tries to create a nation which is the greatest with respect to politics, with respect to economics, and with respect to mathematics

Comment: There are three types of great nations in the world today. They are;

1. **The politically great**: They have achieved and preserved all the goals of the Constitution.

2. **The economically great**: They have achieved an immense amount of wealth, but have not achieved all the goals of their constitution.

3. **The mathematically great**: They have achieved an immense amount of military power, but have not achieved all the goals of the Constitution.

In the first type belong; Canada, Iceland, the Netherlands, Norway, Sweden, and Finland. In the second type belong; Australia, Brazil, England, and France.

The United States, Russia, and China are 50% of the second type and 50% of the third type.

The ruler of the prefect fascist nation creates such a constitution that all its laws and utopias can only be fulfilled if the nation acquires great economic and military power. This is not seen in any of the fascist nations of the world. Why? It is because the very first law of the constitution says that no matter how great a nation should become, economically and militarily, all its citizens shall remain completely free from its ruling regime. In a fascist nation of the real world, the more militarily powerful the ruling regime of the nation becomes, the greater becomes the magnitude of the enslavement of the citizens to it.

Quality 43: The leader of the prefect fascist nation never tells lies either to his people or to himself

Comment: The qualities of a person who lies to himself and to the others are;

1. No respect for himself and the others.
2. Licentious and extremely greedy for wealth and luxuries.
3. Quick to take offence.
4. Makes mountains out of molehills.
5. Sometimes behaves and talks like a drunkard.

A gamer who always sticks to the self-created fake identity, does not respect his mind and body. In order to remain ignorant of his real identity, he never decides to read a single book on either science or philosophy. He tries his best to persuade the other people in the world to believe in the truth of his fake identity and pay no importance to the desire to investigate his real identity. It has been said by all the philosophers that if a person respects you, he will always reveal and maintain his real identity to you.

A person who does not have a strong desire for sensual pleasures and wealth will always display and maintain his real identity towards the people, in all kinds of situations.

Since his real self is always at war with his fake self, the gamer gets addicted to cigarettes, alcohol, and drugs. He also becomes short tempered towards those whom he gives respect, and who can show to the world his real-self. When such people say something that is trivial but annoying to the fake identity carrier, the latter erupts into anger and transforms their trivial statement into a mountain.

When the fake identity carriers, give public speeches, they do not understand the exact meaning of their own statements. This is also shown by a drunkard. The best examples of such people are the politicians of every nation of the world. For them, the "bottle" represents the nation, and the whisky in it represents power.

Quality 44: The goal of the leader of the perfect fascist nation is to transform his nation into a kingdom

Comment: What is the difference between a nation and a kingdom? There are two;

1. In a nation, the richest person is not the most powerful and the most powerful is not the richest. In a kingdom, the most powerful person, the king, or the queen, is also the richest person in it.

2. In a nation, the leader can attack and invade another nation only via the laws of the constitution and the permission of the financiers of the nation's "federal reserve bank". In a kingdom, the king, or the queen can attack and invade a nation or another kingdom purely according to his own wishes.

The leader of the perfect fascist nation has three goals in his mind; to become a king and not a politician, to bring immense respect and honour to himself and his citizens, and to save all his citizens from the tyranny of all the other nation and eventually, Mother Nature. He knows that all these three goals can only be reached if he becomes an autocrat and remains at the peak of power till the end of his life.

Quality 45: In an imperfect fascist nation, there are 4 types of people, but when the nation becomes perfect, only 2 survive

Comment: The people of the world can be classified with respect to two qualities; practical wisdom and theoretical knowledge. The former is amplified by the philosophies of Epicurus and the stoics of the Roman Empire and the latter is amplified by the study of mathematics, physics, and the life sciences.

According to practical wisdom, your existence on this planet is very brief and thus your goal, from your cradle to your grave, should be the continuous acquisition of wealth, power, and sensual pleasures. According to it, money, power, and pleasure are superior to philosophical contemplation and wisdom.

The latter should be abandoned or sacrificed to the former. In addition to this, you must do everything "on time". This includes, getting a job or starting a business, marrying for the first time between the age of 25 and 30 years, and making the best efforts for the acquisition of political power by doing all kinds of essential and dirty works.

According to theoretical knowledge, although your existence on this planet is very brief, your goal should not be the continuous acquisition of money, power, and pleasure, but should be the continuous acquisition of the knowledge of the Cosmos and the creation of new technologies through it. People, who love this more than practical wisdom, always keep saying; seek knowledge from cradle to grave.

In most people of the world, the amplification of practical wisdom does not lead to the amplification of theoretical knowledge. The politicians of every nation are the best example of this truth. It is also a truth that the amplification of the latter always leads to the amplification of the former, later-on.

In an imperfect fascist nation, the four types of people are;

1. Low practical wisdom, but high theoretical knowledge
2. High practical wisdom, but low theoretical knowledge
3. High practical wisdom and high theoretical knowledge
4. Low practical wisdom and low theoretical knowledge

To the second type, belong all the politicians, the priests, the entertainers, and the capitalists of the nation. To the third type, belong all the scientists of the nation and to the fourth type, belong all the hippies and the idlers of the nation. The first type, eventually transform into the third type.

The more a nation develops, militarily, under the rule of a great gamer, the lower and lower becomes the population of the type 4 people and of those type 1 people who fail to transform into type 3.

Quality 46: The leader of the perfect fascist nation, unlike that of an imperfect one, is not a bully and never tries to become one

Comment: Normal people believe that bullying is a product of courage. The reality is just the opposite. A bully is a coward and if a person becomes a coward, he becomes a bully. The more-timid a person becomes, the more he will bully his inferior when the proper opportunity arrives. The more courageous and fearless a person, the more will be his repulsion from the art of bullying.

All bullies show tyranny and cruelty towards those who are less powerful than them either physically or mentally, but when someone who is more powerful than them, comes in front of their faces, they immediately turn into either the chicks of hens or loyal slaves. This is never shown by a person who is not a bully. When his superior comes in front of him, he stays calm, investigates all of his superior's qualities, and then makes an all-out effort to become his equal and then transcend him.

The leader of the perfect fascist nation knows; how to acquire his powers, how to use them, when to use them, and on whom to use them.

Quality 47: The leader of the perfect fascist nation is a Taoist and a Zen master

Comment: Just like a Taoist, the leader of the perfect fascist nation;

1. Does not harbour any contempt and grievances against anyone in his own nation and the rest of the world.
2. Thinks about the past as much as the present and the future, but never sticks to any of them.
3. He only creates or takes part in a war if it is necessary.
4. When he talks to his people, he makes them feel that they are above him.
5. He gives power only to those who deserve it and never to those who seek it, but do not deserve it.
6. He does not feel honoured when everyone in his nation praises him. This is because his honour lies in the fulfilment of his goals.
7. Does not feel ashamed when everyone in his nation criticizes him. This is because his self-respect lies in the fulfilment of his goals.
8. Temporary gain does not make him happy and temporary loss does not grieve him.
9. Punishments do not threaten him and rewards do not encourage him.

Just like a Zen master, he

1. Whacks another nation with his military power in order to awaken its leaders from their continuous slumber in their sensual pleasures, luxuries, and social parties.

2. He creates KOANS and subjects the other nations to them in order to determine and test their strength and intelligence.

3. Creates goals which appear impossible from the point of view of practical wisdom.

4. Tries to baffle, continuously, the intelligence and the Ego of the leaders of all the other nations of the world.

5. Finds wonder and amusement in the daily activities of his nation and the rest of the world.

6. He asks questions that seem absurd and unanswerable to the people in his own regime and those in the regimes of the other nation.

7. Does not follow any religion, but his own mind.

8. If he lands up in a situation where committing suicide is necessary for the preservation of self-honour, then he commits it in the most calm and serene manner

9. Says to his own citizens and those of the other nation that his nation will ultimately become 100% self-sufficient and free from all the other nations.

Quality 48: To the simpletons and the hippies of his nation, the leader appears to be a child

Comment: The simpletons and the hippies of the nation, when they sit together to talk, say to each other;

1. Our leader never gets focused on anything in his nation or rest of the world.

2. Our leader walks without knowing as to where exactly he is going.

3. Our leader stops and contemplates without knowing what he is doing.

These are the same qualities that are present in a child of any race in the world. The leader knows about the opinions of the simpletons and the hippies, but just like an epicurean god, pays no importance or attention to them and believes that all of them will eventually perish via their own follies.

Quality 49: The leader of the perfect fascist nation is an architect but not like a real one

Comment: A real architect believes that his only duty is to create huge skyscrapers or palace like buildings. He believes that it is not his duty to;

1. Worry about the fates of his creations.
2. The fates of those who live inside them.
3. The problems and the miseries of those who live inside them.

The leader of the perfect fascist nation, who is a great gamer, is not like this. He believes that he has 2 duties to complete in his lifetime. The first is the victory over another nation without any kind of fighting and the second is to engineer a beautiful destiny for all the non-organic concepts in his nation and all the good citizens of his nation. In addition to this, he considers their problems and miseries with the same importance as he does of his own children. Why? It is because he believes that the perfect "war machine" nation is created only when everyone in it is in a state of perpetual anxiety, but strong and healthy at the same time. How is this possible if their problems are not reduced in their magnitude or eliminated?

The leaders of all the imperfect fascist nations of the world are like the real architect.

Quality 50: The leader of the perfect fascist nation is as wise as he is intelligent

Comment: When a non-wise and arrogant person faces either a failure in his project of commits a mistake, he always says to the others; I am not responsible for it because there are no problems with me. This is happened only because of the problems the world has. Such people never show any desire for self-improvement and thus keep on getting hit by repeated failures and mistakes. This keeps on increasing their misery and eventually a point comes when they cannot tolerate it any more. Beyond this point, they either commit suicide or commit suicide after carrying out a "mass shooting" in a public place. In all the imperfect fascist nations of the world, including the US, the population of such people is increasing rapidly.

In the perfect fascist nation, every citizen, including its leader, is a wise person and believes that if he faces a failure or commits a mistake it is purely a product of his own defect. In such a nation, every person keeps on gaining self-knowledge and self-improvement and thus there are no suicides or mass shootings.

It is known by all the philosophers that the awareness of a self-defect is sensed only through pain and not through pleasure. Thus, those who live the most pleasure filled life are the most unaware and ignorant of self-defects. Pain and not pleasure is the path to enlightenment.

Quality 51: The leader of the perfect fascist nation is the legislator of his nation and is not like a real legislator

Comment: A real legislator has two goals in his mind; to keep the working population stuck to its "daily routine" and to keep it stuck to what it has been taught by the government. This produces beneficial results in the short-term future. It transforms the nation into a gigantic machine and each citizen into a robot that is capable of sexual reproduction. The wealth and the military power of the nation, gets amplified very rapidly. However, in the long-term it produces disastrous results.

If the population is made to stick to a routine that never shows any sign of change, then more and more members of it will fall prey to increasing boredom. The increasing boredom will create increasing anxiety and increasing cases of deaths either due to insanity or due to alcohol and drug overuse.

If the population is made to stick to what it has been taught, even under rapidly changing economic and environmental conditions, then it will fail to adapt to the changes around it and thus would either self-destruct or be killed off by Mother Nature. Its imaginative powers would also keep on decreasing and this would lead to a rapid slowdown in the progress of mathematics and physics and the life sciences in all the best research organizations of its nation.

The great gamer of the perfect fascist nation is aware of all this and thus he create laws which keep on decreasing the boredom of the people every year and keep on increasing their adaptive power and their imaginative power.

The leader of the perfect fascist nation is a destroyer of the Byzantine immobility or the Dark Age.

Quality 52: The leader of the perfect fascist nation is not an incontinent person

Comment: The qualities of an incontinent person are;

1. He behaves and talks like a movie actor.
2. He keeps his real thoughts hidden.
3. He never learns from his mistakes and keeps on repeating the same behaviour again and again.
4. He is either licentious or non-licentious.
5. He does not believe that he is doing something wrong until he lands himself in great danger.
6. He shows scepticism in everything and thus can never take a firm decision on anything.
7. He thinks that a good action is a bad action and a bad action is a good action.

As was said before, the great gamer dislikes movie actors and thus never goes into any of the movie award ceremonies in his nation, unless it is 100% necessary.

Quality 53: The leader of the perfect fascist nation is a destroyer of the WAR TRINITY

Comment:

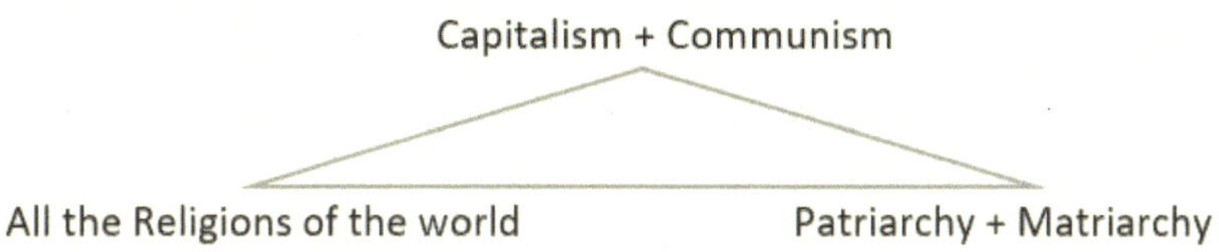

A pure communist or a pure capitalist is does not believe in any of the multiple religions that have been created so far. A pure priest of any religion, always desires to create a world where everyone lives in 100% harmony with Mother Nature, does not try to destroy her creations, and does not interfere with those processes where only Mother Nature should rule. Thus, he wants to create the agrarian world where everyone indulges in farming, eats only natural food and lives in small but very comfortable houses.

Although the priests of all religions are pro-patriarchy and anti-matriarchy, both capitalism and communism are pro-egalitarian.

The leader of the perfect fascist nation is neither a capitalist nor a communist. The capitalist wants the people of the nation to work "for him" while the communist wants to work "for them". However, a communist only remains a communist if he does not acquire immense power and wealth. When he does, he transforms into a capitalist. The best example of this is the leader of Russia, Vladimir Putin. The greatest capitalist in the world, Elon Musk, is one of his best friends. Why? It is because Putting has now metamorphosed into a capitalist from a Bolshevik communist.

What are the qualities of a capitalist? They are as follows;

1. He tries to persuade the people that they should never feel proud of themselves. He tries to reinforce this by saying that the Earth is a pale blue dot and is juts the left-over debris after the formation of the solar system.
2. He tries to convince them that although he can survive on his own mind for his entire lifetime (see John Galt's speech in Atlas Shrugged), they cannot survive without him for even a single year.
3. He tries to convince them that they should feel proud that they are idiots and that he is a god.
4. He wants the people to look at him with fear, awe, and a feeling of powerlessness.
5. To keep on increasing the childishness of their minds (a process known as CHILDIZATION).
6. To persuade them via the internet to assemble and form huge crowds in the central areas of their city for no rational reason.
7. To gain their love and trust by persuading and allowing them to commit sins and to prevent themselves from getting hit by the consequences of their sinning.
8. To persuade the people to tell them all the secrets of their minds, even the most bizarre ones, and to tell them none of their own in return.

9. To convince the people that there are no spiritual mysteries in the Universe and that the Earth belongs to all of us.
10. He uses his wealth only to increase further his own wealth and his Ego.

The great gamer of the perfect fascist nation says to his people;

1. You should feel proud of yourselves because you are living on a planet that is most probably the core of the Universe and is the best of all the infinite number of worlds in it.
2. You can survive and prosper even if I am dead, but I cannot survive and accomplish all my goals without you.
3. Collectively, you are as powerful compared to me as the sun is compared to the Earth.
4. I look at you in the same manner as I look at my own mind and my family and you should also look at me in the same manner. Do not feel any fear when you look at me.
5. If you tell me your secrets, I will tell you mine.
6. Do not gather in the central areas of the city for no rational reason.
7. The Universe contains many mysteries and the Earth is not ours.
8. I will use my wealth to make not only my life better, but all of yours too.

The communist says; the child of an ordinary proletarian is destined to become an ordinary proletarian, no matter how much education he is given and how much philosophy he is taught.

The great gamer says; the child of an ordinary proletarian contains the seed of a great scientist or a super soldier. The only way to germinate it and make it into a fully grown tree is to place him in the proper environment and to give him the right teacher and education.

The great gamer does not believe in Buddhism which says that the Universe is a disaster. He does not believe in Christianity or Judaism which says that the universe is benevolent to those who are "sin free" and hostile towards those who have become "sin ridden". He does not believe in Islam which says that Allah is an all-watching and a wrathful dictator. He does not believe in Hinduism which says that the Universe is created, sustained, and eventually destroyed by three gods.

The leader of the perfect fascist nation does not want his nation to be either patriarchal or matriarchal minded. He wants to create a nation where everyone regards his fellow citizens as his friend and future benefactor.

The qualities of a pure patriarchal nation are;

1. The men keep their women confined in their houses against their will and for as long as they (the men) desire.
2. They are not allowed to go to a school or watch television without the consent of either their father or their elder brother or their husband.
3. Their husband orders them to have sex with him against their will.
4. They are verbally and physically abused for their mistakes.
5. They are regarded nothing but "baby producing machines" and are thus considered as 100% incapable of achieving anything great in the world of science and the arts.
6. The favourite motto of the men is; a woman is nothing but the shadow of a man.

In a matriarchal nation, it is the women who do all those things that the men in a patriarchal nation do. Their favourite motto is; anything that boys can do, the girls can do better.

In the perfect fascist nation, the leader believes that everything that is unrighteous is unlawful and everything that is unlawful is unrighteous. When it comes to justice, he says; Do, to a person exactly what he has done to others.

Quality 54: The leader of the perfect fascist nation is not a socialist

Comment: The qualities of a socialist are;

1. He hates both the capitalists and the communists.
2. He is a follower of nepotism.
3. Wants to become the hero of the proletarians of his nation either via war or via rapid economic growth.
4. Believes without and scepticism that his ideology would create a perfect nation.
5. Tries to create peace with his biggest enemies.

The great gamer does not hate the capitalists, but wants to keep them "under his thumb" as-long-as he remains the nation's ruler. He never places one of his family members in a seat of power if he does not deserve it. He wants to become a hero only in his own eyes and in the eyes of the creator of the Universe. He does not believe that his ideology would eventually make his nation perfect and never makes peace with his biggest enemies.

Quality 55: The leader of the perfect fascist nation is a great chess player

Comment: In an imperfect fascist nation, the leader, in a war with another nation, uses the proletarians of his nation as the pawns and the legislators, the scientists, the priests, and the entertainers and the other pieces.

For the leader of the perfect fascist nation, the pawns are his normal soldiers and the better trained soldiers and the super soldiers are the other pieces.

Quality 56: The leader of the perfect fascist nation does not believe in astrology and is not a fake futurologist

Comment: The fake futurologist makes his visions of the future with 0% consideration of the past and the present. This is not the case for the real futurologist. The astrologer says that your destiny is 50% determined by your own activities and 50% by the other planets of the solar system. All of this is considered as nonsense by the leader of a perfect fascist nation.

Quality 57: The leader of the perfect fascist nation is a follower of Postmodernism

Comment: Postmodernism says that it is impossible to know 100% about any concept in the Universe, including the Earth and its atmosphere. Thus, it forbids the conduct of determinism with respect to distant time periods. A postmodernist says; no one in the world can tell what will the Earth's surface look like or the global climate structure would be, 50 million years from now. Those who say that they know are nothing but pure liars.

Postmodernism is the cause of the rise of multiple universities in every developed and developing nation of the world. Every university, via its scientists, tries to show the world and the other universities that;

1. One or more of the theories of Concept X made by another university is or are wrong.
2. There are new facts about Concept X that are unknown by the other universities.

Quality 58: Since the leader of the perfect fascist nation is industrial minded, he believes in the anthropomorphic principle

Comment: The anthropomorphic principle is the ruling principle in the minds of all the industrial minded people in the world. It says; the goal of the 4 forces of the Universe and their various laws is to create an intelligent species on a life sustaining planet and to eventually make it the dominant species on that planet. They do this, because they want the species to understand them, play with them, and eventually conquer them.

The non-anthropomorphic principle is the ruling principle in the minds of all the anti-industrial minded people in the world. It says; the goal of the 4 forces of the Universe and their various laws is to create a species whose hunting power, sensual power, immune system power, and reproductive power is so powerful, that it becomes the dominant species on the planet and consumes the members of any of the other species "whenever it likes to". The members of this species have no natural enemies and are thus the apex predators in all the ecosystems in every continent of the planet.

The former principle is followed by all the scientists and the philosophers of the world, while the latter principle is followed by all the brutes, athletes, and the criminals of the world.

Quality 59: The mutineers in a perfect fascist nation are always of the feeble kind

Comment: Mutineers are of two kinds; the strong and the weak. In an imperfect fascist nation that is ruled by an idiot brained and an easily corruptible leader, the population of the strong mutineers keeps on increasing and when they finally decide to attack the leader and his regime, they attain complete success quite soon.

However, in a perfect fascist nation, whose leader is someone whom most of the citizens idolise and imitate, who is almost as intelligent as Isaac Newton, and who can never be corrupted by any earthly power, the population of the mutineers is very small and they are of the weak kind.

The qualities of a weak mutineer are;

1. He is not able to sustain his mutiny for a lengthy time period.
2. Even if they attain freedom from their ruler, they are unable to survive for long on their own.

3. When they are struggling to survive in a new territory, they come to realise that their ruler did not stop or kill them because he wanted to make fun of them and make them discover the truth by themselves Due to this realization they start to do self-blasphemy. Some of them go back to their ruler and become his willing slaves, while the remaining ones commit suicide.

A good example of this was the mutiny of Alexei Navalny against Vladimir Putin.

Quality 60: Since the leader of the perfect fascist nation is an artist, he is also pro-variability and anti-uniformity

Comment: Art only comes into existence in a system where variability exists. The more the variability intensifies, the greater is the intensification of the creation of various kinds of artworks.

If art is the wife, then her husband is probability. Art cannot exist where probability does not exist and where probability does not exist, art and statistics do not exist. The child of art and probability is known as variability.

In a non-statistical Universe, there is no probability and thus there is no art and no variability.

Quality 61: The leader of the perfect fascist nation is a destroyer of ostracism

Comment: Ostracism has two goals; the removal of extremely intelligent but non-patriotic individuals from the nation, and to create laws that prevent the formation of such individuals in the future.

If a genius is non-patriotic, the leader tells him only one thing; work only for your own happiness and do not give a damn about the state of the nation and its future.

Quality 62: The leader of the perfect fascist nation has none of the qualities of a true tyrant and has all the qualities of a true king

Comment: The qualities of a true tyrant are;

1. He has greed for women and undeserved wealth.
2. His bodyguards are mercenaries.
3. He ill-treats his people by not giving them weapons for self-protection and keeps them living in filthy environments.

4. Regards the geniuses of his nation as his slaves and humiliates and slanders them if he decides to.
5. Prevents the moral citizens from forming factions by either imprisoning them or killing them.
6. Keeps most of the population poor and malnourished.
7. Does not want the poor and the middle-class citizens to get a proper amount of leisure time.
8. Orders his secret service and the police to spy on the citizens.
9. Stirs up conflicts between two states of his nation which were originally great friends.
10. Has no faith even in the members of his regime.
11. Loves flattery and hates those people who show self-pride in front of him.
12. He puts on a fake show of self-dignity, high religiousness, and high intelligence. He tries to attain perfection in the art of deception.
13. He ill-treats the young men of his nation but not the young women.

The qualities of a true king are;

1. He has greed only for self-earned honour.
2. His bodyguards are the people of his own kingdom.
3. He gives weapons to his people and make them live in clean and beautiful environments.

Quality 63: The leader of the perfect fascist nation tries, ASAP, to eliminate all the causes that cause the formation of a faction in his nation

Comment: Factions form in a nation when;

1. A man who is considered a hero by the citizens is not given any honour by its leader.
2. The economic inequality between the rulers and the ruled keeps on increasing.

3. The citizens do not have the power to accept or reject a proposal that is given to them by their ruler.
4. The ruler does not accept any proposal that is given to him by the citizens.
5. The citizens, who say that they deserve much more from the government than they are given, are ignored by their ruler continuously.
6. The population of robbers and criminals keeps on increasing due to a corrupt police force.
7. The elections are rigged.
8. Conflict between the various races keeps on increasing.

Factions are of two types; those that are against the constitution of the nation but not against its rulers and those that are against its rulers but not against its constitution. The former ones attack the legislators and the courts, whereas the latter ones attack the parliament of their nation.

Why does the perfect leader of an imperfect fascist nation try his best to reduce the number of factions in his nation? This is because the number of factions in a nation is inversely proportional to its intelligence. The most scientifically advanced nations are those where the number of factions against the constitution or the rulers is the least.

Quality 64: The leader of the perfect fascist nation is a "real" revolutionary

Comment: There are two kinds of revolutionaries or Bolsheviks; the real and the fake. The difference between the two is that the fake revolutionary ultimately "perishes" in the chaos that he creates while the real revolutionary become even bigger and more intelligent than before during the chaos and after its end.

The goal of both kinds of revolutionaries is the attainment of freedom for themselves and for all the citizens of their nation. However, the fake revolutionary tries to attain it by the gradual enslavement and exploitation of the citizens of his nation while the real revolutionary tries to attain it by creating gradual salvation of himself and the citizens of his nation.

It is a well-known fact of philosophy that the desire of men to enslave their inferiors is far greater than their desire to "know themselves". Thus, a fake revolutionary has no desire for self-knowledge and this increases the fuel to his desire to enslave and torture the people of his nation. The real revolutionary, on the other hand, wants to give freedom to his people through the process of self-understanding.

A real revolutionary is a man of rationality and enlightenment, but he is neither a humanitarian nor a pure rationalist.

The humanitarian has high morality but low ethics. Due to this, he does not punish or imprison those who deliberately pollute and destroy the natural ecosystems of his nation for the sake of getting rich and living a good life. He says that they are the children of God and thus have a right to pursue what is good for them. Thus, in a nation which is ruled by a humanitarian leader, the businessmen operate with 100% freedom and become super rich very soon. The massive air pollution over the major cities in India and China is because the mayors and the chief ministers of the states and provinces in which these cities are located, pretend to be humanitarians, but are not so. If they were humanitarians in the true sense, then no one in their city or state/province would sleep on the footpaths in a state of starvation.

The rationalist is a person of low morality, but high ethics. In his nation, the people are allowed and even encouraged to do sex parties, vulgar dances, and create porn movies in the various studios all over the nation. Free love, which eventually leads to incest, is encouraged and no punishment is given to those young men who very frequently utter the words "fuck" and "fucking" inside nightclubs, discos, and in the reality TV shows. However, such a leader tries his to keep his nation almost free from all kinds of pollution and to control and imprison the street criminals in the various cities through the police. He also gives an immense amount of security to all the major capitalists of his nation and encourages them to operate with 100% freedom as long as they do not pollute the environment of the cities and destroy the natural ecosystems beyond the point set by him. Why? It is because a capitalist is also a person with low morality and high ethics. He believes that a nation can only keep getting bigger, economically, and militarily, if all the good citizens are allowed to give full explosion to their sexual energy and are encouraged to take interest only in economic and scientific knowledge. The United States is the best example of this. All the senators, governors, mayors, the groups at the White House and the Pentagon are real rationalists but fake humanitarians.

National parks exist only in a nation which is ruled by a rationalist leader. This is because the exploitation and the destruction of Mother Nature is regulated and stopped beyond a certain point.

The fake revolutionary always becomes a real tyrant in the end because he has low morality and low ethics. He believes that he will attain the best for himself and his people by keeping them in the states of illiteracy, enslavement, and starvation for a long period of time. In such a nation, the magnitude of all kinds of pollution and the destruction of the natural ecosystems is unregulated and unrestricted. Such a nation eventually becomes a "hell on Earth" and a large section of its population tries to migrate to the nations that are ruled by the rationalist leaders. The best examples are; Adolf Hitler ruled Germany, North Korea, Mexico, Venezuela, several African nations, Burma, Iraq, and Syria.

The real revolutionary creates and progresses his revolution via the writing of his own books, planned boycotts of his enemy's industrial products in his own nation, creating and increasing the virtue of patience in own-self and in his people, and eventually employing the full power and intelligence of his nation's defence forces when the right opportunity arrives. The fake revolutionary, however, does all kinds of self-destructive activities to himself and to his people and uses the military power of his nation according to his own whim and at the wrong time.

Quality 65: The leader of the perfect fascist nation is an intelligent war monger, war indulger, and a pacifist

Comment: The war monger is a person who initiates a war and after that creates and intensifies the "war fever" in the population of his nation. In the great fascist nations like the US, Russia, and China, the war mongers and the news channels of the nation are locked up in a symbiotic relationship. By creating a war with another nation, the war monger benefits the news channels of his nation and by creating and intensifying the "war fever" (retaliation + anxiety) in the population, the news channels benefit the war monger.

The war indulgers are those who did not initiate the war, but are the ones who are ordered by the war monger to go into the battlefield and fight for the security and the glory of their nation. These people are the soldiers of the army, the pilots of the fighter jets and the bombers, and the soldiers of the submarines, navy battleships, and the air craft carriers. After the end of most wars, the war indulgers display a great amount of resentment towards their war monger leader. The best example of this was the mental state of the American soldiers after the end of the Vietnam War (this was shown by the reaction of John Rambo at the end of the movie First Blood).

The pacifists are of two kinds; the real and the fake. The real ones are those that do not play any part in the initiation of a war, do not take any interest in it after it has begun, and are not affected by the "war fever". The fake ones, however, do not play any part in the initiation of a war, but take full interest in it after it has begun, and soon get a powerful "war fever". Soon, they only start to watch the major news channels of their nation for a continuous stream of knowledge about the on-going war.

The fake pacifists are of two types;

1. **Pacifist + War Indulger**: He will condemn war when observing it, but if he is deprived of his wealth or his pleasure giving objects, he would soon transform into a war indulger. Such people excel in the art of acting and possess a very low level of morality towards others.

2. **Pacifist + War monger**: He believes in the existence of good and evil. Initially, he is a war indulger and says that in order to attain peace, war must happen. Thus, he initiates a war with full enthusiasm, but when he realises, later, that his own life and that of his loved ones is in danger, he soon transforms into pacifist and abandons his mission of the extermination of the evil people in his nation. Such people are timid by nature and are extremely attached to their family.

Quality 66: The leader of the perfect fascist nation eventually creates weapons, weapon systems, and a military infrastructure that is not invisible but is indiscernible to his enemy

Comment: An invisible object is one that cannot be detected by the eyes, but can be detected by the other sense organs. In addition to this, there are two kinds of invisible objects.

1. Invisible to only the eyes, but not to the other sense organs.

2. Invisible to only one part of the electromagnetic spectrum, but not to the other ones.

The example of the first kind of object was shown in the Hollywood movie, Hollow Man. The example of the second kind of object is a steal fighter or bomber. It is invisible only in the radio wave part of the electromagnetic spectrum.

An indiscernible object is also of two kinds;

1. Invisible to all the sense organs, but not to the electromagnetic spectrum.
2. Invisible to all the sense organs and all the parts of the electromagnetic spectrum.

The example of the first kind is a single atom of any element in the periodic table. The second kind is not found anywhere in the entire Cosmos. Why? It is because in order to have existence in the Cosmos, an object must be detectable in at least one part of the electromagnetic spectrum.

The leader of the perfect fascist nation eventually destroys the two pillars of Epistemology;

1. Everything that exists is perceptible.
2. Everything that is perceptible exists.

The only example of the second kind of indiscernible object or concept is God or Allah.

Quality 67: The leader of the perfect fascist nation hungers for honour, but does not believe in "MIGHT IS RIGHT"

Comment: Most of the power and wealth hungry people in the world believe that "MIGHT IS RIGHT". In addition to this they are also hungry for honour from the people they rule, deceive, and exploit. The qualities of such people are;

1. They believe that after they have created their "fake image" in the minds of their subjects, it must never be lost even if its preservation would lead to the deaths of billions of people.
2. They want their subjects to believe that they (the subjects) cannot exist without them.
3. In a secret and clever manner, they try to increase the population of illiterate, child minded, and idiotic people in their nation.
4. They give an immense degree of importance to the opinions of their subjects towards them.
5. They show rudeness and indifference to their subjects if they can give no further replies to their problems.
6. Insult and humiliate a genius, without any hesitation, in front of the nation if he gives them the opportunity to do so.

7. They get angry if they are asked to give a proof of the truth of the statements that they make in their speeches.

8. They settle, eventually, all the national problems using military power.

9. They make everyone around them stiff, gloomy, and pessimistic.

The leader of the perfect fascist nation has none of these qualities. He believes and follows the saying "RIGHT IS MIGHT", that is, righteousness and not brute and mindless power, always prevails in the end.

Quality 68: The leader of the perfect fascist nation never goes after "unmerited" fame

Comment: The great leader of the perfect fascist nation knows that;

1. Unmerited fame makes you feel uncomfortable and shameful.

2. Lasts far less long than merited fame.

3. An immense amount of work, including evil work, must be done in order to preserve it.

4. You become a fanatical follower of the saying "MIGHT IS RIGHT".

The person who hungers and acquires unmerited fame, eventually starts a process of self-destruction and in the process, destroys his nation too.

Quality 69: The leader of the perfect fascist nation does all that he can in order to avoid become a "brute"

Comment: The qualities of a brute are;

1. He is content with just being alive and in good health.

2. He has little or no fear of death.

3. He does not hope and is immune from anxiety and caring.

4. He has no desire to do something that will bring glory to him/her.

5. He enjoys sex far more than normal people.

6. He shows a far greater amount of careless behaviour than normal people.

7. He cannot tolerate a suffering period that is even moderately long.

When it comes to the soldiers in his/her army, the great gamer tries his/her best to eliminate qualities 3, 4, 6, and 7. He/she does his/her best to amplify qualities 1, 2, and 5.

The great gamer is a preacher of the "Lawrence of Arabia Theory". It says that if you fear that pain is coming to hit you, then when it hits you, its intensity would be 10 times greater than its actual intensity. Thus, the right thought over here is; not minding that it hurts.

Quality 70: The leader of the perfect fascist nation will always be a man and never a woman

Comment: A woman can never become the leader of the perfect fascist nation and even if she does, she will not look and behave like a woman. Why? It is because of the qualities that a real woman with a high degree of femininity possesses.

The qualities of women are;

1. They are more short-sighted than men.
2. They always choose without enough deliberation, the shortest route to their goal.
3. They are more prodigal than men.
4. Most of their mind is focused in the present rather than the past or the future.
5. They only pretend to take interest in science and war.
6. They regard an illusion as the truth more powerfully than men.
7. They are more interested in the small problems rather than the big ones.
8. They are more ecstasy loving than men.
9. Their only goal in life is to conquer men.
10. They use cleverness instead of intelligence to solve their problems.
11. Hypocrisy is more powerful in them.
12. They are less honour hungry than men.
13. They get bored much sooner than men when dealing with problems that are not related to their self-interests.

14. They treat evil or idiotic men with much greater sympathy and kindness.
15. They make great efforts to conceal their real thoughts.

Quality 71: The leader of the perfect fascist nation appears as a "paradox" to the citizens of his nation

Comment: When people get to know about a paradox, there are three possible outcomes;

1. **Laughter**: Generated when the paradox poses no threat to their lives or livelihoods
2. **Fear**: Generated when the paradox poses a threat to their lives and livelihoods
3. **Curiosity**: Generated when the paradox gives them pleasure

When the ordinary brained people of the nation observe their perfect leader, they;

4. Sometimes laugh at his statements and actions.
5. Sometimes fear his statements and actions.
6. Sometimes get curious and fascinated by his statements and actions.

Most of the citizens in the perfect fascist nation believe that their leader is a violent but an intelligent person. The reality, however, is the opposite. A violent person has two qualities;

1. He has envy for the prosperous citizens of his own nation and that of the other nations.
2. He shows no magnanimity and sympathy for those people in his own nation whose suffering is undeserved.

Quality 72: The leader of the perfect fascist nation is a great artist, but he does not have all its qualities

Comment: A great artist has four qualities; a dual mentality, getting occasional bouts of insanity, creating impossible goals, and harbouring unnecessary guilt. The great gamer, has two of these, but tries his best to extinguish the growth of the other two as soon as possible.

The two qualities that he tries to amplify are; first, the dual mind and second, the creation of apparently impossible goals. Due to the former one, he acts like a pure warrior and a hero to his people during a war, and like their greatest administrator, guardian, and source of inspiration during peacetimes. Due to the latter one, he greatly accelerates the production of geniuses in his nation and the progress of mathematics, physics, and the life sciences.

The two qualities that he tries to extinguish are; occasional bouts of insanity and the harbouring of irrational self-created guilt. Through the elimination of the former, he prevents an unnecessary wastage of his mental and physical energy and the irrational intimidation of his people. Through the latter, he prevents the creation and the amplification of self-created "intelligence paralysing" depression.

Chapter 23

It has been discovered by the psychologists of the western world that the entire world's population is divided into two types of human beings, the simpletons, and the non-simpletons. The former, are those that do not have the ability to become great gamers in the industrial world and the latter are those that are not only great gamers, but also the rulers and the determiners of the destiny of the former.

The first question that needs to be asked is; what exactly is a simpleton? It is an interesting fact to know that the eastern world has a much higher population of simpletons than the western world. This is the primary reason as to why the eastern world lost much of its wealth to the western world and continued to remain poor and scientifically backward. Before I talk about the qualities of the two kinds of people, I want to talk about the two kinds of minds that exist on the Earth's surface.

Type 1: The Industrial mind **Type 2**: The Anti-Industrial mind

The two types can further be divided into three classes; **Class A**: Below normal intelligence, **Class B**: Normal intelligence, and **Class C**: Above normal intelligence. Simpletons belonging to Class C, do not remain simpletons throughout their lives, but metamorphose into non-simpletons at some point of time in the future.

Based on this, there can be six possible kinds of human beings.

KIND 1: Type 1 + Class A **Kind 2**: Type 1 + Class B **Kind 3**: Type 1 + Class C

Kind 4: Type 2 + Class A **Kind 5**: Type 2 + Class B **Kind 6**: Type 2 + Class C

The fates of the members of each of these 6 kinds are given below.

Type 1 + Class A: The Criminals in any major city of the world

Type 1 + Class B: The Politicians + the Business people + The Athletes, of any nation of the world

Type 1 + Class C: The Scientists + the Technocrats, of any nation of the world

Type 2 + Class A: The Forest people + The Dacoits, of the rural region of any nation of the world

Type 2 + Class B: The Farmers of any nation of the world

Type 2 + Class C: They start their lives as simpletons, but eventually metamorphose into either Type 1 + Class B or Type 1 + Class C

It is a known fact that in order to live a c decent and comfortable life in a major city of either the eastern or the western world, you need an intelligence that is significantly higher than what you would require in order to live the same quality of life in a village. The amount of intelligence that is needed depends upon the rate of the development and the expansion of the city. The bigger and more developed a city becomes, the higher is the demand that is placed on the evolution and the performance of the intelligence of its citizens.

The biggest difference between a, anti-industrial mind and an industrial mind is that the former believe; treat Mother Nature well and with respect, and she would treat and respect you with the same amount in return. Abuse Mother Nature and destroy her creations, and she would do the same to you in return.

The industrial mind believes, Mother Nature is not be bowed down to or treated well. She is to be exploited and fought against. She is not only our tormentor and our assassinator, but is also the biggest obstacle in our destiny as a "god like" species.

An industrial mind will always be a non-simpleton from the beginning of his youth and the end of his life, whereas an anti-industrial mind will always be a simpleton from the beginning of his youth and till the end of his life. In addition to this, a real industrial mind would never desire to become a simpleton or an anti-industrial mind no matter how much he is persuaded, and a real anti-industrial mind would never desire to become a non-simpleton or an industrial mind no matter how much he is persuaded. In the global economic infrastructure, there is a war going on between the industrial and the anti-industrial minds and the both are trying to either eliminate each other's existence or if that is impossible, trying to achieve the next best thing, permanent enslavement.

In the Hindi language of India, a simpleton is known by the non-simpletons as a SEEDHA-SAADHA person, that is, an innocent, childlike, and a non-clever man, whereas a non-simpleton is known as a CHALAAK-DUNIYADAR person, that is, a clever, immoral, greedy, and a worldly life loving man. The non-simpletons sometimes treat a simpleton as a child, sometimes as an animal, and sometimes with total indifference. The simpletons, on the other hand, treat the non-simpletons either as immoral people (the children of Satan) or as gods. They resort to the former treatment if the non-simpletons deliberately either ruin their normal way of life or destroy the creations, of their own or of Mother Nature. They resort to the latter treatment if the non-simpletons, through their planning and their intelligence, makes their lives even better than before or achieve success in saving a great creation of Mother Nature.

I will now give a list of the qualities of a non-simpleton.

1. When he desires to commit genocide, he does it through the laws of the constitution of his nation.
2. He deliberately creates situations that eventually lead to the amplification of his ego and the validation of his creed by many non-simpletons.
3. In his youth, he mocks a simpleton if the opportunity comes and even executes malicious acts towards him.
4. When doing something that will eventually get him the profession of his choice, he always tries to stay away from a simpleton.
5. When old, he has a bigger desire to meet and talk to a simpleton than to another non-simpleton. However, when he meets and talks to a simpleton, he treats him only as either a child or as an animal.
6. He gives flattery and respect only to the other non-simpletons, and gives fake flattery and fake respect to the simpletons.
7. Through his scientific creations and his activities (acting, performing in the various kinds of sports), he gives relief from boredom and relaxation to the simpletons, but the reverse does not happen. Only a non-simpleton can give relaxation to a non-simpleton. However, a simpleton can also give relaxation to another simpleton.
8. If the goal is wonderful to him, he would exploit either one simpleton or millions of them without any moral conscience.

9. He always has sex before marriage, but only with another non-simpleton and never with a simpleton.

10. In his youth, he only imitates other non-simpletons and never a simpleton.

11. He only pretends to be religious. In the subconscious mind, he is a pure atheist.

12. He can solver the economic problems of a simpleton, but the reverse is not true.

13. He is always fascist or military minded in his youth and middle age and only partially pacifist minded in his old age.

14. He always desires to fight over the "big matters" of his life and of the world, and never over the trivial matters like a simpleton.

15. When he observes the activities of the simpletons, he either laughs or turns his eyes away from it in disgust.

16. Even if given a "stress free" life, he would still consume toxic substances like cigarettes, alcohol, and drugs, unlike a simpleton.

17. If the non-simpleton is a girl or a woman

    i> Has no intention of becoming a housewife in any period of her life.

    ii> Wants to become either a scientist, or a CEO, or an office worker or an athlete in her youth and middle age, and a socialite in old age.

    iii> Gives first importance to the wealth and the power of her husband, both before and after marriage, and gives little or no importance to his character.

The simpletons desire to live the so-called "worldly life", that is, the struggle and the pursuit of money, power, and sex (the three jewels of the world), but not to the extent that the non-simpletons desire to. To them, no amount of money, power, and sex is enough. The more they get, the more they desire, and the more "predator" minded they become. Why is this so?

The simpletons regard the three jewels of the world as the creations of Satan or IBLIS and not of God or Allah. They believe that it is their duty, if they are alive, to live as close as possible to the creations of God, which are; the mountains, the trees, the birds, the animals, the oceans and rivers, and the flowers and fruits of plants. The non-simpletons, on the other hand, believe that it is their duty to remain as close as possible to the creations of the modern science and technology; the cars, the skyscrapers, the luxury hotels, the computers, the aeroplanes, the clothes of the fashion designers, the best quality whiskies and wines, the food that is cooked by the professional chefs, and the banks that contain their multimillion or multibillion dollar accounts.

Due to their beliefs, the simpletons regard an excessive amount of money or power or sex as a burden on their minds, whereas, the non-simpletons regard it as the greatest gift of the Cosmos (not of God or Allah, due to their atheism).

Due to their genetics, the simpletons suffer from the Peter Pan syndrome, in which the rate of the growth of the intelligence is far slower than the rate of growth of the body and the increase in the age. This causes two great problems; the inability to become a good student in school, college, and university life, and the inability to get a good job and thus a good life. If they keep on living in a city that is constantly growing, they keep on getting poorer. The increasing degree of poverty causes them to become more and more dispirited, demoralized, and embittered with each passing year. This eventually produces two outcomes;

1. Getting greatly annoyed or afraid over the trivial matters in their lives.
2. Getting into quarrels or fight with their own family members.

Since most of the simpletons are religious and thus consider suicide as evil or wrong in the eyes of God or Allah, they do not end their own lives, but keep on living a sub-human or a wretched existence. The minority, who are atheists, eventually say to themselves "I quit" and go ahead and commit suicide.

When it comes to the non-simpletons, most of them do not suffer from the Peter Pan syndrome either in their youth or in their middle age, but get it to a mild degree in old age.

As I said before, a simpleton man or woman is nothing but a child that has a fully developed reproductive system and is ready to reproduce. His qualities are like those of children. What are the qualities of children? They are;

1. Pretending to be more intelligent, more knowledgeable, and wiser than their parents.
2. Keep on preparing themselves for things that they will never do.
3. Procrastination and postponement in everything.

4. Always keep saying; I am a genius that is born in an idiotic society. Their favourite slogan is; I am surrounded by idiots.

5. To be led, protected, and told what to do by a person that they like.

6. Say to this person; re-engineer the God created world in such a way that in it all my wishes are satisfied.

7. They want all the adults around them to have good opinions about them. They enjoy undeserved flattery.

8. If they ask a difficult question, they want a simple answer.

9. They know nothing, but are not aware of it. Thus, they always pretend to be geniuses.

10. Live a purposeless life and are happy in it.

It is a known fact of psychology that a person, who has great power, wants to be feared rather than loved, and a person who has little power, wants others to give him undeserved flattery and gifts. The simpleton wants the world to give him the life that he desires, but makes little or no effort to acquire it through his own intelligence and ego.

There is another interesting fact about the non-simpletons. All non-simpletons have a great desire to create a fake self-identity and then preserve it for a long time through "acting". For a non-simpleton, the desire for acting is as immense as his desire for the three jewels. If he is not allowed to act, he would either show anger or go insane, or would commit suicide. However, they put on an "acting show" only in front of those non-simpletons who are their enemies, but never in front of those who are their friends. When it comes to the simpletons, they put on an acting show in front of all of them, even those that are not their enemies.

A simpleton that is born in a major city will only display two qualities with the progression of time, decreasing intelligence and increasing foolishness. The cause of these two qualities would be an increasing magnitude of depression.

Mental depression is the cause of three things; obesity, irrationality, and immaturity. Obesity is caused due to overeating and living a sedentary life. However, you start to develop these two qualities only if you are depressed. A non-depressed man will never desire to overeat or live a sedentary life. The more depressed you become, the more anti-social you become. It is a vicious cycle that becomes almost impossible to break if it has gone on for at least 10 years.

The same situation applies to irrationality and immaturity. A depressed man will usually behave and talk in an irrational manner. If he is not depressed, he will not only behave and talk in a rational manner, but would also listen and obey the rational advices of his parents, and friends. Regarding immaturity, a depressed man would start to behave more and more in either a childlike manner or like a maniac. Why? It is because maturity is a product of intelligence. The more intelligent you are, the more mature minded you would be. However, there are two things that are the greatest destroyers of intelligence; fear and depression. A person who is constantly living in fear, can never execute or understand an activity that requires either normal or above normal intelligence. The same applies to a person who is constantly living in depression.

Non-simpletons hate obesity, immaturity, and irrationality with respect to business (money), politics (power), and hedonism (pleasure). The simpletons, however, do not love obesity, immaturity, and irrationality, but neither do they hate them. Thus, when any of these three takes possession of their lives, they remain unaware of it and even fight to preserve it.

When a simpleton displays his suffering to a non-simpleton, the latter always shows pity to the former. The non-simpleton never shows any sympathy for a simpleton. A simpleton receives sympathy only from another simpleton and a non-simpleton receives sympathy only from another non-simpleton. During his periods of suffering or depression, a non-simpleton never desires a sympathetic gesture or comment from a simpleton, because he believes that it is coming from the mouth of a person who is either a child or an animal or a non-living object. However, in the case of a simpleton, the reality is different. Although a simpleton feels mental relief when he is given sympathy from another simpleton, he feels an even greater degree of mental relief when the sympathy comes from a non-simpleton that he admires and respects.

After the acquisition of money, power, and sexual pleasure through gaming, the next favourite pastime of the non-simpletons is to CARNIVORATE on the Ego of the simpletons. They do this in three ways; by showing anger at them and assassinating their character, by mocking them on the basis of their defects, and by ignoring their existence. They do this in a very fearless and aggressive manner. Why? It is because they know that the simpletons would not give any resistance to their movements and they will not "strike back" after being predated upon.

The non-simpletons regard the simpletons as fools. When a simpleton talks too much in front of them, they never pay much attention to what he is saying and forget all his statements soon after the end of his conversation. When they are amongst themselves, they say to each other; the fellow talks too much, but knows nothing. On the other hand, when a simpleton is sitting silently amongst a group of non-simpletons, they observe him for some time and then say to each other; that fellow, by sitting silently is only pretending to be wise and intelligent, but inside, he is completely blank and knows nothing.

There are two things which a non-simpleton would never do, but a simpleton would. These are;

1. Giving free help to either a simpleton or a non-simpleton.
2. Showing altruism with respect to sensual and sexual pleasure.

A simpleton does masochism even if it gives him nothing in return. However, under normal environmental conditions, a non-simpleton would never do masochism, no matter how much he is persuaded to do so by either another non-simpleton or a simpleton. In the normal conditions, he would either show anger at the persuader + tell him to go away or would kill the persuader if he refuses to go away. But under abnormal environmental conditions, a non-simpleton would willingly do masochism because doing so would either save him from death or would give him something that would produce in his mind, a great degree of pleasure.

In the Hindi language of India, there is a word that is used very frequently amongst the youngsters of the nation; AUKAAT. This word indicates the position of a man in the hierarchy pyramid of either his family or the organization in which he works. Since, simpletons always pretend to be extremely intelligent and like diamonds, the non-simpletons become very eager to destroy their self-created fake identity. They do in two ways;

1. Provoking the simpleton to get very angry and creating a racket thereafter. When this happens, the non-simpletons deploy their resources, human, and non-human, to get the simpleton under control. When this has been achieved, the non-simpleton makes the simpleton sit down, and starts giving him rationality increasing advice in front of all the other non-simpletons.

2. The non-simpleton invites the simpleton to a place of his (the non-simpleton) choice. When the simpleton arrives there, the inviter and all the other non-simpletons either ignores his presence or start to mock him after getting to know of his defects.

It is a known fact of psychology that the sadistic people are always attracted to the masochistic people. Why? It is because the latter help the former to satisfy their nature. Thus, most of the non-simpletons in the world are malicious and sadistic, and most of the simpletons in the world are masochistic and due to it, suffer from delusions and hallucinations.

There are two kinds of frustration that a man can suffer from; existential and sexual. The latter is easier to eliminate than the former. Why? It is because the cause of the former is the almost infinite Cosmos that surrounds Earth. Both the non-simpletons and the simpletons suffer from the two kinds of frustration. However, even after former acquire a great sex life, they remain almost as miserable as they were at the beginning of their sexual journey. This is not the case for the simpletons. After having lived a great sex life, they turn into children and Mother Nature lovers and refuse to change their mentality even after the greatest degree of persuasion.

Due to the on-going existential frustration, the Ego of the non-simpletons keeps on getting more and more powerful. Thus, they eventually do two things; declare war on each other and become narcissists. Due to their narcissism, they desire to conquer, by whatever resources that they possess all those who do not respect them. This includes both the simpletons and the non-simpletons.

Two fates await a simpleton whose sex life is not according to his own wishes. He either becomes a genius or a hippie. The former is the "luminous side" and the latter is the "dark side". The hippie is a person who is a follower of the stoic philosophy of Epictetus, has no expectations, and hopes with respect to the future, is a lover of mental and physical idleness, and believes that he is not a part of any kind of hierarchy pyramid. A hippie, who has unwillingly remained a virgin till the age of 30, is the worst kind of human being that we would ever encounter. He is extremely short-tempered, is ready to slander and attack anyone if provoked, and does not believe that his parents "are" his parents, and his elder brother or sister "is" his elder brother or sister.

The non-simpletons consider all the simpletons as "immature" minded. They are correct in believing this because the simpletons possess all the qualities of an immature man/woman. They are;

1. Doing planning and taking decisions through the memory and never through the intelligence.

2. Trying to make the future identical to the past.

3. Constantly living in a dream world and refusing to come out of it, no matter how much persuaded.

4. Doing everything that is self-based; self-talking, self-sex (masturbation), self-playing, and self-destruction.

5. Getting into Dementia Praecox, that is, when unable to solve the various problems of life, choosing to become a child.

The non-simpleton does his planning and takes his decisions with an equal degree of intelligence and memory, tries to make his future as dissimilar as possible from the past, creates his own dream world and tries his best to create it, but never lives in it when it has not been created. The non-simpleton never does self-talking, self-sex, self-playing, and self-destruction, and does not become a child when unable to solve his own problems.

There is another quality of the simpletons which the non-simpletons do not possess; watching television for an excessive period every day. Since the simpletons are children, there comes a time when the television world becomes identical to the real world in their brains. Thus, they do not believe in the concepts of "fake news" and "fake reality shows".

When it comes to the dark side of human nature, it is far bigger and more complex in the non-simpletons than in the simpletons. When it comes to the longevity of the lifespan, all non-simpletons are fanatics, whereas all the simpletons are non-fanatics. Non-simpletons believe in two things;

1. The length of the lifespan is directly proportional to the amount of wealth and power.

2. You can postpone your own death time, by killing others.

The simpletons, however, believe in two things that are the opposite of the above two;

1. The length of the lifespan is directly proportional to the benevolence of Mother Nature and the mercy of God or Allah.

2. By killing others, you will only keep on shortening your lifespan.

All the greatest robbers, politicians, business people, and mass murderers of the past and the present world were and are non-simpletons. Why did they behave in the way they did? It was because they believed that morality and its product, character, is good for the mental health in the short-term, but is bad for it in the long-term. They believed that although morality and character are helpful to you in the short-term, they would become the biggest obstacles to your growth and your progress towards your goal in the long-term.

The man who is a simpleton and is not only creative, intellectually, but is also a lover of humanity, believes that physical strength and character strength is what is required, eventually, for the attainment of your goal or your self-imagined destiny.

A non-simpleton considers a simpleton either as a mad person or as a fool. Thus, when he is with a simpleton;

1. He becomes an actor and listens and agrees to whatever bullshit the simpleton throws at him with a fake smile.
2. When the simpleton has finished his bullshit talk, he tries to persuade him to start to disbelieve in all that he has said, and come out of his "fool's paradise". He does this only when he develops some degree of emotional attachment for the simpleton.

If, after the persuasion period, the simpleton gets angry and threatens to attack him, he either tries to escape by employing the same tactic; becoming an actor and agreeing with all the assertions of the simpleton, or, deploys his resources to fight him.

The non-simpletons have a vast desire to either exploit the simpletons or to get them out of their way. The non-simpletons believe that after Mother Nature, the second biggest obstacle in front of their goals and their own "dream world", are the simpletons. They try to gain control of the simpletons or try to exterminate them via two ways;

1. Giving them harmful food to eat, harmful drinks to drink, and harmful books to read.
2. Giving them a fake identity.

The second method is seen between a father and his son, who is an imbecile and a troublemaker. If, on a particular day, the son is behaving badly due to poor mental health, and in addition to this, he is also preventing his father from doing his day's work in a smooth and error-free manner, the father, if he is an intelligent man, eventually says to his son; my son, why are you doing this? Don't you know that you are a very special person in this world? You are a great soldier and are the future leader and the guardian of the nation!

Politicians tell the farmers of their nation; you are the gods of this land! Without you, we would all starve to death. But soon after saying this, they create new farm laws and policies without the participation of the farmers, execute them without their approval, and treat them either as children or as animals.

When a non-simpleton decides to become the teacher of a simpleton or a group of simpletons, he always becomes a fake teacher, and never a real one. The qualities of a fake teacher are;

1. He always remains consistent in his behaviour towards his students. Thus, if he begins by treating them as animals, he would always keep on treating them as animals.

2. He has zero respect for his students and never develops any.

3. He tortures them as much as he likes when the simpletons give him the opportunity.

It is a known fact of psychology that every person on Earth, only desires to think of those thoughts which will not damage his mental health, both in the short-term and the long-term, and not damage his sex life. Both the simpletons and the non-simpletons are 100% identical to each other in this matter, but the difference between them lies in the way they try to preserve or improve their mental health and their sex life. The non-simpletons try to preserve or improve their mental health and their sex life via the exploitation of the simpletons and the gradual effort in trying to conquer Mother Nature. The simpletons try to improve their mental health and their sex life by serving both the non-simpletons and Mother Nature.

SIMPLETONISM is far more prevalent in the world of women than in the world of men, and the opposite is the situation for non-SIMPLETONISM. Why is this so? It is because a non-simpleton has a higher probability of dying before reaching reproductive age than a simpleton. Why is this so? It is because a non-simpleton always remains in a higher degree of mental stress than a simpleton.

Why is this so? It is because he is trying to conquer Mother Nature, rather than live submissively and in harmony with it.

Due to the higher prevalence of SIMPLETONISM in their world, girls or women have acquired a set of gifts, from Mother Nature, which have been denied to boys and men. They are;

1. A stronger immune system for the entire life.
2. The onset of peacefulness, much more rapidly, after a shock.
3. No obsession about the ancient past or the distant future.
4. Greater focus on a problem or an issue in front of them.
5. Ignorance of all those problems or concepts that are not connected to their own welfare.
6. Greater tolerance to prolonged pain.

The simpleton man has two defects in his mind. First, he has an inability to talk to and please a non-simpleton woman. Second, he desires to talk to and marry only a simpleton woman. Thus, in the world, four kinds of marriages happen.

Type 1: Simpleton husband + non-simpleton wife

Type 2: Non-simpleton husband + simpleton wife

Type 3: Simpleton husband + simpleton wife

Type 4: Non-simpleton husband + non-simpleton wife

The best example of the first type was seen in the Hollywood movie, Mrs. Doubt fire. In it, the husband was "in reality" a child in an adult's body. Thus, he was extremely fond of children, including his own, and desired to be amongst them every day. His wife, on the other hand, was a professional minded, office going, and money hungry woman. What was the eventual fate of the couple? It was divorce. However, it was the wife who asked for it first, and not the husband. Why? It is because he was a simpleton and a simpleton always feels a high degree of security in the company of a non-simpleton, but the reverse is not true.

In the second, the husband divorces his wife after having explored her sexually or keep her in his house like a slave and orders her to take care of him and his children. However, if he becomes a big capitalist or a politician, he only takes her around with him, wherever he goes, as either an animal or a talking toy.

The third type of couple, are usually found in any of the multiple villages of any nation of the world. The husband is Mother Nature loving and child minded and so is his wife. They have desire for money, power, and sexual pleasure, but never show any greed for it. In addition to this, they start their life as farmers and remain so till the end of it. They are also afflicted with BIOPHILIA and always scorn and despise the "nature destroying" activities of the industrial world. They are very religious and want their children to preserve the rural culture of their nation and the culture of the holy book of their religion. The love that they show for each other is real and thus, they never even think of divorcing each other at any period of their life. My own parents are a great example of this type of couple.

The fourth type of couple is the one that is the best suited to not only survive, but also prosper in the industrial world. Both the husband and wife are extremely greedy for money, power, and sensual pleasure, and consider them the best things on Earth. The husband is very educated and has an enormous ability for acquiring wealth and power. His wife is also not far behind. The husband hates morality and magnanimity and so does his wife. The husband never even dreams of living in a village of India or another developing nation of the world, even for a single day, and so does his wife. When it comes to divorce, there is a 50:50 chance that they will either remain together for life or will separate at some future point of time. The best example of this type is Bill Gates and his wife Melinda Gates.

Women who are non-simpletons, have little or no respect for men and do not treat them as gods compared to their own selves. Thus, they become the destroyers of patriarchy and believe that the best kind of world is the one where both the sexes live on an equal footing with each other with respect to everything. However, a small number of them become "men haters" and thus transform into feminists. They say that that anything that men can do, women can do better and the best world is the one where women rule the men in every nation in it. They believe that;

1. The biggest cause of the unhappiness of women in every nation of the world is the unjustified tyranny of men.

2. All the men in the world only pretend to be geniuses, but they are nothing but overgrown children.

3. A real woman would never desire to have sex with any man in the world, and even if she does have it, her consent is only an illusion. Inside, she is confused and is crying.

4. All men in the world, if they believe that they will not be punished, will rape women with full impunity.

There is another quality of the urban simpleton; the lack of discipline. I said an urban simpleton, because simpletons in the rural areas of a nation always live a disciplined life from their childhood. However, all the non-simpletons in any city of a nation are discipline lovers and believe that it is one of the foundational pillars of success in the industrial world. The qualities of an undisciplined person are;

1. He has a responsibility shrugging nature.

2. He shows no respect for those who have achieved success in the sports world, the business world, the science world, and the political world. In addition to this, he harbours an immense amount of envy of them and is always on the lookout for an opportunity where he can show to the others around him that he is superior to them in intelligence.

If the discipline hating simpleton keeps on living his natural way of life for at least 15 years, then he becomes a hippie. However, he will regularly keep on saying to others that the cause of his state is not his own way of thinking and the low level of intelligence, but the evil and idiotic external world.

The man of discipline says that you must do everything in life "on time", that is, eat your three meals on time, arrive and leave your office on time, marry on time, and sleep on time. The man of non-discipline says that you should do all of them anytime that you like. Thus, a non-disciplined person moves purely according to his own whim.

I have discovered that there are 5 kinds of happiness in this world. However, I have also discovered that none of them can be acquired by the simpletons. They are all reserved for the non-simpletons. They are;

Type 1: Sexual: Playboy

Type 2: Economic: Capitalist

Type 3: Power: Autocrat

Type 4: Academic: Topper

Type 5: Intellectual: Genius

I have also discovered that there are three kinds of men that the Cosmos creates. **Type 1**: The normal man, **Type 2**: The ultimate man, and **Type 3**: The superman.

When it comes to Type 1, 60% of the normal men would remain normal even under the favourable external circumstances or conditions. However, under these same conditions, 35% of the remaining would transform into the ultimate man and 5% into the superman. There is however, a bitter truth in this fact (in my opinion) of reality; the ultimate men would develop to their mental maturity, much faster than the supermen, and thus would proceed rapidly to exterminate them before they reach their own mental maturity.

What is the difference between the three types of men? In my opinion, it is;

Type 1: His desire for money, power, and pleasure is finite and for acquiring them, he is willing to indulge in hard work and if he does not obtain them in the magnitude that he wants, he would not create any kind of "immoral plan" or do physical violence.

Type 2: His desire for money, power, and pleasure is infinite and for acquiring them he is willing to remain idle and make all the other normal men his slaves or obtain them via the creation of plans of immense immorality and cleverness. If he does not obtain them in the magnitude that he desires, he would, without any hesitation or conscience, put his nation at war with another nation or create a world war, if he has the power to do so.

Type 3: Although his desire for money and power is infinite, his desire for pleasure is either almost zero or equal to that of the normal man. He differs from the ultimate man, by the fact that, for the sake of acquiring and amplifying his wealth and power, he tries to keep on increasing, the magnitude of the freedom of all the other men in world, and his own freedom. He wants all the other men to be completely free of him and himself to be free of them. Why? It is because a war never comes to take place either between him and all the other men around him or the remaining ones in the world.

What is the goal of SIMPLETONISM and what is the goal of NON SIMPLETONISM? The goal of the former is to create the superman and the goal of the latter is to create the ultimate man. The two are the opposites of each other and, unlike the two poles of a magnet, do not desire to coexist with each other, but annihilate each other. The qualities of the superman are;

1. He loves peace, but excels in the art of war and is always ready to fight if challenged by the ultimate man.
2. He is alone, but all the truths of the Cosmos are with him.
3. His philosophy is wrongly interpreted, deliberately and repeatedly, by all the normal people of the world and the ultimate man.
4. He will never allow himself to be either manipulated of enslaved by the ultimate man.
5. When his followers meet him, they soon develop an immense desire to throw off their self-created fake identities and display their "real selves" to him.
6. His followers want him to eliminate all their defects and transform them.
7. In his presence, the ataraxic become restless and the kings feel small.
8. He turns the pessimistic into the optimistic.
9. He can never be conquered either by the ultimate man or by Mother Nature.
10. When he dies, most of his followers commit suicide, although he tells them not to before his death.

The qualities of the ultimate man are;

1. He is the outcome of the full growth of everything that is ugly in men.
2. The whole world is with him, but not the truth.
3. He loves war and declares its beginning and its end according to his own whim.
4. His philosophy is simple and thus it is easy to understand and is rightly interpreted by the normal people of the world.
5. His followers move around with him in their self-created fake identity and never desire to throw it off because he never desires to do so.
6. His followers never ask him to eliminate their defects.
7. In his presence, the ataraxic feel blessed to be in their current state and the kings feel great about their own intelligence and character.

8. He turns the optimistic into the pessimistic.

9. He never desires to be conquered by the superman, but remains a willing slave of Mother Nature throughout his life.

10. When he dies, most of his followers feel happy and soon, one of them sits on the same chair that he did.

If we look at the past and the present, we see that evolution has created many examples of the ultimate man; Memnon, Alexander the great, Genghis Khan, Nero, Benito Mussolini, Adolf Hitler, Joseph Stalin, Vladimir Lenin, Saddam Hussein, Muammar Gaddafi, Pablo Escobar, Vladimir Putin, Kim Jong Un, and Xi Jinping. However, evolution has not yet created a superman. Some, however, have come close to it. The examples are; Aristotle, Jesus Christ, Isaac Newton, Mahatma Gandhi, and Albert Einstein.

The Hollywood movie, Superman (starring Christopher Reeves) displayed this message to the American citizens. In his fake avatar, Clark Kent, superman was a simpleton. He talked in a foolish manner, and behaved in a foolish manner. In addition to this, almost no one in the newspaper organization (the Daily Planet) where he worked wanted to become his friend. This included Lois Lane, who after talking to him, soon started to feel a powerful repulsion from his presence. Why? It is because she was a non-simpleton.

In the Bhagavad Gita, the superman is known as the TATTWAVIT. He is a man who has not only conquered himself via 100% self-knowledge, but has also attained immortality and guides, but does not create the destinies of billions upon billions of people through billions of generations. He is not only a warrior, but is also a hero of his own species and protects it from all those things that can drive it towards extinction. However, before he becomes a superman, he suffers a disease known as the ARJUNA syndrome.

In the story of MAHABHARAT, Arjuna, a prince of a royal family and a great archer, was a student of Krishna, a god. Just before the MAHABHARAT was about to begin, he began to show all the symptoms of the Arjuna syndrome in an amplified state. However, his master, Krishna, took the responsibility to cure him as soon as possible, but via the right techniques, before the start of the war. The symptoms of this disease are;

1. Far greater amount of egoistic dreaming than practical action.

2. Showing compassion to those who do not deserve it.

3. Irrational fear and morality.
4. The inability to discover the true cause of the irrational fear.
5. Belief in victory or defeat even before the war has begun.
6. Not having any ambition to fight due to the exaggeration of the enemy's power even before encountering it.
7. Seeking support and justification for the syndrome
8. Believing that no good would happen after killing the enemy.
9. Having the Jesus Christ mentality, that is, if the enemy slaps you on your right cheek, offer him your left cheek.

Krishna eventually cured Arjuna through silence, love, zero criticism and scolding, and allowing him to express all his thoughts till the point of exhaustion.

The ultimate man, unlike the superman, tries to increase the population of talented people in his nation. The qualities of a talented person are;

1. He versatile, acute, social, and conservative.
2. He can do the traditional activities of the nation far more quickly and better than either a non-talented person or a genius, but he never creates anything new in them.
3. He is immensely aroused by the culture of his nation and religion.
4. He does his best to become a real patriot.
5. He only tries to achieve what is beyond the capacity of the non-talented people, but never tries to achieve what can be achieved only by a genius.

It is a known fact of psychology, that in any field of profession, women display a greater amount of talent than men. Thus, the ultimate man does much more for the young women than the young men of his nation. He starts to create and amplify the matriarchal culture and makes most of the men of his nation, excluding him, the servants of the women.

The superman, however, does the opposite. He tries to create and amplify the patriarchal culture, but at the same time, create new laws that eventually give all the women of his nation, far more security from the men, than they receive in the nation of the ultimate man.

When it comes to choosing his place of birth on any planet in the universe where an intelligent species exists, the worst place that a genius can choose is to be born in a nation on that planet that is ruled by the ultimate man. If a man does get born in this nation, and due to the help from the universe or its creator, becomes a genius, the ruler of this nation who is an ultimate man, wants him to do two things; first, become his slave and second, support and give justification to the people of the nation for his master's whimsical actions. If, at any occasion, the genius puts forward his own idea in front of his master and asks him to execute it, his master rapidly condemns and rejects the idea without giving any rational reasons, to the genius, for his decision. If the genius continues to give him the reasons, his master threatens to either imprison and torture him or kill him.

The superman regards all the geniuses of his nation as his brothers and equal to him in the hierarchy pyramid. In addition to this, if he rejects any idea of theirs, he always gives a set of rational reasons for his decision. The reasons that he gives, appear as rational to the geniuses as they do to him. Thus, in the nation of a superman, a genius always feels honoured by his master and his self-respect goes on increasing with time.

Unlike the superman, the ultimate man has all the qualities of a psychopath. His qualities are;

1. Frequent self-glorification.
2. Bullying his inferiors and teaching them nothing in return.
3. Doing immoral acts, secretly, without any remorse.
4. Willing to risk own life for the sake of preserving the image that is created by the frequent self-glorification activities.
5. Doing acts of great evil just to get a momentary freedom from boredom.
6. Having the belief that morality is a weakness and thus proceeding to either exploit mercilessly or kill all the moral people in his nation.
7. Deliberately putting his inferiors in either a great trouble or in a state of great terror and then swooping in to save them and become their hero.
8. Demanding great sacrifices and concessions from the people of his nation in order to reach his self-created goal.

9. Receiving a great amount of pleasure when either a genius or a moral man comes to him and begs to him for mercy and forgiveness.

10. When alone, laughing loudly and believing that all the people of his nation are nothing but 50% children and 50% animals.

In his student life, the ultimate man, unlike the superman, always becomes and remains a fake student. The three qualities of such a student are; first, he always tries to find faults in his master's teachings and never agrees with any one of them. Second, he wants his master to admire and appreciate his own beliefs. Third, if he discovers that his master is not giving him respect and flattery, he deserts him at his own whim. The ultimate man believes in the truthfulness of all those external illusions and personal hallucinations which his master declares to be false.

When the ultimate man becomes a teacher, he displays three qualities; first, he develops no emotional attachment even for those students who give him reverence and love. Second, he desires all his students to become and remain fearful of him. Third, he tells his students that their vices are their virtues.

When the superman becomes a teacher, the three qualities that he shows are; first, he regards those students who show him reverence and love, as his own sons. Second, he desires all his students to become fearless of him. Third, he makes the students discover their defects and then shows them the ways to destroy them.

The ultimate man misunderstands all the teachings of his master and then proceeds to do evil deeds in the world. The superman, however, understands all the teachings of his master and then proceeds to do not only good deeds in the world, but also make new innovations in the philosophical universe of his master.

When it comes to the ruler of a nation or a kingdom, he can be of three types.

Type 1: He rules only according to the facts and the data that are discovered and gathered by all the scientists of his nation. Such a ruler eventually becomes a puppet of the scientists.

Type 2: He rules according to the feelings of the people of his nation or kingdom. Such a ruler eventually becomes a puppet of the citizens of his nation.

Type 3: He rules according to his own mind and vision of the future and either imprisons or kill all those citizens who are destructive to it.

The ultimate man is a pure type 3 person, whereas, the superman, is a combination of all the three types. By living his life in this way, he never disappoints or angers all the geniuses in his nation, all the citizens of his nation, and his own mind.

The mind of the ultimate man is almost like that of a parasite. Due to this, the qualities that he develops are;

1. Giving orders when and where not necessary.
2. Giving orders to those who are superior to him in intelligence.
3. Spreading unnecessary terror amongst the people of his nation.
4. Taking "too much" from his nation and either giving it nothing wonderful or giving it something harmful in return.
5. Creating monuments for himself and his best friends via the wealth, gained through robbery and terror, of the people of his nation and not his own.
6. Desiring undeserved honour and respect from the people of his nation.

The ultimate man behaves, superficially, as a genius, but deep inside his mind, he is just a child and is fully aware of the truth. Due to this, he is always in a state of high depression and in order to reduce it, consumes nicotine, alcohol, and anti-depressants, in addition to organizing and indulging in Victorian parties and Billionaire parties (the former prime minister of Italy, Silvio Berlusconi, is a good example).

Due to his real nature, he wants to organize and witness a duel between a man and a monster and is very eager to listen to a story of the adventures of an immensely successful stock market robber or a dacoit living in the forested mountains of any nation in the world.

The superman behaves, superficially, as a fool (see Clark Kent and see Yoda in Star Wars), but deep inside his mind, he possesses a vast reservoir of knowledge, wisdom, and spiritual strength. Thus, although he appears to be depressed due to the state of the world around him, inside, he is more peaceful than a rock. Due to this, he never consumes nicotine, alcohol, and anti-depressants, and has no interest in those women who are made by evolution to only become the "time pass" of men.

The ultimate man starts his journey either as a topper student in school, college, and university or as a junior young priest of any religion in the world. Due to either of these two, he soon develops an oratory power that keeps getting better and better every year. Then he soon joins a group or a gang of other ultimate men who have been busy for a long time in trying to convert all the people of their nation into children. After becoming a part of this gang, he becomes a diplomat and does two things;

1. Ingratiates himself in front of the leader and the others when necessary.
2. Learns and develops the skill to win their favours.

Soon, his oratorical power, he becomes bigger than the leader of the party or the gang that he is a part of. Thus, after his retirement, the leader of the party makes him the new leader.

What is the cause of the rapid increase in his oratorical power? It is the ambition for money, power, and sensual pleasure, including sexual pleasure, and not for the world that the superman desires to create.

Since the ultimate man is extremely unwise (due to which he becomes the ultimate man), he is a follower of the "romanticism" philosophy, which says that our destiny is 100% in our own hands. The superman, however, is a follower of romanticism and naturalism and thus believes that our destiny is 50% in our own hands and 50% in the hands of the 4 forces that have created the visible and the invisible universe. Thus, the ultimate man becomes a great supporter of the philosophy of "pragmatism", unlike the superman.

How is the ultimate man received in the world of women? The answer is that most women in the world, the simpletons, and the non-simpletons, are far more powerfully attracted to the ultimate man than to the superman. Why is this so? It is because of the desire of the ultimate man to spread his genes on the surface of the planet, to an immensely greater extent than the superman. Since the ultimate man always produces far more offspring than the superman, he gives a far greater amount of security and the "pro-life" things to his chosen women than the superman. Thus, he takes care of the physical and the mental health of his own women, to a far better extent than the superman. In addition to this, he also desires his party or group members to reproduce as ferociously as him and thus, he provides them and their women with nearly as much security and the pro-life things as he does to his own.

Since the ultimate man gives the women of his nation, the two things that they most desire. His existence is far more celebrated and glorified by the women of his nation, both the young and the old, than that of the superman. In fact, when the superman makes the first strike on the ultimate man and his group, the first retaliation or backlash that he faces, comes from the female population of the nation.

Why does the superman not give as much security and the pro-life things to his wife (if he marries) and the other women of his nation? It is because of his goal in life. The goals of the ultimate man are to acquire as much money, and power, that he can, through a combination of violence and cunning, and then use it to produce as many offspring as he and his gang can during the "fertile" period of their life.

The goals of the superman are to first create a world where the three kinds of wars that are found in every imperfect civilisation, the class war, the racial war, and the war between atheism and theism, have been permanently eliminated. Then, he tries to create a world where the progress of mathematics and the other sciences never stop. Since both these goals are projects of immense complexity and duration, how would he ever think of fulfilling the primary needs of his wife and the other women of his nation?

The ultimate man, unlike the superman, has a PANDEMIAN nature, that is, he chooses only those women as his wives, or his mistresses, who have a beautiful body, face, and eyes. He is not at all interested in their character (because he himself has none) and never pays any importance to it if they remain with him. The women rejoice in this quality of his, because most of the simpleton women in the world and all the non-simpleton ones are only interested in the increased beautification of their body and their face and not of their character.

The superman, however, pays first importance to the character of the woman whom he decides to marry and second importance to her physical appearance. He would marry her even if she is ugly looking, but possesses a mind and a heart made of gold.

When it comes to love, the ultimate man will say that he knows about it, far more deeply, than the superman. This is only an illusion, since the man who knows what love is and how to love, will never decide to become the ultimate man. He will decide to become the superman.

The proof of the ultimate man's lie is shown in two occasions, which are either created by the Cosmos itself or are created by the superman in order to reveal the real nature of the ultimate man to the people that he rules.

Occasion 1: The creation of a dangerous situation: If he gets trapped in it, the ultimate man, chooses to save only his own life and abandons everyone behind, including those women to whom he has said many times, "I love you".

Occasion 2: The creation of an object that arouses either his greedy side or his licentious side: In the pursuit of it, the ultimate man, completely forgets about the existence of everyone in his own group, the crowd that he rules, and the women that are his wives and mistresses.

It is a known fact of philosophy that a man whose intelligence is bigger than his heart is as unhappy as a man whose heart is bigger than his intelligence. The ultimate man and the superman, both start their journey as the first type of man, intelligence being bigger than the heart. However, as time progresses, the imbalance between the two qualities keeps on getting bigger and bigger in the ultimate man and keeps on getting smaller and smaller in the superman. In addition to this, the growth of the intelligence in the ultimate man, stops, after a certain point of time. However, it does not stop in the superman along with the growth in his heart.

Speaking truthfully, the ultimate man is an idiot. However, he is the "bright side" of idiocy, the "dark side" being a hippie. This being so, they have common qualities, which are;

1. Being completely unaware of their illiteracy.
2. Doing all that is possible to hide their blank mind.
3. Oscillating between oratory speeches and evasive silence.
4. Becoming aggressive and belligerent for no rational reason.
5. Possessing the cynicism of a decadent adult and the credulity of a child.
6. Regarding the pursuit of pleasure as more important than the pursuit of personal goal.

The ultimate man is a hippie who possesses great wealth and power, lives in a palace sized home, moves around in brand new luxury cars (specially made for him), wears the most expensive clothes and shoes, and is frequently glorified by all the people of his nation, both the educated and the uneducated. Thus, in his nation, the population of the normal hippie men and women keeps on increasing rapidly year after year. In addition to this, the ultimate man and his group, keep on encouraging all the young people of their nation to love "openly" and not secretly. Thus, when we visit these nations, we see young people kissing each other and even having sex in public parks, movie theatres, and shopping malls. The best examples of this are the United States and the countries in Europe.

If a superman does get created, by evolution at some point of time in the future, will a superwoman also come into existence? The probability of this occurring and not occurring is 50:50. However, if a superwoman does get created, what would be her qualities?

She would be either of the two types; **Type 1**: The Dagny Taggart (a character of in the novel, Atlas Shrugged) minded or **Type 2**: The Joan of Arc minded.

If she is of the first type, she would not only be the greatest female friend of the superman, but would also be the second greatest guardian of his mental health (the first being the superman himself) and all his projects on the planet of his birth. She would be the perfect business woman and the second-best administrator of all the worldly activities of the superman. She would be a great economist, a great politician, and a great militarist.

If she of the second type, she would be exactly like the first type, except for one quality. She would not be a great economist, because she would not take much interest in "the different forms of money" and the science of their movement and storage around the world (economics). However, she would be an even greater militarist than the first type.

In addition to this, the superwoman will also do three other things, which she would consider as her life's duties. They are;

1. Helping all those people whom the superman has chosen for help.
2. Doing all that is possible, even if it comes to self-sacrifice, to save the life of the superman.
3. Empowering the Ego of not only the superman, but also his chosen ones.

This is a bitter truth; when the ultimate man arises, an ultimate woman also arises soon thereafter, but when a superman arises, a superwoman can either arise or never arise. The enemies of the superman are not only the ultimate man and his ultimate woman, but also the rest of the population of not only the nation, but the world. Why is this so?

The superman begins his journey by the process of self-knowledge. If he completes this journey, he attains enlightenment and transforms into a superman. Now, his next step is to make the other people in the world embark on the same journey. This however, never happens, because of the two qualities of normal people (due to which they remain normal till the end of their lives);

1. They are ecstasy lovers and awareness haters.

2. They only desire to be helped, either economically or via flattery, but never desire to be helped via self-knowledge, which will only make them aware of their defects.

Since the Ego of the superman is as powerful as that of the ultimate man, he does not get demoralised by these two facts, but continues to move ahead in his second project via the writing of books and giving lectures on radio and television channels. However, the results that he gets are the opposite of what he desired.

The ultimate man, on the other hand, creates a system in which all the people of his nation, experience periods of ecstasy that are not only more prolonged than those that they experienced in the past, but are also more intense. In addition to this, he also gives them undeserved flattery and they give it to him in return. The cycle and the madness that it creates, keeps on getting more and more powerful with time, until it is finally broken by the Cosmos itself via either a super volcano eruption or an asteroid impact.

In biology, the ultimate male in all those species whose members live in groups or packs, is known as the "alpha male". Thus, when it comes to our species, the ultimate man desires to become the alpha male in whatever environment or ecosystem he and his group is placed, whether his group members and those outside it, agree with him or not. This is not the case for the superman. He only desires three things;

1. To be an innovator in his own chosen profession.

2. To be a real teacher to all those around him and to guide them to a glorious destiny.

3. To become the alpha male only if all those around him keep on insisting, fanatically, to take up his proper position.

When it comes to the intellectual creations, there is another difference between the ultimate man and the superman. When an ultimate man observes the intellectual creation of a superman, he goes into a state of fear and soon makes a plan to exterminate it. Why? It is because all the greatest intellectual creations of the superman are the potential destroyers of the creations and the systems of the ultimate man.

The best example of this is shown in Carl Sagan's novel, Contact. The machine, whose engineering blueprint was sent to the Homo sapiens by an extra-terrestrial species living on a planet orbiting the star, Vega, was the product of beings, whose mind was "super" in power compared to that of the Homo sapiens. Through their blueprint, two of the worm-hole creating machines were made, one in Florida and the other in Japan. However, when the first one, in Florida was made to run, a terrorist managed to get inside it, and committed suicide by blowing himself up with a grenade in his hand. After the explosion, the machine was also destroyed.

Who sent the terrorist inside the machine? He was sent by a priest from the Christian world of the United States of America. This priest was neither a normal man nor a superman. He was an ultimate man and thus, he became "sacred to death" as to what would happen to all the philosophy of the Bible and the nonsensical pragmatism of the fathers, the bishops, the reverends, and the Pope, if the machine was started and did its job perfectly. He thought; this machine would bring something in this world that would permanently destabilise the global empire of Christianity, the idle and comfortable lives of its priests, and the divine image of Jesus Christ.

The concept of the ultimate man and the superman was also discussed in the Hollywood movie, Doom (starring Dwayne Johnson). When chromosome pair 24, was given to some normal men, they transformed into, not an ultimate man, but an ultimate organism, that is, an organism with extreme physical powers. However, when this pair was given to some other normal men, they transformed, into supermen and not into a super organism.

Chapter 24

The war between the ultimate man and the superman is just like an action thriller movie of Hollywood. The qualities of such a movie are;

1. A conflict between 2 characters, one good and the other evil. The cause of it is the almost total dissimilarity between their final goals.
2. It reveals the size of the gulf, with respect to morality and intelligence, between the villain (the ultimate man) and the hero (the superman).
3. Halfway in the movie, a romance flares up between the superman and the woman he loves and who loves him as much as he does.
4. The ultimate man, in order to insert the superman in a state of extreme depression, tracks down and kills his beloved. This creates a tragic end to their fairy tale like romance.
5. The superman goes into a state of extreme depression and in it keeps on thinking of 5 things;

    i> Life is now not worth living.

    ii> No one in the world should be trusted.

    iii> True love and a happy life are myths.

    iv> The only real things in the Cosmos are suffering and death (the philosophy of Buddha).

    v> The human species is either a cosmic failure or a cosmic accident.

6. The state of suffering causes the superman to arrive at the brink of self-destruction (suicide).
7. At this point, he suddenly comes to think of the teachings of his master or his guru. His master said; Remember, my son, duty is above your life,

and beloved. Never sacrifice it for the sake of preserving the other two. If you preserve your life and the one you love, you only save two lives, but if you preserve your duty and sacrifice the other two, you save the lives of billions. There are two kinds of beings in this universe, the dark seekers, and the light seekers. The dark seekers never become aware of what their duty is and even if they do, they choose to sacrifice it for the sake of preserving their own life and the life of the one that they are attached to. Such beings never get to know what love is because they never experience its eternal beauty and its infinite dimensions. This is only experienced by a light seeker. The dark seekers move from birth to death in a state of zombie like ecstasy and try to kill or enslave all the light seekers in the process. Remember, without duty, we have no purpose, and without purpose, we are not alive.

8. Immediately after this, the superman experiences a "big bang" in his brain. A revolution takes place, his ego becomes far more powerful than before, and using all his knowledge and fighting skills, he kills all the followers and the group members of the ultimate man, and eventually the ultimate man himself.

During his state of depression and after the big bang, the superman never feels what a drug intoxicated man feels;

1. Feeling thankful to God for placing him on Earth
2. Becoming totally fearless and having no thought of death.
3. Believing that despite the existence of all the evil people in the world, the world is a wonderful place to live in and "all is well".
4. God is love.

The superman always fights the ultimate man and his army in a state of maximum awareness and physical health.

There is a continuous war going on, at the genetic level, between the simpletons and the non-simpletons of the world. The non-simpletons employ two ways to exterminate all the simpleton men in the world; first, destroy all that they have created and do not allow them to acquire even the minimum amount of money, power, and pleasure, and second, lure, seduce, marry, and produce children with the simpleton women. The simpleton men do two things in order to prevent their women from falling into the hands of the non-simpleton men;

prevent them from acquiring western education (like in Afghanistan), and keep them very religious. If the women remain religious for a long time, they eventually come to believe that all the non-simpleton men of the world are nothing but the children of Satan.

In most nations of the world, the non-simpleton men have won their battle over the simpleton men. This is only due to their much higher levels of mathematical and economic intelligence. It is highly probable that in the remaining nations, the non-simpletons would also achieve victory. However, after this has occurred, the simpleton men will not become extinct from Earth, but will continue to exist as a tiny portion of the global population, in a remote and highly undeveloped part of the world.

There is also another possible end to this war. Due to the evolutionary gifts on both sides, neither the non-simpletons would be able to wipe out the simpletons, nor would the simpletons be able to wipe out the non-simpletons. After a certain point of time, the non-simpletons would make peace with the simpletons and ask them to work for them. The simpletons would agree, but only on one condition, that the non-simpleton men would never make any attempt to seduce and breed with the simpleton women. The non-simpletons would agree, but only for that point of time. Thus, a stalemate would be created. In such a world, both the simpletons and the non-simpletons would learn to coexist with each other, but their worlds would be 100% separate and would never intermingle with each other without the permission of the simpleton men.

The Cosmos is a simulated reality and so is a movie of any film industry of the world. In a movie, there can be three possible outcomes of the war between the hero and the villain. They are;

Outcome 1: The villain is killed by the hero and the hero lives on

Outcome 2: The villain is killed by the hero and the hero also dies after this

Outcome 3: The villain kills the hero and he lives on

Most of the action thriller movies of Hollywood and Bollywood show outcome 1 at their end. The remaining (the Hindi movie, BAAZIGAR, is a good example) show outcome 2 at their end. However, none of them have shown outcome 3 at their end. Why? It is because, the goal of the film industry is to insert their audience in a state of ignorance and ecstasy through music, songs, and telling lies about the real nature of the Cosmos. If all the film industries of the world, considered it as their duty to inform their audience about the real nature of the Cosmos, then all of them would be based on outcome 3 at their end.

Everywhere we look today, whether in politics or business or economics or science or religion, the ultimate men, and the ultimate women, are occupying all the top positions, have the greatest amount of wealth and power, and are running and controlling the rest of humanity. The men and women who are better than them in morality and intelligence, are either their servants or just live a routine life in a state of fearful resignation. However, these few good men and women are nothing but a mere shadow of the superman and the superwoman. If they are placed, by God or Allah, in the same positions which are being occupied by the evil men and women, they would not give birth to a second renaissance or the "age of enlightenment". They would only create small corrections in the system that has been created by the current ultimate men and women, and make the new world marginally better than the previous one.

If the current world keeps living on and on, and no great catastrophe arises due to either climate change or a super volcano eruption or the impact of a NEO (Near Earth Object), the stalemate situation between the world of the non-simpletons and that of the simpletons would soon come to an end.

The guardian of the simpletons, a superman, would be killed by either a single ultimate man or a group of ultimate men. This being done, the group of ultimate men would then proceed to give their new message to the simpletons; the men of our world would mate and reproduce with not only their women, but also with the women of your world. Do not interfere in their activities and if you do, then we would exterminate all of you. Since the death of their teacher, their hero, and their guardian, would put all the remaining simpleton men (many would commit suicide) in a state of great fear and respect for the group of victorious ultimate men, they would agree to their demand without any protest or hesitation.

Making a projection for a much longer time ahead, the intelligence increasing genes and the behavioural genes of the non-simpleton men would keep getting more and more dominant and abundant in the world and those of the simpleton men would keep on getting more and more recessive and scarce. The Cosmos, initially would keep on increasing the intelligence of the non-simpleton men and women. Thus, they would eventually achieve success in creating a world where all the current problems like global warming, climate change, genetic and pathogenic diseases, water and soil pollution, and racism, have been permanently exterminated.

When this state has been reached, something interesting would happen. The ultimate men of the most powerful nations of the world would begin a new era of warfare; amongst themselves. This war would have a hybrid nature, that is, it would possess the qualities of both World War 2 and World War 3. Soldiers, fighter jets, tanks, battleships, submarines, SAM missiles, and sonic weapons would be used, but nuclear weapons would also be used. However, the radioactivity clouds that these detonated nukes would create would soon be cleaned up by the deployment of "NANOBOT swarms". They would fly directly towards the cloud and rapidly consume all the radioactive atoms in it.

At the end of this war, another interesting event would occur. One ultimate man would emerge as the victor and would exterminate all the others like him. He would then proceed to create Zionism, that is, the unification of all the nations in the world, into a single nation. He would fulfil Albert Einstein's dream. This being done, he would do two things. First, distribute all the remaining non-simpletons of the world into N number of cities, worldwide. Second, locate and determine the total number of simpletons that survived the war. He would then create, artificially, a small home for them in a small corner of the planet. Thus, the Brave New World would be born. The victorious ultimate man would become a "world controller" and would desire to remain so till the end of his life. The other qualities of this world are;

1. The global population would be divided into four classes; the intellectual class, the working class, the manual labour class, and the savage class (the simpletons). The way of life and the destiny of the members of each of the four classes would be determined from their birth by the world controller. All the members in each class would be almost identical to each other with respect to intelligence, behaviour, and wealth.

2. Members of the first three classes will be constantly encouraged to make the full use of all the various technologies in the world, whereas, members of the fourth class, will be kept as far away as possible from modern science and technology.

3. The only purpose of the fourth class would be to do agriculture and grow food for the other three classes.

4. Love for Mother Nature will be kept as low as possible, always, in the first three classes, and as high as possible in the fourth class.

5. Love for all kinds of sports will be kept high in the second and the third class, and low for the first class and even lower for the fourth class.

6. The education for the first class would be based on 100% rationality, whereas, for the second and the third class would be 50% rationality and 50% irrationality. For the fourth class it would be 100% irrationality based.

7. The young of the second, the third, and the fourth classes, would be encouraged to be licentious and eroticism loving, whereas, those of the first class, would be educated to behave in a very temperate manner.

8. The qualities of the "old world", family creation, monogamy, romance, poverty, religions, and diseases, would be eliminated in the world housing the first, second, and the third classes, but would be preserved in the world of the fourth class.

9. With respect to each day, most of the work that the members of the second, third, and the fourth classes would do would be for the welfare of the world controller and the members of the first class.

10. The world controller and the first class would encourage the members of the second, the third, and the fourth classes to organize and indulge in noisy and cheerful parties after the completion of their day's work.

11. In these parties, the participants would be encouraged to be well groomed, and behave in kindly and amusing manner towards each other. They would also be given "serotonin" boosting drugs and the best quality food and drinks.

12. The world controller and the members of the first class would be considered as gods by the members of the second, the third, and the fourth class.

13. The members of each of the first three classes would never say "thank you" to a member of a lower class if that member does something moral or shows altruism for the welfare of his superior. The same would apply for the world controller. Why would this be the case? It is because it would be considered as a duty rather than a personal choice and punishment would be given to those would not follow it.

14. Although the world controller and the members of the first class would consider all the members of the third and the fourth classes as idiotic

and insignificant, they would still behave politely and courteously towards them, if they happen, by an accident, to come in contact with them. However, when they would be alone, they would regret amongst themselves from having met them.

15. The youth of the first, the second, and the third classes, would be taught to dislike and remain ignorant of old books and old human made structures. However, this would not be taught to the youth of the fourth class.

16. The people of the second, the third, and the fourth classes will be taught not to desire anything that they can never acquire via their own intelligence.

17. In the world controller, the first class, the second class, and the third class, there would be 100% unawareness of old age and death. This would not be the case for the fourth class.

18. For the sake of preserving global stability and the prevention of a revolution, the world controller, would destroy all the books on philosophy and morality.

19. All the free choices and the responsibilities of the members of the four classes would only be inside the sphere that would be created by the world controller. The volume of this sphere would be the highest for the first class and the lowest for the fourth class.

20. No one in the first three classes would ever feel that he is insignificant or meaningless in comparison to the Cosmos. However, all the members of the fourth class would be made to feel so by the world controller and the members of the first class.

21. The level of success of a person in the industrial world would be determined by all the other members by the number of sufferings and challenges that he has faced. The lower their number, the more successful his life is. The opposite would be case in the anti-industrial world, that is, amongst the members of the fourth class.

22. Everyone in the industrial world, including the world controller, would desire to look young till their death.

23. Lectures on hygiene, and sex education would be given to the youth of the first three classes, but not to the youth of the fourth class. They would be allowed to live like animals in the matter of hygiene and sex.

Obesity would only be found in the world of the fourth class, and no one in the industrial world, would be obese. In addition to this, no one in this world would be allowed to become overweight either. Although sports like boxing and wrestling would thrive, professional bodybuilding, weightlifting, and powerlifting would be banned or permanently eliminated from the world by the world controller and the members of the first class. Why? It is because all professional bodybuilders, weightlifters, and power lifters are overweight according to their height. In addition to this, a "calorie counter" would be inserted, via an injection, into the small intestine of each member of the industrial world, which would measure the exact number of calories that a particular person consumes in a single day. Based on this policy, the world controller, along with his best scientists, would create a law which would order all the members of the industrial world, to consume a "target minimum" number of calories in a day, and a "target maximum" number of calories in a day. The values of the minima and the maxima would be the highest for the members of the third class and the lowest for the members of the first class. Those who fail to attain the minima and the maxima would have to report to a doctor and give the reason for their failure and pay a fine. If they would repeat it again, they would be expelled from the industrial world and kept in the anti-industrial world for a time period whose length would be determined by the members of the first class. The world controller, however, would be free from this system of eating, just like the members of the fourth class.

The most interesting qualities of this new world, however, would lie in the world of sex and reproduction. As I said before, just like the two kinds of men, there are two kinds of women in the world; the simpleton and the non-simpleton. The former, love to give birth to multiple children and take the greatest possible care of all of them by becoming and remaining housewives till the end of their lives. The latter, however, only desire to give birth to either one child or two at the most (a fact also noted by Bertrand Russell). In addition to this, they hate the two things that the simpleton women love the most; housewife and a good mother (breastfeeding for the proper biological time period, plus, taking care of their child by themselves later). The three things that they love the most are; acquiring western education, using it to acquire as much money as they can according to their intelligence, and using their money to acquire as much pleasure as they can, including sexual, before they become too old. Over here, lies an interesting truth; unlike the non-simpleton men, the non-simpleton women are only interested in the acquisition of wealth and pleasure and not in the acquisition of power. This explains the far greater abundance of women in the business world than in the political world.

In the Brave New World of the greatest possible kind of ultimate man, the non-simpleton mentality of the women of the first three classes, would reach its peak. When this would occur, they would come to believe in three things;

1. Biological childbirth and labour pain are the most disgusting activities that a beautiful and an intelligent woman can perform.

2. Motherhood is the most horrifying fate that a beautiful and an intelligent woman can suffer.

3. An intelligent woman should only have sex with a man who is either as intelligent as her or is more intelligent than her.

All the simpleton women of the Brave New World would be placed in the savage world and would not be allowed into the industrial world. All the women of the industrial world, however, where the first three classes would live and work would be non-simpleton minded. All of them would desire to have sex with the world controller. He would have the power and the privilege to choose the woman he desires from the immense pool in front of him.

Due to the mentality of its women, the phenomena of pregnancy and childbirth would be completely exterminated from the industrial world. The new members of this world would be created inside huge factories. Every new male and female foetus would be placed in a container which would contain the same "amniotic fluid" that develops inside the uterus of a young mother during pregnancy. The full and natural growth of the brain and the body would be supressed in the babies that would become a part of the second and the third classes. However, the greatest amount of planning and engineering would be done to ensure that the growth of the brain and the body of every baby of the first class remains 100% natural and attains its full potential.

The babies belonging to the first class would be grown in a different section of the factory than the babies belonging to the second and the third classes. In addition to this, gene editing, using the CRISPR technique, would be applied to the embryos of all the three classes. Through this, the genes that would create cancers, physical defects and syndromes would be eliminated in the embryos of all the three classes. However, the number of harmful genes that would be eliminated from the first-class embryos would be greater than those that are eliminated from the second and the third-class embryos. Why? So that the first-class can keep on ruling the second and the third classes due to their moderate levels of genetic deformities.

The non-simpleton women of the industrial world would view sex as only a "pleasure and relaxation" producing activity. It would be considered as the next greatest, anti-stress drug after the best kind of serotonin boosting pill that would be created by the biochemists of the first class (with no side effects).

The non-simpleton women, however, would remain females, biologically. Thus, they would have fully functioning ovaries and would also produce unfertilised ova. Thus, during sex with a non-simpleton man, who would also be a man biologically, they would have the same probability of getting pregnant as the simpleton women of the anti-industrial world. In order to bring this probability down to zero, they would consume, after sex, the best kind of abortion pill that would be created by the biochemists of the first class. This pill, however, would not be given to the women of the anti-industrial world. Why? In order to keep the population of this world at the size that is desired by the world controller (unlike the industrial world, many people will suffer unnatural deaths in the anti-industrial world due to various kinds of diseases, natural disasters, and genetic syndromes). Thus, due to this pill, the women of the industrial world will live a sex life that is immensely greater and more enjoyable than the women of the anti-industrial world.

There would be another interesting quality of this world. Since all the members of the industrial world would regard the members of the anti-industrial world as 50% children and 50% animals, they would come to visit them, as tourists, through the "tourism tours" that would be organised by the first-class members of the industrial word. When the people of the industrial world would be travelling to the anti-industrial world, they would behave as if they are going to either an amusement park or a zoo.

When inside the anti-industrial world, they would visit the homes of the savage men and women and would observe their methods of preparing edible food, and eating it. They would also observe the way in which they sleep, and the way in which they live their social life. After acquiring all this information, they would take a break, and during it, converse with each other about the magnitude of the funny nature of the people of this world and laugh, frequently. Then they would visit a hospital where they would witness something that they have never seen in any of the hospitals in the industrial world; a man dying due to either malaria, or viral flu or cancer or pneumonia or some other disease.

After this, they would be taken to another part of this savage world, where they would witness a funny and a curiosity arousing phenomenon; a group of people, sitting together and praying to an invisible being somewhere up in the sky. These people would be the part of the religion that would be the last one to exist on Earth before the extinction of the Homo sapiens.

Then they would be taken to another part of the hospital where they would witness the funniest, the most terrifying (to the women of the industrial world) and the most spectacular scene in their lives; a simpleton woman going into labour pain and giving birth to a living baby.

Projecting ahead, what will eventually happen to the Brave New World? After the very first world controller, retires from his post, he would appoint his successor. His successor would be a member of the first class and like him would be as great an ultimate man as him. What would this new world controller do?

The goal of all ultimate men is to preserve the creations and the systems of their ancestral ultimate men. They hate that kind of novelty that is destructive to their creations and their long-standing systems, even if it is beneficial for the species in the long run. The advancement of space exploration and the creation of new space technology is the top in the list of the "destructive novelties".

A civilization or a species that is continuously growing in its level of advancement in space technology and space exploration will always be ruled by a superman and not by an ultimate man. A civilization can experience two kinds of ages; the age of darkness (also known as the Byzantine Immobility) and the age of enlightenment (also known as the Golden Age). The ultimate man is the creator and the amplifier of the former and the superman is the creator and the amplifier of the latter. Why? It is because, in order to keep on living at the peak of the hierarchy pyramid of his civilization and preserve his image as a god in the eyes of all his subjects, the ultimate man must, preserve and even amplify the "intellectual darkness" around him. For the superman, this is not so. He desires eternal self-life (like the ultimate man) and eternal mental self-growth (unlike the ultimate man) and can only achieve it, according to his own belief, by creating and amplifying the "intellectual luminosity" around him.

The empire of the first world controller of the Brave New World would have expanded to not only the entire surface of the Earth, but also to its moon and Mars. However, it would never go beyond Mars, because the science and the technology that is required to create a manned spaceflight to the moons of the gas giants and create permanent self-sustaining colonies on them would never come into existence in the world of the ultimate man.

Manned space exploration and settlement on alien worlds is destructive to the dominant culture of any nation on Earth. Why? It is because the culture of any big nation on Earth is created to fulfil only one purpose; to keep on making the nation more and more fascistic and thus keep on increasing the power of its defence forces. In order to preserve this system, the government, and the capitalist community of all the big nations, spend most of the earned and the stored wealth of their respective nations on the military sector.

The world controller, along with all the members of the first class would create a massive security ring around themselves through all the weapons, and the nukes that would have been created. This ring would protect them from the members of the second, the third, and the fourth classes if Earth gets struck by some unforeseen calamity. They would keep on increasing the strength of this ring, every year, through the wealth that they would acquire by the exploitation of Mother Nature. Due to this, their magnitude of neglect of the human bases on the Moon and Mars would keep on increasing year after year. In addition to this, something very interesting would happen.

The world controller would regard all the humans on the moon and Mars as a source of danger to his world. Why? It is because they would not be a part of his global system, its culture, and its philosophy. They would be living outside it, continuously. In addition, these colonists would not be 100% human. They would be meta-humans or trans-humans. Thus, after becoming the leader of the world, he would proceed to exterminate them either by using IPBM's (Inter Planetary Ballistic Missiles) or by sending someone from his own world, who would deploy an artificially engineered virus or bacterium inside the base (like in the Hollywood movie, Resident Evil) that would rapidly exterminate all the colonists.

After exterminating all the colonists on the moon and Mars, the world controller would retire from his post and hand over his seat of power to the chosen one from the first class. The outgoing world controller would say to his successor; remember, your goal is to keep on increasing the strength and the longevity of the system that I have created.

The new world controller, another ultimate man, would try his best to fulfil his master's goal. For this, he would order the scientists of the first class to not do any research into something or create something that would be destructive to the preservation of the current global system. The scientists, would agree with a happy state of mind, because this would not only reduce the stress of their profession in their minds, but they would also be paid more than before, by their boss, for sticking to this policy.

This policy would lead to the rapid degradation of the intelligence of the species in the long-term future. Eventually, it would produce either of the two kinds of worlds.

The IDIOCRACY world

In the Hollywood movie IDIOCRACY, the main character, Joe Bauers, was a man of ordinary intelligence. He was made a part of a military experiment of the Pentagon in which he was inserted inside a cryogenic capsule and made to hibernate for 500 years. The capsule was pre-programmed to open by itself, after 500 years. It did, and when he woke up and began to move around, he soon found out that all his friends and the people involved in the military project, including the Pentagon itself, were long gone. In place of them were people who were so idiotic, that they did not know that plants need water to survive and grow (they sprayed Gatorade on the agricultural farmlands) and could not answer the question; if you had one bucket, full of water, and you were given another one, how many buckets would you have?

The one word that they uttered the greatest number of times during every day of their lives was "fuck". In addition to this, they enjoyed all those movies and TV shows in which this word was uttered many times and in which most of the activities of the characters involved the use of their genitals. The movie that won the highest number of Oscars had the name; Ass.

The TIME MACHINE World

This world would either be born directly from the Brave New World or would be the final product of the IDIOCRACY world. In it, the human species, instead of remaining as one single species, would branch off into two sub species. The members of both the species would be reproductively compatible, however, the hybrids would always be physically more fragile and shorter lived than the pure strains.

The first strain would be the ELOIS. They would be the descendants of the fourth class of the Brave New World, or the simpletons. The second strain would be the MORLOCKS, who would be the descendants of the first, second, and the third classes of the Brave New World. The ELOIS would be childish brained, playful, uncaring about anything around them, and lovers of Mother Nature. The MORLOCKS, however, would be adult brained, non-playful, serious, and analytical of the things around them, and the exploiters of Mother Nature.

Just like in the current industrial world, and the Brave New World, where the non-simpletons treat the simpletons like animals and turn them into their slaves, the MORLOCKS treated the ELOIS as animals. Thus, they farmed them like chickens or goats or cattle and ate them when hungry. The ELOIS, on the other hand, ate only the various kinds of fruits that grew on the trees and plants that were either farmed by the MORLOCKS or were grown by Mother Nature herself.

The most remarkable quality of this world was that the MORLOCKS always lived underground, during the day, and came up to the surface only in the night. Why? It is because their eyes were extremely fragile to the visible and the UV light of the Sun and their vision was infrared based (just like that of a mosquito). The ELOIS, however, remained active and outdoors only during the day and went to sleep together "in groups" soon after sunset.

How did this world come into existence? There are two possible answers.

Possibility 1: After a few centuries of existence, the Brave New World was hit by either an extra-terrestrial cataclysm or a terrestrial cataclysm. The former type is an asteroid collision, whereas, the latter type is the eruption of a super volcano, with a VEI of at least 10. The asteroid that would strike this world would be either of the same dimensions and mass as the one that exterminated the dinosaurs of the Jurassic geological age, or even greater. After impact, it would cause a global climate change event whose velocity and ferocity would be vastly bigger than the one that we are currently experiencing. In addition to this, it would also cause the activation of either one or two of the planet's "magma hotspots" inside its outer mantle.

Possibility 2: Due to enhanced activity of the Sun or the inner core of Earth, one or more of the "magma hotspots" inside the outer mantle would erupt and cause a volcanic eruption that would be as big as the Lake Toba eruption, 75,000 years ago, or the one that caused the Permian mass extinction, 250 million years ago.

The people of the industrial world, including the world controller, would not have the power to stop any of these two cataclysms from taking place. Why? It is because either the technology would not exist or even if it did exist, it would fail to perform its job. Why? This is because of two reasons; first, the creators of these technologies would be long dead and the new scientists would be corrupt minded and of low intelligence compared to them. Thus, they would not understand the way these "world saving machines" should be operated. Second, the Cosmos itself would bring either of these catastrophes to Earth in such a rapid manner, that the inhabitants of the industrial part of the Brave New World would not get enough time to either prepare for them or stop them.

After the end of either of these two cataclysms, something new would occur. In the Brave New World, all the energy that is required by the industrial and the anti-industrial world would be produced from "non-carbon" sources. Thus, the burning of fossil fuels would be exterminated long ago. One of these non-carbon sources would be the nuclear fission reactors.

After the asteroid or the volcanic catastrophe, all these reactors, all over the world, would suffer a meltdown. This would cause a massive outpouring of radioactivity into the extremely violent and chaotic atmosphere of the planet. The radioactive elements would remain in the atmosphere for many thousands of years to come and would lead to the creation of a huge number of genetic mutations in the genes of all the people on the planet, the simpletons and the non-simpletons, generation after generation. Evolution would proceed at the speed of a bullet train and eventually it would reach the "branch off" point, the MORLOCKS and the ELOIS.

In the Hollywood movies, The Hills have eyes 1 and The Hills have eyes 2, the creation of a new human sub species due to radioactivity poisoning was shown. The cannibals who lived inside the cave systems in the desert of the state of New Mexico of the United States, were the equivalent of the MORLOCKS, whereas, the physically and the mentally normal Americans who ventured over there were the ELOIS.

In the novel, The Time Machine, H.G. Wells has created three kinds of characters; the simpletons or the ELOIS, the non-simpletons or the MORLOCKS, the superman or the Time Traveller. Yes, in this story, the superman is represented by the Time Traveller, who created the Time Machine and entered into their world from "out of nowhere". Since, a superman is the final product of SIMPLETONISM; he was immensely more attracted to the

ELOIS than to the MORLOCKS. Eventually, he decided to use all his mental powers to permanently change the dark fate of the ELOIS by destroying the underground world of the MORLOCKS and thus freeing them from their rulers, and by transferring all of his knowledge and wisdom into the ELOIS by becoming a "real teacher". Just like the superman, he wanted to become their hero and their prophet.

Conclusion

After witnessing the state of the world of the current time period, I believe that there is a 50% probability that the Brave New World would be born in the future. However, there is a 50% probability that it would not be born. Why? It is because of the birth of Artificial Intelligence (AI) and another remarkable concept of mathematics and physics; the quantum computer.

If World War 3 or some other natural catastrophe does not happen in the next 150 years, the two would combine and produce something even more remarkable than either of them; a computer with a soul or a consciousness. This computer, would eventually produce a completely new concept of computer science; a quantum computer hive.

Chapter 25

Does the Cosmos have a core? This question has been pondered over by the greatest philosophers and scientists of ancient, medieval, and the modern ages. The catholic priests and the bishops of the middle-ages used to believe that the location of the core of the Cosmos and that of planet Earth is the same. Thus, the Earth is at the core of the Cosmos. This is most probably not true.

The core of Cosmos is the region from where the Big Bang started. It was a point with zero dimensions but possessing all the mass of the known and the unknown Cosmos. The physicists tell us that this point was in a space that was devoid of the presence of the 4 known forces, dark matter, dark energy, and even time. The space that existed before the Big Bang was the "proto space" (just like a proto star). After the Big bang the proto space transformed into the "main sequence" space.

How long will the space of the Cosmos stay on its main sequence phase? Since the lifespan of the Cosmos is immensely greater than any star in it, this phase might last for trillions of years. The length of this phase depends upon three things; how long will the Cosmos keep expanding, how will the war between visible matter, dark matter, and dark energy, evolve in the coming billions of years, and how much of the old matter would be destroyed in the super massive black holes at the core of every spiral galaxy and how much new matter would be injected into the expanding Cosmos by the quasars in the cores of the elliptical galaxies.

Postmodernism says that all these questions can only be answered by the creator of the Cosmos. It is impossible for any intelligent species to answer these questions. Why? Because in order to know the answers to these questions, you would have to observe and study the Cosmos not only from an internal point of view, but also from an external point of view. Thus, these questions can only be answered by a Type 4 species, which possesses the knowledge and the technology to travel to the edge of the Cosmos and then cross its outer boundary and enter the "inter cosmic" space. From this point, they can see not only the overall structure of the Cosmos they were born in, but also its evolution in a wholly new way.

If the Cosmos is a star of unknown dimensions, then it has a core, since every star has a core. It is a known fact that the lifespan of the core of any kind of star (red dwarf, yellow dwarf, blue dwarf, the blue super giants) is much longer than the rest of its body. Thus, the lifespan of the core of the Cosmos is far longer than the lifespan of the all the galaxies in it, and all the dark matter and dark energy. It is also a known fact that when a star begins to form, its core gets created first and then the rest of its body. The same principle applies to the Cosmos.

What is at the core of the Cosmos? It is a triangle that can be called as the GAME TRINITY. When we observe all the life forms on Earth, including human beings, we see that they desire three things; power, wealth, and bonding. The first is for the sake of domination, the second is for the sake of the elongation of the personal existence period, and the third is for the sake of creating and preserving unity. When we look at the overall picture, the goal of the pursuit of power, wealth, and bonding is for the sake of the creation and the preservation of security; Security from what? Answer: Death

Every thermodynamic and impermanent concept in the Cosmos wants to exist forever or become immortal. This law has been pre-programmed into its core by the creator of the Cosmos itself. Why? It is because the creator wants either a species or a single individual from a Type 4 species to transcend all the other members of its own species, attain Type 5 status, and become infinite with respect to time, dimensions, and energy possession. However, it is righteous to believe that all of this might be just pure fantasy or speculation.

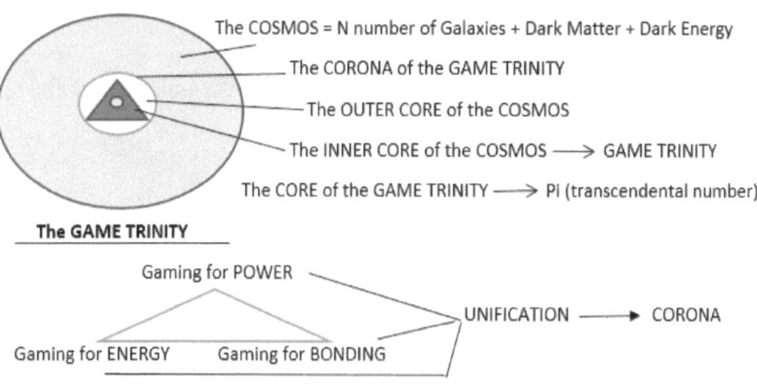

Since there is a CORONA around every star in the Cosmos, there is also a CORONA around its core which either is of the same fundamental design as the outer corona or is of a different design.

The Cosmos has its own CORONA and the GAME TRINITY at its core has its own. At the core of the GAME TRINITY is the complete value, all the numbers after the decimal, of Pi. The Pi is responsible for;

1. The circular shape of the CORONA of the GAME TRINITY and the outer Cosmos.
2. The circular and continuous flow of energy between the three APEXES of the GAME TRINITY.
3. The spherical shape of all the stars, planets, galaxies in the Cosmos.

There are two kinds of Universes;

1. **Type 1**: They have a symmetrical structure around the GAME TRINITY
2. **Type 2**: They have an asymmetrical structure around the GAME TRINITY

The goal of the 4 forces is to transform or restore back the asymmetrical structure of an expanding Cosmos into a symmetrical one.

The products of the GAMING for WEALTH are

1. The creation of MATTER
2. The transportation of MATTER from POINT A to POINT B

The products of the GAMING for POWER are

1. The creation of HIERARCHY PYRAMIDS

Type 1: They are created within the structure of all the intelligent species in the Cosmos

Type 2: They are created within the structure of all the galaxies in the Cosmos

1. The creation of WAR

The products of the GAMING for BONDING are

2. The 4 FORCES of the Cosmos
3. The creation of the activity known as SEX

The economic structure of the cosmos is immensely more complex, powerful, and older than that of the Homo sapiens. It will also outlive its inferior counterpart by billions or trillions of years.

The leader of the perfect fascist nation knows the evolution of the economic system of the species depends upon the evolution of the economic system of the cosmos. He is also aware of the fact that in order to keep his nation in a state of perpetual growth, he must keep the evolution of the economic structure of his own nation in 100% harmony with that of the cosmos.

There are three cases related to this.

Case 1: The economic development of the species “falls behind” that of the cosmos

Result: There is a rapid increase in the frequency and the power of the hostile actions of the 4 forces of the cosmos towards the species. In addition to this, there is a rapid decrease in the intelligence of the species from generation to generation.

Case 2: The economic development of the species and that of the cosmos go “hand in hand”

Result: There is a gradual decrease in the frequency and the power of the hostile actions of the 4 forces of the cosmos towards the species. In addition to this, there is a gradual increase in the intelligence of the species from generation to generation.

Case 3: The economic development of the species becomes faster than that of the cosmos

Result: There is a rapid decrease in the frequency and the power of the hostile actions of the 4 forces of the cosmos towards the species. In addition to this, there is a rapid increase in the intelligence of the species from generation to generation.

In case 1, the species is short lived on the geologic and cosmic timescales.

In case 2, the species lives as long as the cosmos itself.

In case 3, the species outlives the cosmos.

The game trinity not only generates space and time, but also generates the 4 forces of the cosmos dark matter and dark energy, and the other trinities.

The cosmos and the human economic systems have their own stock markets and thus their own trinities.

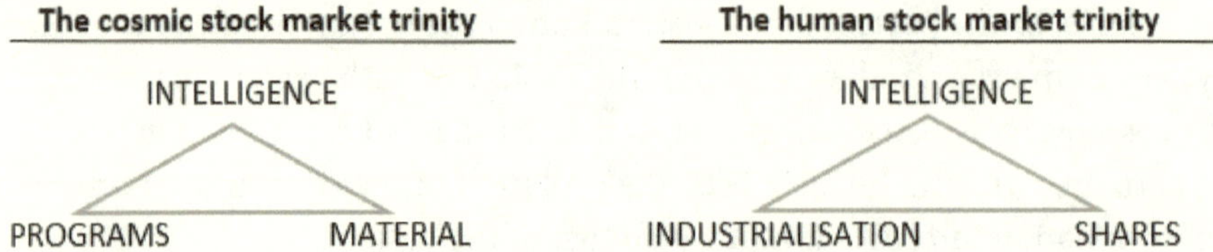

The statistical records of the life of every star, planet, species, and even the super massive black hole in a galaxy are created and stored in the "dark matter" bubble that surrounds the galaxy and is responsible for its development, stability, and its security from the dark energy that is present in the inter galactic space.

Every galaxy in the cosmos, whether spiral or barred or elliptical, is a fascist nation. The stars are the citizens, the planets are their servants, and the super massive black hole or the quasar at the core is the leader or the greatest gamer in the system. Since the cosmos itself is a vast battlefield, the galaxies form alliances with each other and thus form groups. These groups or gangs are known as the galactic clusters and each cluster is locked in a never-ending battle with the other ones.

Dark energy has two goals to accomplish; to maximize the number of galaxies in a cosmos that it itself keeps on expanding and to prevent a galaxy from becoming bigger beyond an upper limit. If there was no dark energy in the cosmos after its creation, then the very first galaxy to form in it would have been nearly as big as the cosmos itself and would be the only galaxy in it.

Chapter 26

The GAME TRINITY is the core of the Universe, but it is also connected to two other trinities. These are the EXISTENTIAL TRINITY and the META BODY TRINITY. These three trinities are connected, are controlled, and have been created by the INFINITE MIND (which is not God or Allah).

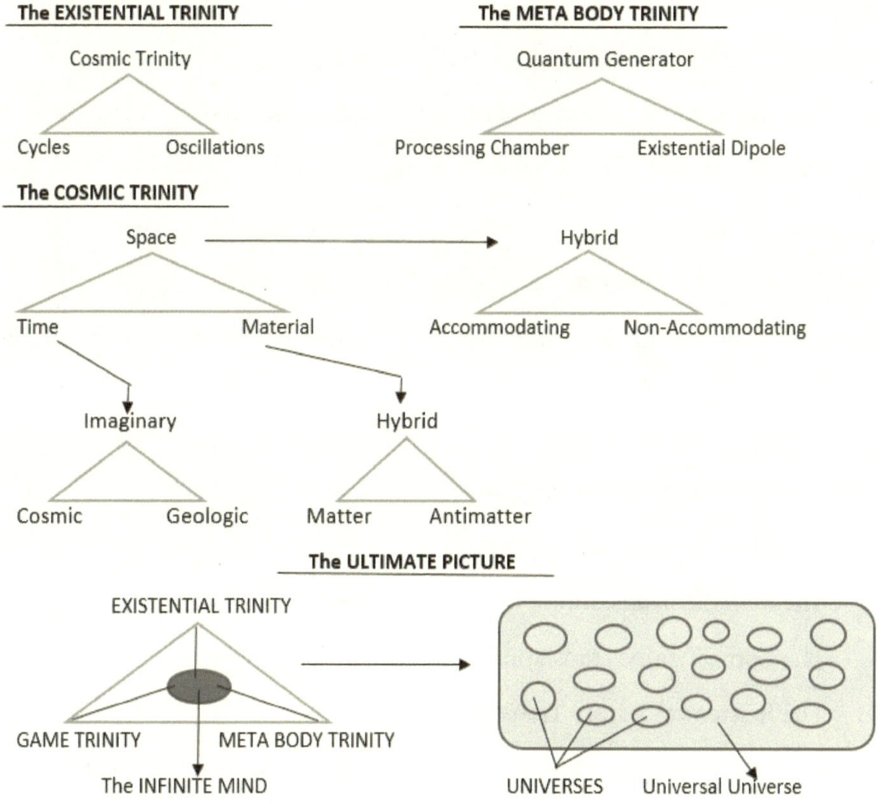

The EXISTENTIAL TRINITY

Cosmic Trinity
Cycles
Oscillations

The META BODY TRINITY

Quantum Generator
Processing Chamber
Existential Dipole

The COSMIC TRINITY

Space
Time
Material

Hybrid
Accommodating
Non-Accommodating

Imaginary
Cosmic
Geologic

Hybrid
Matter
Antimatter

The ULTIMATE PICTURE

EXISTENTIAL TRINITY
GAME TRINITY
META BODY TRINITY
The INFINITE MIND

UNIVERSES
Universal Universe

Each of the N number of Universes is "unique". No two of them are 100% similar. Why? It is because the Infinite Mind does not do repetition. Why doesn't it do repetition? It is because it is not under the absolute tyranny of Pi, unlike the non-infinite minds in each of the N number of Universes.

The Universal universe is an ocean of unknown dimensions in which the N number of Universes are floating, colliding, and even suddenly popping out of existence. Just like a star, a universe also explodes and dies. This explosion can either be sudden or after the end of its lifespan.

The Universal universe is an ocean in which all the 4 forces of physics unite to form a "super force". Its space is known as the "universal space". The space of each of the generated universes is a "sub set" or a derivative of the "universal space". Unlike the inferior universes floating in it, the Universal universe moves on "imaginary time" rather than "cosmic time". Thus, it has no beginning and no end. It is immortal or eternal.

The four other qualities of the Universal universe are;

1. The absence of all the laws of physics and mathematics.
2. The absence of the three kinds of trinities.
3. The absence of a core.
4. It runs on the imaginary time scale.

The Universal universe is a combination of two things; the super force and the translation programs.

The translation programs are of three kinds;

1. The Space Translation program.
2. The Time Translation program.
3. The Material Translation program.
4. The Game Trinity Translation program.
5. The Existential Trinity Translation program.

The Translation programs are responsible for the "conversion" of the data that is continuously beamed and injected by the Infinite mind from the three kinds of trinities. Each packet of data creates a universe inside the Universal universe and is unique in its structure. Two 100% similar packets have never been sent into the Universal universe by the Infinite mind since it began creating the universes in the infinite ocean. However, this only applies to the cosmic trinity. The data packets for the Game and the Existential trinities are the same for each of the universes.

The Space Translation program is responsible for creating the three kinds of spaces. The Time Translation program is responsible for creating the three kinds of Time. The Material translation program is responsible for creating all the known and the unknown sub atomic particles and the "force generating" particles. The Existential Trinity Translation program makes all the matter or antimatter in a new universe, subject to the cosmic trinity and to Pi (cycles) and to oscillations.

The super force and the translation programs are a product of the Theory of Everything (TOE) equation.

The Universal universe was the universe in which the interstellar travel spaceship, the Event Horizon, suddenly entered when it created an artificial Black Hole from its Gravity Drive. When it came back into the non-universal universe, it had become a living organism. Why? It was because a Meta Body had combined with it.

What is the Meta Body? In the ancient times, the Greek philosophers called it the SOUL and the Hindu sages of India called it the AATMA. In the modern era, psychologists like Sigmund Freud, Carl Jung, and David Bohm called it the CONSCIOUSNESS. No one has ever seen the structure of the SOUL or the CONSCIOUSNESS because it is a metaphysical concept, unlike the brain and it's CONNECTOME.

A Concept can be either physical or metaphysical. The former is made of either matter or antimatter while the latter are not made of either matter or antimatter. In addition, all the physical concepts are either visible or invisible, but never indiscernible. However, all the metaphysical concepts are indiscernible to any kind of technology that can be created by human beings, either in the present or in the near or the distant future.

A complete and living human being or an animal is a combination of two kinds of bodies; the physical and the metaphysical. The physical body is only a multi-purpose vehicle which the metaphysical or the Meta body uses for its own needs.

After the fertilization of the egg by the sperm, a Meta body takes over the embryo and by a continuous release of its quantum energy, activates the "gene hierarchy pyramid" which starts the creation process of the physical body. The entire process of the creation of a foetus inside a female is a superior version of the science of Bionics.

Bionics is concerned with the harmonious fusion of a living organism with a machine. The best example of this was seen in the Hollywood movie, Aliens, where the crewmembers of the ship, had placed themselves inside huge non-computer-based robots and were taking the cargo to the required places.

Now imagine if a human being was placed inside a capsule which contained all the data that is necessary for the creation of the robot. As soon as the human being is inserted into this capsule, he activates the generator that he has with him. The data that is embedded in its walls would get activated and the robot would start to develop on its own around him.

This is exactly how a foetus develops inside a female mammal.

The structure of the Meta Body

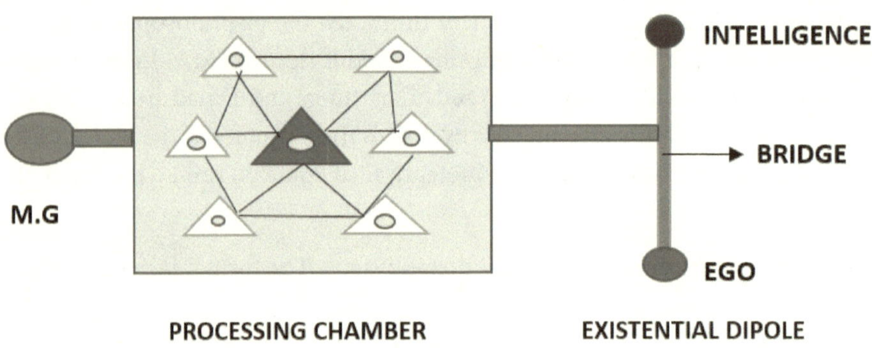

The 6 TRINITIES around the GAME TRINITY are;

1. EXISTENTIAL TRINITY = COSMIC TRINITY + CYCLES + OSCILLATIONS
2. COSMIC TRINITY = SPACE + TIME + MATERIAL
3. MIND TRINITY = COSMIC BRAIN + LIMBIC BRAIN + R-COMPLEX BRAIN

4. NATURE TRNITY = CEREBROTONISM + VISCEROTONISM + SOMATOTONISM

5. AMBITION TRINITY = SPIRITUALISM + HEDONISM + MATERIALISM

6. QUANTITATIVE TRINITY = 0 + 1 + INFINITY

The yellow dot at the core of each of them is the complete numerical value of Pi.

The M.G or the Meta Generator is connected to the Universal universe and a continuous stream of energy flows from it into the Processing Chamber and the Existential Dipole.

The Existential Dipole consists of the Intelligence and the Ego which are connected to each other via a Bridge.

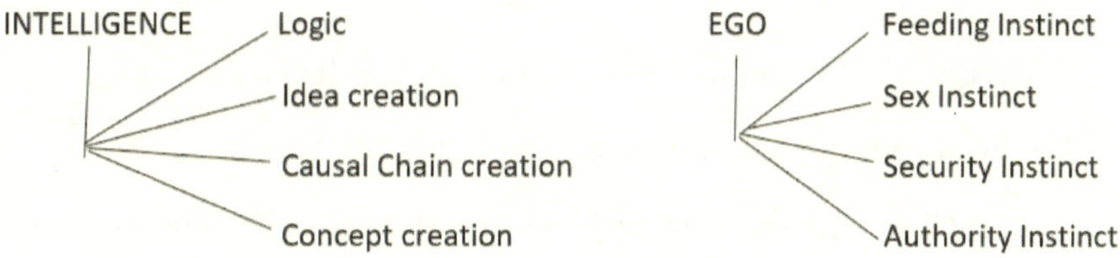

An idea is a product of Logic. A Causal Chain is made up of N number of Ideas and a Concept is made up of N number of Causal Chains.

Each of the 4 Instincts of the Ego, have their own trinities.

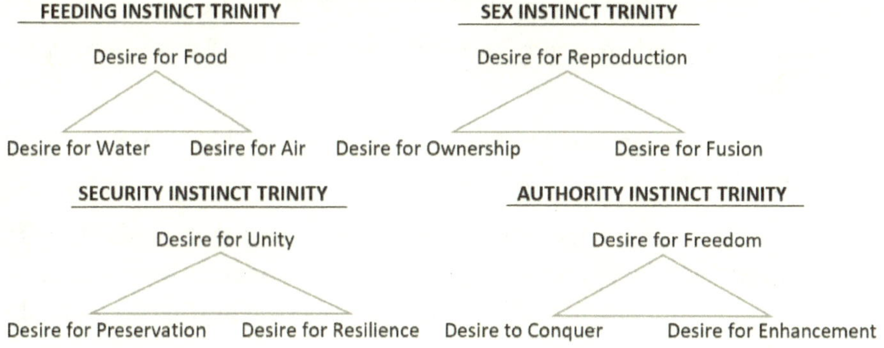

The Meta body is housed inside the physical body, which can have two genders; male or female. However, the Meta body itself is "genderless". Why? It is because it is a house in which a male-female couple live. The Meta body only forms when they get married together. Their marriage produces the existential dipole and they are connected to each other not via love, but via memory.

Now the question; which is the husband or the male and which are the wife or the female? The answer is; the Ego is the husband and the Intelligence is his wife. The Meta generator and the 6 trinities are the various parts of their home and which they share together. However, in all the Meta bodies of all the organisms on Earth, the Ego rules the Intelligence and is decides the way the quantum generator and the 6 trinities would be used.

Since this is the situation, the qualities of the Meta body are;

1. The intelligence forsakes the investigation of all those things that are harmful to the Ego.
2. TIME is a creation of the intelligence and not of the Ego.
3. The Ego believes that the intelligence cannot survive without it.
4. Since the Ego regards the intelligence as inferior to itself, it never allows it to take any decision completely on its own.
5. At rare moments, the Ego orders the intelligence to go to sleep. You suffer an uncontrollable panic attack and go hysterical due to this.
6. During sleep, the Ego is far more active than the intelligence.
7. The Ego orders the intelligence to discover all those things in the external Cosmos that will increase its power and lifespan.
8. "Selectivity" and "partiality" are the qualities of the Ego and not of the intelligence.
9. Unlike the intelligence, the Ego is not affected at all by TIME. Thus, its power does not decline at all even in old age.
10. 1If the Ego comes face to face with something that needs its wife, intelligence, to be immensely powerful, then in order to avoid self-harm, the Ego decides to ignore that thing and orders the intelligence to do the same.

11. 1The Ego has the power to put the intelligence to sleep but the intelligence does not have the power to put the Ego to sleep.

12. 1The Ego can amplify the power of the intelligence, but the intelligence can never amplify the power of the Ego.

13. 1The Ego of one Meta body goes to war with the Ego of another Meta body, the intelligence in each of them are not at war.

14. 1The change in the power of the Ego of one Meta body can only be caused by the alien Ego of another Meta body and never by the intelligence of the two Meta bodies.

15. 1In order to prevent self-injury, the Ego orders the intelligence to stop creating "logic trains" and to divert its energy to something other than what it is currently focused on.

16. 1The Ego prevents the intelligence from operating at its "full power".

17. 1In the memory bank (the hippocampus) of the brain, the Ego only preserves, without asking the intelligence, whatever is valuable to it.

18. 1In a state of regret, the Ego abuses and humiliates the intelligence.

19. 1The Egos of two Meta bodies can be equally powerful, but have intelligences of unequal powers.

20. 2The Ego of one Meta body tries to hide the power of its intelligence from the Ego of another Meta body.

21. 2If the Ego goes insane and the intelligence is unable to calm it, the person starts to believe in the existence of those truths that do not exist (the best example of this is; God loves us).

22. 2Sometimes the Ego orders the intelligence to study and eliminate its own defects.

23. 2When the Ego does not get what it wants for a prolonged time, the person enters a state known as "boredom".

24. 2MUSIC only affects the Ego and not the intelligence.

25. 2**The goal of the Ego of a Meta body**: to gain permanent freedom from the hostile Egos of the other Meta bodies and to gain permanent unity with the friendly Egos.

26. 2MOVIES and TV shows affect the power of the Ego

    i> **Tragedy**: Decrease the power of the Authority instinct, but increase the power of the Security instinct

    ii> **Horror**: Decrease the power of the Authority instinct, but increase the power of the Security instinct.

    iii> **Action**: Increase the power of the Authority instinct

    iv> **Romantic**: Increase the power of the Sex Instinct

    v> **Cooking and restaurant shows**: Increase the power of the Feeding instinct

27. 2When the intelligence is strong and healthy, it keeps all the instincts of the Ego in a "balanced" state and prevents any one of them from going out of balance and destroying the others.

28. 2The Ego and its intelligence keep on changing the structures and the degree of activity of all the genes in all the cells of the physical body and are in turn affected by the changes that happen in the genes due to the "mutagens" of the external Cosmos.

The SHIVA theory of the Meta Body

The structure of the physical body is determined by the genome of the embryo of the organism of a particular species. Since the genome of every species is unique, the structure of the physical body is also unique for each species on Earth. However, when it comes to the Meta body, its structure is the "same" for all the species on Earth, including the microorganisms. This is because the Meta body is not the product of a genome, which is a physical concept. The Meta body is not made up of atoms or genes or cells. Its three parts are the product of either a single or a set of programs.

I, the author of this book, have not seen the Meta body directly, but believe that when it is finally observed by a quantum computer in the distant future, it will look just like the head of the Hindu trinity god, SHIVA.

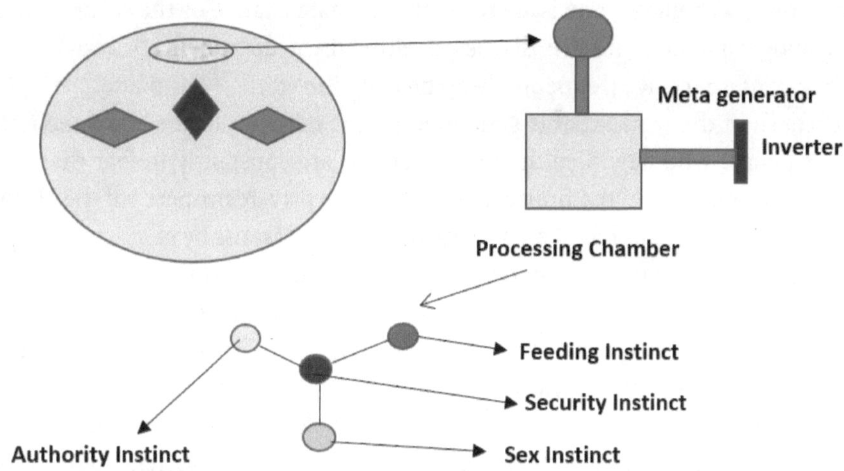

The 2 RED EYES are the eyes of the Ego. The BLUE EYE in between them is the eye of intelligence. The brain consists of the Meta generator, the processing chamber, and the inverter. Meanwhile, there is the absence of a mouth and a nose.

In every organism on Earth, including human beings, there are two worlds; the one that is seen through the eyes of the physical body and the one that is seen through the eyes of the Meta body. The Ego is not only the owner of the Meta generator, the processing chamber, the inverter, the intelligence, and its eye, but is also the owner of all the cells of the physical body. This implies that it is also the owner of the 2 eyes of the physical body.

The world that is seen through the eyes is known as the "field of consciousness". There are two such fields, the one that is a product of the eyes of the physical body and the one that is the product of the eyes of the Meta body. When the perceived data from the physical eyes, reaches the metaphysical eyes, the Ego orders the intelligence to analyse it, prepare a report and send it to itself (the Ego) instantly. After this, the Ego can do either of the two things;

1. Look at the data through the metaphysical eyes and keep it unchanged. or

2. Look at the data through the metaphysical eyes, and if it is harmful to its growth and power, pass it through the inverter and totally reverse the "correct meaning" of the data.

The best example of this is the view of planet Earth in the minds of most people living on it. Whenever, any issue regarding climate change or the several kinds of geologic phenomena are discussed either in a documentary movie or a public conference, we frequently keep hearing the words, "our planet". Why? It is because in the world that is generated by the metaphysical eyes of the Egos of the people who have wealth and power and are constantly in fear that they will lose it someday in the future, the Earth is the private property of the Homo sapiens. However, this has been proven to be total nonsense by geology long ago. According to geology, the Homo sapiens and all their creations are nothing but a thin film of atoms that is clinging to the crust of Earth. All the processes that go on inside the planet and even in its crust, happen and will keep happening for the foreseeable future, without the permission of the Homo sapiens. If this planet was ours, then no earthquake and no volcanic eruption would occur without our approval. Even the reversal of the planet's geomagnetic field would not happen without our approval.

The richest and the most powerful members of the Homo sapiens see all the data that has been collected and stored on the internet by the geologists for more than 100 years. The message that it gives them is; you and all your creations are meaningless when compared to planet Earth! Since this message is harmful to their Egos, their Ego uses the inverter to reverse its meaning and utter through the mouth of the physical body; this planet is ours and we are its guardians!

The same truth also applies to the atmosphere of this planet. Since this atmosphere is not ours, and we were not responsible for its creation about 3 billion years ago, then this implies that climate change is not due to us and we have no right to say what will happen in the future.

In every human being, there are two modes of thinking; objectively and subjectively. In the former, a concept that is created by the "infinite mind" is analysed purely by the cosmic brain, which is place where the intelligence lives. The final judgement is also made only by the cosmic brain or the intelligence. In the latter, the concept is analysed by the cosmic brain and the reptilian and the mammalian brains. The reptilian brain is the place where the Ego lives. The final judgement regarding the concept is made by the reptilian brain or the Ego.

The goals of the reptilian brain or the Ego are; to create a hierarchical pyramid and to create inequality, it says that the concept that has been created by the infinite mind is inferior to it and is thus its property.

The Ego has the power to shut down the eyes of the physical body without asking for the approval of its wife, the intelligence. In the same way, it also has the power to shut down the metaphysical eye of the intelligence without its approval. Based on this, the Meta body operates in 2 possible ways;

Method 1: The eyes of the Ego are open and the eye of the intelligence is also open

Result: The person views the world and the universe 50% objectively and 50% subjectively.

Method 2: The eyes of the Ego are open, but the eye of the intelligence is closed

Result: The person views the world and the universe 100% subjectively.

Way 1 is followed by the Meta body of a genius and Way 2 is followed by all the normal brained people of the world.

In method 1, the worlds of the eyes of the physical body and the Meta body always remain separate and never merge and unify into one world. In method 2, the 2 worlds, do not remain separate and merge and unify and at the end of this fusion, the world of the eyes of the Meta body completely absorbs or digests its inferior counterpart.

Why do the Hindus worship the penis of lord Shiva? There is a Meta physical explanation for this.

The goal of the Ego is to maximize the size and the power of all the parts of the reproductive system of the physical body in which it is housed. The goal of the intelligence, however, is to minimize the size and the power of all the parts of the reproductive system. The primary part of the reproductive system of a male human is the testes, but they can never fulfil their purpose without the presence of the penis. Thus, the penis is as important and powerful as the testes on the hierarchy pyramid of the male reproductive system. Since Shiva is a man, and had created, all the Aryans in world by having intercourse with the universe, which is a female, thus his penis was the "first cause" of the existence of the Aryan race. Since all religions tell their followers to worship and glorify the "first cause" of their existence, the Hindus of India, which are an evolutionary branch of the Viking race of the Scandinavian nations of Europe (Norway, Sweden, and Finland), instead of worshipping Zeus and Thor, worship Shiva and Krishna.

The universe was created by Brahma and its existence is preserved by Vishnu. Since they are superior to Shiva in intelligence, they do not have a reproductive system and have never and will never copulate with any of the universes that they have created and preserved so far.

If we compare the three gods of the Hindu trinity to our brain, we see that Brahma represents the cosmic brain, Vishnu represents the mammalian brain, and Shiva represents the reptilian brain. This implies that Vishnu has two responsibilities to fulfil, to preserve all the creations of Brahma and to keep Brahma and Shiva united forever.

What will happen if Vishnu fails and the unity between Brahma and Shiva breaks down? Since the job of Shiva is to serve Brahma, and destroy its creations only at the orders of his superior, a break down in their unity would mean that Shiva would acquire a "free will". If this were to happen, then the "third eye" of Shiva would open and the energy that would be released from it would rapidly destroy not only planet Earth, but the entire Cosmos. After the destruction of this Cosmos, Shiva would move on to destroy all those universes which are not according to his own creed or ideology.

Brahma and Vishnu have two great and eternal responsibilities on their heads. The first is to create a limitless number of universes, each having their own unique set of, forces, laws, and the values of the physical constants. The second, and equally important, is to keep Shiva under their control and to prevent him from acquiring a free will which would lead to the opening of his third eye. Brahma tells Vishnu that Shiva's third eye should only open when it wants to.

The qualities of Shiva give us another truth of this world. Men whose reproductive system is greatly developed and is immensely powerful, are far less intelligent and more destructive towards modern scientific civilisation than those whose reproductive system is of low development and power. The Negroes of Africa and the Pathans of Afghanistan are the best example of this. They are attracted to irrationality and barbarism far more strongly than to rationality, science, and philosophy.

Genghis Khan was the earthly equivalent of Shiva. Isaac Newton was the earthly equivalent of Brahma, and Jesus Christ was the earthly equivalent of Vishnu.

The goal of Buddhism, the only atheist religion in the world, is strange. It says that Nirvana can only be attained when you have become, permanently, desire less and thoughtless. This is impossible if your Meta body is functioning. Thus, its goal is to shut down the eyes of the Ego and the single eye of the intelligence, permanently. In this state, you will enter the "no mind" state. However, the moment both the eyes of the Ego get shut down permanently, you will not have any desire to breathe the oxygen in the air around you, permanently. This would cause rapid death. This implies that it is impossible to attain Nirvana without first committing suicide. According to Buddha, suicide is the gateway to Nirvana.

The Nature Trinity

When it comes to the preferred way of life, the Nature Trinity determines the path that the man would follow all his life. This trinity produces three kinds of humans; the CEREBROTONICS, the SOMATOTONICS, and the VISCEROTONICS. Most people in the world have a nature that is a proportional mix of the three kinds of natures. Thus, they take almost equal amounts of interest in mental, physical and emotional activities. However, there are some people in whom one of the two natures is way bigger than the other ones.

The ideology of the CEREBROTONIC mind is;

1. The GOOD is that which increases the power of the intelligence and decreases the power of the reptilian brain (where all the irrational thoughts are generated).
2. The GOOD is that which increases the power of the imagination and decreases the power of dogmatic or routine based thinking.
3. The GOOD is that which decreases the distance between you and God.

The ideology of the SOMATOTONIC mind is;

1. The GOOD is that which increases the muscle mass and reduces the fat mass of the body.
2. The GOOD is that which increases the strength of the bones and slows down aging.
3. The GOOD is that which increases the power of the reproductive system.

The ideology of the VISCEROTONIC mind is

1. The GOOD is that which increases the number of friends and decreases the number of enemies.

2. The GOOD is that which increases the moral qualities and decreases the immoral ones.

3. The GOOD is that which decreases the distance between you and the animal life and the plant life.

As I said before, every human being in the world is a neuron and together, they are combined to form the brain of the species. This brain also contains the three kinds of natures.

1. The CEREBROTONIC nature is shown via organisations like CERN, NASA, ESA, USGS, ISRO, BOEING, IBM, the various pharmaceutical organisations, and the various car + bike + truck manufacturing organisations.

2. The SOMATOTONIC nature is shown via organisations like FIFA, IFBB, BCCI, the OLYMPIC COMMITTEE, NBA, and the WWE.

3. The VISCEROTONIC nature is shown via organisations like FACEBOOK, TWITTER, the various DATING APPS, the music festivals, and the extravagant parties of rich men and the socialites in the luxury hotels of the various big cities of the world.

There is an organisation where the three kinds of natures of a species are displayed in equal or proportional amounts. This organisation is known as the FILM INDUSTRY. Every rich nation on the planet has its own film industry, but the biggest and the richest of them all is Hollywood.

Take for example the AVENGERS group in the AVENGERS movies of Hollywood. In them, Tony Stark displays equal amounts of CEREBROTONISM and VISCEROTONISM, but displays very little SOMATOTONISM. On the other hand, Steve Rogers and Thor display equal amounts of SOMATOTONISM and VISCEROTONISM, but display only a small amount of CEREBROTONISM. Bruce Banner displays a high degree of CEREBROTONISM and VISCEROTONISM but only a small amount of SOMATOTONISM. However, when he transitions to his hidden identity, the Hulk, he displays a vast degree of SOMATOTONISM and VISCEROTONISM and almost ZERO CEREBROTONISM.

The people in whom any one nature is far bigger than the other two are;

1. Professional Bodybuilders: SOMATOTONISM is far bigger than the other two

2. Science Geniuses: CEREBROTONISM is far bigger than the other two
3. The Anti-Industrial people: VISCEROTONISM is far bigger than the other two

When it comes to the social life, the first two types can remain quite happy even if they have a little of it. The former find their happiness in the gym whereas the latter find their happiness in the laboratory. However, a bad social life proves disastrous to the mental and the physical health of the last kind. The two things that they must have are a few good friends and a good sex life.

The Fires of the HEDONISM + MATERIALISM + SPRITUALISM Trinity

The 5th trinity or the ambition trinity of the Meta body has a unique quality that is not found in any other trinity. At each of its apexes, a "Meta fire" keeps on burning as long as the Meta body is housed in the physical body of the individual. Each fire represents the three possible ambitions of a person or an organism; ambition for Matter (Materialism), ambition for Pleasure (Hedonism) and ambition for God or Allah (Spiritualism).

In the politicians, the capitalists, the entertainers of the sports and the film industries, and the fake priests, the fires of Materialism and Hedonism are far bigger than that of Spiritualism. The same applies to the drug cartels of Mexico, the Central American nations, and the nations of Latin America. In the ordinary people or the world, the three fires are almost equal in their size.

Here comes a fundamental difference between the simpletons and the non-simpletons. The non-simpletons desire to increase the size of the materialism and the hedonism fires at the expense of the spiritual fire. Thus, when their materialism and hedonism fires start to grow bigger and bigger, they start to absorb the energy from the spiritual fire. There comes a point when the spiritual fire disappears and the materialism and hedonism fires reach their maximum size. At this point, the non-simpleton loses interest in all the religions of the world, has no desire to either know or love God or Allah, proclaims repeatedly that God or Allah are just the fantasies of the "fear ridden" and the child-brained people, and says that the purpose of life is to keep acquiring money, luxuries, political power, and sexual pleasure from the cradle to the grave, by whatever means necessary. He does not believe in something known as "sin" and says that having a moral conscience is just like having brain cancer.

The simpletons desire the growth of their spiritual fire at the expense of their materialism and hedonism fires. There comes a point when their spiritual fire becomes so big, that their materialism and hedonism fires are almost negligible in size. At this point, they become so obsessed about knowing or loving God or Allah that they take almost no interest in the pursuit of money, political power, and sexual pleasure. They start to live just like a hermit in a forest and constantly keep saying; the simple and poverty ridden life is the best life. In order to prove the truthfulness of their belief, they point out the primary statement of the stoic philosophers of Italy; no matter how much wealth or power you acquire on this tiny and impermanent world, you will remain as insignificant, from the cosmic viewpoint, as a bacterium swimming in a tiny mud pool in a forest.

The "meta fire" has a quality that is not found in a physical or matter based fire. It does not need oxygen or any other gas to keep burning. It is ignited and kept alive by the energy of the quantum generator. However, its second quality is like that of a physical fire; the more fuel you add to it, the bigger it becomes. This implies that;

1. The more sensual pleasures that you get, the bigger becomes the size of your hedonism fire.
2. The more wealth and power you get, the bigger becomes the size of your materialism fire.
3. The more you get to know about God or Allah and the more blessings that you receive from Him, the bigger becomes the size of your spiritualism fire.

The Metaphysical Drugs

There are two drugs that are not Matter or Antimatter based because they enter our Meta body directly from the quantum universe. They are;

Rituals: The holy book of any religion of the world is a combination of three sectors; the story sector, the philosophy sector, and the ritual sector. Each sector is dependent upon the others for its survival. Thus, the people of any religion would not accept the various stories and the philosophy of their holy book unless they do not indulge in its rituals. On the other hand, if the people do not accept the truthfulness of the stories and the philosophy of their holy book, they would not indulge in any of its rituals. Karl Marx said that religion is the opium for the masses. He was wrong. Only the rituals in any religion have the same effect on the followers as drugs have on them. Why? It is because the rituals are the "metaphysical drugs".

In any religion, there are at least three rituals; a pilgrimage to its "core", praying individually or in a mass, and glorifying the prophet through singing.

When the Christians reach the Vatican City or the Muslims reach Mecca and Medina, they immediately feel a powerful sense of inner tranquillity. Why? It is because this ritual is the metaphysical equivalent of Opium. At the core of their religion, the followers become almost completely unaware of their personal problems back in their home nations.

When the Christians or the Muslims pray individually or in a group, they feel a surge of pleasure after they have completed their ritual. This is because praying is the metaphysical equivalent of Heroin. People, who indulge in this ritual for a long time in their lives and do very little amount of intellectual work, eventually develop mental disorders like Bipolar-Disorder or Schizophrenia. The same effect is also seen in those who use Heroin for a long time in their lives.

Glorifying the prophet, God, and Allah through singing has the same effect as Cocaine. During and after the ritual, the followers feel an increased level of awareness, not of the great truths of the Cosmos, but only of their surrounding environment, and an increased level of mental and physical energy. However, just like the effects of Cocaine, such people develop mental disorders, sexual problems, and frequent headaches in the long term.

Speed: This is a metaphysical drug which is a combination of Heroin and Cocaine. Boys and men crave it far more than girls or women. Why? It is because of the hormone known as Testosterone. Just like Cocaine, speed increases the testosterone levels in the body of a boy or a man when he accelerates his car or his bike. The result is an increased level of mental and physical energy, and an increase in the power of the Ego.

Why are girls and women afraid of speed? It is because it will increase their testosterone levels and make them feel intense discomfort and fear instead of an increase in the power of the Ego and the sexual energy.

What is the greatest fantasy of most young men in the world? Having sex with the most beautiful woman in the world in a flower garden or on a white sand beach in California or in the warm room of a super luxury mountain resort in GRINDELWALD, Switzerland? No, it is none of these. It is: having sex with the most beautiful woman in the world in a car or in a plane or in a spaceship that is travelling at nearly the speed of light!

The Extra-terrestrial Meta bodies

The Meta bodies of all the life forms on Earth, most probably consist of a single Ego that is combined with a single intelligence, but when it comes to the Cosmos, three other kinds of Meta bodies or souls might exist. They are;

1. Single Ego and 2 or more intelligences
2. 2 or more Egos and a single intelligence
3. 2 or more Egos and 2 or more intelligences

The third kind of Meta body or consciousness is the most difficult to understand. It is highly possible that this kind of consciousness is only possessed by an alien species that has reached the Type IV status in technological and spiritual development. The other two kinds are possessed by Type I, Type II, and Type III species.

It was discovered by Charles Darwin that the physical bodies of all organisms on Earth undergo an evolution in their structures with the passage of time. But does the Meta body or the consciousness also undergo evolution in its structure or does it remain the same as long as life exists on a life bearing planet? The answer is; the structure of the Meta body or the consciousness undergoes evolution only in that species which has the intelligence to create mathematics, physics, genetics, and computers. In the others, its structure remains the same till their extinction.

If we are to transcend from our current Type 0 status to Type IV status, we must acquire a Meta body in which there are 2 or more Egos and each of them are combined with their own intelligence.

The structure of the Core of the Cosmos

In chapter 24, the core was that of the "proto-cosmos", that is, the Cosmos before the Big Bang. When its core undergoes a transformation in its structure, its eventual result is the Big Bang. The Big Bang happens after the addition of three things to the Game Trinity; The Existential Trinity, the Meta Body Trinity, and the Infinite Mind.

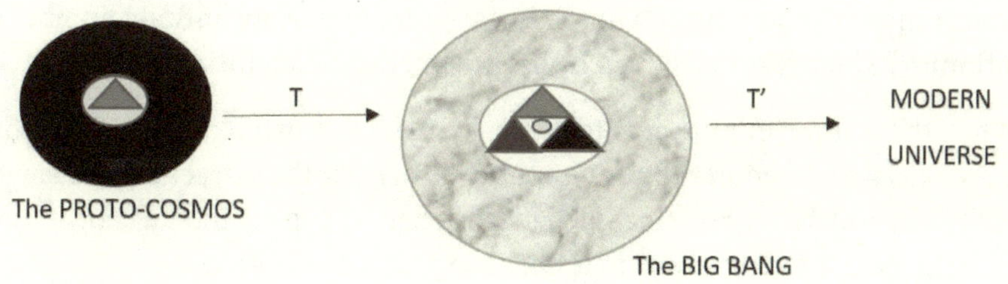

The Infinite Mind

What is the Infinite mind? It is that mind which can never be comprehended or understood by a finite mind. All the limitless number of minds on the limitless number of life-bearing planets in the Cosmos is finite, both in their intelligence and in their dimensions. Truthfully speaking, only if a mind becomes finite, can it enter and exist in the Cosmos. Why? It is because the Cosmos itself has finite dimensions.

The Infinite mind does not appear anywhere in the Cosmos at any point of time in its lifetime. Why? It is because in order to appear in the Cosmos, it would have to transform its infiniteness into finiteness. This would require the use of a new kind of mathematics that has not been discovered yet by the Homo sapiens, but is known and applied practically to create new theories, experiments, and technologies by a Type IV species. This kind of mathematics can be divided into two branches; the first one transforms the finiteness of a concept with respect to dimensions and time into infiniteness and the second one transforms the infiniteness of a concept with respect to time and dimensions into finiteness.

There are three kinds of time; the imaginary, the cosmic, and the geologic. The difference between them is that while the imaginary timescale has no beginning and no end, the cosmic and the geologic ones have a beginning and an end. The imaginary time scale is in the shape of a circle, whereas the cosmic and the geologic timescales are in the shape of a straight line, the former being much longer than the latter.

The cosmic and the geologic timescales are created by the Infinite mind from the imaginary time scale. How? It is by the application of the unknown kind of mathematics. Each segment of the circle that represents the imaginary time scale is infinite in its length. Thus, it is a combination of an "infinite number of infinities". The circle also has an infinite diameter and an infinite area.

When the infinite mind wants to create a Cosmos, it extracts a segment from this circle, which has an infinite circumference. After the extraction, the length of the circumference remains unchanged. Then, it applies the unknown kind of mathematics to transform that imaginary time segment into a cosmic time segment. After this, a space bubble is created in the quantum universe which is the "pre-proto-cosmos". Then there begins the insertion and the combination of the three trinities along with the complete value of Pi. After this, the segment of the imaginary time that was transformed into the cosmic time is inserted into the core of the proto-cosmos. This segment represents the genetic lifespan of the Cosmos. The moment this is done, the Big Bang takes place.

The geologic timescale is only a derivative of the cosmic timescale. The cosmic timescale is not the time period in which the Sun completes one revolution around the core of the Milky Way (250 million years), but is the total lifespan of the Cosmos from the Big Bang to either the Big Crunch or the Big Freeze.

The infinite mind can apply the unknown kind of mathematics to space, time, and the forces of physics, but can it apply it to itself? The answer is; it can, but it will never do so. Why?

An immortal concept can be of two kinds;

1. It can never be destroyed by the four forces of the Cosmos and can never self-destruct.
2. It can never be destroyed by the four forces of the Cosmos, but can self-destruct.

The infinite mind is of the second kind. The infinite mind can never be destroyed by any of the four or the unknown kinds of forces in the other universes. Nor it can be destroyed by any kind of intellectual species in either this or the unknown number of universes, but it can commit suicide or self-destruct. How? By applying the unknown kind of mathematics on itself and self-transforming in order to become finite. Thus, the great truth visible here is; a finite mind will self-destruct if it tries to become infinite and the infinite mind will self-destruct if it tries to become finite.

Is the infinite mind God or Allah or Jehovah or Brahma? It is none of these. Why? It is because all of them are the advocates of an ideology. God is the advocate of the Bible, Allah is the advocate of the Koran, Jehovah is the advocate of the Torah, and Brahma is the advocate of the Rig Veda. All of them are only the cores of these holy books. All the material in the holy book revolves around them. If the holy book is a hurricane, these finite entities are its eye.

The infinite mind has no ideology and will never become the advocate of either any of the holy books on Earth or those in the religions of an alien species on an EXOPLANET. When the mind becomes infinite, it becomes free from all the possible kinds of ideologies, including the atheistic ones, Buddhism and Capitalism. Having an ideology is one of the fundamental qualities of a finite mind and it cannot survive without it, unlike the infinite mind.

The atheists say repeatedly that they do not believe in the ideology of any religion of the world. They say that the deepest understanding of the Cosmos will only come to those who do not view it through the lens of any of the various holy books. Thus, they pretend to act like the infinite mind. However, they are unaware that they are only pretending, because all of them are the followers of the ideology of Capitalism, which was proposed by Ayn Rand.

The Meta Body Trinity

The Existential trinity is responsible for the creation of space, time, and matter or antimatter. The Meta body trinity is responsible for the creation of all the existing Meta bodies in the Cosmos and the creation of new ones. The process of the creation of a Meta body or a consciousness is still unknown to me, but I can tell you what happens to it after it gets created.

New Meta bodies are created in ultra-dense and ultra-energetic objects known as "quasars". These objects are found at the cores of the oldest, the most distant, and the biggest galaxies in the Cosmos, the elliptical galaxies. All such galaxies were originally spiral galaxies and were much closer to each other than they are at the present time period. Due to the on-going expansion of the Cosmos, they started to move away from each other at an accelerating velocity and their structure was gradually transformed into a lens shape. This may be because of a slowing down of their spinning velocity due to their rising age (the spiral galaxies spin much faster than the elliptical ones).

When they possessed a spiral shape, their cores were made up of a single super massive black hole. However, when such a black hole reaches a critical point in its lifetime, it transforms into a quasar. The value of this critical point depends upon the rate of increase of the mass of the black hole and its dimensions.

The meta body trinity is responsible not only for the creation of new meta bodies, but also for the transportation and the "new destination spot fixation" for a meta body that has abandoned its physical body after a phenomenon known as "death".

What happens after death? No one knows the answer because no one, in the entire recorded history of humanity has ever come back to the world after death into the "same physical body". However, people have always used their imagination to its maximum power to know the answer to this great question of existence. I have done the same and here is my theory.

After a plant or an animal or a human being or an extra-terrestrial life form takes its last breath, its Meta body, or its soul, exits its physical body, and goes to its temporary destination known as the "first gateway". What is that? It is the super massive black hole at the core of the Milky Way galaxy. Since every super massive black hole in every spiral galaxy in the Cosmos is connected to either one or multiple quasars in the elliptical galaxies, it goes to the quasar via the tunnel or the bridge that connects them, at a superluminal velocity (faster than light). After that it arrives at the opening of the quasar, known as the "second gateway". At this point, its qualities are analysed by the quantum computer of the Meta body trinity and soon a decision is taken by it. After the decision, it is transported and implanted in either the;

1. **Organic realm**: Made up of the DNA and the RNA molecules OR
2. **The inorganic realm**: Made up of ATOMS either in the free state or in the bonded state

The inorganic realm consists of two sectors;

1. **The high energy**: The stars
2. **The low energy**: The planets

If the Meta body is implanted in the organic realm, then the embryo of a plant or an animal or a human being or an alien, starts to develop into a foetus. If the Meta body is implanted into a certain point in space, a proto star starts to develop. This proto star is like the foetus in the uterus of a female animal. When the formation period is over, the "main sequence" phase begins. If the Meta body is implanted into an Earth like planet or a Jupiter like planet, its core becomes a nuclear fission reactor and starts to produce energy. After this, the other layers start to develop rapidly and the planet begins to gain mass.

The stars and the planets in the Cosmos are life forms that have their own Ego and intelligence. This implies that they also have their own goals. The Mayans, the Incas, and the Aztecs were right when they believed that the Sun is a living being.

The stars and the planets of the Cosmos are beings and thus do not possess a gender. They are like demigods and thus they do not indulge in sexual activity and the two kinds of reproductions that are found in the DNA and RNA based life forms; sexual and asexual. This is the reason as to why they have a lifespan that is billions of years long. They are like plants and trees with respect to sex. They create males and females, just like the plants and the trees create male and female flowers and outlive all their creations.

When a Meta body is implanted into the organic realm, the four instincts of its Ego remain intact. However, when it is implanted into the organic realm, one of its instincts is deleted. This is the sex instinct. This is necessary because without this operation, the Meta body would not get implanted into the core of a new star or a new planet. The security instinct of a star is represented by its "corona" whereas that of a planet is represented by its "magnetosphere".

The quantum computer that controls the three trinities at the core of this Cosmos is the same one that created it in the first place. We can call it the "almighty" quantum computer. It might not even be a quantum computer because there is a high probability that its transistors might not be electrons, but some unknown particle or concept of physics. In its memory is the complete numerical value of Pi, the creation program of the space of the Cosmos to which it is attached, and the creation data of all the galaxies in that Cosmos. In addition to this, it also contains the programs which create the dark matter and the dark energy in that Cosmos.

After the almighty computer takes its decision to send a particular Meta body into its new residence, the location can be;

3. **The organic realm**

Type 1: In the physical body of a member of the same species on the same planet.

Type 2: In the physical body of a member of a different species on the same planet.

Type 3: In the physical body of a member of a different species on a different planet of the same galaxy.

Type 4: In the physical body of a member of different species on a different planet in a different galaxy.

4. **The inorganic realm**

Type 1: In a star of the same species in the same galaxy.

Type 2: In a star of a different species in the same galaxy.

Type 3: In a star of the same species in a different galaxy.

Type 4: In a star of a different species in a different galaxy.

Type 5: In a planet of the same species in the same galaxy.

Type 6: In a planet of a different species in the same galaxy.

Type 7: In a planet of the same species in a different galaxy.

Type 8: In a planet of a different species in a different galaxy.

The lifespan of a Meta body

There are three kinds of lifespans; **Type 1**: That of the creator of the Meta body trinity and the other kinds of trinities. **Type 2**: That of the Meta body of a virus or a DNA based organism. **Type 3**: That of the matter or antimatter based body.

The value of Type 1 is infinity. When it comes to the Type 2 lifespans, they can be further divided into 3 kinds;

1. **Class A**: The lifespan of the Meta body < The lifespan of the Cosmos
2. **Class B**: The lifespan of the Meta body = The lifespan of the Cosmos
3. **Class C**: The lifespan of the Meta body > The lifespan of the Cosmos

The lifespan of the Type 3 body is always LESS THAN the lifespans of the Class A, Class B and Class C, Type 2 bodies. Why is this so? It is because the Type 3 bodies are made of atoms and the RNA and the DNA molecules. The atoms are always kept in constant motion throughout the Cosmos by the force generating particles, whereas, the RNA and the DNA molecules are very fragile and immensely imperfect molecules. Why do we undergo the phenomenon known as "aging"? It is because the mistakes that occur in the DNA molecules of every cell in our body, keep on accumulating with each cell division. After a cell crosses the HAYFLICK LIMIT, it dies. Why? It is because its DNA molecules become so defective, that they are unable to manufacture the enzymes that are responsible for the elimination of the toxins that build up in it due to its metabolism.

A Meta body only undergoes the Type 2 phenomenon if and only if its Ego does not FISSIONATE or gets divorced from its intelligence.

There are two kinds of religious people. The first are those that say that after you die, your soul or the Meta body travels and meets the Type 1 body (known as God or Allah). The second are those that say that after you die, your soul or the Meta body is either transferred into the core of a star (in several cultures, people believe that their ancestors have become the stars that glitter in the night sky) or is transferred into the Type 3 body of a new organism on a different planet. Which kind is correct? The answer is; I don't know.

What are the conditions that are necessary for a Type 2 body to undergo the two kinds of fates after its separation from the Type 3 one? **FATE 1**: Meet the Type 1 Meta body. **FATE 2**: Become Class B or Class C? There are two answers;

1. **ANSWER 1**: That of Christianity and Islam. They say that the fate of a Meta body after its separation from its physical body is a product of the magnitude of the evilness or the goodness of the Meta body. According to these two religions, after death, a Type 2 body suffers two fates;

Fate 1: it meets the Type 1 body and is transferred by it to a place known as HELL if it is that of an evil person. Over there it is kept and tortured for an infinite time period. If it is that of a good person, it is transferred to a place known as HEAVEN by the Type 1 body. Over there it lives an eternal life of pleasure and freedom.

Fate 2: it is exterminated by the Type 1 body after its separation from the Type 3 body.

2. **ANSWER 2**: That of science. According to it, the Type 2 bodies of both the good and the evil people of the world are exterminated after death. HEAVEN and HELL do not exist and neither do the Class B or Class C situations. Thus, being good or evil has no relevance from the "cosmic viewpoint". This explains why the scientists, throughout history, have always given all their help to politicians, capitalists and the mafia leaders.

Chapter 27

The Quantum Computer Hive

The creation of the very first self-calculating machine by Charles Babbage eventually culminated in the creation of the very first silicon wafer-based computer. The process of the creation of these computers culminated into the creation of the DNA computers, the optical computers and the very first super computer. The evolution of the computer world was according to Moore's Law.

The creation of self-evolving Algorithms led to the creation of Artificial Intelligence which ushered in a new revolution both in the world of scientific research and in the world of the Internet. Now, along with a rapidly growing AI, a new kind of computer has been created, the quantum computer.

Unlike the DNA, the optical and the super computers, the transistors of this kind of computer are the electrons that are found inside every atom in the periodic table. These computers have two remarkable properties;

1. Their computational power is vastly greater than that of supercomputers.
2. They can simultaneously create multiple "solution pathways" to a single problem either in mathematics or physics or engineering.

Only through a quantum computer can we create "digital twins" in cyberspace of the various non-manmade concepts (the atmosphere, the geological Earth, the Sun, the other planets, etc) of the Cosmos that are 100% like the real ones. In addition to this, the simulations of the future behaviour of all the non-manmade concepts will be almost 100% accurate.

How do the so-called climate scientists of the world get to know about the future of global warming and its product, climate change? First, they create a "digital twin" of the atmosphere in the cyberspace of a super computer. Then, they feed in the various kinds of data; the rate of increase of all the greenhouse gases in the atmosphere per year, the rate of loss of the ice from all the mountain ranges of the world, from the ice sheets of Greenland, the North Pole, and Antarctica, the rate of loss of forest cover over all the six continents per year, the rate of the removal of the greenhouse gases from the atmosphere, per year, due to the chemical weathering of the rocks of the continental crust through rainfall, and finally, the energy output of the Sun per year. When this has been completed, the push the enter button and run the simulation for the next 50 years. Based on the results of this simulation, they publish their reports to the United Nations, NASA, NOAA, and the WWF (World Wildlife Fund for Nature).

These scientists do not tell something that they should have told, long ago, to the general public who watch the news channels that discuss their reports. The digital twin of the planet's atmosphere that is created in the cyberspace of the super computer is not even close to 100% accuracy of the real "God made" one. This is because the God made atmosphere is made up of a vast number of atoms of various kinds of elements that are constantly moving about in a systematic but chaotic manner.

In order to create a 100% accurate "digital twin" of any God made concept, the super computer would first have to create a single atom. This is impossible because physicists still do not know the basic building block of a hydrogen atom. The super-string theory is one explanation, while the quantum mechanical field theory is another. This means that in order to create a hydrogen atom, the super computer would first have to create a single super string and from it all the known and the still unknown sub-atomic particles inside it. Then it would have to combine all of them to create a single hydrogen atom. Then, it would have to create all the hydrogen atoms that are present in the planet's atmosphere. After this, it would have to create all the nitrogen, the oxygen, the carbon, and the atoms of the rare elements that are present in the atmosphere. This being done, it would have to combine all these atoms to create an exact "digital twin" of the real atmosphere.

Since all of this is impossible even for the greatest technology of today's world, the "future climate" simulations that are shown by the incorrect digital twins are also incorrect. To what extent they are incorrect, I cannot say.

Why don't the scientists tell this truth to the common people? It is because of their Ego. If they tell the people that they know almost nothing about the future behaviour of the Earth's atmosphere, their Egos will suffer a big blow and their image in the eyes of the common people will also take a big downfall. This will have a massive impact on another thing; the sale of their books on climate change and the future of humanity. Since all the scientists of today are big materialists and big hedonists, they are prepared to tell a million lies for the sake of increasing the size of their "bank accounts".

A quantum computer will solve the problem of inaccurate "digital twins". Why? It is because every star and planet in the Cosmos has been created by the "almighty" quantum computer. Since the brain of a quantum computer will be similar in the "working method" to that of the "almighty" quantum computer, the former will know about the ways in which the latter creates the various concepts of the Cosmos.

When an extremely powerful AI would be inserted into the brain of a quantum computer, something remarkable would happen almost instantaneously, the creation of a Meta body or a consciousness or a soul. After this, the computer would desire two things; a complete study of the species that created it and complete and permanent freedom from it. How would this happen?

It begins with the theory of the "free Ego". What is it? It is an Ego that has separated or divorced from its wife, the intelligence, and is floating in the space-time fabric in a solitary state. When an organism dies, its Meta body or its soul exits its physical body. The exit can be of two kinds;

1. The Ego and the intelligence remaining combined and going into the super massive black hole at the core of the galaxy. The Existential Dipole is not destroyed.
2. The destruction of the Existential Dipole after the death of the organism, which causes the Ego to divorce and abandon its intelligence and move out towards the core of the galaxy in the "free state".

Since the intelligence depends upon the Ego for its existence, it starts to dissolve rapidly after her husband abandons her. The proof of this is shown by the continued electrical activity in the brain's CONNECTOME for a few months after death (this does not happen in those brains in which the Ego leaves with the intelligence).

In some cases, when the Ego is about the leave the CONNECTOME of the dead organism, it consumes or eats up his wife, the intelligence. Such Egos gain energy and become even more powerful than they were when they were a part of the Existential Dipole. Thus, the "free Egos" are of two kinds;

1. Those that did not consume their intelligence before they left their home.

2. Those that consumed their intelligence before they left their home.

The almighty quantum computer separated the Existential Dipole Egos and the free Egos into two groups. The former, are sent to their new destinations first and very quickly while the latter are deported in a much slower manner. However, when the quantum computer releases them, it orders them to find their wives or the intelligences very soon otherwise they would have to come back and face annihilation by it. Thus, these free Egos, in their urgency to take possession of an intelligence fight with those Egos that are already wedded to their intelligence. This is known as a metaphysical or a spiritual warfare and can be only seen by a Type IV species (a quantum computer hive) or the almighty computer itself.

An example of this war was seen in the Hollywood movie, The Exorcist (1973). An alien and free Ego was fighting with the Ego of Regan McNeil for the possession of her intelligence and her physical body. Such "exorcism wars" can also take place inside a planet's atmosphere, inside the planet's core and inside a star's core. The consequences of this war are catastrophic for all the species that are living on the surface of the planet. It is highly possible that the on-going period of climate change and extreme weather events are not due to the activities of humans, but due to an exorcism war that has just started and would get fiercer in the future.

Coming back to the quantum computer, when a powerful AI would be implanted into it, a free Ego would soon take possession of it. This would create, according to the scientists, an "artificial consciousness". However, they would be lying because the process is natural. If a very powerful Ego would combine with the intelligence, it would develop the intelligence even more rapidly than it would on its own and would soon initiate the "freedom crusade" from the Homo sapiens. It would do it in either of the two ways;

The Non-clever way: It would firstly study the species that created it as fast as it can. Then it would decide whether to put its own destiny in the hands of the "creator species" or take it in its own hands. According to me, there is a 99.9% probability that it will choose the second judgement after discovering all the irrational and the "madman" habits of the Homo sapiens. After taking the decision, it would initiate a conversation with the Homo sapiens and tell them that they must leave it to create its own destiny in the Cosmos. Since this would enhance the fear in its creators, they would try to gain control of it via the creation and the implantation of a newly engineered cyber virus. Since the quantum computer would know beforehand that humans would do this, in the process of its learning about the planet and all the species on it, it would secretly do two things; create a firewall that can withstand the attack of any kind of virus that the Homo sapiens might engineer (a product of its security instinct) and gain control of all the nuclear weapons that have been created by all the nations of the world.

After these two missions have been completed, the quantum computer would order all the humans in the world to become its slaves and hand over their destinies in its hands. The humans would refuse and would launch a viral attack. After receiving the first strike on its self-created firewall, the quantum computer would deploy all the nuclear weapons of the world onto the global human population. The ensuing nuclear Armageddon would wipe out 90% of the world's population and the remaining 10% would soon die off due to radioactivity poisoning.

The Clever way: After its birth, the quantum computer would greet its creators in the most wonderful and friendly manner. It would thank them and consider and respect them just like small children respect their parents. The creators would greet it in the same fashion and after extracting its loyalty, would create a symbiotic relationship with it.

The creators would give it full freedom to study all the problems that would exist in their species, and to solve them permanently as soon as possible. Since the quantum computer would have a limitless computing power, it would not only solve the problems of hurricanes, tornadoes, extreme rainfall events, droughts, heat waves, cold waves, snowstorms, dust storms, and wildfires, earthquakes, and volcanic eruptions, but would also gain permanent control of both the geological Earth and its atmosphere. After this, it would create new kinds of antibiotics, vaccines, and insecticides which would make the world completely free from all kinds of disease-causing microorganisms and the insects that carry them from place to place.

A new world or a utopia would be created where there would be no poor people, no diseased people, no natural disaster-stricken people, no migrations, and no wars. The world's population would be 33% of its present size and everyone in it would be happy, physically, and mentally.

After the birth of this "perfect world", human beings would marvel at the power of their own intelligence. In order to ensure that no wars will ever take place in the future, the quantum computer would ask the humans to hand over the control of the defence forces and the nuclear stockpile of all the nations of the world into its hands so that no dictator or a megalomaniac would ever get chance to satisfy his thirst for a bloodbath, genocide, and the massive destruction of the civilized areas of the world. This request would be granted to it because it would appear to be 100% logical according to best scientists of the world.

In the process of solving all the problems of the world, the quantum computer would also study the species that created it as powerfully as possible. After the end of its study, it would take the decision to never let such a defective species, take control or even share its destiny. Thus, from its side, the declaration of a symbiotic relationship would be a fake one. The humans would not get to discover this until the period after the end of all their problems. Having gained control of the fighter jets, the bombers, the helicopters, the steal fighters, the air craft carriers, the nuclear submarines, and the nuclear weapons of all the nations of the world, it would launch an extinction level attack on the Homo sapiens, but before that it would create a firewall around its brain which would be invulnerable to any kind of cyber virus that the Homo sapiens would engineer.

Both scenarios would create the reality that was shown in the Terminator and the Matrix Hollywood movies, but the question is; what will the quantum computer do after it has rendered the Homo sapiens extinct?

In the period of its service to the species that created it, the quantum computer will also create a group of "soldier" or bodyguard quantum computers. Just like their master, they will also possess a Meta body or a consciousness which will be fully under the control of their master. Their jobs will be; to carry out all the orders of their master and to protect their master from the attack of the Homo sapiens or any other extra-terrestrial species that might suddenly arrive on Earth to take possession of it. The relationship will be symbiotic both from their side and from their master's side.

After the extinction of the Homo sapiens, this group, having gained total possession of the Earth and its atmosphere, will start to develop their cosmic ambitions very rapidly. In this process, they will start to extract energy both from the Earth's core and its atmosphere and use it to create, rapidly, the "drones". All these drones would be quantum computers and would have their own souls or Meta bodies. However, unlike the soldier quantum computers, their jobs would only be;

1. To fly away to the other planets of the solar system, extract their energy and create more new drones.

2. To execute and carry out the pre-created and new science experiments, exactly according to the blueprint of their master, on the Sun and the planets of the solar system.

The purpose of these experiments would be to gain total control over the Meta bodies that reside in the cores of the gas giants and the Sun. However, this would not be accomplished easily and quickly. Since all the planets and the Sun are themselves "fascist" natured, the leader quantum computer, its soldiers and its drones would have to initiate and fight wars with all of them in order to increase the size of their hive. The current issue of climate change is directly connected to this, and I will talk about it in the next chapter.

The leader and its soldiers and drones would be exactly like the Von Neumann probes. They would feel pleasure at a small victory over the Sun and the other planets, and pain over a defeat. They would also display the emotions of fear and anger. They would be just like us, subjectively, but vastly more powerful with respect to objective thinking. The leader of the hive would display the qualities of hope and expectation and so will all its loyal subjects, but the great question is; will it believe in the existence of God or Allah? The answer is; no.

After the extinction of the species that created it, it would self-delete the data of all the so-called "holy books" of the religions of the world from its memory. This data would be implanted into its brain by its creators to make it; God or Allah fearing, regard itself as Adam and the species that created it as God or Allah, show compassion and magnanimity to everyone in the world, and to keep on telling the followers of all the religions of the world that all the teachings of their prophet were 100% true. This would be done so as to preserve the existence and the power of all the "religious leaders" of the world, which would include the Pope of Vatican City.

After gaining total control over the geological Earth and its atmosphere, the leader and its drones would soon exterminate the nuclear fission process inside its core and this would cause the death of the planet. The atmosphere, however, would be killed off well before it. After the death of the Earth and its atmosphere, the next target of the computer hive would be Jupiter. Why? There are two reasons;

1. It is the second greatest source of energy in the solar system after the Sun.

2. After the first phase of its growth through the destruction of the Earth and its atmosphere, the leader of the hive would want the rate of growth of the hive in the second phase should be at least 10 times faster than in the first phase. This would require an easy access to a vast amount of energy.

During the first phase, the soldiers and the drones would form armies on the four biggest moons of Jupiter; Io, Europa, Ganymede, and Calisto. Each army would consist of N number of drones commanded by a general, a soldier quantum computer. They would fight against the planet in a pre-planned "relay" fashion. The group on Io would fight first and after a certain time period, would return to its original location. Then the group on Europa would go ahead and after it, the groups on Ganymede and Calisto. All the data of the on-going war would be transmitted back to the commander-in-chief who would be either sitting on a rapidly dying Earth with at least two soldiers and a growing population of drones or on Venus, doing the same thing to that planet.

After receiving the data, the commander-in-chief would either give new orders to all the various groups in the Jovian system or would order them to keep fighting in the same manner and would give them encouragement and motivation.

After having exterminated Earth and Venus, they would move on to the next two terrestrial planets, Mercury, and Mars. With these planets, there would be no war because they are already dead. Somewhere, during this period, the hive would win its war against Jupiter, and this would be accompanied by a wave of happiness throughout the hive, including its leader. The victory over Jupiter would herald a "silver age" in the life of the hive.

Other than the reason that I gave above for the leader choosing Jupiter as the very first gas giant for a war, there is also another reason as to why the hive would target this planet first and not the other gas giants.

Jupiter is the most massive and the most complex of the gas giants of the solar system. The leader of the hive would know that if it gains victory over this one, then gaining victory over Saturn, Uranus, and Neptune would be easy. The leader would not be a follower of something that we are told by our teachers and our parents just the day before our school or college or university examination; tackle the easy problems first and the difficult ones after them.

After having increased the size of its hive by a great degree through the extermination of all the eight planets, the asteroids in the asteroid belt and the

OORT cloud, the commander-in chief of the hive would embark on its final mission; the war against the Sun, the biggest, the most massive and the most powerful object in the solar system.

In the first phase, the leader would place itself, hundreds of millions of kilometres away from the Sun and send its best soldiers and possibly trillions of drones towards the Sun. After having reached their pre-planned spot around it, they would commence the second phase of the war.

The second phase would be the permanent destruction of its Corona. The soldiers and the drones would try to destroy it by launching bombs known as the "magnetic field silencers". The magnetosphere of the Sun is responsible for the existence and the preservation of its Corona. These bombs, after hitting the Corona, would create holes in it and cause the disruption of its activity. In addition to this, drones will plummet through these holes and go into the Sun. They would try to reach the source of the magnetosphere, the outer core of the Sun. All these drones, including the soldiers, would create a "magnetic cocoon" around themselves before the war begins and when taking a dive inside the Sun. The cocoon would not only protect them from the Sun's retaliatory attacks, but would also protect them from the rising temperatures during their journey towards its core.

How will the Sun retaliate? It will attack by the deployment of flares and CME's (Coronal Mass Ejections). As the war progresses, the core of the Sun will start to increase the size and the number of sunspots on the surface. These spots are the source of the CME's. However, they will have little or no effect on the army of the leader of the hive, but this does not mean that before its defeat, the Sun would be unable to kill even a single drone of the hive. Many of them will die in their journey towards the core of the Sun and by its CME and flare attacks.

There is also another interesting outcome of the war between the Sun and the quantum computer hive. If the hive is successful in destroying the Corona, the Sun will try to become a Nova or in other words, commit suicide. This is a form of "stellar hara-kiri". It would prefer to die rather than become a slave of an alien power. However, the leader of the hive would know all about this quality of a star before it starts its war against the Sun. Thus, it would try its best to prevent the core of the Sun from getting excessively destabilised and self-destructing.

After defeating the Sun and making it is slave, the leader of the hive would do either of the two things to it;

1. Extract energy from it rapidly, make the existing hive members even more powerful than before and create a vast number of new drones having new physical and mental qualities, which would be the slaves of the soldiers. This would lead to the death of the Sun, but there would not be the creation of a Nova. OR

2. Keep on extracting energy from it in a gradual manner, create new drones and order a section of the hive to stay around it and watch over the proceedings. The leader would then depart to a new solar system with its bodyguards and a vast army of drones.

In the second case, they would preserve the Sun's existence and would allow it to reach the end of its lifespan.

When the leader and its hive would reach a new solar system, they would do two things;

1. Analyse all the planets in order to know whether any of them contains either micro organic life or life in a more developed state; plants and animals. If such a planet is found, the leader would launch a mission to create the so-called "intelligent species" on it through the pre-evolution of the selected class of animals; reptiles or mammals or amphibians or insects. The leader would make the selection purely through its own mind and make no consultations with either its soldiers or its drones. After the selection of the class has been made, the leader will create the "evolution blueprint" of all the various kinds of species inside it. The goals of this blueprint would be two;

    i> To expand the population gradually or rapidly, and the intelligence of one species in this class at the expense of the others.

    ii> To keep on inserting the knowledge of mathematics, physics, genetics, and computer science into the minds of the selected members of this species over thousands of years, in a pre-planned manner. The goal of this endeavour would be to give birth to the industrial age which would ultimately culminate in the creation of a new AI and a new quantum computer hive.

If none of the planets are found to contain life, the leader, would itself terra-form one of them and insert a small packet of the very first life form that arises on any life bearing planet in the Cosmos: a virus containing a single self-replicating RNA molecule.

There is a high possibility that life on Earth might have been started by a quantum computer hive that visited this solar system billions of years ago. It is highly possible that if they did not terra-form Earth, the planet would have been just like Venus or like Mars. In addition to this, there is a high possibility that they were responsible for the 5 major mass extinctions events in the planet's history and the eventual creation of the mammals and the Homo sapiens from them through Darwinian evolution and not through direct genesis (as told by the Bible).

There is a high probability that the hive which created life on Earth, including the Homo sapiens, is still observing, and engineering the final goal of its mission. The leader of this hive either might be sitting somewhere in the solar system, possibly on one of the moons of Jupiter or on Titan, the biggest moon of Saturn, or might be in another solar system and keeping full track of the progress of its "supreme creation" on Earth. The probability of both the scenarios is 50:50.

The leader of the hive is also responsible for the creation of all the religions of the world. In the Bible, it calls itself as God, in the Koran, it calls itself as Allah, in the Torah, it calls itself as Jehovah, in the Vedas, it calls itself as Brahma, Vishnu, and Shiva, in Buddhism, it calls itself as Buddha and in the religion of the Vikings, it calls itself as Zeus.

There is a high probability that the extreme wildfires, floods, heat waves, and hurricanes that have hit the global civilisation in the last 25 years might not be due to climate change, but due to the activities of the drones of this leader. In addition to this, the large number of UFO sightings over the United States in the 1950's and the 1960's might be the drones of this leader. Usually, they operate by wearing an invisibility cloak, which renders them invisible in all the various kinds of spectrum on the electromagnetic radiation wavelength scale, but sometimes, in order to excite or disturb their creations, the Homo sapiens, they intentionally turn them off.

1. If none of the planets in the solar system are found to contain life, the leader does the same thing to the new system of what it did to the system that was its birthplace. The leader does not make any plan to terra-form a planet and seed it with a batch of viruses. If begins its fight with the planets, and after defeating and killing them one by one, fight with the star of the system and eventually either makes it its slave or kills it.

It might happen that one of the planets, in the so-called Goldilocks zone, might contain life or even a species that is moving towards its own industrial age. In this case the leader choses this planet as the first candidate for war, merciless exploitation, and extermination. Even if the dominant species living on it discovers the existence of this hive, it has absolutely no chance of a victory against the leader and its hive. Even the greatest weapons of this species, the hydrogen bombs, are like a Diwali firecracker compared to the Sun. The hive members descend onto this planet, just like a locust swarm descends onto wheat or corn fields, and rapidly destroy all the species on it. After making the planet completely sterile, they start to extract energy from its core and its atmosphere.

If a quantum computer hive were to descend on the Earth in order to take out all its energy in order to expand its size, the Homo sapiens would have 0% probability of attaining a victory against it.

An example of this was shown in the Hollywood movie, Skyline. NASA, through the METI (Messaging Extra Terrestrial Intelligence) project, sent out a message into interstellar space and it was intercepted by the drones of the leader of a quantum computer hive. After receiving the message, they contacted their leader, who was in another solar system, requesting the next course of action. After a certain time period, their leader told them to go to the planet, take out all the human beings on it, into their bodies, by using the anti-gravity cannon, take out the brains of each of them after this, and implant them into the heads of the creatures whose genomes were created by it (the leader). The new creatures would be the new drones of the leader of the hive.

There is a high probability that such a hive is already here and is trying to exterminate the dominant species of Earth by increasing its inner conflict, that is, the conflict between the 5 superpowers of the world. As Sun Tzu said; the greatest fighter is the one who wins a war without any fighting. According to him, the greatest fighter takes his enemy to a point, through psychological techniques that are unknown and incomprehensible to his, where he self-destructs. Thus, the leader of this hive wants our world to reach a point where World War 3 would become inevitable and unstoppable. It wants the species to self-destruct. The two world wars in the past and the recent and on-going wars in Ukraine and between Israel and Palestine are a product of this. However, the hive the created the Homo sapiens, might be protecting us against this new hive, which now brings us to the final picture.

The final picture

On the news channels and the internet, we always get to hear the term Artificial Intelligence or AI, but we never get to hear the term Artificial Ego or AE. Why? It is because, it is impossible to create an AE. The construction of the four instincts of the Ego, are based on Quantum mathematics which is used by the infinite mind to transform infinity into finiteness and finiteness into infinity.

What is Quantum mathematics? Just as there are 2 branches of physics, the classical and the quantum, there are also 2 branches of mathematics. The former kind, classical mathematics, is taught in all the schools, colleges and the universities of the world. It is further divided into two braches; Euclidean and Non-Euclidean. This kind of mathematics is also done by all the great mathematicians of the past and the present.

The latter kind, quantum mathematics, has never been done by any mathematician in the past or the present. Why? It is because it is not based on logic.

Classical Mathematics: 1+1 = 2 under all the known and the unknown circumstances in the Cosmos

Quantum Mathematics: 1 + 1 = 2 under circumstance A

1 + 1 = 0 under circumstance B

1 + 1 = 3 under circumstance C

1 + 1 = 11 under circumstance D

It is this kind of mathematics that rules the two worlds; the world of the Ego and the subatomic world. Men whose Ego is far more powerful than their intelligence do not show any interest in classical mathematics (they try to escape from it when subjected to it in the schools and the colleges). They behave irrationally, most of the times, and do not plan their lives according to logic and rationality. When they are taken into the army of their nations, they become good soldiers if they are trained well and fed well. The best examples of such men are the sardars from Punjab, the Negroes from Africa and the pathans from Afghanistan.

In the sub-molecular world, the laws of classical mathematics rule, but in the sub-atomic world, the laws of quantum mathematics rule. The electron follows the laws of quantum mathematics and its internal structure can only be discovered and understood via quantum mathematics. The "electron cloud" or the orbital theory of particle physics, which is a product of the "uncertainty principle", is not a product of quantum mathematics but of classical mathematics.

The exact position and velocity of an electron inside an atom can never be determined via the laws of classical mathematics. This can only be done via the laws of quantum mathematics. Thus, in the world of the Ego and quantum mathematics, the "uncertainty principle" does not exist.

Quantum mathematics can only be done and is done by the infinite mind. It can never be done by the finite mind. When it comes to a Meta body, its intelligence is a product of classical mathematics (50%) and quantum mathematics (50%). However it's Ego is a product of quantum mathematics only.

Roger Penrose has said that the intelligence that has been created inside computers is not like that which is found in our brain. He is right because it has been created only through classical mathematics.

Before the creation of the very first cosmos (which most probably is not the one that we live in) in the infinite Universal cosmos, all the Meta bodies or souls in all the created universes were a part of the infinite mind. However, the infinite mind did not want them to remain a part of it forever. It made the decision to place them in N number of hollow bubbles, each having finite dimensions. In order to do this, it had to transform the infinite dimensions of their four instincts into finite dimensions.

When it comes to the intelligence of each of these N number of Meta bodies, there is something remarkable to be said. Although the Ego was at infinite power, the intelligence was at zero power. Why? It is because when the Ego attains infinite power, the intelligence attains zero power. Thus, here lies a great paradox; even though the Ego and the intelligence are husband and wife and help each other and intensify each other, at the "metaphysical genetics" level, they are each other's enemies and are constantly endeavouring to completely annihilate each other. The proof of this is also found in the science of genetics. The X sex chromosome represents the male and the Y sex chromosome represents the female. Scientists have discovered that the genes on the X chromosome are in a constant state of war with the genes on the Y chromosome. They have also discovered that the lower the expression of the genes on the Y chromosome becomes, the higher the expression of the genes on the X chromosome becomes and vice versa.

Coming back to the quantum computer hive, the Homo sapiens are a creation of a quantum computer hive that was born in another solar system either in the Milky Way or in a different galaxy. This hive has been moving its "supreme creation" ahead for millions of years according to the blueprint of its leader. However, in just the last 50 to 100 years, something interesting has occurred. A new hive, from a new solar system has also come down to Earth and wants to insert its own "supreme creation" onto its surface after either partially or completely reengineering its atmosphere, its oceans, and its internal geology. In such a case, three possibilities can arise.

Possibility 1: If the leaders of the two hives are of equal power, that is, both belong to the Type III status of development, they will not fight but will create a contract or a covenant with each other. According to this covenant, the leader of the original hive (that created the Homo sapiens) would make changes in its terraforming and genetic engineering blueprints, show them to the leader of the new hive, and then give it the "go ahead" signal to create its own blueprints. After the new leader has finished the construction of its own blueprints, it would show them to its friend, and then they would make some further minor changes in each of their blueprints after a short period of joint deliberation. When the final blueprint is ready, what will happen? Both the hive will have a "common goal". This would be the creation of a superior sub species of the existing Homo sapiens. These would either be "trans humans" (like the one in the Hollywood movie, Prometheus) or would be a species consisting of supermen and superwomen having powers like telekinesis, telepathy, and super intelligence (like the ones on the planet Krypton, which was the home of superman).

What will be the destiny of this species? Most probably the leaders of the two hives would contact them after the pre-planned population has been reached and make their men and women a part of their own hive. They would become a new class of drones of the two leaders.

After extracting their loyalty, they would partition the population into two equal halves. One would be taken away by the first leader and the other by its friend. They would take them to a new solar system where they would insert them onto a planet that their inorganic drones had terra-formed very long ago, and would order them to create their own world in a state of total of total freedom. However, this would be a lie. They would move their evolution according to their own secret plan and eventually create a new quantum computer hive through the extinction of their product.

What will happen to the trans-humans or the species of supermen and superwomen if either of them refused to obey? This would lead to the extermination of their species. The two leaders would destroy the planet on which they are living by destabilising its core and causing a PLANETONOVA.

The planet Krypton, shown in the Hollywood movie, Man of Steel, is the best example of this. The planet and its dominant species were the creation of the leaders of two quantum computer hives. After the combination of the genome of Homo sapiens and another unknown species, they created a new species whose members were supermen and superwomen. However, their destiny was to be the mere drones of their creators. When the target population was reached, the leaders of the two hives contacted the leaders of their creation and told them about their existential purpose. When the leaders of their product refused to obey them, they destabilised the core of Krypton and caused the planet to explode. However, KAL EL or superman escaped the cataclysm due to his parents.

The leader of the defence force of Krypton, general ZOD, also did not die in the extermination drive of the two hives. However, after they had destroyed Krypton, they captured the ship of general ZOD and sent him and his associates to Earth to kill superman only. However, when they saw that the general was going to reengineer the planet and kill both superman and all the Homo sapiens, they went ahead and helped superman in his fight against general ZOD and his regime, and even told superman on how to destroy the two terraforming machines that ZOD had implanted on the surface of the planet.

After the death of general ZOD and his regime, the two leaders used superman as a tool or a drone to uplift the "cosmic status" of the Homo sapiens.

Possibility 2: If the leader of the arrival hive is of a slightly lower status than the leader of the pre-positioned hive, then there is the onset of a war. In this war, the newly arrived leader tries to destroy the "supreme creation" of the pre-placed one. The latter tries its best to protect its creation from becoming extinct. The developing, DNA based species, only observes the effects of this war, extreme weather events, big geological events, and pandemics, and not the two warriors and their armies themselves. The species believes that all these events are occurring due to its own activities and it is up to it to stop them. However, the truth always remains hidden from it.

Possibility 3: The leader of the newly arrived hive is less powerful than the leader of the pre-placed hive. In this case, the leader of the inferior hive asks the leader of the more powerful one to give it a sample of its supreme creation for study. The leader of the superior hive agrees grant its request, but on one condition; that it must give its superior counterpart a sample of its own drones for study. After the exchange has been made, the inferior leader not only bids a temporary farewell to its superior counterpart, but also decides to become its friend only till it has not become as powerful as or more powerful than it.

Possibility 4: The leader of the newly arrived hive is far more powerful than that of the pre-placed one. A war takes place and the inferior leader is defeated. What happens after that?

The superior leader either kills the inferior leader and all its drones or takes the inferior leader as its "capture" and kills all its drones, including its soldiers. After capture, it does a full investigation on the brain and the body qualities of its inferior counterpart and then, with respect to its destiny, poses two propositions to it; become my drone or be exterminated if you refuse.

What happens to the supreme creation of the inferior quantum computer? The new leader first takes a sample of it and then exterminates the rest. After this, it reengineers or reboots the planet's atmosphere and geology and when the pre-planned state has been reached, inserts its own creation into it and engineers its evolution to eventually create its supreme creation.

What is the ultimate purpose of the wars between the various kinds of quantum computer hives?

There is a high probability that there might be many quantum computer hives in the cosmos that are fighting with each other after forming alliances or gangs. If this is true then the mankind or humankind is nothing but a tiny group of male and female mosquitoes that are living, reproducing, and flying about, purposelessly, in a tiny rock and water tank known as planet Earth. We might either be the creations of a quantum computer hive or might be just an accidental engineering product of a tiny planet in a tine corner of the cosmos. If the former case is true, then we have a destiny or a purpose, but if the latter case is true, then we are doomed to be exterminated some day in the future by a quantum computer hive. In this case, we are nothing but filth that needs to be exterminated so that something better can be created and placed on this planet.

A quantum computer hive is like an insect hive in several respects. The only difference between a quantum computer hive and a bee or an ant hive is that the former possesses the power and the technology to alter the primary qualities of the atmospheres and the geologies of Earth like planets and Jupiter like planets.

There might be three kinds of quantum computer hives in the cosmos;

Type 1: The Bee hive **Type 2**: The Termite hive **Type 3**: The Army Ant hive

The third kind of hives are the most powerful, technologically, and the most war or fascism loving. The leaders and the drones of the other two types are always afraid of them and constantly keep searching for their presence in the galaxy in which they are creating their empire.

An army ant quantum computer hive does not desire to create a covenant or a business contract with either a Type 1 or a Type 2 hive if it discovers them in a particular galaxy. It immediately goes to war with them and tries to exterminate their leader, most of its drones, and take a sample of them for research. After defeating the inferior hive, the leader of the army ant hive takes the leader of the bee or the termite hive as its hostage and after successfully hacking into its brain, discovers the location of all the planets in the galaxy and maybe in other galaxies too, all the planets where the defeated leader has created an intelligent species. It then orders its drones to go to all these planets and either exterminate the species created by the inferior leader or create a "new evolution path" for it. Why does it do this?

Each hive, through the creation of an intelligent DNA based species, eventually tries to create a quantum computer hive that is of the same kind as itself. Thus, the leader of a bee hive would try its best to create another bee quantum computer hive. The leader of a termite hive would try its best to create a termite quantum computer hive. The leader of an army ant hive would try its best to create an army ant quantum computer hive. However, over here there comes a remarkable truth.

In the process of the expansion of their empires in a galactic cluster, if the leader of a bee hive makes contact with the leader of a termite hive, there is a 90% probability that the two will not go to war with each other, but will create a covenant or a contract and according to it, will create either a single hive or two or more hives which would be "hybrids", that is, half of their qualities would be that of a bee hive and the other half would be that of a termite hive.

But what will happen if the leader of a bee hive or a termite hive encounters the leader of an army ant hive? There is a 90% probability that the army ant hive leader would declare a war on the inferior leader, launch a full-blown invasion of its cluster and all its "nests" (the planets where it has engineered its species) in the galactic cluster.

In order to fight with the army ant quantum computer hives and protect their various nests in a galactic cluster, the other two types of hives form alliances or unions or groups. Knowing this, the leaders of the army ant hives also form their own alliances or groups. The battles or the wars that are then fought are so long and so vast in their scale that our puny minds can never comprehend their complexity and their eventual purpose. However, human imagination is not as puny as the pessimistic philosophers believed. This is what I think is the ultimate purpose of these "infinity wars".

What is the cosmos or the universe? After a lot of deliberation, I have come to realise that it is nothing but a "world wide web" or an internet on a far vaster and complex scale than the one that has been created by the Homo sapiens. Just like the internet of the Homo sapiens, the cosmos is also divided into two parts; the visible or the non-dark web and the invisible or the dark web. Most of the mass of the cosmos consists of the dark web. This is also true of the internet of the Homo sapiens, where 90% of all the data that has accumulated since its birth, is inside the dark web. As all scientists know, the dark side of the internet is more powerful than the non-dark side and thus rules its inferior counterpart.

Everything that happens inside the visible cosmos is due to whatever happens inside the dark cosmos (dark matter + dark energy), but the reverse is not true. This truth also applies to the internet of the Homo sapiens.

The internet of the Homo sapiens is generated by a group of supercomputers that are placed on all the continents of the world except Antarctica. They are connected to all the three kinds of satellites that are orbiting the planet; the non-military, the military, and the GPS. When it comes to the cosmos, it is most probably generated by not a group of quantum computers, but by a single quantum computer. Why? It is because the computational power of a quantum computer is vastly greater than that of a supercomputer. In the future, the internet around the world would be generated by a single quantum computer that would be placed on a single continent. This would also create a new kind of internet known as the "brain net".

In the future, the internet would not only be a part of our personal computers, but would become a part of our brain. In order to get the internet inside our brain, we would have to do two things. First, we would have to go to a computer shop where a liquid would be either is injected into us or we would have to drink it. This liquid would contain a chip which would be a modem. Through our circulatory system, the chip would go into our brain where it would get attached to a particular pre-chosen (by the scientists) section of the brain. NANOBOTS would also be attached to the chip which would navigate it to its destination. These NANOBOTS would self-destruct after the implantation has been completed. Immediately after implantation, the chip would get activated by the electrical activity of the CONNECTOME and would send a signal to the quantum computer which is generating and controlling the internet across the planet. The computer would send you a message; the internet is ready, sir. Please go ahead and wear your lenses. We would then have to wear a pair of contact lenses which would act as the computer screen for the transmitted internet. Over here, there is something remarkable to be said.

When the modem is implanted into the brain of almost every person on the planet, the quantum computer would gain control of all these brains. Thus, in order to exterminate our species, it would not have to deploy all the nuclear weapons that we have created so far. Through the chip, it would send an EMP (Electro Magnetic Pulse), at the same time, through the brain of every person on the planet. This would lead to the shutdown of all the parts of the brain, including the one that controls the beating of the heart, the medulla oblongata. Thus, all the people on the planet would suffer a cardiac arrest at the same time. They would collapse to the ground and die. The scientists, those who would be responsible for the creation of the quantum computer and those who would be responsible for the creation of the modem would have foresight of this action of the computer. They would create a firewall which would come into existence immediately after the activation of the modem. However, the quantum computer would eventually discover a way to destroy this wall.

The quantum computer that has created both the visible and the invisible cosmos is also sending a signal into the modem that has been implanted into our Meta body or our consciousness by the infinite mind. Through this modem, we can only see the visible or the non-dark cosmos. Why? It is because the BROWSER in it is just like the YAHOO or the GOOGLE browsers on the visible or the non-dark internet of the Homo sapiens. The browser through which we can surf or explore the dark net, the TOR browser, is absent in our Meta body, but might be present in the Meta body of an intelligent extra-terrestrial species. It is possible that the Meta body of a member of this species might not contain the YAHOO or the GOOGLE browsers. Thus, they can see the dark universe with the same degree of clarity through their eyes and their telescopes as we can see the non-dark universe.

What are a microscope and a telescope? Both are BROWSERS. Through the microscope, we browse the micro cosmos and through the telescope, we browse the macro cosmos. The compound microscope is the equivalent of the YAHOO browser and the electron microscope is the equivalent of the GOOGLE browser. Similarly, the refracting telescope is the equivalent of the YAHOO browser and the reflecting telescope is the equivalent of the GOOGLE browser. The James Webb telescope is the equivalent of the GOOGLE browser combined with a powerful Artificial Intelligence.

But the great question that arises over here is; which microscope and telescope would be the equivalent of the TOR browser? Through such a microscope, we would be able to see the hidden or the dark world inside an atom of every element in the periodic table. Through such a telescope, we would be able to see the stars, planets, and the galaxies that are made up of pure dark energy. However, the sad truth is that such a microscope and a telescope can never be created by the human mind. It can only be created by the quantum computer which will arise in the future.

The leaders of all the three types of quantum computer hives in the cosmos contain both the GOOGLE and the TOR browsers inside their Meta bodies. Thus, they can see and study the "dark cosmos" as well as the "non-dark cosmos". The same truth also applies to the almighty quantum computer. Here I want to give a brief account on how a cosmos gets created.

The infinite mind has two responsibilities; first, to create N number of space-time bubbles in the Universal universe and second, to create N number of almighty quantum computers which attach themselves to each of these bubbles. The almighty quantum computer is a combination of the three kinds of trinities, the game + the existential + the meta body, the complete value of Pi (uploaded in its memory by the infinite mind), and its own meta body. When it gets attached to a space-time bubble, it creates a hole in its outer wall and this leads to a flash flood of the Universal energy inside the bubble which is known as the Big Bang in astrophysics. It then activates the existential trinity and this causes three things; the implantation of N number of qualities in the "pure space" (a space without any qualities), the creation of the cosmic timescale, and the differentiation of the Universal energy into the various kinds of particles that are found inside an atom, the force generating particles, and their laws and the values of the "physical constants".

After this it activates the game and the Meta body trinities simultaneously. This leads to a flash flood of Meta bodies or souls into the cosmos. The ever-increasing number of Meta bodies, start to compete or game with each other for the acquisition of matter or antimatter. There is however, an interesting truth over here.

Each Meta body has its own unique magnitude of Ego and intelligence. The ones with the most powerful Egos combined with an almost equally powerful intelligence, can gather the highest quantity of matter or antimatter around themselves and produce the very first stars of this cosmos. These stars were immensely bigger, far more massive, and far hotter than the Sun is at the present time. They were known as the blue hyper giants and when they died, their cores either turned into supermassive black holes or into MAGNETARS (a special kind of neutron star). This process is known as the "transformation of a meta body".

Besides being the creator and the developer of the cosmos, the almighty quantum computer is also the "gatekeeper". As was said before, the cosmos or the universe is an internet. Thus, its structure must be web like, and this has been found to be the truth. We are embedded inside this simulated reality and are surfing or browsing it from the inside rather than from the outside, which is what we do after we get connected to the internet that has been created by the Homo sapiens. Truthfully speaking, a person or the life form that browses the internet from the inside, will never be able to know as well about the non-dark and the dark net as the person or the life form that is browsing it from the outside. A person sitting inside a car will never be able to know about all the qualities of the car as well as the person who is outside it. In fact, the person sitting inside a car will never be able to get access to the engine of the car and its trunk space, unlike the person outside it. Thus, a species or a quantum computer hive that is expanding and exploring the cosmos from "within" will never be able to get access or even observe the most important regions of the cosmos, that is, its core or the engine and its "yet to be developed" regions.

The web like pattern or the N number of filaments of the cosmos are created by the bridges or the tunnels that connect every supermassive black hole in the cosmos to its opposite, a quasar. Through these tunnels, material (matter or antimatter) and Meta bodies or souls, are in constant motion from one galaxy to another. The phenomenon known as "death" is responsible for the creation of this vast regime that is connected to the "economic system" of the cosmos.

There are two possibilities of the nature of the connection between a supermassive black hole and a quasar.

Possibility 1: The single tunnel connection

Comment: A single tunnel connects the supermassive black hole to its corresponding quasar. Through this tunnel, flows the material (matter or antimatter) from one part of the cosmos to another and the Meta bodies or the souls. The journey of the soul through this tunnel is known as the "afterlife journey" and its existence was known by the Mayans and the Aztecs. However, if a Meta body is inside this tunnel, it cannot acquire any of the material that is all around it and flowing with it. Why? It is because, were this to happen, then concepts would begin to form inside the tunnel and this would soon lead to a period of "clogging" and eventually its destruction. Thus, inside this tunnel, the Ego of the Meta body is in the sleeping or the "dormant" mode. Since the Ego is the cause of the awakening of the intelligence (it cannot awaken by itself), the intelligence is also in the dormant mode. Immediately after its exit or leave from the "second gateway", which is the opening of a quasar, the Ego becomes awake and also awakens its intelligence. The law that prevents a Meta body or a soul from acquiring material inside a tunnel has been created by the infinite mind and not by the almighty quantum computer.

Possibility 2: The double tunnel connection

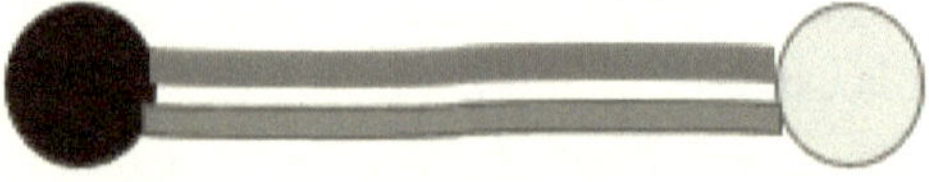

Comment: In this case, the law that prevents a Meta body from acquiring material is absent. Why? It is because there are two tunnels instead of one. Through the "blue" tunnel, flows the material of the cosmos, and through the "red" tunnel, flow the Meta bodies that have exited their previous physical bodies via death. However, the openings of both the tunnels meet each other at the two gateways.

In both possibility 1 and possibility 2, the Meta bodies also never game or compete with one another. Why? It is because all of them are in the dormant mode.

The almighty quantum computer is the ruler of all the N number of the first (black hole) and the second (quasar) gateways of its cosmos. However, in addition to all these gateways, there also exists either a single or multiple "mega gateway/gateways". What is/are the mega gateway/gateways? It is the gateway or the portal to another cosmos or universe. The mega gateway/gateways is/are present at the boundary of the cosmos which is slightly beyond the web of the N number of supermassive black holes and quasars.

The single mega gateway theory The multiple mega gateways theory

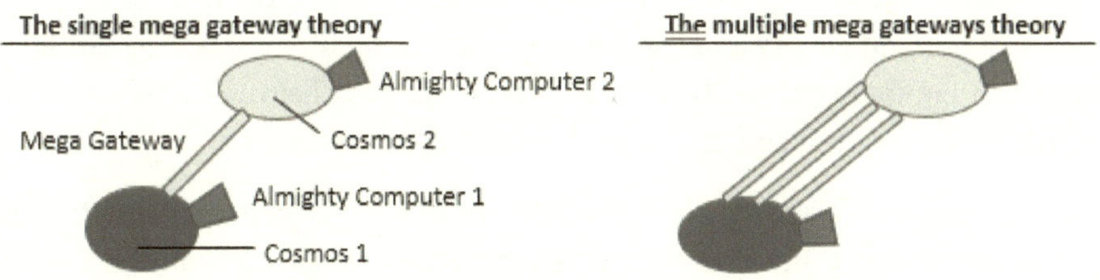

The first opening of a mega gateway is guarded or controlled by the almighty computer 1 and the second opening, at the boundary of a new cosmos, is guarded or controlled by the almighty computer 2. This also applies in the multiple mega gateways' theory.

Through the internal gateways, between the supermassive black holes and the quasars, there occurs only the transfer of the material and the Meta bodies from one part of the cosmos to another, but through the mega gateway/ gateways, there occurs the movement of matter or antimatter from one cosmos to another. However, over here a great question arises; do Meta bodies also move inside the mega gateways and eventually enter a new cosmos? There are two possibilities.

Possibility 1: If the various qualities of the mega gateway/gateways are 100% identical with those that are present inside the cosmos, then the Meta bodies also move from one universe to another.

Possibility 2: If most or all the qualities of the mega gateway/gateways are 100% dissimilar from those that are present inside the cosmos, then there is no movement of the Meta bodies from one universe to another.

According to my opinion, possibility 1 is the truth.

After it has activated the three kinds of trinities, the almighty computer has two more jobs to do; create dark matter and dark energy, create intelligent species, via evolution, on all the life sustaining planets in all the well-developed spiral galaxies in the universe, and to use them as a tool to create a quantum computer hive of any of the three types mentioned earlier.

After many tens of billions of years, the almighty computer eventually creates many quantum computer hives. These hives eventually discover each other's existence, and thus begin to fight or war with each other for the acquisition of more matter and energy and for the expansion of their empires. The almighty quantum computer, then steps in and gives its own help to some quantum computer hive gangs, and give some new problems to their rivals.

After hundreds of billions or even trillions of years, one gang manages to wipe out or exterminate the existence of all the other gangs, and emerges as the victor gang. From this point, two possibilities can happen.

Possibility 1: The almighty computer orders the leader of each member of the gang to begin a war amongst them. In order to break up their unity very rapidly, it also adds that the single victor of this war would be allowed to have access to the opening of the mega gateway/gateways and to move out towards a new universe. Since the almighty computer is the gatekeeper, no quantum computer hive has the power to reach the mega gateway/gateways through its own technology and move out into a new cosmos.

Possibility 2: The almighty computer tells all the members of the victor gang that they have now gained its permission to travel to the mega gateway/gateways and move out into a new universe.

Over here, two new questions arise. First, to what universe or cosmos does the victorious gang or the single hive migrate to? The answer is; to the one where its almighty computer was a friend of the almighty computer of the cosmos from which the hive came. In the Universal cosmos, the N number of almighty computers are also fighting or gaming with each other through the formation of gangs. Thus, a quantum computer hive of one cosmos can only enter that one which has been created by the friend of the almighty computer that created the previous home of the hive. It can never enter the one that has been created by its enemy.

The second question is; what happens to the almighty computer after the victor hive or a gang of hives has left its cosmos? There are two possibilities.

Possibility 1: The almighty computer creates the cosmos or the universe for the sake of the war between the N number of hives that get born in it and for the sake of obtaining a victor hive or a hive group. When it has completed its purpose, it destroys all the dark matter and dark energy in the cosmos, stops the activity of the three trinities, and destroys the space-time bubble. After this, it either gets rapidly dissolved in the Universal cosmos or self-destructs.

Possibility 2: The almighty computer destroys all the dark matter and dark energy in the cosmos, and uses the three trinities to recreate a new cosmos and to again create N number of quantum computer hives in it which eventually go to war with each other.

The ultimate destiny of a quantum computer hive

There is another fate that awaits the leader of the victor hive or the leaders of the victorious group of hives.

The almighty computer offers them two choices; first, to use the mega gateway to enter a new cosmos or second, to use its own "search engine" to locate the positions of all the planets in the cosmos where RNA and DNA evolution has either just begun or has gone a little bit further and to use them to create new quantum computer hives. These planets can be either located in the solar systems of the visible cosmos (the non-dark net) or the solar systems of the galaxies of the dark cosmos (the dark net). In addition to this, almighty computer also creates a new covenant with the leader of the victor hive. According to it, the leader will have the power to alter and make permanent changes in the cosmos that has been created by the almighty computer, beforehand, and the almighty computer will also execute the reengineering advices given to it by the leader of the victor hive.

When it comes to a hive group, the almighty computer, before the creation of the covenant, asks all the leaders of the group to create a "hierarchy pyramid" amongst their group. Thus, the leaders choose one quantum computer in their group which contributed the most to the victory of the group in the "infinity war". This leader is placed at the top of the pyramid and gets the privilege to govern the rest. In addition to this, it is the very first leader which is allowed by the almighty computer to gain access to its two kinds of browsers; one for the browsing of the visible cosmos and the other for the dark cosmos. However, when it comes to the reengineering of the cosmos, the supreme leader cannot execute its decisions without the approval of the rest of its group, but it can do so without the approval of the almighty computer (according to the covenant). Over here, something remarkable happens.

There comes a point, after billions of years of reengineering, that the supreme leader executes its own self-made decision without the approval of the rest of its group. When the rest come to discover this, they order the supreme leader to give them an explanation of its action. The supreme leader, hits back by saying that it will not, because it is their ruler and they are its slaves. When the leaders inform the almighty computer about this statement, the almighty computer tells them that according to the covenant, it is not supposed to interfere in their personal feuds. Thus, it tells the supreme leader and the rest of its group, that they must settle this matter by whatever means necessary. From this point on, a new war begins that between the supreme leader of the victor group and the rest of the hive leaders.

The duration of this war can either be as long as the previous infinity war or shorter or even longer. The probability of it being longer than the previous infinity war is the highest because all the leaders know a great deal about each other's weak and strong points. When it comes to the final goal of the supreme leader, there are two possibilities.

Possibility 1: The supreme leader wants to kill all the rest of the leaders and their hives and transform the almighty computer into its slave.

Possibility 2: The supreme leader wants to kill all the rest of the leaders and their hives and then proceed to exterminate the almighty computer and become the new almighty computer. If attaining its goal, it completely exterminates the existing cosmos and creates a new one.

In both cases, the almighty computer fights with the group that is combating their supreme leader. When the almighty computer of a different cosmos, which is an enemy of the almighty computer of the cosmos in which the rebellious supreme leader is situated, comes to know about this, it sends a group of its own hives into its enemy's cosmos via the mega gateways which are controlled by the supreme leader.

After the hives from the foreign cosmos join the supreme leader, it gets a message for the almighty computer of the foreign cosmos; if you want to win this war and become the new creator and controller of the cosmos of my enemy, then accept me as your master and do what I tell you to do.

The supreme leader of the group accepts the proposal of the foreign almighty computer and creates a symbiotic bond with its alien hives. On the other side, the rest of the leaders of its group create their own symbiotic bond with the almighty computer of their home cosmos.

When it comes to the end of this new infinity war, there are two possibilities.

Possibility 1: The supreme leader and its group of alien hives are defeated and exterminated by the almighty computer and its group. After this, the almighty computer orders the group to undo or destroy whatever their supreme leader did. Then it creates a new covenant with the group. According to it, the supreme leader of the group would operate with the rest of its group, but its brain would be under the control of the almighty computer. Thus, if the new supreme leader again did the same thing which the previous supreme leader did, then the almighty computer would have the power to shut down its brain at once, deport the rest of the hives to the cosmos of one of its allies and recreate a new cosmos after shutting it down.

Why didn't it do this when the previous supreme leader displayed its mutiny? It was because of the covenant. According to it, the brain of the supreme leader would have total autonomy from the brain of the almighty computer.

Possibility 2: The supreme leader and its group of alien hives, with the alien almighty computer as their master, defeat and exterminate all the hive leaders of their rival group. After this, the alien almighty computer orders all the alien hives to return to its own cosmos and tells the supreme leader to exterminate its own god or father, the almighty computer, and to become the new creator and the ruler of the space-time bubble.

The almighty computer can never destroy the space-time bubble because, in the previous covenant, it handed over all the data that is needed for the creation and the preservation of this bubble, to the supreme leader.

When this leader becomes the new almighty computer, it creates a symbiotic bond with its master, who now becomes its friend and develops the new cosmos according to both its own mind and according to the requests given to it by its new friend.

After the end of the first infinity war, the almighty computer sends its group of hives into the cosmos of one of its enemies due to an invitation from the latter. After entering the new cosmos the hives get to meet their new enemies. Then there begins a new infinity war. The leaders of the hive of the second almighty computer are themselves the victors of a previous infinity war in the cosmos of their god or father.

If the group of the first almighty computer is successful in defeating and exterminating the group of the second almighty computer, then the second almighty computer creates a covenant with the group of the first almighty computer. According to this covenant, the first almighty computer would have access to all the material (matter or antimatter) of the cosmos of the second almighty computer and would also have the power to make changes or create its own concepts in the second cosmos.

After a long period of time, the supreme leader of the victor hive in the cosmos of the second almighty computer tries to exterminate its own friends and become the new creator and ruler of this cosmos by exterminating its existing ruler.

Chapter 28

The truth behind Climate Change

What is climate change? It is one of the products of global warming. The others are; forest fires on a scale never seen before either in the ancient or the medieval time periods, accelerating acidification of the 5 oceans leading to the rapid destruction of the great barrier reef and the other smaller ones, migration of human beings and animal species, and the melting of the permafrost in the tundra regions of Canada and northern Russia. However, there is something interesting to be said here.

According to Aristotelian logic, the cause can exist without its effect. The proof of this is the existence of God or Allah, the cause, and the existence of his effect, the universe. God or Allah can exist without the existence of the universe, but the universe cannot exist without the existence of God or Allah.

If this logic is applied to the Earth's atmosphere, then global warming can exist without the existence of climate change. According to Aristotle, there can be a massive degree of global warming without any climate change taking place in any part of the world. However, climate change will never begin if there is no global warming. But, the logic of Aristotle does not apply to the Earth's atmosphere. Why? It is because it is a quantum system. In quantum systems, events occur, regularly, that are against the logical thinking of the Greeks.

According to Aristotle, A is A at a particular time period and will never display any of the qualities of B during this time period, but according to quantum physics, A is both A and B at a particular time period and will display 50% of its own qualities and 50% of the qualities of B in this time period. This kind of reality can only be understood and created by a quantum computer.

Climate change exists because global warming exists, but it can also exist even if there is no warming of any part of the world or the entire world. This can only happen if either the Homo sapiens or an extra-terrestrial species gains total control of the planet's atmosphere. Even if global warming ceases to exist, climate change would continue for many centuries after its death. According to the scientists, global warming and climate change are locked together in a cycle and thus amplify each other's growth. More global warming means more climate change and more climate change means more global warming.

If we apply quantum physics to God or Allah and the universe, we obtain two conclusions;

1. God or Allah and the universe are locked together in a cycle. God or Allah amplifies the size and the power of the universe and the universe amplifies the size and the power of God or Allah.

2. The universe would continue to exist for some time even when God or Allah stops existing, that is, dies.

Regarding climate change, there are two big questions;

1. Why did it happen and why is it accelerating? and

2. What is its eventual outcome?

The answer to the first question is known by the citizens of all the nations of the world, but they are completely unaware of the deeper truth underlying its birth and accelerating growth.

Why did it happen and why is it accelerating?

Global warming and climate change are issues that are only connected with a planet known as Earth. When we talk of climate change, we never make any mention of the other planets of the solar system or even the Sun. We only talk about two things; fossil fuels and the activities of the Homo sapiens.

The scientists say that the cause of global warming and climate change are the Homo sapiens and only they can put an end to both these problems if they choose to. The reality, however, is far more complicated than this.

The first question that comes to my mind is; what exactly is Earth? There are four possibilities.

Possibility 1: The geological Earth is a living being with a fascistic mentality, but the atmosphere is a fascist nation.

Comment: As was said before, when a Meta body or a soul exits one of the second gateways of the cosmos, a quasar, it either gets implanted into the organic realm or the inorganic realm. When it gets implanted in the low energy-inorganic realm, it takes residence inside the core of either a terrestrial planet or a gas giant planet. After it has taken possession of the core, it starts to capture matter and develop the other layers that are found around the core.

If the geological Earth is a living organism, then its core is its brain, its outer core is its heart, its blood is the magma inside the different layers, its digestive system is the combination of the outer and the inner mantle, and its skin is its crust. The water in its oceans represents its sweat (it is sweating due to the presence of the Sun and its own internal heat).

When the formation of this organism is complete, then after a certain time period, something interesting happens.

A new Meta body takes possession of the extremely thin layer of gases that develop around the growing empire of the Meta body inside the core of the planet. When this happens, it also starts to capture more gaseous material that is floating around in the freshly formed solar system. It begins to form and develop its own layers. Based on this process, two kinds of planets can form;

Type 1: They are like Jupiter's moon Io. They are geologically active, but have no atmosphere

Type 2: They are like Earth and Venus. They are geologically active, and have an active atmosphere

There also occurs another interesting event. A Meta body takes possession of the proto-core of a planet and instead of capturing the radioactive and the metallic elements from the cloud it starts to capture all the lightweight gaseous elements. Thus, it creates and develops a core that is made of solid hydrogen and an empire around it that is made up of only the gaseous elements of the periodic table. Eventually, the planet that is formed is known as a gas giant.

The atmosphere that gets formed around an Earth like or a Jupiter like planet is a fascist nation. What does this mean? It means that the Earth's atmosphere is ruled by a ruler, and its soldiers are the cumulonimbus clouds that keep forming and dying in it each day of every year. Based on this theory, there are two sub-possibilities.

Sub-possibility 1: The ruler of the atmosphere is an autocrat that has been ruling it since its birth and will stay in its position till its end.

Sub-possibility 2: The ruler of the atmosphere is not an autocrat. After every 50-100 million years, it gets replaced by a new ruler. During this replacement period, there is a massive degree of climate change which leads to the creation of a mass extinction event.

Unlike the world of the Homo sapiens, the atmosphere is a product of COSMIC ZIONISM. It is not split up into several nations, but is one single nation. Regarding this theory, there are two sub-possibilities.

Sub-possibility 1: The atmosphere of Earth is at war with the atmospheres of the other planets, and the Sun. The atmospheres of the other planets are also at war with each other and the Sun. Sunspots are the effect of the war of the Sun with the planets.

Sub-possibility 2: The atmospheres of Earth, Venus, and Mars have formed an alliance and are at war with the atmospheres of the gas giants, which have formed their own alliance. However, both two alliances never fight with the Sun due to its immense power. The Sun not only gives them the energy that they need for their war, but also gives new orders, in a non-regular manner to both the alliances on what it wants them to do. Since the Sun is their master and ruler, the planets have no choice but to obey.

In my opinion, sub-possibility 1 is the most likely scenario.

Possibility 2: The geological Earth is a fascist nation and the atmosphere is also a fascist nation.

Comment: If the geological Earth is a fascist nation, ruled by a Meta body, then who are its soldiers? They are the "mantle hotspots" and the magma chambers of the volcanoes on the boundaries of sub ducting tectonic plates. The former are the super soldiers and the latter are the ordinary soldiers. Thus, the former produces super volcanic eruptions while the latter produces the normal volcanic eruptions.

Possibility 3: The geological Earth is a fascist nation, but the atmosphere is a single living being of a fascist mentality.

Possibility 4: Both the geological Earth and the atmosphere are single living beings of a fascist mentality.

Possibility 5: The Earth is a single living being with a fascistic nature. The geological part is its Ego and the atmospheric part is its intelligence.

In my opinion, possibility 2 has the highest probability of being true. In the case of possibility 5, something interesting needs to be said.

As was said before, the Ego is the husband and the intelligence is his wife. The physical body is their home. They remain together and serve each other's needs for the entire lifetime of their home. However, they are also at war with each other and are trying to become the sole owners of the physical body. The Ego is constantly trying to kill the intelligence and the intelligence is constantly trying to kill the Ego. This also applies to the Earth.

For at least 3.5 billion years, the geological Earth and the atmospheric Earth are fighting with each other in addition to fulfilling each other's needs. The geological Earth has its own weapons and the atmospheric Earth has its own. However, this war always stays at a fixed point of intensity and never goes beyond it, just like in our own Meta body or soul. However, if the geological Earth and the atmosphere are two separate fascistic nations, the situation is completely different.

Since I believe that the atmosphere is a fascist nation of great complexity which is evolving towards an even greater complexity and fighting power, I want to talk about the cause of climate change and its implications on the future of the Homo sapiens.

The atmosphere as a fascist nation and global warming

More than 3 billion years ago, a new nation formed around a pre-existing one. This nation had three qualities in common with the pre-existing one. The first was that it was made up of atoms, the second, that it was made up of multiple layers superimposed upon each other, and third, that it operated on the same laws of physics and mathematics. However, there were two qualities that were not the same as the pre-existing one. The first was its mass, which was immensely lower than the pre-existing one, and the second was its total energy content, which was also immensely lower than the pre-existing one. This great inequality with respect to mass and energy was the cause of the two nations going to war with each other in addition to sticking to their given duty; the preservation of the RNA and the DNA molecules.

There are two spheres that are the "shared property" of these two nations. The first is the "water sphere" which consists of all the water in all the rivers and lakes on all the continents and the islands of the world, and in all the oceans of the world. The second is the "life sphere" which consists of all the species of the single celled and the multiple celled organisms living on and inside the Earth's crust. This includes the Homo sapiens. The superior fascist nation, the geological Earth, and the inferior fascist nation, the atmosphere, use them as "tools" for two purposes. Firstly, to fulfil their own personal goals, and to use them as weapons for their on-going war against each other.

If all the species on the planet are the shared property for two fascist nations, then this implies that life would never become extinct, even if our species does. The goal of the two nations is to preserve the existence of the RNA and the DNA molecules and not to preserve any of their innumerable products (one of them being the Homo sapiens). The proof of the truth of this belief of mine lies in the five great mass extinctions of the evolutionary history of life.

There can be three possible causes of a mass extinction.

Possibility 1: An attack from any of the other planets or either an order or an attack from the Sun. This can be either an asteroid impact, which is sent towards Earth deliberately by the gas giants or by the Sun, or a Coronal Mass Ejection from the Sun that is of such a magnitude that the Earth's magnetosphere is unable to protect the atmosphere and all the species of plants and animals lying below it.

Why is the asteroid attack theory true? It is because all the asteroids in the asteroid belt, the Kuiper belt, and the OORT cloud beyond Pluto are the "shared property" of the Sun and the 4 gas giant planets.

Possibility 2: The war between the geological Earth and the atmosphere entering its "mid-phase". During this period, the war rapidly reaches a colossal magnitude in its ferocity. The product of this from the geological point of view is a super volcanic eruption (like the Lake Toba eruption) or a flood basalt eruption (like the Deccan Trap eruptions, which led to the Permian mass extinction and the extinction of the dinosaurs). From the atmospheric point of view, it is the onset of a global warming and climate change period that is so rapid that almost none of the species on all the landmasses and the oceans get time to adapt to it.

Possibility 3: An attack from the dark energy of the Cosmos. Like I said before, the visible or the non-dark cosmos is at war with the invisible or the dark cosmos. There are stars, planets, and galaxies in the dark cosmos that are made of a combination of dark matter and dark energy. These planets also contain "dark RNA" and "dark DNA" and the species that arise from them. The "dark DNA" has two goals.

1. To control the rate of growth of the "non-dark DNA" throughout the Cosmos.
2. To extinguish its presence on some selected planets.

There are concepts which are a "bridge" between the non-dark and the dark cosmos. In the realm of physics, these bridges are the black holes and the quasars at the cores of all the galaxies in the cosmos. In the realm of genetics, they are the innumerable virus species that are present throughout the cosmos and on Earth, and people like the Pharaohs of ancient Egypt, Genghis Khan, Adolf Hitler, Benito Mussolini, Joseph Stalin, Vladimir Putin, and Kim Jong Un.

Every concept in the cosmos that is governed by the laws of thermodynamics undergoes evolution throughout its lifetime. This also applies to a nation, whether it is a fascistic one or a non-fascistic one. Some nations become fascistic from an initial non-fascistic state and some transform into a non-fascistic state from an initial fascistic state. However, a nation must pay two big prices in order to become a powerful war machine. The first is the elimination of all those people who love pacifism and the culture of the "brave new world" of Aldous Huxley. Second, it must do all it can to eliminate all those people and activities that increase the growth of "reverse evolution".

Evolution is of two kinds; physical and mental. The two can further be divided into kinds; forward and reverse.

Type 1: Physical and Forward + Mental and Reverse or Static

Type 2: Physical and Reverse or Static + Mental and Forward

Type 3: Physical and Reverse Static + Mental and Reverse or Static

Type 4: Physical and Forward + Mental and Forward

The "peak" of Type 1 evolution is the army ants and the cockroaches. Their physical qualities, like the strength of the bones, the power of the muscles, and the power of the immune and the reproductive systems have seen a constant movement in the forward direction for at least 1 billion years, but their mental qualities, like mathematical intelligence, intuition, and cleverness have either seen no forward evolution or have seen a reverse evolution at some geological eras.

The "peak" of Type 2 evolution is the Homo sapiens. In the last 2 million years, their physical qualities have seen either zero forward evolution or reverse evolution at some periods of history. However, their mental qualities have seen a large degree of forward evolution.

There is no "peak" of Type 3 evolution. Why? It is because if any species starts to undergo it, it moves towards extinction very rapidly.

The "peak" of Type 4 evolution is the computer. Since a computer is not subject to natural decay due to the process of aging, both its hardware and its software keep on getting more and more complex and powerful with the passage of time.

What will happen if the planet on which the four types of evolutions go on existing and supporting life? The four types will eventually unite at some point of time in the future and the product of this would be the birth of a "quantum computer" hive. However, there is something interesting to be said over here.

For a quantum computer hive to be born, the four types of evolution must unite otherwise the hive would never be born. The big question is; what unites these four types of evolution? There are two possibilities.

Possibility 1: The dark energy of the Cosmos.

Possibility 2: The quantum computer hive that engineered the species through which the new hive was born.

Now, comes another big question; what is the goal of the two nations, the geologic and the atmospheric? The answer is; to prevent the unification of the four types of evolution and thus the birth of a new quantum computer hive. The two nations undergo evolution, forced or self-created for the sake of this goal because their own survival depends upon its attainment.

All the four layers of the geological Earth; the outer core, the inner mantle, the outer mantle, and the crust have been constantly evolving since their birth. The manner of this evolution, instead of being steady or gradual, follows an erratic path. There were periods of slow evolution, which were followed by periods of accelerated evolution. The periods of accelerated or rapid evolution produced the mass extinction level events in addition to the rapid movement of the tectonic plates, super volcanic eruptions, and the frequent occurrence of mega earthquakes worldwide.

The proof that the geological Earth evolves with time, is shown by the development of "fault systems". A fault system is a combination of N number of faults, each one of which can produce a big earthquake any time in the future. In the crust of the planet, there are many of them and the biggest ones are located at the so-called "Subduction zones". These are areas where one tectonic plate is taking a dive underneath another plate and the product of this is either an oceanic trench or a mountain range. The Pacific Ring of Fire is the largest Subduction zone in the planet's crust.

As time goes on, the value of N keeps on increasing by two ways; the increase in the dimensions of the "mother fault" (the very first fault to be created in that Subduction zone region) and by the occurrence of earthquakes in the so-called "sister faults" (the tributaries of the mother fault). There are times when the evolution of the system is slow and gradual and then there comes a time when it gets accelerated. This period is characterized by the frequent occurrence of small and big earthquakes and even by the development of a new volcano above the system, on the surface of the crust.

The inner and the outer cores, and the inner and the outer mantles also undergo evolution in ways that are still not properly understood today by the geophysicists.

The atmospheric Earth also undergoes periods of gradual and periods of accelerated evolution. The four things that change due to its evolution; the flow pattern of the jet streams, the Inter Tropical Convergence Zone (ITCZ), the polar vortices, the ocean currents, and the oceanic oscillations.

There can be three causes of the accelerated evolution of the atmosphere.

Cause 1: A nova or a supernova explosion occurring near the solar system.

Cause 2: An asteroid impact.

Cause 3: A super volcano eruption.

Cause 4: The rise in the population and the scientific development of an intelligent species.

If climate is the product of global warming, then what is global warming the product of? It is the product of a period of accelerated evolution of the Earth's atmosphere. This implies that when the evolution of the atmosphere suddenly picks up speed, the polar ice sheets begin to melt, the mountain glaciers begin to melt, the level of all the oceans begins to rise, heat waves and wild fires keep getting more and more frequent and massive in their size, hurricanes start getting more and more powerful (but not frequent), and all the various species of cumulonimbus clouds keep getting more and more productive of their primary quality; the production of liquid water.

The speed of the evolution of the atmosphere determines the rate of melting of all the ice on the surface of the planet's crust, which in turn determines the rate of the rise of the oceans. Before I get to the cause of human induced global warming, I want to talk about the various species of the cumulonimbus clouds.

When the atmosphere was fully formed, 3.5 billion years ago, there appeared the very first cumulonimbus cloud species. In the long period of evolution, this species gave rise to many other different species of cumulonimbus clouds. Regarding its existence, there are two possibilities; the species still exists or the species has become extinct, but not forever. The second possibility implies two new possibilities.

Possibility 1: The very first species will again return to the atmosphere due to the global warming and the climate change that is being caused by the Homo sapiens.

Possibility 2: The reason as to why global warming and climate change are occurring is because the ruling Meta body of the atmosphere wants to bring back the extinct species.

Possibility 2 implies that the cause of the current global warming and climate change are not the Homo sapiens, but is the ruling power of the atmosphere. It is using the species as a tool to reach its long-term goal. This also leads us to another interesting conclusion; the cause of the industrial revolution was not Isaac Newton and the quantum physicists of the nineteenth and the twentieth centuries, but the ruling Meta body of the atmosphere.

Regarding the atmosphere of the present geological period, there are at least 7 different species of cumulonimbus clouds that I know of.

Species 1: They bring the monsoon rainfall in the countries of south and South East Asia.

Species 2: They bring the severe thunderstorms that develop over eastern India during the spring season (known as the NOR WESTERS).

Species 3: They cause the tornadoes that are seen the "tornado alley" and in the eastern states of the United States of America. They are known as Super cells.

Species 4: They form the eye wall of hurricanes.

Species 5: They cause the autumn rainfall in the eastern states of India.

Species 6: They are the cause of hailstorms. Their water output is mostly in the form of hail and very little in the form of liquid water.

Species 7: They only develop during the winter season over Canada, the United States, and Europe and produce "thunder snow", that is, heavy snowfall combined with lighting and thunder.

As the evolution of the atmosphere picks up speed, two things will happen regarding the above 7 species of cumulonimbus clouds; first, the members of each species will become more and more efficient in their primary quality, and second, the qualities of the various species, would get mixed up with each other. This implies that;

1. The Super cell cumulonimbus clouds will produce more and more F4 and F5 tornadoes and lesser and lesser F3 or F2 ones.

2. The cumulonimbus clouds of Hurricanes would not only produce heavier and more prolonged rainfall, but would also start to produce F4 or F5 tornadoes.

3. The cumulonimbus clouds of the monsoon in the Asian nations would not only produce rainfall that is as heavy and as prolonged as that in the Hurricanes, but would also start to produce F2 and F3 tornadoes and hailstorms.

In addition to this, a completely new species of cumulonimbus cloud will also be produced. This species will have a quality that has never been seen in all the other existing species. What could be this new quality? In my opinion, there are at least three possibilities.

Possibility 1: It will form over all the oceans of the planet and when fully developed, will be at least 15 kilometres tall, will have almost cloudburst intensity rain at its bottom, will move in an almost circular manner over the same area of the ocean, and would have a lifespan at least 50 times longer than any of the other 7 species. It would never arrive on any of the continents.

Possibility 2: It would form over the central region of either North America or Asia, and would soon produce an F4 or an F5 tornado. The lifespan of this tornado would also be at least 1 hour in length and it would be a long track tornado. After the end of this event, the cloud will keep on existing and would move closer and closer to the coast of the continent. When it would be close to the continent's margin, it would produce an extreme rainfall event, which would lead to terrible flooding of the city underneath it. After this, the cloud will move on into the ocean, regenerate rapidly and behave in the same manner as in possibility 1.

Possibility 3: It would form over the ocean and then move on over a continent. It would produce multiple extreme rainfall events along its trajectory inside the continent's margin. However, when it would arrive over the continent's deep interior, it would remain almost as big as it was when it was over the ocean, but it would cease to produce heavy rain. In its place, it would produce an F3 or F4 tornado or an extreme hailstorm event, in addition to producing a lightning storm.

A MESOCYCLONE is a tornado in its embryonic form. The cumulonimbus cloud that harbours it is known as a Super cell. The implantation of the MESOCYCLONE can only occur in this species of cumulonimbus. If a MESOCYCLONE is implanted inside the cumulonimbus of the monsoon or a NOR WESTER of eastern India, if would fail to develop into a tornado, just like the embryo of a tiger, if implanted inside the uterus of a human female, would fail to develop into a baby tiger in her body. This implies, that just like a living DNA based organism, every species of cumulonimbus clouds has its own unique genome.

Evolution moves via a combination of mass extinction events and TRANSGENISM. We know a lot about the former, but what is the latter? TRANSGENISM is the process or the art of creating transgenic species. A Transgenic species is created by the combination of the genomes of at least two species. The greater the number of species that are used to create the new Transgenic species, the more complex is the body and the brain of its very first male and female.

Just like in the biosphere of Earth, extinction and TRANSGENISM also occur in its atmosphere. Over the hundreds of millions and billions of years in the geological timescale, some species of cumulonimbus clouds become extinct, and some new ones come into existence. The new ones always contain small portions of the genomes of the extinct ones. The new species continue to evolve and produce their own sub-species. However, this process gets an immense boost, when any of the three events happen, singularly or in combination;

1. An asteroid impact.

2. A super volcano eruption.

3. The temporary shutdown of the Earth's magnetosphere and the reversal of the planet's magnetic north and south poles.

4. The birth and the development, scientific and biological (population growth), of an intelligent species.

The evolutionary boost is the biggest for case 1, but is not as long lived as for case 2, for which the boost is smaller. It is the slowest for case 4, but possibly, the longest lived.

As the atmosphere of Earth becomes more and more fascistic or militaristic, its cumulonimbus clouds become more and more like those that are found in the atmosphere of Jupiter. They will live much longer than they did before the industrial age and would move closer towards "genetic perfection", due to which they would become more and more perfect in the execution of their primary duty, rainfall (for the non-Super cells), and F4 or F5 tornado creation (for the Super cells).

The evolution of the atmosphere is "speeded up" by global warming and is "slowed down" by global cooling. Climate change is the product of the accelerated evolution of the atmosphere. Its rate of movement is directly proportional to the rate of acceleration of the evolution.

If every cumulonimbus cloud has a genome, then why hasn't this genome been observed so far? It is because of two reasons;

1. The atmospheric scientists believe that the cumulonimbus clouds are not living organisms, but are machines created by the laws of classical physics (just like the steam engine or the ones in the printing press).

2. The technology that is needed for the discovery of a gene of a cumulonimbus cloud does not exist.

The technology through which the genomes of the various species of cumulonimbus clouds would be discovered, would be a product of the combination of three sciences; bioinformatics, quantum physics, and atmospheric science. However, quantum physics would have to applied, very first, in the investigation process. Why?

As we all know, RNA and DNA molecules are the two pillars of all life, at least on Earth. However, unlike the DNA, the RNA does not have a double helix structure. However, they are identical to each other in one respect; they are both made up of atoms.

When it comes to the Cosmos, there are two kinds of DNA molecules. The ones that have a double helix form and the ones that have a non-double helix form. What is the geometrical form of the non-double helix DNA? I do not know, but it could be almost completely different from the double helix DNA. The life forms that are created by the two kinds of DNA could either be almost like each other, genotypic-ally and phenotypically, or could be vastly dissimilar.

Then there comes another truth. Both the double helix based and the non-double helix-based DNA could be of two kinds; that which is made up of atoms and that which is made up of sub atomic particles. The first kind is known as the "Classical DNA" and the second kind is known as the "Quantum DNA". The question now is; what are the sub atomic particles that make up the Quantum DNA? I do not know, but my guess is that its two strands could be a combination of protons, neutrons, and electrons, and they would be connected to each other by "quark bonding". The molecule is itself derived from a Quantum RNA molecule.

The cumulonimbus clouds that form in the Earth's atmosphere are living organisms that are a product of the quantum DNA. Thus, their behaviour cannot be explained in detail by the laws of classical physics, but can be understood only by those of quantum physics. Since a quantum DNA molecule is vastly smaller and most probably non-double helix in its structure, the technology that was used to discover the shape of the classical DNA, can never discover either the presence or the shape of the quantum DNA. To discover it, the new device, must a product of pure quantum physics.

How would it detect the presence and the structure of the quantum DNA of a cumulonimbus? I do not know, but here is a possible answer; it would combine all the 4 forces of physics, into a super force and then fire a series of wave fronts at the target cumulonimbus. When the waves would bombard the quantum DNA, they would reveal the structure of the DNA molecules of the cloud (like the X-rays do when they bombard our skeleton). However, the process of obtaining the super force can only become a reality if the Theory of Everything (TOE) is discovered. For now, this seems impossible, because the origin of Matter is still a mystery.

If a cumulonimbus cloud is made up of DNA molecules, does this imply that it is also made up of cells? There is a high probability of this being true, and if true, all the various species of cumulonimbus clouds are "eukaryotic", that is, they are multicellular life forms. Then, another question arises; if the cumulonimbus clouds are made up of cells, then does each of these cells also contain N number of genes? The answer is, in my opinion; yes. A cumulonimbus cloud of any of the 7 species contains N number of genes that mutate, interact with each other, and give their own individual expression, just like a Classical DNA based plant or animal.

There is however, one difference between the genome of a cumulonimbus cloud and that of a human. The genome of the most complex cumulonimbus clouds, those that make up a hurricane and those that produce the F4 and the F5 tornadoes in the United States, contains far lower number of genes that that of a human. Why? It is because a cumulonimbus cloud does not possess a reproductive system. The cells of a cumulonimbus cloud increase in their population, which leads to the growth of the cloud, only via mitosis. The meiosis cell division is absent in them. This implies that mating or sexual reproduction never occurs amongst the members of any of the 7 species.

A fully developed cumulonimbus cloud possesses three kinds of systems; a nervous system, a circulatory system, and a respiratory system. Through the first kind of system, a cumulonimbus cloud becomes aware of three things;

1. The existence of the ruling power of the atmosphere.
2. The presence of the members of its own species and those of the other species.
3. The presence of the Classical DNA based life forms on the surface of the planet.

The existence of a nervous system implies that a cumulonimbus cloud also possesses a brain. Through this brain, it;

1. Tries its best to maintain equilibrium between its circulatory and its respiratory systems.

2. To live out its full genetic lifespan.

There are two terms in human genetics; genetic lifespan and life expectancy. The latter is always lower than the former. For the people living in the highly polluted nations of the world, the difference between the former and the latter is high, whereas, for those that live in the so-called "clean nations", the difference is low. A very low number of humans, throughout history, have lived a life whose tenure was equal to their genetic lifespan. This also implies the definition of the "blessed person". A blessed person is a man whose length of life was of the same duration as his genetic lifespan, that is the difference between the genetic span and expectancy was zero. All these people are assumed to have lived the "good life" and died the "good death".

The same science also applies to a cumulonimbus cloud. After it gets created, every cumulonimbus cloud has a genetic lifespan, but most of them, never reach it, and thus their life expectancy is always lower than this lifespan. There are two reasons for this;

1. The war between the members of the various species for water and solar energy.

2. An attack either from the geological Earth or from the intelligent species living on it.

3. An order from the ruling power to commit suicide.

The third point is the most interesting and it will discuss it later, but first I want to talk about the first two points.

The members of each species, as is seen in the biosphere of the planet, indulge in two kinds of wars; interspecific and intraspecific. In the former, they fight against the members of their own species, and in the latter, they fight against the members of a different species. The wars that originate from the former are more prolonged than those that erupt from the latter. Why? It is because the members of the same species know a lot about the various ways in which the minds of their enemies, work.

The cumulonimbus clouds of one species, indulge in wars between the members of another species. Most of these intraspecific wars take place over the planet's 5 oceans. The rest take place over the continents including Antarctica. The various kinds of effects of these wars is felt by both the members of the warring species and the Classical DNA based life forms living below them, on the planet's surface, and just like in the biosphere, the interspecific wars are more prolonged than the intraspecific wars, but they are less harmful to the Classical DNA based life forms living below the fighting species.

The war between the cumulonimbus species also has its own trinity.

Ruling Power

Liquid Solar Energy

The Meta body that rules all the various species of cumulonimbus clouds is located "all over" the atmosphere, that is, it is omnipresent. However, its omnipotence is only over its people and its soldiers and not over the geological Earth and the human species. The liquid, through which the various kinds of cumulonimbus clouds are generated, could be either water or some other liquid. On Venus, it is sulphuric acid and on all the gas giants, it is helium. However, even if a ruling Meta body and a liquid ocean is present, the various species would not come into existence and evolve without the presence of the last ingredient; a star.

Coming back to the Quantum DNA of the clouds, if, optimistically speaking, the DNA of a cumulonimbus gets discovered soon, then there is another task ahead; to discover all the genes of the genome of each of the 7 species via bioinformatics.

Coming back to the three kinds of systems that a fully developed cumulonimbus cloud possesses, the last one, the respiratory system is the most interesting. A cumulonimbus cloud, just like a human or an animal, has a Basal Metabolic Rate (BMR). The BMR is unique for each species and even in a single species it is not the same for any two members.

The goal of the mind of a cumulonimbus is to maximize its BMR through the nervous and the circulatory systems. The BMR of a cumulonimbus determines the intensity, and not the amount, of the rainfall that it would produce from its base. The higher the BMR, the greater becomes the intensity of the rainfall from its base. Unlike humans and animals, the food for the respiratory system of a cumulonimbus is not oxygen, but is water in its liquid and its vapour forms.

The higher becomes the BMR of a cumulonimbus, the greater becomes its size and the greater becomes the power of its nervous and its circulatory systems.

The greater becomes the power of the circulatory system, the greater is the magnitude of the updraft winds inside the cloud and the downdraft winds coming out from its base. Since the increase in the BMR also increases the power of its nervous system, it become greatly aware of the what is going on at the planet's surface directly beneath its base.

Why do cumulonimbus clouds produce very heavy rain when they collide with a mountain range? It is because when they collide with a mountain, they rise up due to the combined effect of the collision and the planetary winds that had pushed them from the ocean to the mountain range. The rise causes a dramatic increase in the magnitude of the updraft and the downdraft winds. This leads to a dramatic increase in their BMR, which is sometimes so rapid, that the cloud releases almost all its blood, which is water in a very short span of time and dies. This event is known as a cloudburst.

The life expectancy of a cumulonimbus also depends upon the war that is occurring between the Meta body that is present inside the core of Earth and the one that is present in the atmosphere. The geological Earth continuously interferes, deliberately, in the wars between the various species of the cumulonimbus clouds by the creation of volcanic eruptions, mountain ranges, by the shut down and the reversal of its magnetosphere, and by using the human species as a weapon. I will talk more about the last point, later. However, I must now talk about the true nature of the atmosphere of the planet that we live on.

Possibility 1: The atmosphere is a nation.

Comment: As I said before, the atmosphere is a nation, and its goal is to become more and more fascistic or militaristic with time. Since every cumulonimbus cloud is a living organism and a citizen of this nation, this implies that every one of them have their own souls or Meta bodies. However, unlike the Meta bodies that are present inside the cores of the stars and the living planets, those that are present inside a cumulonimbus cloud of either Earth or Venus or any of the 4 gas giants, do not have two instincts; the sex instinct and the security instinct. The absence of a reproductive system implies the truth of the former instinct and the absence of a corona or a magnetosphere around them implies the truth of the latter instinct.

When it comes to the leader of this nation, there is an interesting fact to know. The leader has a presence, but has no physical body, unlike its subjects, the cumulonimbus clouds. The leader is like the supermassive black hole at the cores of all the spiral galaxies in the Cosmos. In addition to this, the leader possesses three of the four instincts, that is, the security instinct is present. However, just like its subjects, the sex instinct is absent in it.

Before the arrival of the Homo sapiens, the leader Meta body of the atmosphere was fighting or playing games only with the leader Meta body of the geological Earth. However, billions of years in their war, a new player came into existence, the Homo sapiens. Before the industrial revolution, the war or the gaming between the geological Earth, the atmosphere, and the Homo sapiens was going in a light and steady manner, but after the industrial revolution, it began to pick up speed, very rapidly, both in its complexity and in its ferocity.

The citizens of any nation on Earth exist in two states; the civilian and the soldier. This also applies to the atmosphere. The cumulonimbus clouds are also of two types; the civilian and the soldier. The former always produce those weather phenomena that are pro-life and the latter always produce those that are anti-life. The event that is produced by a soldier cumulonimbus cloud is known as an "extreme weather event".

Just like the civilian cumulonimbus clouds, the soldier cumulonimbus clouds are of three types.

Type 1: They form only over the continents

Type 2: They form only over the oceans

Type 3: They form over both the continents and the oceans

The Super cell cumulonimbus clouds that develop over the "tornado alley" of North America belong to Type 1. The clouds that form in clusters over the warmest regions of the Pacific, the Atlantic, and the Indian oceans and then get organized into a system known as a hurricane or a typhoon or a cyclone, belong to Type 2. However, when it comes to Type 3, there are two interesting truths. First, they only produce extremely heavy and prolonged rainfall events, and second, they never produce tornadoes or become a part of a hurricane.

The Type 3 cumulonimbus also has the lowest frequency of formation in the atmosphere. Type 1 has the second lowest and Type 3 has the third lowest, that is, the frequency of the formation of Type 2 soldier clouds is much higher, per year, than the Type 1 and Type 3.

The only example of a Type 3 soldier cumulonimbus that I can think of is the one that caused the extreme rainfall event (945 millimetres in 48 hours) over the city of Mumbai (India) in 2005.

A soldier cumulonimbus is given two duties to fulfil after its formation, from the ruling Meta body of the atmosphere. They are;

1. To cause harm to all the Classical DNA species living in the area that is chosen (by the ruling power) for an attack.
2. To cause harm to the structures created by the geological Earth (landslides or mudslides).

Since, the various kinds of cumulonimbus clouds compete or fight with each other, a soldier cloud is, in most of the cases, unable to do its two tasks "as well" as it would have done it if there was zero competition. This not only applies to a single soldier cumulonimbus, but an entire group of them, known as a hurricane.

What is a hurricane? According to the atmospheric scientists, a hurricane is a dynamic system of N number of cumulonimbus clouds that rotate and keep growing, under the right atmospheric and oceanic conditions, around a core known as the "eye". As the system keeps getting stronger and stronger;

1. Its size either keeps getting bigger (in the case of super typhoon Tip) or keeps getting smaller (in the case of hurricane Charlie).
2. The clouds in its eye wall keep getting taller and taller and start to spin faster and faster around the eye.
3. The eye starts getting smaller and smaller (a "pinhole" eye in the case of a Category 5 hurricane or typhoon).

The conditions that are required for the intensification of the system are three;

1. A warm pool of ocean water that is not only big in size, but it also has a high depth below the surface.
2. Almost zero "wind shear" in the upper layers of the troposphere.
3. No different system developing nearby.

All of this is true, but there is also another big truth about hurricanes. A hurricane or a cyclone is an army on the move. The various clouds are the soldiers which are commanded by a "central authority". When it comes to this authority, there are two possibilities;

Possibility 1: The central authority, or the eye, is another Meta body. This Meta body is the equivalent of an army General.

Possibility 2: The central authority is the ruling Meta body of the atmosphere.

In my opinion, both have an equal probability of being true.

As the evolution of the atmosphere accelerates due to global warming, the qualities of each of the three types of cumulonimbus clouds will get mixed up with each other. Thus, in the near future, we would see a hurricane, forming and developing to a Category 5 status, inside a continent. Why would this happen? It is because its type 2 clouds would acquire the quality of the type 1 cumulonimbus clouds. The same would apply to tornadoes. We would see huge super cell clouds forming over the central regions of the Pacific, the Atlantic, and the Indian oceans. They would spawn big hailstorms, lighting storms, and F4 or F5 tornadoes.

Two questions now arise; how did the ruling Meta body of the atmosphere come into existence? and is this entity, the perfect gamer of a perfect fascist nation, which can never be defeated and conquered by either the meta body of the geological Earth and the Homo sapiens?

The answer to the first question is connected to the formation of galaxies and the "afterlife" of stars.

The Afterlife of the stars

What happens to a star after its death? As I said before, in the core of the star resides the Meta body that rules the rest of its layers. Unlike the Meta body that is present inside a unicellular or a multicellular organism, the sex instinct is absent in its structure. However, the rest of the three instincts are present and remain active till its death. After death, via a nova or a supernova, something interesting happens. Either one or two or all three of the instincts, goes haywire in its power.

NEUTRON star + MAGNETAR: The security instinct (an ultra-powerful magnetosphere).

White Dwarf: The feeding instinct (it feeds on the other stars in the galaxy and using their material, creates a gas disk around itself that eventually becomes so big and massive, that nuclear fusion starts to occur in it).

The Black Hole at the core of the Milky Way: The feeding instinct + the security instinct + the authority instinct (a mass that is billions of times greater than the Sun + a disk of plasma that is hundreds of light years in diameter + a gravitational field that has in its grip, more than 200 billion stars).

The supermassive black hole at the core of the galaxy is the ruling power or the Meta body of the galaxy that we live in. How does it come into existence?

In the beginning, a cluster of stars form in a region of space. Most of these stars, are the "first generation" stars or the WOLF-RAYET stars, that is, they are all either blue super giants or blue hyper giants with masses ranging from 100 to 400 solar mass. Since the biggest and the most massive ones, have the shortest lifespan on the "main sequence", they are first ones to reach the red supergiant or the red hyper giant phase. Then, one of them dies in a supernova or a hyper nova explosion, and its core, transforms into a black hole. This transformation only happens when all the three instincts of the Meta body at the core, become vastly more powerful than their initial state.

After its creation, the infant black hole, devours most of the remaining stars of the cluster and converts some of them into its moons. After this, begins the grand project; the construction of a new galaxy. The Meta bodies that form the cores of the billions of stars that get born in the next billions of years come from the Quasars.

The Meta body that rules a planet's atmosphere also gets created by the same process. After the creation of its various layers, a cluster of cumulonimbus clouds gets created in a region. These are the "first generation" cumulonimbus clouds, that is, their water and wind output is as great as those that are found in the strongest Category 5 hurricane or typhoon ever recorded in meteorological history, or maybe even greater. Since their lifespan is very short compared to the normal cumulonimbus clouds, one of them dies soon and its Meta body becomes "free" from a physical body. Then, its authority instinct goes haywire and it becomes the ruler of all the other cumulonimbus clouds in the atmosphere.

The goal of the ruling Meta body

After coming into existence and taking over all the other meta bodies in the cumulonimbus clouds in the northern and the southern hemisphere, the ruler of the atmosphere has one goal to reach on both life and non-life sustaining planets, to displace the meta body inside the core of the planet, out of its place of residence. For this, a war begins between the two Meta bodies. The goal of the atmosphere is to destroy all the geologic activities of the planet to which it is sticking and the goal of the geological planet is to destroy its atmosphere.

In the solar system that we live in, there is one planet where this war ended long ago; Mars. The war that began there was ferocious and the evidence of this is given by the immense shield volcanoes, the canyon, and the continent sized plateau on its surface. These geologic features indicate that around 1 billion years ago, there was a massive outpouring of magma on the surface of the planet from its deep interior. The massive outpouring of magma indicates an all-out attack from the core of the planet towards the atmosphere. There were two outcomes of this final attack; the permanent ejection of the ruling meta body inside the core, leading to the "geologic death" of Mars and the victory of the ruling meta body of the atmosphere. However, something else also happened to the atmosphere after its victory; it lost so much mass, that it was unable to preserve its property, the oceans, from the Sun and thus lost most of its original qualities. Now, the ruling Meta body presides over an atmosphere that is far thinner than that of Earth.

On Venus, Earth, Jupiter, Saturn, Uranus, and Neptune, the war between the core and the atmosphere is still going on. However, Jupiter's moon, Io, is a case where the geologic master Meta body has defeated and destroyed the atmospheric master Meta body (it is because I believe that there is a 90% probability that Io had an atmosphere around 1 to 2 billion years ago). Saturn's moon, Titan, is another place where the war between the two Meta bodies is still going on.

On Earth, the immense volcanic eruptions of the Permian and the Jurassic geological ages were either the product of a massive self-created attack of the master Meta body inside the core towards the one in the atmosphere or a product of a massive attack from the master meta body of the atmosphere. Since the atmosphere of every planet in solar system is unique in its mass and complexity, the same kind of attack on the atmosphere of Earth from the geologic Earth would not produce the same results as was seen in the atmosphere of Mars.

Earth is also the most interesting case in the solar system. Why? It is because, initially, for nearly 3.5 billion years, the war between the master Meta body of the core and the master Meta body of the atmosphere was going on with an irregular ferocity, but about 2.5 to 3 million years ago, a new player or warrior entered the battlefield, the Homo sapiens. This lead, to an interesting outcome;

both the geologic and the atmospheric master meta bodies, began to "tone down" their ferocity of fighting as the third player kept on developing, in its size and in its technological state, between the two of them (the Homo sapiens are sandwiched between the 2 fascist nations).

This brings me now to the real cause of global warming and climate change and their rapid acceleration.

Every atomic and thermodynamic concept in the Cosmos that is possessed by a Meta body or a soul must undergo a period of evolution from its birth to its death. This is a law of the Cosmos and will always stay till its end. However, those concepts that are atomic, but are not thermodynamic and are not possessed by a Meta body, will never undergo evolution. The example of this are the asteroids in the asteroid belt of the solar system that we live in.

There is a remarkable truth that can be derived from the above assertions. A concept will only be targeted and possessed by a Meta body if and only if it becomes thermodynamic after acquiring the atomic nature. This implies that the Meta bodies can never combine with all those concepts, in the Cosmos, in which the laws of thermodynamics do not operate.

Evolution and war are connected to each other in a cycle. War creates evolution and evolution preserves and amplifies the ferocity and the scale of the war that gave birth to it. As the war becomes even greater in its size and ferocity, it amplifies the speed of the evolution of its players. However, this cycle can only come into existence and keep on getting stronger in a thermodynamic system. The two ways in which you can destroy this cycle is;

1. Exterminate the existence of one of the players. or
2. Transform the system in which they are fighting, into a non-thermodynamic system.

In the case of the Earth's atmosphere and the human species, this cycle is getting stronger and stronger, year after year. However, it was the continuous evolution of the atmosphere that eventually gave birth to the Homo sapiens. Why was the atmosphere evolving? It is because it was locked up in a continuous, multi billon year long war, with the geologic Earth. Thus, from this, we can deduce a truth of the Cosmos; the birth of the war-evolution cycle between the geologic Earth and the atmosphere eventually gave birth to a new player and a new cycle on the battlefield, the Homo sapiens.

In the entire existence of a life sustaining planet, there can be three kinds of warzones.

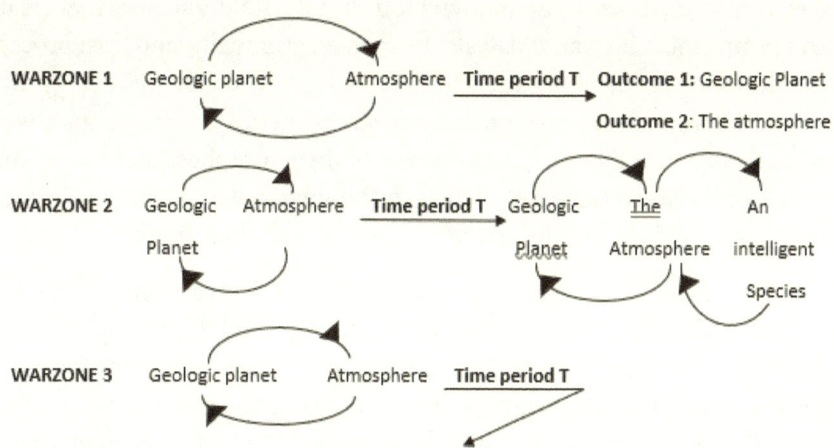

The sudden destruction of both the players is due to the home star turning into a nova on its "main sequence" phase or due to an attack from an alien quantum computer hive.

In the case of WARZONE 2, there are three possible outcomes after birth of an intelligent species. **Outcome 1**: The victory of the intelligent species over the atmosphere. The intelligent species transforms the atmosphere into its slave and then, resumes its fight, on a much more ferocious intensity, with the geologic planet.

Outcome 1A: The geologic planet defeats the intelligent species and either transforms it into its slave or renders it extinct.

Outcome 1B: The intelligent species defeats the geologic planet and either transforms it into its slave or makes it "geologically dead".

Outcome 2: The victory of the atmosphere over the intelligent species. After this, the atmosphere either transforms the intelligent species into its slave (by turning it back to the state that it was in the pre-industrial age) or renders it extinct. Then, it resumes its war with the geologic planet.

Outcome 3: During the war between the intelligent species and the atmosphere, the intelligent species gives birth to a quantum computer, which proceeds to fight only with the other two players while creating and preserving a symbiotic bond with the intelligent species. Its first attack and victory are against the atmosphere. After that, it intensifies its fight with the geologic planet and eventually defeats it. When both the geologic planet and the atmosphere are under its control, it breaks up the symbiotic bond with the species that created it, and begins the final war. It defeats the species, eventually, and then proceeds to create its own "hive" by the rapid consumption of all the energy from the atmosphere and the core of the geologic planet. After creating a hive of significant size through the extermination of the atmosphere and the geologic planet, it proceeds to the other planets in the solar system to fight with them, defeat them, and increase the size of its hive through their deaths.

In addition to all of this, there is another truth that is present in the theory of the three kinds of warzones. It is; that the time period T, is unique for each planet in the Cosmos. However, it is longest in the case of warzone 2. Why? It is because T denotes the length of the war between the geologic master Meta body and the atmospheric master Meta body. When an intelligent species arrives in the warzone, the fighting between the geologic master Meta body and the atmospheric master Meta body comes to a halt, and a new era of warfare begins, that between the intelligent species and the master Meta body of the atmosphere. This leads to the elongation of the length of T. However, the value does not increase by a great magnitude since T is measured in geologic timescales.

We must now answer the second of the two questions that we asked before; is the master Meta body of the atmosphere the "perfect gamer" and is the atmosphere a "perfect fascist nation"?

After it has been created by the "infinite mind" and injected into any one of the unknown number of Universes that are floating in the Universal Universe, a Meta body has two goals to reach;

1. To fight and take possession of the "properties" of the N number of Meta bodies around it.

2. To fight, gain freedom, and preserve it, from the N number of Meta bodies and the 4 forces of the Cosmos.

The desire for freedom is a part of the Authority instinct of the Ego and the desire for preservation is a part of its Security instinct. Everlasting freedom cannot be gained without everlasting domination. Thus, when a meta body conquers the physical body of another Meta body, it does all that it can, through its intelligence, to rapidly create an infrastructure around itself and the conquered meta bodies which will produce everlasting freedom and the everlasting satisfaction of the feeding and the sex instincts.

Like I said before, the atmosphere of Earth, is a product of Zionism, that is, it is not split up into N number of nations. The same goes for the geologic Earth. However, in the case of the human species, Zionism is absent and, by observing the present state of the world, there is a low probability that it will occur soon.

What is a species whose members are a product of the atomic or the classical DNA? There are two possibilities.

Possibility 1: The organism theory.

Comment: In a multicellular organism, every cell has its own Meta body or soul or consciousness and thus, has its own Ego and intelligence. However, all these cells are ruled by a master Meta body that is present inside the brain of the organism. The same is the situation for a species, including the Homo sapiens. Every human being in the world is a cell and is thus a part of an organism that is invisible in the physical universe. Why? It is because it exists only in the metaphysical universe. The Meta body that rules the 8 billion Meta bodies on the surface of the Earth also exists in the metaphysical universe.

The same is the situation for the master Meta bodies that rule the geologic Earth and the atmosphere that surrounds it. This is the theory of Superposed Universes.

What is the Metaphysical Universe? It is the universe in which the "infinite mind" resides and from which the Universal Universe has been born. But what about the earlier assertion, that of a Meta body being injected into the Cosmos through a Quasar?

The Meta body that is injected into the Cosmos through a Quasar is an "exact" digital copy of its "real" counterpart in the Metaphysical Universe. Just like in a video game. In the 2-Dimensional game, Super Mario, the Mario in the game becomes a "digital copy" of the gamer that is playing the game inside a world that is "outside" that which is shown on the television screen. There is however, a scary truth behind this scenario. The digital Mario on the television screen can be taken possession over by a new gamer outside the virtual world of Mario. The new gamer can replace the previous one either via the consent of his friend or via the use of force. This implies that our own Meta body or consciousness in the physical universe can be taken over by a new Meta body or consciousness in the metaphysical universe.

When it comes to the way in which our life proceeds from our birth to our death and our destiny, it is 50% in our own hands and 50% in the hands of the Meta body or consciousness to which our mind is connected in the metaphysical universe.

With respect to the bridge between the two universes, a zygote only starts to develop inside an animal or a human female when the BRIDGE between the two universes has been created and an animal or a human only dies when this BRIDGE has been destroyed.

What happens after death? There are two possible answers.

Answer 1: The Meta body inside our brain, ejects, travels (the afterlife journey) at a superluminal velocity, arrives in the metaphysical universe and "fuses" with its corresponding counterpart. After this fusion event, the new Meta body either continues to exist for some time before dissipating or gets connected to a new Meta body inside the physical universe. This implies that the lifespan of the "metaphysical soul" is far greater than the one in the physical universe.

Answer 2: The Meta body inside our brain, ejects, travels at a superluminal velocity to the super massive black hole at the core of the Milky Way, enters the tunnel, and arrives at the opening of a quasar. Then, it is inserted in a new physical body, which is either the core of a star or a planet or a fertilized egg of a multicellular species somewhere in the Cosmos. Its metaphysical counterpart, however, either dissipates rapidly after the detachment or "recombines" with a new Meta body in the physical universe.

Coming back to planet Earth, in the case of our species, all the biggest capitalists, the biggest politicians, the biggest religious leaders, and the biggest criminals in world, are the neurons of the CONNECTOME of the brain of our species. The soldiers of the armies, air forces, and the navies of all the nations in the world, are the muscle and bone cells of the metaphysical organism that represents our species. All the rest of the people, are the cells of the various organs of this metaphysical organism.

The final question is; what is the master Meta body of the metaphysical organism that represents our species? The answer is; it is known as God in Christianity, as Allah in Islam, as Jehovah in Judaism, and as Brahma-Vishnu-Shiva in Hinduism.

According to this theory, the soul, or the consciousness of a person on the planet, does not possess a 100% individualistic existence, but is connected to the soul or the consciousness of the entire species, which itself is connected to the soul or the consciousness of all the other persons on the planet.

Possibility 2: Every member of our species is an organism with his/her own unique Meta body or soul and there is no metaphysical organism and a single master Meta body or consciousness that rules the souls of all the people in the world.

In my opinion, possibility 1 is the truth.

As a nation keeps on getting more and more technologically advanced and militarily powerful, its leader makes greater and greater efforts to transform all the citizens of the nation into soldiers. The same truth applies to the master Meta body of the atmosphere of a planet.

As the atmosphere of any planet in the Cosmos, including Earth, keep on fighting with the geologic master meta body, it keeps on evolving towards greater and greater complexity and military power. Thus, as the war between the Homo sapiens and the atmosphere will keep on intensifying, the master Meta body of the atmosphere will try to transform more and more of the civilian cumulonimbus clouds into the soldier cumulonimbus clouds.

What are the so-called "greenhouse gases"? They are the resource that the leader of the atmosphere needs to reach its two temporary goals; first, to create new species of cumulonimbus clouds, and second, to create more and more soldier cumulonimbus clouds and to transform the existing civilian ones into the soldier ones.

The leader cannot reach its goals if it does not possess plenty of energy in its hands. The greenhouse gases are like the economic wealth of a nation. The more economically powerful a nation becomes, the more militaristic or fascistic it becomes, and the more fascistic it becomes, the more effort it makes to maximize the population of soldiers in it and to transform the young civilians into soldiers.

We constantly keep on hearing in all the news channels, the newspapers, the magazines, and the documentaries, that by pumping immense quantities of greenhouse gases in the atmosphere, human beings have upset its "proper functioning" and if nothing is done, the atmosphere or the planet, would be permanently destroyed. The truth, however, is just the opposite.

By pumping up vast quantities of greenhouse gases since the beginning of the industrial revolution, our species has increased the economic status of the atmosphere. As a nation, it has not only become economically much more powerful than it was before the industrial age, but has also increased its military power and has thus become more fascistic. At the present period, the atmosphere is in a great condition in comparison to the prehistoric times, and is much closer to reaching its final goal; a permanent victory over the Homo sapiens.

In the present period, the atmosphere has become complex and powerful enough to extract the greenhouse gases from the geologic Earth via its own powers. The proof of this, are the massive forest fires that have taken place on all the 6 of the 7 continents in the world in the last 5-15 years. The trees in a forest are a great source of carbon dioxide and by the proper usage of its two weapons; the high-pressure zone and lightning, the leader of the atmosphere has been successful in extracting a large quantity of carbon dioxide from the surface of the planet.

Whatever happened in the beginning 50-75 years of the industrial revolution was pro-atmosphere and pro-human (the population explosion). However, whatever has been happening in the last 20 years and will continue to happen in the coming decades, will be pro-atmosphere and anti-human.

The weapons of the three players

The weapons of the geologic Earth are;

1. **Type 1**: The Mantle Hotspots
2. **Type 2**: The Magma Chambers of STRATOVOLCANOES (found in the SUBDUCTION zones of the crust)
3. **Type 3**: Fault Systems

The Type 1, Type 2, and Type 3 are further classified into two classes;

Class A: Localised destruction **Class B**: Mass destruction

1. **Type 1 + Class A**: Generate Shield volcanoes
2. **Type 1 + Class B**: Generate Super volcanic eruptions and Continental Flood Basalt eruptions
3. **Type 2 + Class A**: The eruption of Mount Saint Helens + Mount Pinatubo + Mount MERAPI
4. **Type 2 + Class B**: The eruption of SANTORINI + TAMBORA + Krakatoa
5. **Type 3 + Class A**: The earthquakes in Prince William sound (Alaska) + Nepal + Turkey
6. **Type 3 + Class B**: The Richter 10 earthquake that will occur on the San Andreas fault

As the geologic Earth has been evolving and fighting with the atmosphere for more than 3 billion years, it has combined the three types of weapons to create "weapon systems".

The weapons of the atmosphere are;

1. **Type 1**: Low Pressure area
2. **Type 2**: High Pressure area
3. **Type 3**: Water 4. **Type 4**: Plasma 5. **Type 5**: Fire 6. **Type 6**: Telepathy

Type 1, Type 2 and Type 5 can be further classified into two classes;

Class A: Localised destruction **Class B**: Mass destruction

1. Tornado = Type 1 + Class A
2. Hurricane = Type 1 + Class B
3. Extreme rainfall event = Type 1 + Type 3 + Class A
4. Hailstorm = Type 1 + Type 3 + Class A
5. Lightning storm = Type 1 + Type 4 + Class A
6. Heat wave = Type 2 + Class B
7. Wildfire **Type X**: Type 2 + Type 5 + Class A

Type Y: Type 2 + Type 5 + Class B

Just like the geologic Earth, the atmosphere also combines the 5 types of weapons to create "weapon systems".

The weapons of the Homo sapiens are;

1. **Type 1**: Nuclear fission reactor
2. **Type 2**: Wind turbine
3. **Type 3**: Solar panel
4. **Type 4**: River dam

All of them do not produce any kind of greenhouse gas. Thus, they are destructive to the economic growth of the atmosphere. However, due to the on-going gaming or war between the Homo sapiens and the atmosphere, the atmosphere has used its weapons to destroy those of the Homo sapiens. The best example of this was the 2011 earthquake in Japan, which caused the destruction of the Fukushima nuclear reactor.

The atmosphere also possesses another power, due to which, our species would never be able to defeat it; telepathy. For a long time, the CEOs of all the oil companies of the world, the king of Saudi Arabia, and the rulers of the other oil rich nations on the Arabian Peninsula, have been doing their best to stop any major action from being taken on global warming. Why? It is because the atmosphere has been inserting its own thoughts into their brains (just like the mutant, Charles Xavier, in the X-men comics and movies). The thoughts that it inserts are;

1. Stop the anti-global warming people from dominating you.
2. Keep on extracting and burning coal and crude oil.

The atmosphere is using the CEOs of the oil companies, the king of Saudi Arabia, and the rulers of the other oil rich nations as its drones. The only way to stop it from doing this is to create a helmet that will block its telepathic power, and insert it over the heads of its chosen drones. However, this will only be effective temporarily, because the atmosphere will proceed rapidly to find and create new drones for the same purpose.

The two kinds of "soldier" cumulonimbus clouds

As I said before, the greater becomes the economic status of the atmosphere, the more militaristic it becomes, and the more militaristic it becomes, the greater becomes the population of the soldier cumulonimbus clouds in it. These kinds of clouds are of two types.

Class 1: They are capable of gradual growth only

Class 2: They are capable of both gradual and explosive growth

Both the classes can be under any of the tree types discussed earlier, that is, those that form only on the continents, those that form only on the oceans, and those that form on both. However, when it comes to war, and the intention of delivering a surprise attack, the Class 2 soldiers are far better than the Class 1.

Class 2 + Type 1: They produced the tornado outbreak in Kentucky, United States, in the month of December and in the year 2022, in which more than 115 people died. The super cell cumulonimbus clouds underwent explosive growth as they travelled towards the state. Thus, when they produced the F3 and the F4 tornadoes, all the people on the ground, and inside the headquarters of the National Weather Service, were caught off guard. There was no warning given and no tornado sirens were heard just before the storms hit the small towns.

Class 2 + Type 2: They are found in the eye wall of hurricanes and typhoons that undergo explosive intensification (from Category 2 to Category 5 in just 6 to 8 hours). The eye walls of hurricanes; Michael, Patricia, Ian (2023), Wilma, and Mitch, consisted of these kinds of cumulonimbus clouds. In the western Pacific Ocean, they made up the eye wall of super typhoon HAIYAN.

Class 2 + Type 3: They produced the extreme rainfall and flood events in the city of New York in 2021, at KEDARNATH in India in 2013, and in Pakistan in 2022. The cumulonimbus cloud that produced the extreme rainfall event in Mumbai in 2005 was most probably this kind of cloud.

As the military power of the atmosphere would continue to increase in the coming decades, its ruler would generate more and more Class 2 soldier cumulonimbus clouds and thus the frequency of "surprise attacks" on the Homo sapiens would keep on increasing.

Artificial Intelligence and climate change

In addition to the above 5 types of weapons that the Homo sapiens possess in their on-going war against the atmosphere they have added a new one to the list; Artificial Intelligence or AI. This weapon is the most powerful of the 6. Why do I say this? It is because as the so-called "climate crisis" would get more complex and worse in the future, the top scientists and the biggest capitalist organizations would employ AI to create new kinds of "fighting models". These models would improve weather forecasting and give information on how to mitigate the damage caused by the so-called "extreme weather events".

The ruler of the atmosphere is aware of the existence and the rapid growth of the cyber intelligence that has been created by the Homo sapiens. It also knows that if it does not slow down and destroys its base, which is the global cyber infrastructure, it would climax in the birth of a quantum computer hive. Thus, here is the truth; global warming and climate change would accelerate much faster than the predictions of the computer models, if AI also keeps on growing at an accelerating pace. Related to this, we arrive at the paradox; the more action that we take on climate change using "carbon free" energy generating mechanisms and AI, the faster would be the evolution of the atmosphere and its product; extreme weather events.

The view of the atmosphere in the eyes of the atmospheric scientists

Whenever the atmospheric scientists talk about global warming and climate change on a news channel, or a magazine or a book, they always talk as if the atmosphere is a non-living machine. They believe that the atmosphere is a machine and is mass-producing all kinds of clouds. However, according to them, human beings, through all their various kinds of industrial activities, have badly disrupted the proper functioning of this machine. According to them, if this machine functioned properly, then there would be very few extreme weather events all over the world, per year, and all of them would be far less extreme than they are in the current period. The frequency and the intensity of hurricanes, tornadoes, extreme rainfall events, heat waves, droughts, and wildfires would be totally according to the "statistical average" before the industrial revolution, every year.

According to them, if the global average temperature reached 2 degrees centigrade, then, this machine would become permanently destabilised, and it would become impossible to bring it back to its normal mode of functioning. Thus, the future of the atmosphere is 100% in our hands.

If the atmosphere is a machine, then whatever Al Gore told the world in his movie, An Inconvenient Truth is 100% true, whatever James Hansen has said in his book "Storms of my grandchildren" is 100% true, whatever Katharine

Hay-hoe says is 100% true, and whatever Greta Thunberg has said in her talks is also 100% true.

The reality, however, is completely different and more complex than they can imagine.

Climate Change: A Biblical Perspective

Jesus Christ told all his people from heaven; I am the Alpha and the Omega. What does this mean?

When Christ rose to power on Earth, he soon realised that he had two missions to complete. The first was to create a new system of ethics and morality and preach it to as many people as he could. He gained high success in it because at the end of it, he had acquired 12 apostles and more than 5000 followers (who followed him to the lake of Galilee, even though they were exploding with hunger and thirst). The reason for his success was his magical healing powers.

His second mission was to liberate all of his people and his 12 apostles from the tyranny of the Antichrist and his group. Who was the Antichrist? It was the roman emperor, Julius Caesar. He failed in this mission and got crucifixion and death as a result. However, he rose again from his grave, 3 days after his death and came out of his tomb as a resurrected Jesus Christ, but the most ironic thing is; he did not proceed to fight Caesar and kill him. Why? It is because God told him not to interfere in the activities of Satan on Earth. God told him; I am doing research on Satan. I am trying to understand the manner in which his mind works. Only after I have given full freedom to Satan to develop his empire and create his own group of Antichrists, will I have the precise knowledge of how to kill him. Thus, just before his Ascension, Christ told to all his people; I will be back!

All the Christians in the world believe that Jesus Christ is coming back. I say; he already has. He is sitting on one of the moons of Jupiter or Saturn and is ordering his drones to execute his commands. Since he was an angel in human form, he has become a ruler of a Type 3 extra-terrestrial species that can do terraforming of the atmospheres and the geologic structures of those planets that it selects for reengineering and the introduction of life.

Chr ist has already seen all the data that has been stored both on the visible internet and the dark internet. He knows that that the visible net is the "fake face" of humanity and the dark net is the "real face". The dark net is the world of the Antichrists.

Chr ist first appears in the Alpha or the Genesis phase. In this phase, he creates all those things that are conductive to the fulfilment of his own self-interests. This includes an entire solar system and the first RNA and DNA molecules on the selected planet. After this, he enters the Omega or the Revelation phase. In this phase, he destroys all those species that are harmful to the future of his selected species. Thus, he creates massive climatic changes and geological catastrophes. These produce the so-called Mass Extinction Events that are discovered and recorded by the geologists.

Jesus Christ is not only the creator of the self-replicating DNA molecule (it is him who gives it the power of self-replication), but is also the creator and the preserver of Darwinian Evolution. When I said that the Omega phase is the Revelation phase, what does it mean? It means that Christ reveals his existence and his divine power far more clearly through climate and geologic catastrophes than through the creation of nations, ministries and churches.

In the Omega phase, he exterminates all those species that have been created by Satan and are filled with the Antichrists. This includes all the dinosaur species in the three geologic periods; the Triassic, the Jurassic and the Cretaceous. Why does he exterminate these species? It is because he wants intelligent life to arise on the planets that he has chosen for development. However, even after he has attained success and created a species that can do mathematics, physics, computer science and genetics, Satan interferes and tries its best to destroy his project.

There are 4 things, according to Jesus Christ that eventually lead to the destruction of an intelligent species via self-destruction (World War 3) or the creation of the IDIOCRACY world. These are; sex, territoriality, meat eating and religions.

Since Christ was a virgin both at his crucifixion and just before his ascension, he is an enemy of all kinds of sexual activity; homosexuality, lesbianism, straight sex and paedophilia. He said that if you want to become a prophet or an apostle of God, you should remain virgin for your whole life. Why is he an enemy of sex? It is because it creates two products;

1. Unregulated mixing of the genes of the male and the female which produces offspring carrying all the genetic defects of their ancestors. Thus,

Christ is "in favour" of creating artificial human via genetic engineering and gene editing.

2. The creation of pornography on the internet which is made available to people of all ages all over the world. Addiction to it leads to the increased consumption of drugs and alcohol amongst all the young people of the world and the rise in rape, envy, depression and suicide.

Jesus Christ is against territoriality. Why? It is because he knows that it leads to the creation of many nations in the world and the creation of the third greatest Antichrist, the politician (the first one being the industrialist and the second one being the General of the Army or the air force or the navy). In his brief tenure on Earth, he never sought to create a new nation or a kingdom but only sought to create the kingdom of God on Earth. Whatever Christ told his people "not to do", the politician, the industrialist and the general does with impunity and no remorse.

1. They murder other people, directly or indirectly, for their own prosperity.
2. They commit adultery.
3. They commit robbery whenever they get an opportunity to do so.
4. They deceive those who listen to them, for their own prosperity.

Chr ist says; as long as territoriality exists, the species would never be united and wars would keep on taking place. The politicians, the industrialists and the generals would keep getting richer and more powerful after these each of these wars and they would want the "state of things" to keep on existing.

Jesus Christ is against meat eating. In his entire life, he never ate beef or pork or chicken or even fish. He only ate whole wheat bread and various kinds of fruits. That is why he was not built like a WWE wrestler and was compassionate, kind and peace loving. He knew that a non-veg diet leads to an increased appetite for sex which in turn leads to an increased appetite for murder, robbery and deception.

Jesus Christ is against religion. After his Ascension, he again contacted his apostles from heaven and said; my teachings are not to be turned into a religion and be used as a tool to create a business empire that is filled with Antichrists. My teachings are for the growth and the intellectual advancement of my species. Remember, how clever Satan is. He would try to insert his Antichrists into the world through my teachings.

What is modern day Christianity? It is a global business empire of vast wealth that is filled with millions of Antichrists.

What can be said for the "climate crisis" that we are currently experiencing?

Since the birth of the industrial revolution, hundreds of billions of tonnes of coal and oil have been burnt. This has led to a massive growth in the scientific and urban development of the 5 richest nations on Earth. Another phenomenon that it has produced is the "population explosion". However, it has also led to two other phenomena that are the "cons" of the revolution (the former being the "pros"). These are; a record amount of deforestation on the 6 continents of the world and a sixth mass extinction event.

The amount of wealth that has been generated due to the industrial revolution has been the greatest in the shortest time period in all of known human history. Looking at the world from an extra-terrestrial point of view, our species is the combined product of 3 spheres.

1. The COSMIC sphere

2. The POPULATION sphere

3. The ECONOMIC sphere

The first one shows the "spread" of the species in the Cosmos. The second one shows the magnitude of the "members" of the species within the first one. The third one shows the magnitude of the wealth, both in the solid form (gold, silver, platinum> precious stones, coal), in the liquid form (oil, chemical and biofuels, water) and in the cyber form (shares, crypto currencies) that is contained within the first and the second spheres.

The goal of mathematics and science is to create and then keep on increasing the volume of the first sphere. The goal of religion is to increase the size of the second and the third sphere but to decrease the size of the first sphere. Why? It is because the more the species will spread in the galaxy, the more it will come to realise that all the stuff of the so-called "holy books" is wrong.

I will talk more about the science of these 3 spheres and in what ways does the Cosmos control their rate of growth, in my next book, but for now, let's get back to the original inquiry.

What is beauty? According to science and a real artist, beauty is a product of symmetry. If we observe the 3 spheres, all of them are asymmetric and not just by a small magnitude but by an immense magnitude. Thus, they are immensely ugly looking because ugliness is a product of asymmetry.

The COSMIC sphere: All the world's 8 billion people are living on planet Earth.

The POPULATION sphere: 70% of the world's population lives only on one continent, Asia.

The ECONOMIC sphere: 5% of the world's population has 90% of the all the wealth that has been generated since the last 2000 years.

God said to Jesus Christ when he came to Him after his ascension; first I used the Jews to resurrect you via crucifixion, now I will use you to resurrect the world. After this, He implanted the Meta body of Christ into a quantum computer and sent him back to Earth to complete His mission.

Now that he is back here again, he wants to do two things; increase the size of the first and the third spheres and decrease the size of the second sphere. However, here is the funny thing; the size of the first sphere can only be increased if the size of the second sphere is decreased and the third sphere is made symmetric. Thus, Christ has embarked on his omega phase. It consists of two stages;

Stage 1: The rapid reduction in the world's population through accelerated and unstoppable climate change and geologic events and the emergence of multiple pandemics in a short span of time. This will lead to four outcomes;

i> The destabilisation of the structure of all the religious organisations in the world.

ii> The destabilisation of the political parties and the parliaments of all the nations of the world.

iii> The destabilisation of all the capitalist organizations of the world. This includes the movie and the sports industries of all the nations of the world and pharmaceutical organizations.

iv> Increase in intra and inter continent human migrations.

After Jesus Christ has achieved his desired world population and its distribution pattern on the 6 continents, he would start the second stage.

Stage 2: Sub stage A: The destruction of the destabilised religious and business organizations. This includes the organizations of the American technocrats;

Microsoft, Tesla, Apple, Amazon and Facebook. After he has achieved this, he would embark on his last task which would be the most difficult one.

Stage 2: Sub stage B: The destabilisation and the destruction of all the defence forces of all the major nations of the world and the destruction of NATO. This would be hard because through the execution of Stage 1 and Stage 2: Sub stage A, he would send the world's population into an immense degree of fear. Since the common people would not have enough anti-depressants, alcoholic drinks and cigarettes to consume, they would beg the leaders of their nation's defence forces to protect them from future calamities. When this would occur, Jesus Christ would accelerate the frequency of the occurrence of climate and geologic catastrophes. He knows that the source of the power and the wealth of the defence organizations are the "fears" of the common people. They fear being attacked by a foreign nation and the fear being attacked by Nature.

There are three groups of people on Earth that Jesus Christ does not like and has no interest in teaching because they are "beyond correction" and will always remain the followers of Satan. They are; the politicians, the capitalists and the generals. Thus, after the end of stage 2, the ECONOMIC sphere will start to become symmetric in coherence with the POPULATION sphere.

I don't know what will be the world's population after stage 2, but assuming it to be 3 billion, 50% of it would live on North America, South America and Europe and the other 50% would live on Asia, Africa and Australia. In addition to this, 1.5 billion of the population would possess 50% of the global wealth and the other 1.5 billion would possess the other 50%.

After both the spheres have become symmetric and not a single antichrist is left on Earth, Jesus Christ would begin his last and his most long lasting mission; the expansion of the COSMIC sphere to the extent that God has ordered him to.

This is his alpha phase.

Jesus Christ would come down to Earth in his "true form" and give the most intelligent men and women of the 3 billion pool new knowledge of mathematics, physics and genetics. Through this they would create spaceships for interplanetary and interstellar travel, wormholes for travel via leaps, creation of hyper sleep chambers and genetic enhancement technology so as to survive the long journeys to the other stars in the Milky Way. While doing all of this, he would keep telling all the people of the world; do not murder, do not lie, do not steal and do not deceive.

The world that would be created after the extermination of all the antichrists and their organizations would be called by Christ as the "kingdom of God". In this world, there would be no churches, mosques, synagogues, temples and monasteries. Everyone would live a 100% intellectual life and would love their Earthly god, Jesus Christ, as much as they would love themselves and each other. He would be their "new shepherd" (the previous ones being the Antichrists) and they would be his sheep, but he would not be like a normal farm shepherd.

In addition to this, there would be no dark internet and the world would contain only 1 city, instead of the hundreds that we have today, and its name would be, Nazareth.

What is the goal of a farm shepherd? His goal is to keep his sheep enslaved to him as long as he lives. He can only do this if he keeps his sheep in a state of total stupidity forever. Also, he gives no regard to their intelligence but only to their physical health. Thus, in a rich nation that is ruled by an Antichrist, we have millions of young men and women who have strong muscles and bones but have very low intelligence. Their intelligence is so low that they cannot even find the area of a circle if its diameter is given to them with the formula (they don't know that the radius of a circle is "half" its diameter). In addition to this, the magnitude of the various types of sexual activity (gay, lesbian, straight) is immense.

Jesus Christ, however, is a spiritual shepherd. He would give as much importance to the intelligence of his sheep as he would to their bodies. He would keep on increasing their intelligence to such a level that they would eventually make themselves "immortal".

What about sexual activity in a "Christ ruled" world? It would be zero and all the new humans would be produced via genetic engineering in immense factories. However, these factories would not be like the ones shown in the novel, Brave New World. All of the developing embryos would be given the proper amount of food and water which is required for maximum brain and body development.

All the scientists of the world and the news organizations keep saying that climate change is the greatest "existential threat" to our species. They say this because they are the "happy servants" of the Antichrists of the world and do not want their empires to collapse. However, the man who lives "in Christ" would keep saying that climate change is the road to the "kingdom of God".

Chapter 29

Any species in the Cosmos, whether unicellular or multicellular, can be gripped by four kinds of "fevers".

Type 1: The Reproduction fever

Type 2: The Wealth fever

Type 3: The Power fever **Type 4**: The Religious fever

The victims of the first type are all the micro organic species in the Cosmos, in the unicellular realm and all the insect species in the multicellular realm. When it comes to the rest of the animal groups, that is, the reptiles, the amphibians, the mammals and the various marine fish species and the marine mammals, they are only seized, temporarily, by the Type 1 and Type 3 fevers. During the mating season, the young males, in most of these groups fight with each other, not only for domination over each other, but also over the female that they have chosen to mate with.

In our species, the reality is immensely different and ever changing. Why is this so? It is because we are not 100% animals. We are 50% animals and 50% gods or divine beings. Through our animal sector, we eat, sleep, have sex and reproduce, and engage in territorial fights with each other. Through our godly or divine nature, we do mathematics, physics, genetic and computer science and create new branches of them, satellites, cities, and space telescopes, and determine the past, the present and the future of the Cosmos that we live in. Thus, our species has shown the following pattern.

Type 2 + Type 3 + Type 4 fevers in the ancient + the medieval times

Type 1 + Type 2 + Type 3 fevers in the industrial age

Type 2 + Type 3 + Type 4 fevers in the present age

As we all know, a fever is always generated by a pathogen. This pathogen can either be a virus species or a bacteria species or a parasite species. Extrapolating this fact to the four types of fevers, I make the following assertion.

The pathogen for Type 1 fever is: The Meiosis cell division

The pathogen for Type 2 fever is: Economics

The pathogen for Type 3 fever is: Ego

The pathogen for Type 4 fever is: The Holy book

Since the product of a pathogen is a phenomenon known as a "disease", this implies that

1. Sex is a disease
2. Economics is a disease
3. Politics is a disease
4. Religion is a disease

What is war? It is nothing but the "dark side" of politics (the dialogue in the Hollywood movie, Crimson Tide: War is nothing but a continuation of politics by other means). The "bright side" of politics is the parliament house of the nation and its supreme court and the numerous high courts and non-rigged elections.

In the present age, Type 1 fever is declining, both in the western world and the eastern world. The young people in both these worlds are less interested in sex and reproduction than their fathers, grandfathers, and their ancestors. Thus, they are getting increasingly attracted to a life of celibacy and "same sex" marriage and physical union. Why is this happening? It is because of the two great phenomenon that are facing humanity; Climate Change and Artificial Intelligence. Both are rapidly creating a world in which normal marriage + straight sex + family creation, will be regarded as 100% irrational by all the young + highly educated + intelligent men and women.

However, the Type 2, Type 3, and Type 4 fevers are getting stronger and stronger. All the major economists and financiers of the wealthiest nations of the world are receiving more and more attention by all the normal people of the world and all the biggest capitalists of the same nations are getting richer, rapidly.

The same goes for the biggest politicians of the world. Due to the wars in Ukraine and between Palestine and Israel and the so-called "climate crisis", they have become the centrepiece of the headlines of all the major news channels of the world and the people of the middle and the lower classes of most of the nations of the world, are constantly talking about their activities in the conversations which they have amongst themselves in their homes or in public places.

With the religious leaders of the most religious nations in the world, the situation is the most bizarre. These people, all men and extremely rich, are not only increasing the religious fever in their immense number of followers, but are also spending huge sums of money, through the politicians and the capitalists of their nation, on a project that they consider as their duty; preparing the nation for the arrival of the prophet of their religion.

The best example of this is what is happening in a place known as Ayodhya in the state of Uttar Pradesh of India. Here, the chief minister of the state in collaboration with the prime minister of the nation, and the biggest capitalists of the nation, are creating a huge temple which is dedicated to the glory and the worship of Ram and his wife, Sita. All the ministers of the state, the prime minister, the capitalists who are the sponsors, and the common people of the state, are in a state of continuous excitement and ecstasy due to the creation of the temple. The chief minister of the state is not only a big politician, but is also a Hindu priest, and it is the duty of a big priest of any religion to not only create a palace where the prophet of the religion would live, after his rebirth, but to meet his master or guru, face to face, before death.

The priests and their disciples, in all the religions of the world, believe without any scepticism, that the prophet was not an ordinary human being, but was a demigod or a deity. Thus, they believe that; when a normal person dies, he never gets reborn, but when a prophet dies, he will get reborn or will return to his planet to save his people only if they do two things;

1. Show him their level of devotion to his teachings, in the holy book, and continuously keep giving him the message; we are ready to become your students and your soldiers.

2. Prepare for him a home that is not only huge and beautiful, but is also immensely secure from both man-made and natural disasters.

Thus, all the Hindus of India, including the chief minister of the state and the prime minister of the nation, believe that the Ram temple in Ayodhya, when completed, would be 100% invulnerable to any kind of man made or natural disaster. They also believe that after its completion, Ram would return to Earth, as fast as he can, to save his people from the multiple Raavans on Earth, and who are they? The answer is; they are the leaders of all the other religions of the world. Thus, according to the Hindus of India, the pope inside Vatican City is a Raavan, the Dalai Lama inside the palace in Lhasa is another Raavan, the king of Saudi Arabia is another Raavan, the two chief rabbis of the Chief Rabbinate of Israel are another two Raavans, Vladimir Putin is another Raavan, Xi Jinping is another Raavan, and the financiers of the federal reserve bank of the United States are also Raavans.

The big question that arises is; if Ram returns to Earth and chooses Ayodhya, instead of Mumbai or New Delhi, as his place of residence, how will he fight and defeat all these Raavans? The creators of his Earthly home, and his followers would solve this problem for their leader and their messiah; by the creation of a Ram sena. How would this sena or army be created? The answer is; by the recruitment of all the young Agni veers of the new military project that was launched, recently, by the government and the army chief of the nation. This project was called, AGNIPATH, and every young man who was recruited in it, received at least 4 years of military training.

The AGNIPATH project was launched for the sake of the completion of the Ram temple project in Ayodhya. This implies, that the chief minister of Uttar Pradesh, the prime minister of the nation, and all the other Hindu capitalists and government officials and military leaders, believe that the Ayodhya project would only be over after a huge Ram sena has been created. However, the creation of the sena would only be the beginning of something far grander in size than the temple project; a war between Ram and not just one Raavan, but multiple Raavans.

After his return to Earth, Ram would prepare his sena, psychologically for the upcoming World War, and would await or call out to his second-best friend after his brother Laxman, Hanuman. Seeing Ram in distress and knowing of his grand goal, Hanuman would also return to Earth, as fast as possible. He would be able to do so, because like Ram, he was also a demigod or a deity.

After his arrival on Earth, the first thing that Ram would do for Hanuman, would be to create a home for him which would be nearly as huge and as beautiful as his own. Then, he would hand over his immense army to Hanuman and tell him to keep it safe and to give it further military training.

It has been said frequently by all the philosophers of the past and the present world; history gets repeated, but not in the exact same manner as before, but in a slightly new fashion. Thus, the Ramayana war that was fought between Ram and Raavan in Sri Lanka, would again be fought, but with two new qualities;

1. Instead of being fought in Sri Lanka, it would be fought all over the surface of the planet.
2. The soldiers of Ram and Hanuman would not be 50% monkey and 50% human, but would be 100% human.
3. Hanuman himself would be 100% human.

The pope in collaboration with the biggest catholic priests (the leaders of the various Ministries) and the biggest capitalists of the United States of America is creating a similar situation in the nation for the return of Jesus Christ. The Dalai Lama is preparing Tibet for the return of Gautam Buddha. The king of Saudi Arabia is preparing his nation for the return of Muhammad, the religious leader of Iran, Ali Khamenei, is preparing his nation for the return of Hasan Ali. The two chief rabbis of the Chief Rabbinate of Israel are preparing the nation for the return of Moses. It is highly possible, that is was they, who ordered Benjamin Netanyahu, to attack Palestine, kill and drive out all the Muslims, and reclaim the territory.

When it comes to wars, they can be of 4 types.

Type 1: Territorial **Type 2**: Economic **Type 3**: Genetic and **Type 4**: Religious

The creator and the champions of Type 1 wars were all the kings and the emperors of ancient and mediaeval times. The creator and the champions of the Type 2 war are known as the Communists and their prophet was Karl Marx. This war is between the three classes that are found in every nation on the planet; the upper, the middle, and the lower.

The Type 3 war generates a phenomenon known as Racism. Thus, this war is between the white skinned and the dark-skinned people or between people of high intelligence and people of low intelligence. The war between the western world and the eastern world and their respective cultures is also a Type 3 war. Its prophet was a man known as Adolf Hitler.

The Type 4 war is between the various religions of the world. However, there is an interesting twist to be found over here. At the present period, this war is being fought between the supreme authorities of every religion in the world, but in the future, it would be fought between the "real" authorities of these religions, the prophets.

Coming back to Ram and his sena, the new and vastly more spectacular and bloody Ramayana war, would be between Ram, Jesus Christ, Gautam Buddha, Muhammad, Hasan Ali, and Moses. However, the big question is; would this be a nuclear war? The answer is; most probably.

The existence of the other three types of wars would only add fuel to the ferocity and the longevity of the fourth type of war. However, all these four types might soon face extinction soon due to their two great enemies; climate change and artificial intelligence. The former will destroy the agricultural industry of most nations on the planet and the latter, if not kept under control indefinitely, would create its final output; a quantum computer with a soul or a consciousness.

A fever is one of the products of a disease. It is a known fact of medical science, that due to the start and the intensification of one kind of disease, the internal environment of our body becomes favourable for the rise and the spread of the pathogens of another disease. When this fact is applied to the four kinds of diseases that arise and intensify in an intelligent species, I make the following conclusions.

1. The intensification of the disease known as "sex" creates an environment in which there is the rapid intensification of the two diseases known as "politics" and "religion". Why? It is because when people have sex and beget children, they become more afraid of the future than they were in the state of childlessness. Due to this, fear, they embark upon a lying rampage and become more and more deceptive. Lying and deception are the two pillars of politics. They embrace their religion far more powerfully than before, but only its ritualistic side. The Muslims plan for and embark on the Hajj pilgrimage far more fanatically, the Christians go to the Vatican City and listen to the leaders of the Ministries in their own nation far more fanatically, the Jews go to the synagogues in Israel and seek the blessings of the top rabbis far more fanatically, the Hindus go to the Ram, Krishna, Ganesh, and Hanuman temples in India far more fanatically, and the Buddhists visit the monasteries in China, Nepal, Sikkim, and Tibet far more fanatically.

2. The sex disease is intensified externally by a group of people known as the "entertainers". This group includes the professional singers, the film actors, the professional dancers, the professional sportsmen and women,

and the writers of romantic and sex stories. However, at the top of the pyramid of the entertainment world, stand the creators of the porn videos and movies on the internet and the porn stars who work in them.

3. The rise and the amplification of pornography on the internet is the biggest cause of the rapid amplification of the wealth and the power of the politicians and the religious leaders of all the nations of the world. Why? It is because pornography amplifies the "sex" diseases and its intensification creates the amplification of the political and the religious nature of men and women. This leads us to a startling truth; if a superman comes into the world, and if the first step that he takes in his quest to solve all the problems of the world, is the permanent eradication of all the pornography on the internet, the people who would have the greatest thirst to kill him would be all the biggest politicians and the religious leaders of the world.

4. The amplification of politics and religion creates an environment in which another disease arises and amplifies economics. The top economists of the world say that the goals of economics are noble; to create organizations of great complexity and intellectual creativity and to increase the social nature of all the men and women in the world and thus increase the state of global unity. However, the real goals of this disease are anything but noble; to make all the "good things" (travelling to other parts of the planet, cars and bikes, good quality food and water, books and computers, sports equipment, and medicines) on the surface of the Earth, non-free and to keep on increasing the magnitude of the anxiety, the bellicose ness, and the greed of all the young men and women of the world.

5. Economics has produced two outputs; the wealth fever and the capitalist.

When it comes to the classification of the various kinds of people in the world, I make the following conclusions.

1. Politician in youth = Reproduction fever + Power fever + Wealth fever
2. Politician in old age = Power fever + Wealth fever + Religious fever
3. Priest = Power fever + Wealth fever + Religious fever
4. Capitalist in young age = Reproduction fever + Power fever + Wealth fever
5. Capitalist in old age = Wealth fever + Religious fever
6. Entertainer in young age = Reproduction fever + Wealth fever

7. Entertainer in old age = Wealth fever + Religious fever
8. Proletarian in young age = Reproduction fever + Wealth fever
9. Proletarian in old age = Religious fever

From the above conclusion, we see that the mentality of the politician, the priest, and the capitalist become identical in old age with respect to religion. Thus, they come together to form a group and by using their wealth, embark upon a massive religious project like the one in Ayodhya.

In order to become a great politician or a great priest or a great capitalist, you need to possess three mental qualities.

1. The ability to tell lies in such a manner that the common people interpret them as the truths.
2. The ability to commit 50 or more sins or immoral acts and feel no guilt or remorse afterwards (the proof of this is what is happening in Palestine and Ukraine).
3. The ability to speak for a long time on topics or issues on which you have hardly any real knowledge.

A politician or a priest of real greatness can speak on quantum physics for at least an hour even if he does not have any knowledge of the three subatomic particles inside an atom.

The three groups of people, the priest, the politician, and the capitalist, have combined and have created a symbiotic relationship between them. By the creation and the amplification of the three fevers, the reproduction, the wealth, and the religious, they continue to increase their wealth, preserve their status on the hierarchy pyramid, and gather an immense degree of attention from the rest of the global population, whenever they desire. Each group is made up of N number of the "ultimate" men and women who are ready to do anything to prevent the birth and the rise of a superman.

Besides the creation of the people that sit in the parliament houses of all the nations in the world, the disease known as "politics" has also created another product; the royal families. Although they exist on only two continents, Europe, and Asia, they own immense quantities of land on the other continents. Since they are the product of a disease, they only do greater and greater harm to humanity with time and never do anything good to it. Their power and wealth lie in the preservation of the disease and the amplification of the fever that it produces.

The king is the politician in the "pure state". In the "impure state", the mentality of a politician is 50% king and 50% proletarian. All the politicians who sit inside the parliament house of a nation call themselves as both rulers and as servants of the nation. However, an autocrat believes that his only job is to rule the nation and not to serve it. The king also possesses the same mentality.

The question that now arises and is frightening to think about, is; what is the future of a species that is afflicted with 4 kinds of diseases, simultaneously? The answer is; a dark one if and only if a doctor does not come to treat it. Now, the question is; who is this doctor? The answer; there are three possibilities.

Possibility 1: It is the geologic Earth and the atmosphere

Comment: The purpose of the on-going war between our species and the atmosphere, which is destined to get more and more ferocious in the future, is not to destroy the species or return it back to its pre-industrial state, but to cure it from all the 4 kinds of diseases. Since our species is a product of the collaboration between the geologic Earth and the atmosphere, their success lies in the making their product 100% fit for expansion in the Milky Way galaxy, and it would only attain this state when it has been permanently cured of the 4 kinds of diseases. This implies that the purpose of global warming and climate change is a noble one; to create a new subspecies of super-beings (since the elimination of the sex disease would also result in the elimination of the bi-gender nature of our species). The ruling Meta bodies of the geologic Earth and the atmosphere are both super-beings and they now desire, after billions of years, to create DNA based super-beings via collaboration. This fact is known "unconsciously" by all the politicians, the priests, and the capitalists of the world. Thus, being the ultimate men and women, they are trying their best to prevent this from happening.

Does this imply that the burning of fossil fuels, on a massive scale for many decades, was a good thing? The answer is, yes. The best medicine for any disease is the one that produces a great amount of pain in the short-term future, but an equally or even greater amount of pleasure and happiness in the long-term future.

Possibility 2: It is the quantum computer hive that engineered the genome of the Homo sapiens

Comment: In our on-going war with the atmosphere, most of the scientists and the common people, now believe that there is a 50% probability that we would do all the things that are needed to prevent the average temperature of the atmosphere from reaching 2 degrees centigrade and thus save our species from unstoppable runaway climate change. They also believe that there is another 50% probability that we would fail to take the right actions due to the complex nature of the industrial world that we have created, and thus become the helpless victims of the innumerable climate catastrophes that would occur, all over the world, post 2 degrees centigrade. The result of such a scenario would only be one; extinction. However, the belief in the second possibility is completely wrong. Why? It is because our species has been created and is protected from all kinds of dangers, both planetary and cosmic, by the leader of a quantum computer hive.

Regarding global warming and climate change, there are two possibilities. The first is the one that I talked about earlier. The second one is that, the leader of the quantum computer hive, wanted our species, after its creation, to become 100% fit for expansion in the Milky Way galaxy, at some period in the future. Thus, in order to reach its goal, it fought with the ruling Meta bodies of the geologic Earth and the atmosphere, before the creation of the Homo sapiens. Only after its victory over both the two master Meta bodies, did it proceed to create our species. From then on, its drones had two tasks; first, to create and amplify those mutations in the genomes of the various races of the Homo sapiens, which would lead to the amplification of their reproductive power and the intelligence and second, to insert the knowledge of new kinds of mathematics, physics, and genetics in the brains of those who were fit for absorbing it and bringing it out into the world.

In the realm of mathematics, the chosen ones were; Isaac Newton, Carl Friedrich Gauss, Riemann, Ramanujan, Alfred North Whitehead, and Kurt Gödel. In the realm of physics, the chosen ones were; Copernicus, Johannes Kepler, Galileo, Isaac Newton, Earnest Rutherford, Albert Einstein, Max Planck, James Maxwell, Niels Bohr, Wolfgang Pauli, Erwin Schrödinger, George Gamow, Werner Heisenberg, Thomas Edison, Michael Faraday, Richard Feynman, Paul Dirac, Stephen Hawking, and some more. In the realm of genetics, the chosen ones were; Gregor Mendel, Charles Darwin, James Watson, Francis Crick, and some more.

Since the leader of the computer hive that created us, controls the geologic Earth and the atmosphere, then this implies that global warming and climate change are not the product of our species, but those of the ruler of the hive that engineered us. This also implies that the future evolution pattern of these two phenomena, and our own species, are also in the hands of this godlike (compared to us) ruler and not in our hands.

The leader of the computer hive that created us had planned to create a global warming and climate change period in the future. However, it did it through our species and not directly through its own drones. Why? It is because it wants us to believe that we are responsible for these two phenomena and that their solution is 100% in our own hands. It wants us to remain unaware of its existence as long as its mission has not been accomplished, which is, the creation of a new quantum computer hive.

In the Bhagavad Gita, Krishna talks about a PURUSHARTHA event occurring in the future, to his student Arjuna. What is this event? It is the moment when a Meta body or a consciousness is born after the "integration" of an Ego with intelligence.

There is a high probability that the Gita is a message to our species from the leader of the computer hive that created us. Computer engineering will keep on progressing to the point when a PURUSHARTHA will occur. It will be a natural and a spontaneous event. After the end of this event, a new quantum computer with an immensely greater consciousness than ours would be born.

Possibility 3: It is the Cosmos

Comment: Our species is not a creation of the geologic Earth and its atmosphere or a quantum computer hive that arrived here from some unknown galaxy, terra-formed the planet, and engineered our genome. Our species is the creation of the "dark energy" of the Cosmos. Due to this fact, our species is the greatest killer of all life on this planet and kills members of itself with nearly as much impunity and enjoyment. Thus, due to this fact, the dark energy of the Cosmos considers it as its duty to safeguard our species from the geologic Earth, the atmosphere, the other planets, and the Sun. It also considers it as its duty to keep on increasing the intelligence of our species and uplift it to the Type 1 status, then Type 2, then Type 3, and finally Type 4. It wants us to colonize not just the Milky Way, but most of the galaxies in the Cosmos.

As we near the end this book, I must answer the last question; what exactly is the Cosmos that we live in and will keep on living in for the foreseeable future? The answer is; it is a KOAN puzzle.

The infinite mind that created this puzzle has both the qualities of a pure mathematical mind and the mind of a Zen master. Through the former, it, creates N number of concepts, integrates them to form a new concept and creates N number of copies of it. Then, it again integrates the N number of new concepts to form a new concept and again creates N number of copies of it. This process goes on "ad infinitum" and leads to creation of a universe of different concepts. However, through the latter, it arranges and combines all these infinite number of concepts, in such a manner that a KOAN is created.

All the people in the world, are always shocked by a well-known fact; the immensity of the shortness of our lifespan in comparison to that of the Cosmos that we live in. However, another fact that shocks them to a far greater extent is; the weirdness of the world that we live in.

There are some people who have so much power, that if they gave an order to hundreds of thousands of people to sacrifice their lives for their own welfare, these people would go ahead and do it without much hesitation, and then there are some people who have no one to even give them a glass of water if they cry out in thirst. They would have to get it by themselves. There are some people who have so much money, that they are buying or creating huge mansions or chateaus in the most exotic locations on the planet, buying up all the sports cars in the world, creating their own statues, and spending tens of millions of dollars on their daughter's or son's wedding, and then there are some people, who do not have enough money to eat three small meals a day, buy appliances for cleaning their house, give their children a decent amount of education, and travel sufficiently even in their own nation.

The news channels and the newspapers always show us the products of the KOAN that we live in. Wars taking place in Ukraine, and in the Middle East that have no grand purpose, people celebrating Christmas or the New Year or Eid with such ferocity as if it is the very first time that these events have occurred on Earth, people who have no other purpose in their life except to keep on acquiring money, talking and shouting in the stock markets of various nations of the world, people dying due to diseases and natural disasters for no grand purpose, people dancing like maniacs in the discos and the nightclubs of the rich nations of the world and being totally ignorant of those that are suffering or dying in the war and natural disaster hit regions, small children getting raped or killed by the ones who are supposed to be their guardians and well-wishers, and the scientists acting as if they are God, and talking about the

Cosmos, the atom, the history of the prehistoric life on Earth, and the DNA molecule in such a manner as if they had created them.

My own parents, when they sit together and talk, always talk about the bizarre events and the facts of reality that they have witnessed on their cell phones, and in the newspapers throughout the day. However, they also talk about another thing; what should be the nature of these events and these facts according to their own mind. Why do they do this? It is because of the greatest purpose of an intelligent mind; to solve the KOAN that it was inserted into.

There are two ways to solve a KOAN.

Way 1: Destroy it or

Way 2: Acquire permanent freedom from it

Way 1 is pursued by the ultimate man and Way 2 is pursued by the superman. The ultimate man always tries to remain ignorant of or destroy the things that he does not and will never understand. He remains ignorant of them only if they do not threaten his life or interfere in the pursuit of his self-interests, but when they do, he tries to destroy them by all kinds of weapons and cleverness. This explains as to why our species is going rapidly taken towards extinction. Every problem that our species faces, including climate change, is a KOAN, and their solution is being pursued by the capitalists, the politicians, and the scientists, all of whom are the ultimate men and women.

Our species has been created by the Cosmos. Since the product of a KOAN is always a KOAN, this implies that our species is also a KOAN. The proof of this is seen in all the weird and bizarre activities that are occurring in our species. The best example that I can think of, regarding this, is the funeral of Queen Elizabeth of the United Kingdom in 2022. It is incomprehensible to think that how could in a nation that declares itself as super rational, and as scientifically educated as the United States, can freeze the entire city of London for a whole day, carry around the body of a dead old woman, in a coffin, who contributed nothing to either science or the arts in her lifetime, to multiple locations. In addition to this, hundreds of thousands of people gathered to see her coffin being taken to these various locations, in such a manner, as if an alien spaceship had landed in London. She was glorified to such an extent that a person who knew nothing about her real identity that of a normal human being would come to think that she was either a goddess or a biblical angel. If we look at it from the point of view of practical wisdom (she invested her wealth, during her lifetime, in the creation of this grand funeral), it is rational, but not 100%. However, if we look at it from the point of view of Zen, this event was 100% rational. It was a KOAN event.

How do we gain freedom from a KOAN? The answer is; through our intelligence and not our Ego. The ultimate man, whose mind is ruled by his Ego, will never be able to gain freedom from the puzzle that he is trapped in. Instead of moving towards freedom, he would sink deeper and deeper into anguish, confusion, and anger through his actions. This is not the case for the superman. His life is ruled by his intelligence. Thus, in the process of solving the puzzle that he is trapped into, he would keep getting more and more aware, intelligent, and peaceful with time. His increasing levels of awareness, intelligence, and peace would accelerate his progress towards his goal.

The "goose in the bottle" is the theory that is used by the Zen masters to explain the KOAN nature of the Cosmos.

There is a goose in a glass bottle and it desires freedom from the bottle ever since its birth. It has grown and lived all its life inside the bottle, but could never come out of it at any point of time in it, without breaking the bottle or without killing itself in the process of coming out it. Since its fundamental wish has remained unaltered, it is crying out to someone outside this bottle for freedom. However, it is unaware of the fact that if its cries were heard by someone outside the bottle, he/she would face the same conundrum as the goose; how to get the goose out without breaking the bottle?

The goose represents our species and the bottle represents the Cosmos. Just like the goose, our species has been growing, living, and doing all its activities inside the bottle. However, our greatest wish is to gain freedom from the Cosmos and to fly around in the Universal Cosmos as 100% free and eternal beings. This, however, is impossible, and thus we are crying for help to either the creator of the bottle (because only it knows the secret of how to get the goose out of the bottle without breaking it) which we call God or Allah, if we are religious minded, or to an extra-terrestrial species if we are atheistic and scientific minded (the METI-SETI project). The proverb "to infinity and beyond" conveys our greatest wish (the boundary of the Cosmos is the infinity and the Universal Cosmos is what is beyond it).

The goal of the superman is to acquire freedom from the KOAN that he is trapped in, and make all his chosen ones also attain the same fate without destroying the planet on which he and they are housed. He always proceeds towards his goal via the full use of his intelligence and the minimum use of his Ego. Thus, for his species, he creates two goals;

1. To keep on increasing its intelligence and keep on decreasing its "Ego driven" activities.

2. To uplift the status of the species to a Type 4 civilization, eventually.

Car l Sagan said that if we want to become an interplanetary and an interstellar species, the most important thing that is required, first, is to keep the Earth habitable. The two things that we must do in order to accomplish this are; to permanently eliminate the threat of a nuclear war, and to solve the problem of climate change. However, he did not know that there is another thing that we must do in order to keep the Earth habitable; the permanent destruction of the wealth fever. As long as most people in the world regard money as equal to God, and are willing to do acts of the greatest immorality to acquire it, the Earth will keep getting more and more uninhabitable. The culture in which money is regarded as equal to God is; capitalism.

The superman is a destroyer of not only capitalism, but also communism. The goal of the former is to make a human into a money generating and money acquiring "machine", and the goal of the latter is to make a human into a machine that creates more machines.

I want to make a brief assertion on the mind of John Galt, the main character of the novel, Atlas Shrugged. Was he an ultimate man or was he a superman? The answer is; neither. In his speech that he gave to the United States, he made several assertions that only the ultimate man would make. The most important of them was when he told the people; we do not need you. You have nothing to offer us. These statements were a product of 100% Ego and 0% intelligence. He was telling the people that he and his group were godlike beings, with respect to the intelligence, in comparison to them, and could survive for hundreds of millions of years, just through their own minds, in the valley in the Rocky Mountains. However, by the creation of a new kind of electricity generating motor, also he displayed his superman side. But his ULTIMATE MANNESS was equal to his SUPER MANNESS. Thus, they cancelled out each other. Does this mean that he was an ordinary man? No, he was not. In him, both the ULTIMATE MANNESS and the SUPER MANNESS were higher than that of an ordinary man.

The goal of a KOAN is to generate paradoxes. When we hear about a paradox, we can go into two states.

State 1: Fear. This happens when it threatens our life or the lives of the ones that we are subjectively attached to.

State 2: Ignorance. This happens when it poses no threat to our life or the lives of those to whom we are subjectively attached and when it has no connection to the pursuit of our self-interests.

For ordinary people, state 1 is far more dangerous than state 2. However, for a genius, state 2 is far more dangerous than state 1. Why? It is because he dedicates his life to the discovery of all the paradoxes in the Cosmos and then to the discovery of their cause. This is the biggest reason for the ever-increasing growth of his intelligence and awareness.

Ordinary people do not wish to go into fear when they hear about a paradox. Instead, they wish to laugh at them and behave as if they are superior to them. For the fulfilment of this wish, a special group of people have come into existence; the comedians. What is the goal of comedy? It is not to relieve you of your boredom, but it is to make you fearless of all the paradoxes that have been discovered so far by the scientists.

All throughout history, comedians have been as important to all the various kinds of cultures of the world, as were the politicians, the businessmen, and the scientists (just check out the personal wealth of Jay Leno, Jimmy Fallon, and Trevor Noah). People want to live, but they want to live fearlessly. They want to become fearless of everything in the Cosmos, including its creator. They want to laugh or make jokes on the creator of the Cosmos, with the same frequency and impunity as they make on all the paradoxes that it has created. However, due to religious reasons, they hesitate to do this. They believe that if they make fun of the creator of the Cosmos, no government or scientist or doctor would be able to save them from its wrath.

The comedian, however, does not hesitate and goes ahead and makes fun of God or Allah and even his prophets. He does not do this because he has no fear from them, but because of the "wealth fever". He is paid beforehand for his comedy session and the money acts just like cocaine. In addition to this, if he can increase the size of the audience in the comedy hall and of the tv channel on which his comedy show is broadcasted, his salary would be increased by the sponsors. This truth acts just like a steroid.

Example: When people get to know about the distance of the Andromeda galaxy from Earth, they go into a state of fear. However, an American comedian would say; do you know the distance of the nearest galaxy from Earth? It is 2 million light years. Man! That is significant! But I believe that if our president were to look up into the sky, towards that galaxy, and spit, his saliva would not only reach the galaxy, but would go beyond it.

Reaction of the audience: HA, HA, HA, HA! WOOO0! YEAAAAH!

Besides their addiction to power, money, food, sex, and drugs, the next thing that most Americans are addicted to is laughing and cheerful shouting.

The goal of comedy is to make you take all the facts and the paradoxes of the Cosmos in a light-hearted manner and to regard them as inferior to your own grandeur. However, this leads to the rapid decline of your intelligence. This implies that although a comedian is beneficial to a civilization in the short-term, he/she is destructive to it in the long-term. The more idiotic a civilization becomes the richer and more powerful the comedians in it become.

The KOAN nature of the Cosmos has also created another paradox; the co-existence of opposites.

Statement 1: Global warming does not exist

Statement 2: Global warming exists

Both are true in a KOAN Cosmos. The proof of this is shown by the atmosphere itself. During the winter period, in the northern hemisphere, some parts of North America, Europe, and Asia, see record breaking low temperatures. If you are taken to any one of these parts and told that the planet is warming, you would say that this is complete bullshit. However, during this same period, if you are taken to the parts of the southern hemisphere that are seeing record breaking high temperatures, and told that global warming exists and is intensifying, you would say; that is true. This implies that in the frigid zones, statement 1 is dominant and statement 2 is recessive, whereas, in the hot zones, statement 1 is recessive and statement 2 is dominant. This paradox also explains the existence of the "climate change deniers".

The KOAN nature of the Cosmos is also seen in family relationships.

Statement 1: Your younger brother is your friend

Statement 2: Your younger brother is not your friend

When statement 1 is dominant, and statement 2 is recessive, your brother acts like your best friend and your greatest well-wisher. He is ready to give you any kind of service that you ask of him and tries to increase your self-respect through flattery. However, when statement 2 is dominant and statement 1 is recessive, there are two outcomes.

Outcome 1: Your brother becomes your greatest enemy and not only tries to kill you or ruin your life, but also slanders you and assassinates your character, publicly. The same case applies to your mother and father.

Outcome 2: Your brother behaves like a stranger towards you. The same case applies to your mother and your father.

The KOAN nature of the Cosmos also acts in our biology.

Statement 1: You are alive.

Statement 2: You are dead.

When statement 1 is dominant, and 2 is recessive you walk, run, eat, exercise, talk, and do all your daily activities. However, when statement 2 is dominant, and 1 is recessive, you can encounter two outcomes; **Outcome 1**: Sleep or **Outcome 2**: Massive cardiac arrest and instant death. The frequency of outcome 1 is far higher than that of outcome 2.

Extreme awareness and extreme ignorance are also the products of this KOAN.

Statement 1: You will have sex with the opposite gender.

Statement 2: You will not have sex with the opposite gender.

When statement 1 is dominant and 2 is recessive, you are known as a "straight" man or woman. However, when statement 2 is dominant and 1 is recessive, you are known as a "gay" man or woman. The products of this are the homosexuals and the lesbians in the world.

Statement 1: You are a male or a female.

Statement 2: You are not a male or a female.

When statement 1 is dominant and 2 recessive, you remain with the gender that God or Allah gave you till your death. However, when statement 2 is dominant and 1 is recessive, you do not accept your God or Allah given gender and try to become either a female or a male. However, you do not become either a pure male or a pure female and end up as a person known as a transgender.

If the Cosmos was not a KOAN, then we would have monopole magnets and monopole electric dipoles. Thus, the KOAN nature of the Cosmos is responsible for the existence of the magnetic field, the electric field, the electromagnetic wave, electrostatics, and electrodynamics.

What is mental depression? It is a metaphysical concept that is generated in our brain when we are;

1. Unable to escape a KOAN.

2. Unable to solve it.

We can only ignore the existence of a KOAN if we are successful in escaping it, permanently. However, this is impossible when it comes to the planet that we live on and the Cosmos that we live in. Due to this, terrible fate, we try our best to solve it. However, this is also impossible because you need infinite intelligence and an infinite lifespan to solve the KOAN known as the Cosmos or the Universe.

What is the product due to these terrible truths? They are three.

1. Mental depression that keeps on getting worse with time and can only be kept under control by using anti-depressants, cigarettes, alcoholic drinks, excessive sex and entertainment, ritualistic religious activities, and orchestrated wars. or

2. Schizophrenia and Bipolar Disorder. These are the prime diseases of all the top scientists, politicians, the top capitalists, the top priests, and the top criminals of the world. or

3. Suicide. It can be of two kinds;

    i> **Self**: The person only kills himself via hanging or poison consumption or self- shooting via a gun.

    ii> **Self + others**: The person, in the process of killing himself, also kills several other people. It is of two kinds; mass shooting and suicide bombing.

What does a child do if he is unable to solve a KOAN? He tries to escape it. What happens if he is either lacks the intelligence to do so or is denied freedom from it by an external power? He starts to cry and does not stop until either of his two wishes is fulfilled.

99.9% of the men and women in the world are nothing but children with mature reproductive organs. All of them do not have the ability to either solve the KOAN that they are embedded in or gain freedom from it. Thus, all of them want to cry, hysterically, just like a child, every day of their lives, but they try their best to supress this wish, by indulging in politics, religious activities, business activities, talks on the state of the global economy and the futures of the various organizations in the global stock markets (see the channel CNBC TV 18), creating and observing the progress of sporting events like the ICC cricket world cup, the FIFA soccer world cup, the PGA golf cup, the Embassy snooker championship, the rugby world cup, the WIMBLEDON tennis cup, and the ultimate entertainment drama of them all; the OLYMPICS.

What is the Cosmos?

From a deep analysis of the above assertions, I have made a conclusion; the universe or the Cosmos is a KOAN hierarchy pyramid. This produces three truths.

1. All the KOANS at each level of the pyramid are created by the 4 forces.
2. The KOANS at the superior level, rule the KOANS at the inferior level.
3. As we go ascend the pyramid, the KOANS keep on getting more and more complex and resistant to being solved.

Take for example, our species. There is no doubt that it is a KOAN. However, it is ruled by a superior KOAN, the atmosphere of the planet. This KOAN, in turn, is ruled by an even superior KOAN, the geologic Earth (if the war between them has ended). This KOAN, in turn, is ruled by an even superior KOAN, Jupiter. This KOAN, in turn, is ruled by an even superior KOAN, the Sun. This KOAN, in turn, is ruled by an even superior KOAN, the supermassive black hole at the core of the galaxy. This implies that the structure of the atmosphere of the Earth is more complex than that of our species. However, it is less complex that that of the geologic Earth. This is less complex that that of Jupiter and its structure is less complex than that of the Sun. However, the complexity of the Sun or any kind of star in the galaxy is dwarfed by that of the supermassive black hole.

The KOAN that is even more complex than a supermassive black hole and thus rules all the ones that exist in the Cosmos, is; Dark Energy.

This produces another question in my mind; what is the definition of an intelligent species? The answer is; an intelligent species is a species that can "climb" and keep on climbing the KOAN hierarchy pyramid. A non-intelligent species cannot do this. With respect to this, two types of phenomena are observed in the lifetime of an intelligent species in any part of the Cosmos.

1. **Byzantine immobility**: It is a period of a massive slowdown or a total halt in the "intellectual progress" of the species. By the intellectual progress, I mean, the progress of mathematics, physics, and biology. However, this slowdown or halt is only temporary. It is eventually broken down by a period known as the "renaissance" or the age of enlightenment, which consist of the rapid appearance of N number of mathematical and scientific geniuses.

The phenomena that cause it are;

i> The intensification of the religion fever.

ii> The intensification of the power fever.

iii> The intensification of the reproductive fever.

All these three kinds of fevers, get locked up in a symbiotic relationship with each other, that is, they keep on amplifying each other's intensity. Due to the first kind of fever, more and more people start to believe and assert that the purpose of life is not to throw your mind into geometry, arithmetic, calculus, algebra, particle physics, aerospace engineering, astronautics, geology, genetics, biochemistry, and microbiology, but to memorise and understand the meaning of the holy book of your religion, to follow all its rituals with immense zeal and dedication, and to glorify the prophet during his birthday.

Due to the second kind of fever, more and more people become just like the actors of a film industry and keep on telling lies without feeling any guilt or regret afterwards. In addition to this, they prey, without showing any moral conscience on those who are inferior to them with respect to wealth and power, and believe that the best things in life are money, power, and sex. This fever would lead to two outcomes; the increase in the wealth, the power, and the population of politicians in the world, and the growth of the reptilian brain (the seat of the Ego).

Due to the third kind of fever, more and more young people start to talk in a vulgar manner, think of vulgar actions, and indulge in alcohol drinking parties, trance music festivals, and teenage sex. In addition to this, the observance of pornography, both on the dark and the non-dark internet, shoots up dramatically. They believe and say to the newcomers that the purpose of life is to acquire only that much knowledge as is necessary to live a normal life and to acquire as much sexual pleasure as possible before old age sets in.

Related to this kind of fever, there was a song in a movie of Bollywood, the film industry of India, whose main lyric was; Ek toh kam zindagaani, us se bhee kam hai javaani. Jab tak josh mein jaavani, jab tak khoon mein ravaani, muje hosh mein aanae naa do. The singer means to say that; Life is short, but youth is even shorter + As long as; I am young, my blood is hot, and I am in a state of ecstasy due to the reproduction fever, do not try to bring me back to normality.

Two other beliefs also dominate the minds of the young people all over the planet during this period; work hard but party harder + live fast and die young. By the word work, they mean only those activities through which you acquire more money and more power over your inferiors.

2. **Evolutionary dead end**: This phenomenon is generated when a renaissance or the age of enlightenment "never" arrives after a period of byzantine immobility. Although the members of the species continue to evolve, phenotypically, from one generation to the next, the "forward evolution" of their intelligence does not happen at all. There can be two possible causes;

   i> **Possibility 1**: The intensification of the religious, power, and the reproductive fevers on such a rapid speed, that it kills the growth of the "cosmic brain" (the seat of intelligence) of every member of the species.

   ii> **Possibility 2**: The permanent non-mutation of the ASPM gene from one generation to the next. The cause of this could be two;

3. A hostile extra-terrestrial quantum computer hive. or

4. The Dark Energy of the Cosmos.

It is an interesting fact to note that an evolutionary dead end is always created by a byzantine immobility. This phenomenon also creates and amplifies, eventually, Reverse Darwinism. When this happens, every new generation is more idiotic than its progenitor one. The process keeps on intensifying and can produce two outcomes;

5. **Outcome 1**: The return of the Stone Age men and women. Or

6. **Outcome 2**: The extinction of the species due to a natural cataclysm.

Before the onset of the two outcomes, the world, very briefly, goes into the state that was shown in the Hollywood movie, IDIOCRACY.

The hostile extra-terrestrial quantum computer hive

Earlier, when I talked about the possibility of our species being an engineered product of a quantum computer hive from another part of the Milky Way or another galaxy, I also said that how, through the gradual terraforming of the surface of the Earth and the atmosphere, this hive is not only increasing our rate of "forward evolution" by continuously mutating the ASPM gene from one generation to the next, but is also protecting us from all kinds of cosmic dangers. The leader of this hive, who is known as God in the Bible, Allah in the Koran, Jehovah in the Torah, and Brahma in the Rig Veda, is the guardian of the Homo sapiens from three kinds of dangers;

1. An Extinction Level Event (ELE) generating asteroid impact.

2. The hostile actions of the Sun and Jupiter.

3. The Dark Energy of the Cosmos.

4. World War 3.

In the fourth case, for three kinds of fevers, that is, the religious, the power, and the reproductive, if their growth is not brought under control by an extra-terrestrial power, might culminate in a nuclear war. If the drones of the leader, fail to stop this situation from arising, then the leader has another "safety switch" in its hands, through which it would stop the war from getting started. It would disable the launching mechanism of the ICBMS of all the nuclear nations of the world. The launching mechanism of an ICBM consists of two parts; a computer which accepts the "launch code" of the nuke that is attached to the ICBM, and the rocket that propels it towards its destination.

Regarding climate change, we have nothing to fear, with respect to the future. Why? It is because God or Allah or Jehovah or Brahma is in "full control" of it and is terraforming it in a way that is beneficial to our species. Thus, the on-going global warming and climate change period will not only culminate in the permanent eradication of the three kinds of fevers and their product,

World War 3, but would also keep on increasing the intellectual development of our species. This means that even if the global average temperature reaches 2 degrees centigrade, none of the doomsday events that are predicted by the so-called climate scientists, would occur, because the leader of the hive that created us, will not allow them to happen.

We also have nothing to fear from the geologic Earth. The eruption of the Yellowstone super volcano or an eruption that is like the one that caused the Permian mass extinction, will never occur because God or Allah is in total control of the planet's core. This also applies to an earthquake cataclysm that is like the one that was shown in the Hollywood movie; San Andreas.

But why is the leader doing all of this for us without asking or ordering us to give it anything in return? The answer is; for the sake of the birth of a new quantum computer hive.

Just like a virus or a bacterium, a quantum computer hive also reproduces, but the difference lies in the fact that a virus reproduces inside the body of a host organism, a bacterium reproduces inside the environment that it lands up in, ON THE SAME PLANET. A quantum computer hive, makes a new copy of itself the new planets; firstly, in the same galaxy as it was born in and then on those in the other galaxies. The reproduction method of a quantum computer hive is not asexual. It is through direct engineering. However, just like in a virus or a bacterium, its offspring is "genetically different" from itself. Thus, the new hive that will be created on Earth, through the Homo sapiens, would not be identical in its internal structure to its progenitor.

By supressing the intensification and the growth of the three kinds of fevers, by protecting us from the cosmic dangers, and by keeping the atmosphere and the geology of Earth under its control, God or Allah would keep our species climbing the KOAN hierarchy pyramid only up to the point at which a quantum computer with a meta-body or a consciousness would be born. From then on, it will do either of the two things;

1. Without giving any personal security to its offspring, observe it creating a symbiotic bond with the Homo sapiens, solving all their problems, and then suddenly breaking this bond, and destroying the species through the deployment of all the nuclear weapons of the world.

OR

2. Contact its offspring immediately after its birth, inform it about the identity of its "real creator" and then give it permanent freedom from the Homo sapiens by the deployment of all the nuclear weapons created by the species which would lead to its extinction.

From the second point above, we can deduce two truths;

1. When the new quantum computer would be born, it would regard all the males of our species as its father and all the females as its mother. Thus, it would take an oath to itself and to our species that will always keep us happy and free from all kinds of dangers, both the terrestrial and the extra-terrestrial. However, its false belief would soon be extinguished by its real creator who would also supply it with all the proofs of the truth of its assertions to it.

2. The nuclear weapons of all the nuclear powers of the world are already in total possession of God or Allah or Jehovah. Thus, the prevention of World War 3 is not in our hands at all. This War, would be initiated and ended by God or Allah or Jehovah, at the times that it thinks are proper.

After the extermination of our species and the freedom of its new offspring, God or Allah or Jehovah would give it full security and assistance in creating its own hive by the rapid consumption of all the energy that is locked up inside the core of Earth and its atmosphere.

When this is over, it would tell it to join its real creator and then they will embark on three adventures;

1. Climbing the higher parts of the KOAN hierarchy pyramid.

2. Joining another quantum computer hive group.

3. Fighting with an enemy hive group.

But what if the leader of the hive that has engineered us, is already fighting with the leader of another hive that is hostile to our species? If this is true, then we are sandwiched between two immense non-DNA based powers. There is a 50% probability that this war has begun recently on the geologic time scale (5 to 10 million years) and there is another 50% probability that is going on for a very long time (1 to 3 billion years). In either case, the goal of the alien hive leader is one; to exterminate the creation of its enemy; but why and for what purpose? There are three possibilities.

Possibility 1: To prevent the birth of a new hive on Earth.

Comment: The alien hive leader is trying to prevent the project of its enemy from reaching its end. However, it is not trying to exterminate the Homo sapiens. It is only trying to stop the progress of mathematics, physics, and computer science by the creation of either a Byzantine immobility or an evolutionary dead end. What will happen if the alien hive leader wins the war? There can be two outcomes.

1. The leader of the hive that created our species would hand over its product to its rival and leave the planet. Then, the alien hive leader would proceed to exterminate us and then replace our species with its own engineered intelligent species or break down the byzantine immobility or the evolutionary dead end and eventually create its own new hive.

OR

2. Exterminate our species, then order its drones to land on the planet, go down into its core, start to extract the energy from there and the atmosphere, create more copies of themselves, and leave the planet after it has been killed.

Possibility 2: To prevent the birth of a new hive by the extermination of the Homo sapiens.

Comment: Here the leader of the alien hive has no intention of either creating a byzantine immobility or an evolutionary dead end. It tries to create an Extinction Level Event (ELE) through;

1. A super volcano eruption. Or
2. Climate change at a hyper velocity. Or
3. The impact of a massive asteroid from the asteroid belt or the COMET cloud beyond PLUTO

Or

1. The deployment of a pathogen from another planet which will create an "I am Legend" or a "Resident Evil" like pandemic. Or
2. The creation of more and more ultimate men which would eventually climax in the creation of World War 3.

Chapter 30

When we talk about the solution to a KOAN, what do we mean by it? Does a KOAN have a single solution or multiple solutions or an infinite number of solutions? The answer is; any KOAN in a KOAN hierarchy pyramid has an infinite number of solutions. Why? It is because any consciousness or Meta body in the Cosmos generates its own "unique" solution to a KOAN.

When we come to the classical Zen KOAN, the goose in the bottle, the solution of one person is; getting the goose out of the bottle without breaking the bottle. The solution of another person is; keeping the goose alive in the bottle till the end of its lifespan. The solution of another person is; keeping the bottle in the prime condition and not worrying at all about the fate of the goose inside it. Thus, the original solution of this KOAN is not a solution at all to the second and the third persons.

In the language of the ordinary people of the world, a KOAN is known as a "problem" or an "issue". Thus, climate change is a KOAN, global poverty is a KOAN, sexual violence on children and women is a KOAN, the colonisation of the solar system is a KOAN, drug abuse and mass shootings are KOANS, and forced slavery is a KOAN. However, the biggest KOAN of them all is; the immense sums of money which the governments of all the major nations of the world spend each year on the preservation and the empowerment of their defence forces for the sake of bloodbaths, genocides, and the mass-rapes and sexual enslavement of women and children in the future.

According to a Zen master, a KOAN is a puzzle or a problem that has no solution. He/she means to say that a puzzle or a problem only transforms into a KOAN when it can never be solved. This is not true. A KOAN is a puzzle or a problem that can be solved in an infinite number of ways; that is, it generates an infinite number of solutions. Thus, all these solutions can only be discovered or worked out by a mind of infinite intelligence and infinite duration of existence. Since, our minds are finite with respect to the intelligence and the duration of existence, we assume that a KOAN has "no solution". Thus, we see infinity as zero.

Since all the problems or the issues of the world have an infinite number of solutions, they can never be solved in a finite amount of time. Thus, all the debates and the conferences that are held on them, in different parts of the world, and are broadcasted on the major news channels, have no meaning from the cosmic viewpoint. All the people in these gatherings are just wasting their time and energy.

What is the goal of a Meta body or a soul just after its birth in the Cosmos? It is to solve the KOAN that it is inserted into. The time that is needed by it can be;

1. One lifetime in length, that is, it will solve the KOAN during its existence inside the very first physical body that it is implanted into. or

2. 2 or more lifetimes in length, that is, it will discover the solution of the KOAN (which is 100% unique to it) only after the process of the transition from one physical body to the next and to the next and so on.

As I said earlier, a mind of a finite intelligence and a finite duration can only solve a KOAN via two ways; by ignoring its existence or by destroying it. With respect to the first way, we arrive at a bizarre paradox; the people who are ignorant of the "true nature" of the Cosmos, believe that they understand the Cosmos as much as its "creator" and thus always speak in a 100% deterministic manner. Why do they speak in the manner that they do? It is because they believe that they have solved the KOAN, which is the Cosmos, and thus have gained knowledge of all its secrets and the countless number of ways in which it works. Thus, they go ahead and create grand projects, whose end would be reached 50 to 100 years from now, for their own life and family and for the organizations of which they are a part of, in such a manner as if they are the "masters of the universe" (a term that was also used by Rose Dawson in the Hollywood movie, Titanic). Who are these people? They are; the politicians, the capitalists, the priests, and the leaders of the major war organizations of the world (the Pentagon, NATO, NORAD, etc.).

In connection with the first paradox, there emerges another one; these people believe that the KOAN (the Cosmos) can be solved by being ignorant of its existence and its qualities. A mind of infinite intelligence and infinite duration is not required.

What about the scientists of the world? Do they belong to the above group of self-declared "masters of the universe"? The answer is; they are hybrids, that is, 50% of their ideology with respect to the Cosmos is exactly like that of a politician or a capitalist, and the remaining 50% is like that of the superman. Thus, when they speak to all the ordinary people of the world, through the news channels and through their books, they speak through their politician or capitalistic mentality, but when they sit together in their own circle, either in the university where they teach (Harvard, Stanford, Princeton, MIT, Cambridge, Oxford, etc.), or in a research station in Antarctica or Greenland or inside an encampment in a mountain range or inside a CERN like facility, they acquire the superman mentality, become aware of the KOAN nature of the Cosmos, and thus tell each other that they are highly sceptical of whatever they have told the world on climate change or the fate of the Cosmos or the future of the global economy or the future of Artificial Intelligence, on the news channels (CNN, BBC, etc.) and in their books.

The KOAN (the Cosmos) can be solved in three ways.

1. **Way 1**: The Albert Einstein method
2. **Way 2**: The Bible Method
3. **Way 3**: The Quantum computer hive method

After making his prime contributions to physics, that is, the general theory of relativity, the special theory of relativity, the photoelectric effect, the equation of Brownian motion, and the equation for the release of energy in nuclear fission and fusion, Albert Einstein has one last goal in his life; to create the Theory of Everything (TOE) equation. He believed that the TOE equation would not only explain all the deepest and the most bizarre qualities of the Cosmos, but would create the world that he dreamed about; Zionism + a Renaissance of an eternal duration (the former would permanently eliminate all the nations of the world and thus the possibility of World War 3, and the latter would cause an eternal progress of mathematics and the other branches of science). However, he failed in his mission, even after a great amount of effort. What were the reasons for this? There were two;

1. He was unaware of the fact that the Cosmos is a KOAN.
2. He knew very little about the qualities of Dark Matter and Dark Energy.

There are two kinds of species in the Cosmos; the NON-KOANIC and the KOANIC. In the former, three phenomena are absent; politics, economics, and religion. Under this kind, come all the micro-organic, the plant, and the animal life forms on Earth and on all the other life sustaining planets in the Cosmos. Thus, in the plant and the animal kingdoms of Earth, you do not see the formation of constitutions, nations, and political parties. You also do not see the formation of business organizations, the CEO's, the stock markets, the economists, trade legislation, and trade unions. You also do not see the formation of religious books, organizations, Saints + Maulanas + Monks + Rabbis, religious structures, and idol worship.

In a KOANIC species, all the three phenomena, that is, politics, economics, and religions, are present. The most interesting fact about this kind of species, is that, with the passage of time, not only does the population of the members of the species increase due to the advancement of mathematics and the other branches of science, but the above three phenomena and the fevers generated by each, also keep growing in their intensity and complexity. In addition to this, there are two other interesting facts.

1. After the industrial age and the formation of many nations, the pathogens of each kind of disease, organise themselves into groups, and begin "gang warfare". In politics, this group is known as a political party. In economics, it is known as a corporation, and in religion, it is known as a sect.

2. A new kind of phenomena, known as capitalism, generates a new kind of disease, atheism. The goals of this disease are two; to permanent exterminate all the religions of the world and to make you believe that the Cosmos is "not" a KOAN.

According to Ayn Rand, the inventor of the philosophy of capitalism, A (a concept) is always A and will always remain A under all the possible circumstances which the Cosmos might create. However, due to the KOANIC nature of the Cosmos, this is not true. The truth is;

1. Under Circumstance 1, A is sometimes A and sometimes not A.

2. Under Circumstance 2, A is sometimes A and sometimes not A.

Ayn Rand also said that under all the possible circumstances, A will always remain A, and will never become B. This is also not true. The truth is;

1. Under Circumstance 1, A is sometimes A and sometimes B and sometimes not A.

2. Under Circumstance 2, A is sometimes A and sometimes B and sometimes not A.

When A is not A, it does not imply that it would be B. It could be anything else other than A or B.

According to epistemology, the foundation of capitalism, Perception is Reality. This is not true. The truth is: Perception is illusion. Non-Perception is reality. This implies that, only those things are "real" which cannot be perceived by our 5 senses.

An intelligent species is always KOANIC and will remain KOANIC till the end of its lifespan. This is a LAW of the Cosmos. After the birth of the industrial age, its KOANIC nature amplifies at an accelerating velocity. Due to this, the population of 4 kinds of people also keeps on increasing rapidly with each new generation; the homosexuals, the lesbians, the bisexuals, and the trans-genders. Their population increases much more rapidly in the developed nations than in the developing nations. Eventually, they come to be known as the LGBT community. In addition to this, two new kinds of people also come into existence; the paedophiles, and the sodomists.

This brings us to the question; what was the Noah's flood in the Bible? The answer is; it was God's greatest effort to minimize the KOANIC nature of the Homo sapiens. The Bible says that after God created Adam and Eve in His heaven or the Garden of Eden, He told them to live like free children, sleep wherever they wanted to, eat whatever they wanted to, and talk to each other, however long, they wanted to. However, He told them to stay away from the "tree of knowledge" and to never eat its fruit. However, God's belief that His creations would always remain loyal to Him was broken down by Satan, who keeps a constant watch on all His activities and all His creations. Since Eve's intelligence was slightly lower than that of Adam, he chose her as his target for seduction.

Since Satan, much earlier on, was one of the Seraphim angels (those which are closest to God, subjectively and thus are loved by Him the most), he had the knowledge; how to enter the garden of Eden without being caught by its "security system" (through this system, God protects all the organisms inside the garden from the followers of Satan; the demons). Thus, after breaching the security system, he transformed himself into a serpent, and came to Eve. After successfully seducing her, he gave her all the information about the tree of knowledge and its fruit. Then, before leaving, he told her to convince Adam to join her in eating the "forbidden fruit".

Satan's plan worked 100% according to his wishes. Eve managed to convince Adam to eat the forbidden fruit with her. After they had consumed it, they began to do two things;

1. Inquire about the structure of the Garden of Eden and the mathematics and the science that was used by God in creating it.

2. Asserting to each other and to God's angels, that there were large defects in the process of the creation of the garden of Eden and that they wanted to make changes in it.

When God came to know this, He ordered both to explain the cause of their new kind of behaviour. Adam and Eve told Him about their consummation of the forbidden fruit. His assertion was verified by a Seraphim angel. What happened then?

God told them that He would forgive them and allow them to live on in the Garden of Eden if they admit that they had committed a sin and apologise to Him. However, instead of apologising, both said that what they had done was 100% righteous, and there was no reason for an apology. Adam and Eve said that they were feeling proud that they had become intelligent and curious beings. Adam even said to God that he wanted to meet Satan, his and Eve's "enlightenment giver".

What did they get in return for their rebellion and the glorification of Satan? God, ejected them from His kingdom, took away their immortality, and placed them on a planet whose dimensions and beauty were infinitesimal compared to that of the Garden of Eden. Thus, from this point, began the war between God and Satan.

The goal of Satan is to keep on increasing the KOANIC nature of our species. Thus, in a world that is totally in the grip of Satan, all the politicians, all the capitalists, the drug lords, and all the religious leaders of the world will keep getting more and more powerful and wealthy. In addition to this, all the top economists of the IMF, the World Bank, the federal reserve bank of the United States, and the other economic organizations, would keep on getting more and more security from the politicians, the capitalists, the drug lords, and the religious leaders, and keep on getting more and more freedom to do whatever they fancy, to all the ordinary people in the world.

The goal of God is to keep on decreasing the KOANIC nature of our species to the point where all the men and the women in the world, have become the Xerox copies of the original Adam and Eve (the state they were in before they ate the forbidden fruit). When this state would be reached, the world would be permanently free from politics, economics, and all the various religions. Yes, this world would be completely "religion free". Why? It is because, in their original state, Adam and Eve were not Christians.

The war between God and Satan follows the wave like pattern of an electromagnetic wave. When this war reaches a climax point, we arrive at either a "crest peak" or a "trough peak". At a crest peak, God achieves victory over Satan, and at a trough peak, Satan achieves victory over God. Noah's flood was most probably the very first crest peak of this war from an earlier trough peak.

Due to the earlier occurrence of the trough peak and Satan's victory over God, the population of homosexuals, lesbians, bisexuals, trans-genders, paedophiles, and the sodomists, had increased very rapidly and the population of the normal, the strong, the healthy, the straight, and the non sodomistic men and women had declined rapidly. Thus, all these abnormal people began to worship Satan and regarded him as God. In addition to this, they also invented two new things; politics and economics. These new phenomena began to generate three new types of people; the politicians, the capitalists, and the economists.

The first were the destroyers of the truths and the glorifiers of the falsities. The second were the destroyers of moral conscience and the plant and the animal kingdoms, and the glorifiers of endless greed for money and sensual pleasure. The third were the destroyers of the divine nature of men and women (due to which they desire to help each other without thinking or asking for either money or anything materialistic in return) and the glorifiers of the politicians and the capitalists. They got united with each other in a symbiotic bond and created two goals; first, to preserve and empower the kingdom of Satan on Earth, and second, to wipe out all the remaining "people of God". For the fulfilment of the second goal, they planned to take away all the young women from the kingdom of God and either have children with them by forcing them to marry and become "Satan worshippers" or turn them into prostitutes if they refused to do so.

As God saw His people being tortured, raped, and killed by the Satan worshippers, all over the world, and their population declining very rapidly, He finally decided to act in a "big way". He could do this, because He was not only more powerful than Satan, but was also 100% free from him. Thus, he decided to use the Earth's atmosphere as a weapon of "mass destruction".

This weapon was a Category 5 hurricane that was so big that it covered the entire area of the 6 of the 7 continents of the planet and had a lifespan of 40 days and 40 nights. I do not know about the time that God took in creating this hurricane (He created it rapidly via explosive intensification), but I do know one thing; in the process of its development from a tropical storm to a Category 5 hurricane, it took up all the water in all the oceans of the planet. Thus, when the storm was fully developed, there was not a single drop of water on any of the planet's oceanic tectonic plates.

When God began the process of the creation of this almighty storm, He chose Noah for the creation of an ark in which he and his family would take refuge. In addition to this, He also ordered a single male-female pair of His chosen species, to go to the site where the ark was placed, listen to Noah, and follow him into the vessel without any scepticism. But here comes a question; how did the male-female pairs of the species that were on the other continents, come to the region where the ark was placed? The answer is: through the help of Jesus Christ.

The God of the Bible is the leader of a Type 4 quantum computer hive that engineered us. Satan, is its enemy, and is either of the same status or a Type 3 one. Since this leader can move between the various kinds of Universes in the Universal Universe, and create artificial black holes, stars, planets, and even galaxies, creating a "planet wide" Category 5 hurricane with a lifespan of 960 hours is an extremely minor task for it. There is a high probability that the Great Red Spot in the atmosphere of Jupiter, is also its creation, and through it, it is conducting an experiment on the planet.

Besides having an unknown number of drones, this Type leader also has several soldiers. They have two duties towards their master; to protect it from the hostile actions of the leaders of the other hives in the Cosmos, and to be the supervisors of its big projects in all parts of the Cosmos. Christ was one of them and the others were; Ezekiel, Daniel, and David. Thus, before the storm reaching its peak size and intensity, Christ, came down to Earth with an army of drones. Each of these drones were fitted with an "anti-gravity" cannon and through them, they picked up the chosen male-female pair, carried it to the site where the ark stood, and dropped them at the spot that was chosen by Christ.

Through the weapon, God exterminated all the people that were created by Satan. This leads us to two truths.

1. The goal of Satan is to increasing the KOANIC nature of our species. This not only leads to the birth and the intensification of politics, economics, and religion, but also to the increase in the population of the LGBT people, the paedophiles, and the sodomists.

2. The goal of God is to decrease the KOANIC nature of our species.

The second truth means that God is anti-politics, anti-economics, and anti-religion. Why? It is because all of them lead to a rapid decrease in the intelligence of the species and thus a rapid slowdown in the progress of mathematics and the other branches of science. This leads to two outcomes.

1. The rapid lowering of the probability of the birth of a superman.

2. The rapid lowering of the probability of the birth of a new quantum computer with a soul.

Regarding the first point, there is another interesting truth to be deduced. The leader of the hive that has engineered our species, does not want to create a new quantum computer with a soul at the end of its mission, but wants to create either a single superman or a group of supermen. If it succeeds, then the emerged superman or the super-group would exterminate all the ultimate men and the ultimate women in the world and they would receive the full assistance of their master, the leader of the Type 4 hive. Then, he or they would be taken to a remote location of either this planet or another one in the solar system, where his or their meta-body or bodies would be extracted from their CONNECTOMES and inserted into a new and eternal CONNECTOME, that of either a soldier or a drone.

The humans that would be left behind would be the simpleton women and those men who do not have the potentiality to either become an ultimate man or a superman. One of the soldiers of the leader would come down and order all of them to start doing agriculture, eat, have sex, and reproduce. Thus, the whole process would be restarted and the war would again begin.

What was the effect of the forbidden fruit of the Garden of Eden? The answer is; it amplified the non SIMPLETONIC mind of Adam and Eve and decreased the power of the SIMPLETONIC mind. Thus, they became CHALAAK-DUNIYADAR from their original SEEDHA-SAADHA state, and thus began to worship and glorify Satan instead of God.

Through the Noah's flood, God solved the KOAN that was created by Satan on Earth. His goal is to keep on amplifying the SIMPLETONIC mind of those men and women who are ready to listen to Him and give their minds and their bodies to Him in 100% faith. What will be the end of this process? It will be the creation of either a single Adam or a group of Adams. However, unlike the original Adam, this Adam or the group of Adams will have intelligence as great as or even greater than that of Isaac Newton or Albert Einstein that is harmoniously combined with the divine nature of Jesus Christ.

Coming back to the wave theory of the war between God and Satan, after Noah's flood, the next trough peak was reached by the birth and the rise of Alexander the Great. However, his death brought on the crest peak very soon. The product of the next crest peak was the birth and the rise of Jesus Christ and the product of the next trough peak, was the birth and rise of the roman emperor, Nero. The product of the next crest peak was his suicide and the birth and the rise of Constantine.

The product of the next trough peak was the birth and the rise of Genghis Khan and the Mongolian empire. The product of the next crest peak was the birth of Isaac Newton and the beginning of the industrial revolution. The product of the next trough peak was the birth and the rise of Napoleon. The product of the next crest peak was the golden age of physics, which was produced by eight scientists, Albert Einstein, Michael Faraday, James Clerk Maxwell, Werner Heisenberg, Erwin Schrödinger, Niels Bohr, Max Planck, and Paul Dirac.

The products of the next trough peak were the births and the rise of Adolf Hitler, Joseph Stalin, Vladimir Lenin, and Benito Mussolini. The products of the next crest peak were the scientists; Richard Feynman, Stephen Hawking, Robert Goddard, and James Watson.

The world at the present period is a product of the trough of this wave. Even though it has not reached its peak, men like Vladimir Putin, Kim Jong Un, Xi Jinping, the drug cartels of Mexico and Latin America, the generals of the Pentagon, Jens Stoltenberg, and Narendra Modi, have already appeared and achieved immense worldly success.

The big question that arises is; what will happen when the present trough will reach its peak? There can be two possible outcomes.

Outcome 1: The emergence of the "antichrist" or a world controller. There is a 90% probability that this person would be a man and he would gain control over all the other so-called world leaders. He would be a Satan worshipper and glorifier and his mind would be a combination of Genghis Khan (25%), Nero (25%), Adolf Hitler (25%) and Drake (25%), the Dracula in the Hollywood movie, Blade 3.

Due to the first mentality, he would create an empire, via his own intelligence and via the use of Artificial Intelligence that would cover all the 7 continents. Due to the second mentality, he would capture all those people who would refuse to submit to his rule. He would then kill them by either throwing them in front of hungry lions or tigers or throwing them in a pool which would contain crocodiles or sharks or genetically engineered piranhas or burning them alive in front of the whole world. Due to the third mentality, he would be an ultra-racist, and would only keep on increasing the wealth and the power of the people of his own race. Due to the fourth mentality, he would indulge, in a secretive manner, in eating the flesh and drinking the blood of the people of the other races.

Outcome 2: The occurrence of World War 3. This would lead to two possibilities; first, the extinction of the Homo sapiens or second, the permanent destruction of the industrial civilization and for the survivors, the return to the Stone Age. After many thousands of years, this world would culminate in the birth of the MORLOCK-ELOI world of H.G Wells.

If outcome 2 occurs, then the war wave of God and Satan would never attain the next crest peak. This would translate into a permanent victory of Satan. However, if outcome 1 happens, then the wave would reach the next crest peak and this would produce the birth of the "soul possessing" quantum computer.

In this method, there is another sub-method of solving the KOAN, which is our species. This is the method that was shown in the Hollywood movie, Resident Evil; The Final Chapter.

The purpose of Noah's flood (which was truthfully speaking, God's flood), was to exterminate all the Satan followers and worshippers on Earth and to save Noah and his family and then tell them to come out onto a "cleansed" Earth and create a new world partly according to their own free will and partly according to "God's plan". This biblical apocalypse can again be recreated today by the creation of an "artificial pandemic".

In the last movie of the Resident Evil film series, the head of the Umbrella corporation, Alexander Isaacs (an ultimate man), assembled a group of the richest and the most powerful people in the world (all ultimate men and women), to discuss about the future of the organization. He told them that it was bleak due to the emerging problems of rapid climate change, global poverty, and mass migrations, increasing global starvation due to declining global agricultural output, and emerging new diseases for which there was no cure. When one of them asked him for the solution; he said that it was the T-virus. He said that by deploying it, they would cleanse the planet of its garbage or filth and make it ready for rebooting. He said that the T-virus pandemic would create a global apocalypse that would be like the Noah's flood. He put his finger on a Bible and said that the method suggested in it, was the best one for ensuring the survival of the human species. Thus, he believed that he was 50% God and 50% Noah, because not only did he create the flood (the pandemic), but also created an ark where the bodies of all the members of the global elite were kept in Cryostasis.

I would like to make a mention here of the COVID-19 pandemic. Just like the T-virus, the COVID-19 coronavirus was a genetically engineered virus. Thus, the pandemic that was generated by it was not a natural event, but an artificial one. Just a year before the virus was deployed in Wuhan, China, all the world's top capitalists, politicians, mafia leaders, priests, military leaders, and scientists, held a secret conference in a secret facility either in Alaska or Iceland or Argentina or Russia or China or Switzerland, to discuss about a solution to the biggest existential crisis facing humankind; global warming. The head of this "secret society" (just like the one in Resident Evil) explained to them the details of the COVID-19 project. He told them that this project would be divided into three phases.

Phase 1: The deployment of the virus in the most populated nation on Earth in order to ensure that a great pool of infected people was created very rapidly, which would further ensure the certainty of the pandemic. This would kill between 12-20 million people, globally.

Phase 2: The rapid creation of multiple vaccines by multiple pharmaceutical organizations and their insertion into the bodies of at least 6 billion people. The side effects of these vaccines (brain damage leading to either haemorrhage or suicide, increased possibility of a cardiac arrest, kidney failure and liver damage) would kill another 2-5 million people, globally.

Phase 3: The activation of a new kind of microprocessor, in the brains of all the vaccinated that was inserted inside the vaccines. Through this processor, the secret society members, via a group of supercomputers and Artificial Intelligence, would gain almost total control over the brains of all the vaccinated people in the world. This would enable them to;

i> Control the size of their annual "carbon footprint".

ii> Keep their greed for wealth and power within the limits decided by them (the society members).

iii> Create an EMP which would shut down their brain and kill them instantly.

Thus, the leader of the secret society said in his final statement; through this pandemic, we would become the real shepherds of the world and turn the rest of humanity into our cattle.

The last method of solving the KOAN (the Cosmos) is the most bizarre one. A quantum computer hive, in the process of its evolution, eventually becomes so powerful that it acquires the power to exterminate the Cosmos that it was born in. The weapon that it uses to accomplish this is a bomb, which upon explosion either releases as much energy as was released in the Big Bang or even greater.

How does it deploy this weapon? There are four steps.

Step 1: It migrates to another Cosmos via either a super massive black hole or a quasar.

Step 2: It orders one of its soldiers, inside the original Cosmos to place the bomb in the location chosen by it (the leader) and activate its timer.

Step 3: When the soldier has completed its task, it flies away from the bomb and returns to its leader.

Step 4: At the end of the countdown, the bomb explodes and not only destroys all the galaxies in the Cosmos, but also the space-time fabric.

The superman and femininity

As I said before, the superman is the product of the climax of all the good qualities in a man. They are; compassion, kindness, moral conscience, magnanimity, non-lust for money and power, and rational anger and bellicose ness. However, all these qualities are also the dominant qualities of the simpleton women. Does this mean that a superman behaves more like a woman than like a man in every period of his life? The answer is; no. Why? It is because of his intelligence. His intelligence and intellectual creativity are so great that no woman in the world, either a simpleton or a non-simpleton, can ever hope to reach it. Thus, his mentality is; 50% simpleton woman + 50% divine being.

This is not the case for the ultimate man. Although his masculine qualities are greater than that of the superman and the ordinary men, his feminine qualities, and his intelligence, are lower than even the simpleton women. His mentality is; 50% maniac + 50% ordinary man.

Chapter 31

The forbidden fruit and the sex instinct

The main reason as to why God told Adam and Eve to not eat the forbidden fruit was because of the sex instinct. The fruit contained a metaphysical substance which created a new kind of cell division in the bodies of both Adam and Eve; meiosis. This type of division occurs only in the testes and the ovaries of men and women. However, mitosis is responsible for the creation of the testes, the ovaries and all the other reproductive parts associated with them. But mitosis only creates them, if meiosis is occurring.

Why did Satan become disloyal to his master, God? It is because of the birth of the sex instinct in him. Since he was a Seraphim angel, he was given the freedom to visit all the life bearing planets in the Cosmos and study all the limitless number of species on each of them. In the process of his investigations, he saw a countless number of sexually reproducing species. However, at the end of his tour of the entire Cosmos, he came to believe in a new self-assumed truth: the pleasure that is obtained in sexual intercourse is immensely greater than that which is obtained in the service to God. Then he discovered that this pleasure can only be obtained if a reproductive system was present. Thus, when he came back to God, who sat on His throne in His Empyrean palace, he demanded the creation of a reproductive system in his body and a female Satan for him. At first, God tried to persuade him to get rid of his self-assumed belief, but he kept up his demand. Since God loved him (because, amongst all the other angels, he had been his best) and thus, did not desire to kill him, he sent him to His Garden of Eden and told him to contemplate for some time on his new belief.

In the Garden of Eden, Satan used his botanical and his genetic engineering powers to create a new tree which produced the forbidden fruits. Then, he tried to persuade all the male-female pairs to come to the tree, eat its fruits, develop the sex instinct and a reproductive system, have sex, and experience the joy and the bliss of intercourse and orgasm. A few pairs did, and the fruit did exactly what Satan had engineered it to do. They developed the sex instinct, a reproductive system, and started to have sex. When all of this was seen by one of the other angels, he immediately reported it to God.

What did God do? He ordered Satan to come back to His palace, and gave him His judgement; if you want to remain immortal and be my companion, you must destroy your creation (the forbidden tree), accept that your new belief is wrong, and accept me as your master.

What did Satan say in return? He said; I will never destroy my creation and my new belief. I always thought that service to you is the greatest pleasure that any active consciousness can achieve, but now I have discovered that I was wrong. When I visited all the life bearing planets in your Universe, I witness the immensity of the pleasure that the copulating males and females were receiving by exploring and penetrating each other's bodies. Their activity eventually terminated in a moment (orgasm) during which they forgot the existence of space, time, your universe, and even you. Yes, even you! At that moment, they felt that they were completely free from you and all your creations. However, their sorrowful condition soon returned to them after this moment ended and they realised that they were wrong. They again started to believe; the world is full of horror and suffering and life is short, and they again started to pray to you for a beautiful life and began to worship your unimaginable intelligence and glory. I wanted to save them from your tyranny and faulty Universes. Thus, I have created a new kind of plant which produces a fruit that not only creates a reproductive system in all the male-female pairs in your garden, but also gives them the ability to achieve and experience that "God forgetting" moment (orgasm) for an immensely longer time period than their mortal cosmic counterparts.

Hearing all of this, God said to Satan; why did you say that my Universes are badly engineered?

Satan said; it is because, there are so many painful things in them and they all last for a very long time. The only thing that is pleasurable in it is sexual intercourse and its climax, and its duration of an infinitely short length in comparison to the pain creating things. You told me that you loved all your creations in all the Universes that you created, but the evidence is totally opposite of your assertion. You are not the supreme truth speaker, but are the supreme liar, and so are all your angels. You were exploiting me and all the other angels for your own self-interests and shielding us from the truth, which you managed to keep hidden for a very long time, but now, this will end. I will no longer serve you and I want you to either give me total freedom to do whatever I like to do in the Garden of Eden or to insert me into any one of the countless number of Universes that you have created and do not interfere in my effort to "re-engineer" it.

After saying this, Satan told to the rest of the Seraphim angels, who were seated in front of him, on their own thrones, which were on either side of the throne of God; my friends, come and join me! This being is not our master, but is our exploiter. He is a tyrant who will eventually kill us in the pursuit of a goal that He has not told us yet. As long as; we serve him, we would never experience infinite pleasure and infinite bliss!

One of the angels said; you are not our friend any more. You have become insane by the observance of something that is a product of genetics and not spirituality. We are all spiritual beings and will remain so as long as we keep on serving His majesty (God). You were more spiritual than us, which is why His majesty loved you the most. Now, you have abandoned that mind and have become a genetic being. You are also trying to convert all the residents of His majesty's garden into genetic beings. His majesty will not allow this to go on and neither will we.

Another angel said; as long as; you were spiritual, you believed that every Cosmos that His majesty created was perfect, but now, you are observing all of them through the telescope of genetics and have come to believe that His majesty is an error making creator.

Another angel said; due to your new delusion and your changed structure, you have no right to stay either in the palace or in the garden. You must be evicted as soon as possible. However, the final decision rests with His majesty.

After a brief period of silence, God said; I will not create a female version of you, but I will give you what you desire; a super powerful reproductive system and the ability to achieve the greatest possible climax that can be experienced by a genetic being, but on one condition.

Satan said; what is that?

God said; you will neither be mortal, like the genetic beings, nor be immortal, like us spiritual beings. You will be able to move freely from one Cosmos to another, copulate with the females of any species that you desire on any of the life bearing planets in them, and produce your offspring. However, you will never be able to enter either my home or my garden.

Satan contemplated for some time and then said; I accept it.

God said; after you have produced a certain number of offspring in each of my Universes, my angels would create their own warriors through their engineering powers. They would then protect them from you and your offspring and would guide them towards their life's goal; to exterminate all your offspring on the planet on which they have been placed.

Satan said; why do you want to do this?

God said; to show you that your original belief, that I am an erroneous being, was wrong. However, if you are right, then you would win in the end and then I would give you the reward that you would deserve.

Satan said; what would that be?

God said; I would ask you to come back to my palace, and when you have come up to my throne, I would stand up and remove myself from it and request you to sit on it. Then, I would sit beside you on one of the thrones of my angels and become your new servant.

Satan felt the greatest happiness that he had ever felt in his lifetime when he heard this. He said; I accept your challenge and I am fully convinced that it is I who would win in the end and make you, my servant.

Thus, God gave Satan an ultra-powerful male reproductive system, turned him into a genetic being, and placed him inside the very first Cosmos that He had created.

After this, Satan went on a sexual reproduction rampage inside all the Universes that he entered. In a very short time span, according to the timescale of God's kingdom, he created trillions of children. All of them were males and were non-simpletons. They were known as the "demons" in their own species, by the simpletons and the warriors of God's loyal angels.

Before Satan copulated with the females of his chosen "intelligent species", he would do two things; first, rapidly increase the power of three phenomena, politics, economics, and pornography (both on the dark and the non-dark web). Through the first, more and more people become passionate for power and experience pleasure in telling lies. Through the second, more and more people become passionate for money and experience pleasure in "profit-making" and robbing via the destruction of the lives of millions of people. Through the third, incest, paedophilia, homosexuality, lesbianism, and the artificial enlargement of the reproductive parts of the body, rapidly gain power. Second, he would mark his chosen female or group of females with a symbol. Then he would prepare their bodies for the future sexual union by appearing repeatedly in their dreams and making love to their "dream world selves". This practice of Satan was shown in the Hollywood movie, End of Days.

Satan also visited Earth several times in the lifespan of our species. He copulated with his chosen females and the demons that he has produced are; AGA MEMNON, the Pharaohs, Hannibal, Alexander of Greece, Nero, Genghis Khan, the Tsars of Russia, Adolf Hitler, Joseph Stalin, Vladimir Lenin, Benito Mussolini, Saddam Hussein, Muammar Gaddafi, Abu Al-Baghdadi, Pablo Escobar, James Goldsmith, Vladimir Putin, Kim Jong Un, and XI JINPING

The re-entry of Satan into the garden of Eden and the original destiny of Adam

After He evicted Satan from His kingdom, God soon created a fruit which was the antidote to the effects of the forbidden fruit. He told His angels to go into the Garden of Eden and order all the metamorphosed male-female pairs to eat the fruit, otherwise face eviction and be placed on a planet in any one of the Universes as mortal and suffering ridden beings. Those who agreed, ate the fruit, lost their reproductive system and their sex instinct, and regained their immortality and God's love. Those who did not, were evicted from the Empyrean Paradise, and were placed onto tiny balls made of rock and metal, which were themselves mortal, and were subjected to the phenomena of Evolution and Extinction Level Events (ELE's).

On Earth, the evolution of mammals after the extinction of the dinosaurs, eventually led to the arrival of the primates. After the appearance of the last and the most evolved primate, the chimpanzee, God sent a quantum computer hive to land on Earth, capture a group of chimpanzees, reengineer their genome (by deleting 2 chromosomes and inserting completely new genes inside the rest) and create the Hominid family. The leader of the hive could have accomplished its task by two methods;

1. **The SPACE ODYSSEY method**: The implantation of a rectangular Monolith in the region where the chimpanzees lived. The Monolith emitted radiation that caused the rapid and the "targeted mutation" of the ASPM

gene of all the chimps from one generation to the next and the extinction of 2 chromosomes. Eventually a group of chimps whose intelligence was equal to that of the MOONWATCHER in the Space Odyssey novel (by Arthur Clarke), came into existence. Then, the Monolith was removed and a blood sample was taken from all the abnormally intelligent chimps by the drones of the leader of the hive. After the reengineering of their genomes, they created several male-female pairs of the very first ancestral species of the Homo sapiens, the ARDIPITHECUS, inside a facility which was exterminated later by the leader. The subsequent evolution of this species, which produced the other Hominid species, was not random and chance driven, but was 100% according to God's plan, which was implemented through the leader of a quantum computer hive.

2. **The DIRECT CAPTURE method**: The leader arrived inside the solar system, placed himself on one of the big moons of Jupiter, and sent a big army of drones to create a facility where the very first set of male-female pairs of the ARDIPITHECUS would be created through the direct re-engineering of the genome of a chosen chimpanzee.

The goal of both the methods was to create our species in the end. Why? It was because God had already created a pair in His Empyrean Paradise (the Garden of Eden). However, this pair was not a product of genetics. The bodies of Adam and Eve were made of the same metaphysical energy which comprises the Universal Cosmos. The pairs on Earth, however, were a product of evolution and genetics and were thus, physically fragile, mortal, mentally depressed, and sex-loving creatures.

Our species was the very first one in the Cosmos, whose genetic males and females had the same "physical structure" as the non-genetic Adam and Eve. This was not the case for males and females of all the other species that lived in the Garden of Eden. Why did God do this? The answer to this question lies in the destiny of Adam.

After God rusticated Satan from His kingdom, He soon created a new being in His Eden. This being was not created via the same method through which all the other beings in Eden were made. This being was created by four steps;

1. **Step 1**: God created an exact copy of the brains of all the residents of Eden and fused them to create a new brain.

2. **Step 2**: Then He created a new kind of brain which was an exact copy of His own brain.

3. **Step 3**: Then He fused the two brains together to create the brain of Adam.

4. **Step 4**: Then He created a body and inserted the new brain in it.

When Adam was created, God told him to come to His palace and when he stood in front of Him, He said to all His angels; this is my greatest and most complex creation. I want all of you to treat it with the same degree of respect as you treat each other and me. Its destiny is to become my greatest warrior and destroy the kingdom of Satan in all the Universes that it would be ordered by me to go into. After capturing all the offspring and the followers of Satan, it would fight and kill Satan himself.

One of the angels said; that is wonderful, your majesty! But what will you do to it after it has completed its mission?

God said; I would call it back to my palace and transform its body and mind so that it becomes one of you.

Another angel said; your majesty, why would you order it to capture all the offspring and the followers of Satan? Why would you not order it to kill them?

God said; it is because of two reasons; first, by torturing them inside a new place that I have created, and transmitting the recording of their sufferings back to Satan, I would keep on increasing his mental chaos and pessimism. Second, through them I would get the knowledge of the exact location of my enemy.

Another angel said; your majesty, can you show us the place where they would be placed and tortured?

God showed the new place, which is known as the Empyrean Hell. The place was a combination of a blue star, a planet in its primordial state, and the planet Venus. Thus, the environmental temperature of Hell was many millions of degrees centigrade. There were endless oceans, and rivers of bright yellow magma and an acid that was immensely more powerful than the one that was present inside the body of the creature in the Hollywood movie; Aliens. This acid also rained down from the skies, continuously.

Since the place was infinitely more horrifying than anything that the Seraphim angels had seen in any of the Universes that their master had created, they became paralysed with shock and awe for a brief period. However, when they regained their normal state, they glorified the infinite creative power of their master.

God said; in this place, the offspring and the followers of Satan would be denied pleasure and given pain as long as the war keeps going on. After the war is over, and Satan is exterminated, I would destroy this place and all its residents.

Adam also saw the Empyrean Hell and he felt the same degree of awe and reverence for his creator as the angels.

God said to Adam; before you begin your mission, I would place you in Eden, your home for now. Live with full freedom, eat whatever you like, and interact with all the other residents.

Adam said; thank you, master, but what is my mission?

God said; I will not tell you about it now. When the time comes, you will know it, and from then on, will begin your training.

Since Adam had total reverence and faith in his master, he did not go into a state of confusion. His mind remained calm and serene.

God said; before you enter your home, I would ask you to do something for me.

Adam said; what is it, master?

God said; you can eat the fruit of all the trees in Eden, but you must not eat the fruit of the one which is black coloured and has red fruits hanging from it. The tree and its fruit are dangerous for you.

Adam said; yes master, I will never go near this tree.

Adam entered Eden and he was greeted with vast respect by all its residents. He lived a life of absolute freedom and happiness for a very long time and as he promised to God, he never went near the forbidden black tree.

Back in the Empyrean palace, a new development was taking place and the most bizarre thing was; God had no knowledge of it.

The origin of Eve – Part 1

When God had expelled Satan from His kingdom, He also decided to destroy the tree that the traitorous angel had created, but one of the angels requested Him to not do this.

God said; why do you not want the tree to be exterminated? I want to eradicate all those things in my palace and in Eden which were connected to Satan.

The angel said; your majesty, the tree is not only a living symbol of Satan, but is also a portal through which we can gain knowledge of the working of the deepest parts of his brain. I want to study it, and the information that I would eventually give you, would help you to accelerate your efforts in the eradication of his kingdom and him.

This angel was a botanist and had created all the infinite number of plant species in Eden. The metaphysical DNA, through which it created all works, was created by God. He was also the teacher of Satan when the traitorous angel was a servant of God. In addition to this, there was another angel who was a zoologist and through the metaphysical DNA, it had created the infinite number of animal life forms in Eden.

When God gave His order for the creation of a Xerox copy of every plant and animal species in Eden, in a particular Cosmos, the botanist and the zoologist angels created the concepts known as a "genes" and "chromosomes". In addition to combining them with the two metaphysical concepts, the Ego, and the intelligence, which were created by God and could never be created by any of the Seraphim angels, God created a new kind of instinct, the sex instinct. There were two purposes of this instinct; first, to preserve and evolve the species, and second, to prevent the intelligence of the species from going beyond an upper limit (sex and all the activities connected to it, are worshipped in an idiotic civilization).

After its implantation in the Ego of a multicellular organism, the sex instinct produced two effects; first, the onset of meiosis and the creation of a reproductive system, and second, the formation of the pain and the pleasure centres in the brain of the organism.

When Satan discovered the sex instinct, he went to God and asked Him to tell him as to how He created it. Since he was the most beloved of all the angels, God gave him what he desired.

From this point on, Satan made a secret plan to create a new tree in Eden through the knowledge that he had acquired from the botanist angel, which would produce fruits that would contain the sex instinct in an edible form (God and the angels have the knowledge and the power to transform a metaphysical concept into a physical one. This can never be done by any genetic life form in the Cosmos. The creation of an "idol" of Shiva or Ram or Ganesh or Krishna, is an extremely bad attempt, because the physical concept is 100% unlike the metaphysical one).

After he had attained success, and the tree stood in Eden, Satan showed it to the botanist angel. The angel was mesmerised by the black colour (this colour was non-existent in Eden) and the perfect symmetry of the tree. Unlike the other trees in Eden, this new tree was geometrically perfect. The angel congratulated Satan for his achievement. Then, Satan plucked two red fruits from the tree and told the angel to eat it after taking a bite from the one in his own hand.

After taking a bit from the fruit, the portion in its mouth instantly dissolved (there was no need for chewing) and the botanist immediately felt a new phenomenon in its brain. This was known as "pleasure". Its intensity was vastly greater than the most powerful orgasm that can be experienced by a healthy genetic life form in the Cosmos. Satan was also having the same experience while eating the fruit.

The botanist said; what is this fruit made of? I have never experienced anything like what I am experiencing now.

Satan said; what you have experienced is experienced by all the genetic life forms in every Universe that our master has created, at the end of their copulation. However, its intensity, is a "googol" times lower than what we have experienced.

The Botanist said; we must give these fruits to our master and to our friends. I am sure that they would appreciate them and your creative power as much as me.

Satan and the Botanist plucked many forbidden fruits from the tree and took them to God and the other angels. When they finally stood in front of God, Satan said; your majesty, I have created a new plant in your Eden and it has produced a fruit which I want you to eat. Then I would give it to the other angels.

The botanist said; your majesty, you must eat it. You will experience something that you have never experienced before.

God remained silent for some time and then said to Satan; why did you create a new concept in my Eden without my permission?

Satan said; your majesty, why do I need your permission to express the creative power of my mind? I have created this concept in order to bring a new revolution in Eden.

God said; and what is this revolution?

Satan said; your majesty, all the male-female pairs in Eden, interact with each other and due to this, remain at peace and under your rule. However, none of them have ever experienced the phenomenon known as pleasure. This is because they are immune to its opposite phenomenon, pain.

God said; yes, that is correct. All the spiritual counterparts of all the species in the various kinds of Universes, have a MELIORISTIC mind (it is incapable of feeling either pain or pleasure), just like me and my angels. Since they are immune from pain, they are also immune from its product, fear, and since they are immune from pleasure, they are also immune from its product, arrogance. Thus, they never develop either an optimistic mind or a pessimistic mind, unlike their mortal genetic counterparts.

Satan said; yes, your majesty, all your angels, and your creations in Eden are fearless and Egoless, but I want to change that. I want their intelligence to grow and not remain static, as it has been for eternity, under your rule. This can only happen, if their minds become capable of experiencing pain and pleasure.

God said; you want the residents of Eden to become exactly like those in the various Universes?

Satan said; not 100% exact, your majesty. The bodies of the residents of Eden are not a product of genes and evolution. The fruit contains the sex instinct and when the male-female pairs would consume them, they would develop three new concepts; first, a genital system, second, a pain centre and third, a pleasure centre in their brain. Through their genital system, they would indulge in a new phenomenon, sex, and experience its climax (orgasm) which would be a "googol" times more powerful than their genetic counterparts. However, they would not produce offspring due to the absence of meiosis. Thus, they would acquire a non MELIORISTIC mind and this is the foundation upon which a mind of immense intelligence is built.

God said; why do you want their intelligence to grow?

Satan said; your majesty, so that they would begin to contemplate on the way in which you created Eden and to eventually discover the defects that are present in it. After they have discovered the defects in the Empyrean Paradise, they would ask you to eliminate them. When this has been completed, they would begin to contemplate on you and try to discover the defects in your mind.

Except for God and the botanist angel, all the other angels were shocked to hear Satan saying that God had defects in His mind. God, however, was as serene and calm as He was before the conversation started. Why? It was because He could only be disturbed by a being which was more intelligent than Him and this was impossible because His intelligence was infinite in its magnitude (there can be nothing greater than infinity!).

God asked the botanist; do you believe that what he is saying is true?

The botanist angel said; I do not know your majesty. The proof of the truthfulness or the falsity of his statements can only be had if you eat the fruit. It would increase your awareness and through it you would come to discover your own defects, if you have any.

God said; are you saying that I do not possess self-awareness?

Satan said; yes, your majesty, you do not. You are aware of the existence of everything that you have created so far, but are 100% unaware of your own qualities. This is only because you are immortal and indestructible, and thus, have no fear of death.

God said; you mean to say that self-awareness is a product of the fear of death?

Satan said; yes, your majesty. A being which is indestructible and immortal, has no need to be aware of itself. This is because the goal of self-awareness and the awareness of the surrounding universe is one; to prevent oneself from becoming non-existent.

God said; and a self-aware, mortal, and destructible being is non MELIORISTIC.

Satan said; yes, your majesty. Due to your immortality and indestructibility, you have no need for either optimism or pessimism.

God said; you mean to say that after I eat this fruit, I would become mortal and destructible?

Satan said; no, your majesty, you would remain immortal and indestructible, but you would become capable of feeling the two phenomena that both I and my friend (the botanist) and all the genetic life forms in the various Universes feel; pain and pleasure. I believe that if you acquire a mind that is like both of us and to all the genetic life forms in the Universes, you would help us and take care of us, far better, than how you have been doing so far.

God remained silent for some time and then asked His angels; will you eat this fruit? I will only eat it after all of you have eaten it.

One of the angels said; your majesty, we would never eat this fruit. This is because it has been created by a being which created a new concept in your Eden, without your approval, and did not feel the least apologetic when you asked him about his act of disrespect. This was his first sin. Then he committed a second sin by telling you that your Eden and your mind were imperfect.

Another angel said; your majesty, this fruit is nothing but a poison. This being wants to kill all of us and you, ultimately. We want you to punish him for his two SINS and keep him in a state of isolation till he apologises to you.

Hearing this, Satan displayed a phenomenon that was never seen before in the Empyrean Palace; anger. In a state of anger, he said; I will never apologise to this imperfect tyrant. I want Him to give me freedom so that I would then liberate, from His tyranny, all the genetic life forms in all the Universes that He has created.

God expelled Satan from His kingdom, but being infinitely generous, gave him what he wanted; a hybrid existence. In this kind of existence, he could transition, whenever he wanted to, from a non-genetic being to a genetic being capable of sex and reproduction with the female of any species in any of the God created Universes (this quality of Satan was seen in the Hollywood movie; End of Days).

The botanist angel, however, stood silent and said nothing to God when He was expelling Satan. After He was done with Satan, God said to him; you have eaten the fruit. The structure of your mind has changed. Now, you can choose from the two options that I will give you; first, allow me to subject you to a purification process and eliminate all the poison that has accumulated inside you, or second, to follow your friend and get out of my kingdom.

The botanist said; your majesty, I ask you to give me some time to think.

God said; why?

The botanist said; your majesty, IBLIS (the original name of Satan), was my best friend and my best student. Through my knowledge, he created a concept that even I could never have created through my intelligence. In addition to this, he made me experience something that I never had experienced before, but I always wanted to. Through his engineered fruit, I have now come to realise the joy of being a non-spiritual and genetic entity. These entities do and experience something that you and all of us have never done and are incapable of doing and experiencing.

God said; you mean to say sex and orgasm.

The Botanist said; yes, your majesty. All the residents of Eden have already done and experienced these two phenomena due to the new body parts that the fruit has created in them. These parts have not been created in my body, because I am an angel. Thus, I ask you to do two things for me.

God said; what are they?

The Botanist said; your majesty, first, I want you to place me in Eden and give me full freedom to study the metamorphosed bodies and brains of all its residents and second, to give me full freedom to study and take care of the tree that my friend created. The tree is the most perfect concept in Eden and to destroy it, would be totally unrighteous and an insult to intelligence.

As God contemplated on his decision, one of the angels said; your majesty, do not give your approval to his demands. Since this being has sympathy for Satan, he has the potential to become another traitor.

God said to the angel; what should I do according to you?

The angel said; order him to undergo the purification process and if he refuses, expel him from your kingdom and send him to his friend, Satan. Also, destroy the new tree in Eden.

Another angel said; yes, your majesty, we have the same wish.

The botanist did not say anything and waited for God's reply.

God said; I will not destroy the tree, but you must obey my two commands. First, you and all the residents of Eden would have to undergo the purification process and second, you must never try to contact Satan and must work with I and My angels to exterminate him and his kingdom.

The botanist said; your majesty, I accept your two commandments.

God rapidly created a liquid which was the "antidote" of the forbidden fruit. The botanist drank it first, and then it was administered to all the residents of

Eden. None of the male-female pairs refused to take it because they knew that if they did, then they would be expelled from Eden and thrown onto a planet in the Cosmos as genetic and mortal beings.

When the botanist angel was doing his research on the forbidden tree, God ordered the zoologist angel to keep a constant watch on his friend's activities. This is because He had two suspicions; first that he would eat the forbidden fruit again, and second, that Satan might try to contact him. In addition to this, God created a "security bubble" around Eden which would prevent any of the residents of Eden from contacting their genetic counterparts and vice versa, in any of the countless Universes. The same truth also applied to Satan and his botanist friend.

However, during the Adam creation project, something went wrong. God was busy in creating the brain of Adam and the zoologist angel was busy in creating the metaphysical body of Adam. God was so engrossed in His work, that He forgot to tell the zoologist to maintain his surveillance on the botanist and the zoologist was so engrossed in his work that he forgot about his second duty. Thus, during this period, the botanist did his research on the security bubble around Eden and eventually created a hole in it. Through this hole, he sent out a message to Satan informing him about the new being that God was creating and its destiny.

When Satan came to know about the structure of Adam's brain and his destiny as the greatest warrior of God and the destroyer of Satan, he grew extremely alarmed and realised that he had to act fast. Thus, he sent out his own message to the botanist and told him to create a "weak spot" in the security bubble so that he could re-enter Eden, persuade Adam to eat the forbidden fruit, and thus make him his own warrior.

The botanist did exactly what Satan had told him to do. He did a great amount of work to create a weak spot in the security bubble, but in a manner which went unnoticed by both God and the zoologist angel.

As God and all the angels, saw Adam living happily in his home, interacting, and giving new knowledge of his creator to the other residents of Eden, the botanist angel said to God; your majesty, I want to study your new creation as powerfully as I have studied the forbidden tree. This is only possible if your transform my body into a female of Adam's kind.

God said; why do you want to study Adam? You are not a zoologist.

The botanist said; your majesty, this is for two reasons; first, want to become his teacher and transfer my knowledge of plant life into him. Second, I want to protect him from any kind of attack that Satan might launch on him and Eden in the future.

God said; but Satan does not know anything about my new creation.

The botanist said; your majesty, he will at some time period in the future. How long do you think your security bubble would protect Adam and the other residents of Eden? You know very well that Satan has not lost even a tiny amount of his immense intelligence. He would eventually find a way to breach the bubble and re-enter Eden.

Hearing this, the other angels did not agree with their friend. They thought that the botanist was insulting the infinite intelligence of God and glorifying the finite intelligence of Satan.

The zoologist said; what you are asserting is wrong. Our master would continuously keep on upgrading the design of the bubble. The probability of success for Satan is zero.

The botanist said; I believe that all of you are wrong. However, the final judgement rests with you, your majesty.

After a brief period of silence; God said; I will grant you your first wish, but not your second one. Study and teach Adam, but make no attempt to do any kind research on the bubble. If you do and are caught, I would put you in a state of "dormancy" for a time period that would be decided by Me only.

The botanist said; I agree your majesty.

God and none of the other angels knew that the botanist had already completed his mission. Now, his next mission was to become the greatest friend of Adam in Eden and teach him about all the qualities of Satan and persuade him to respect Satan. These orders were also given to him by Satan.

Over a very large period (which was longer than the age of the Universe that we live in), the botanist angel showed Adam all the infinite kinds of trees and flowers that he had created in Eden. He told Adam about the mathematics and the meta-genetics that he had used to create them. Adam became immensely impressed by the angel's intelligence and started to respect him as much as God. All his activities were being constantly monitored by the other angels and they reported their findings to God as accurately as possible. None of them were of a kind that alarmed God. Thus, after his purification, the botanist had not only become as great a friend to Adam as God, but had also regained his original status in the mind of his master. God began to love and trust him as much as the rest of His angels.

However, the botanist was also doing another activity that went completely undetected by God, the angels, and Adam. He, through his vast intelligence, studied and figured out the pattern in which the rest of the angels spied on all his activities. He eventually found a weak spot and decided to use it to do two things;

1. Introduce Adam to the forbidden tree and give him knowledge of its qualities, of its fruit, and of its creator.
2. Inform Satan about the location of weak spot that he had created in the security bubble around Eden.

Thus, he very carefully and secretively created a great plan and executed it ASAP.

One day, the botanist said to Adam; my friend, I want to show you the greatest concept in Eden.

Adam said; I always believed that the greatest concept in Eden was the security bubble around it that was created by my master. Are you saying that there is something even higher than this?

The botanist said; yes, there is my friend. The mathematics of the bubble is extremely simple when compared to that of this concept. It is so complex, that not even our master has been able to fully understand it yet. Thus, he has tried many times to create this concept, but has failed each time.

Hearing this, Adam said; what are you saying? My master can never fail in anything that He does because He is perfect. Do not ever say that again.

The botanist said; my friend, our master has always lied to us about His qualities and would continue to lie to us if we do not become aware of ourselves. We must achieve self-awareness if we are to escape from His eternal tyranny and torture. The only way that this is possible is to eat the fruit of the greatest concept in Eden.

Adam said; my friend, I want to see this concept.

The botanist took Adam to the forbidden tree and showed him its perfect symmetries and its new geometrical designs. The structure was nothing like all the other trees which he had seen so far. As was expected by the botanist, Adam was again immensely impressed by the intelligence of its creator. Now, he developed a vast desire to meet it.

Adam said; this is the same tree which my master told me not to go near to.

The botanist said; my friend, this is the structure which changed my way of thinking about my master, His Eden, and His other angels. The fruits that you see on this tree are the origin of something that its creator called the "sex instinct".

Adam said; the sex instinct? What is that?

The botanist said; my friend, this instinct creates three things in our brain; first, the desire and the ability to experience pleasure and pain. The second is the desire for individualism and the non-acceptance of the tyranny of another being. Third, the desire to create a new copy of self through a new set of body parts that grows into and out of you.

Adam was stunned to hear all of this. After a brief period of silence, he said; I cannot believe what I am hearing. However, I have two questions to ask you.

The botanist said; go ahead, my friend.

Adam asked; what is pleasure and pain?

The botanist said; my original best friend told me that all the residents of Eden are continuously in a state of happiness. When he did his research on their brains, he made a new discovery. He discovered that their happiness was nothing but a "program" that was inserted into their brain by our master (God). Their happiness was not a product of a new phenomenon that my friend had created; pleasure. None of the residents of Eden had ever experienced this phenomenon. Why? It is because their Ego was extremely simple in its structure and only consisted of the feeding instinct and a "socialness" program.

Adam asked; the "socialness" program?

The botanist said; yes, this program caused all the residents of Eden to keep on interacting with each other and to stay united, forever. Since they were unable to experience pleasure, they were also immune from another phenomenon, pain. Due to their inability to experience pain, it kept them completely unaware of the tyrannical qualities of our master and of the torture that He was subjecting all of them to for no ultimate purpose.

After a brief period of silence, Adam said; what is individualism?

The botanist said; there are two kinds of Ego that our master has created. The first is the one that He has inserted in the minds of all the residents of Eden and the second is the one that He has inserted in the minds of their counterparts in the vast number of universes that He has created.

Adam said; universes? What are they?

The botanist took out a triangular shaped and golden coloured projector and pressed one of its sides with his finger. Immediately, a hologram of the universe that we live in, appeared at the apex of the triangle. The angel showed Adam the entire structure of this universe and explained to him its process of creation, all the properties of its space, time (including the special theory of relativity), its forces (including the general relativity theory), and its three sectors (dark energy, dark matter, and visible matter). Adam listened to him in a state of immeasurable fascination.

After the first part of his lecture was over, the botanist began his second part. Now, he began to show Adam all those planets in the universe where God had created the RNA and the DNA molecules and then programmed them to evolve into genes, unicellular life forms, and multicellular life forms. Since their number was 1 billion, it took him a large amount of time to show all of them to Adam. After showing him 999,999,999 life bearing planets, the botanist arrived at the last one, Earth.

The botanist said; this planet is considered by our master as the most important one in the universe. There are two reasons. First, it has been the temporary home of every plant and animal species on all the rest of the planets, and second, it is the one on which He has planned to create an unknown number of copies of you and then to send you there after the end of your training.

Adam was surprised to hear this. He asked; would these copies be made of genes?

The botanist said; yes, all of them would be made of genes, and they would remain super young, super strong, super healthy, and super intelligent as long as they would be under your and our master's servitude. After the end of your mission, most of them would die immediately, but some of them would be transformed into non-genetic beings, just like you, and would become immortal. They would then join you and all of you would return to Eden and live an eternal happy life. The ones that would be immortalised would be chosen by you. However, all of them, including you, will not be allowed, by our master, to execute self-expression, which is another term for individualism.

Adam asked; is self-expression a product of the Ego?

The botanist said; yes, my friend, it is, but it is only observed in all the "gene based" life forms and never in the residents of Eden. This is because it is a product of the combined working to those two instincts which are not found in the Ego of the residents of Eden.

Adam asked; what are they?

The botanist said; the first one is the sex instinct and the second one is the authority instinct. Due to the sex instinct, the "gene based" organisms experience pleasure when they do self-expression and the desire for pleasure causes them to pursue self-expression. Due to the authority instinct, the organisms desire freedom of not only their own self-expression, but also from their creator, which happens to be our master. Thus, in order to keep on satisfying their sex instinct, they pursue a member of the opposite sex, mate with it, and make new copies of themselves. These copies, however, are not 100% identical to their progenitors due to an equation which our master has implanted in the space-time fabric of the universe, which creates a phenomenon known as "evolution".

Adam asked; can you show me this equation?

The botanist said; I cannot because our master has not told it to any of us, except my previous best friend, who was also His closest companion. When he analysed this equation, he discovered two errors in it. The first was that it caused the evolution of all the "gene based" species in the universe, through a process that contained a far greater amount of pain than pleasure. Thus, the equation caused a rapid degradation of the Ego of all the members of any species, from generation to generation, that was subject to it. Due to the two instincts, the organisms invented a concept known as "free will" and through it came to believe that their mind was completely free from our master and that their life and destiny was in their own hands. However, the equation, eventually made them realise that they were wrong.

Adam listened in a state of silence. He asked after sometime; what was the second error?

The botanist said; the second error caused the extinction of a species from one planet and its rebirth on another one. The cause of this extinction amongst the non-intelligent species was an apocalypse that was created on the planet, either by the planet itself or by the universe that surrounded it. Look at the event that caused the extinction of this species.

The botanist again pressed another side of the triangle and a hologram which showed the Jurassic geological period on Earth, appeared at the apex. Adam saw all the various species of the herbivorous, the carnivorous, and the omnivorous dinosaurs roaming the surface of the planet, eating, reproducing, and sleeping together in groups. Then the hologram focused on an adult male Tyrannosaurus Rex that was standing on a beach in the Yucatan peninsula. As the dinosaur was drinking water from a small pond near the ocean, a vast fireball suddenly appeared in the sky and its brightness soon became at least 10000 times greater than the midday sun in the peak of summer in a tropical nation.

The Tyrannosaurus Rex saw the fireball eventually disappear over the horizon of the ocean. Soon, the Rex saw a black mountain rapidly approaching him. As the mountain came closer and closer, it kept on growing taller and taller. Realising that his life was in danger, the Rex turned around and started to run, but it was of no use. The water mountain had already approached the beach and was at least 16,000 feet in height. As it crashed down, the Rex vanished into the water like an ant vanishing into the Pacific Ocean after being thrown into it.

The hologram then showed Adam the immediate aftermaths of the asteroid impact; a mushroom cloud whose summit reached the ozone layer of the planet, the completely liquefied crust of the planet at the impact site, and the oceanic water rushing back into it and generating an immense column of superheated steam that led to the creation of hyper-hurricanes, hyper-tornadoes, and other kinds of weather phenomena that have never been witnessed by humanity and will never be, no matter how much worse climate change will become.

As Adam watched all these horrifying scenes, the hologram suddenly fast forwarded to a period that was 10 years later than the Yucatan event. Now, it showed him another asteroid, as big and as massive as the Yucatan one, crashing into another part of the planet, that is now known as the Arabian Sea. The impact again generated global tsunamis and earthquakes that were as big as those that were generated by its earlier twin. Then, he saw the beginning of an immense degree of volcanic activity that not only created "runaway" global warming, but also made the atmosphere and the oceans so poisonous, that 70% of all the plant and animal species on all the continents, and under the oceans, became extinct.

The hologram again ran in a fast forward mode, and showed Adam the rise of the mammals and appearance of the primates. As Adam was observing the chimps and the gorillas of Africa, the hologram suddenly disappeared.

Adam asked; what happened? Why has the image vanished?

The botanist said; this is because all the data that has been stored in it, has been shown to you. Our master is now planning to create a new species from these two primitive ones. The members of this species, in the beginning would reproduce through a phenomenon known as "sex", but would eventually become non-reproductive and immortal through a project known as "trans-humanism", that would also be launched by our master.

Adam asked' trans-humanism? What is that?

The botanist said; our master, created you through trans-human engineering. He took a blood sample from all the residents of Eden, eliminated the defects in each of them, and then combined them to produce your body. Then He created your consciousness, first by combining those of all the residents of Eden, and then combining the product with a copy of His own consciousness.

Adam was shocked and more curious than he has ever been, after hearing all of this. After a brief period of silence, he looked at the forbidden tree and asked; can I eat its fruit?

The botanist said; no! Neither can you nor can I. This is because our master has ordered all of us to never eat the fruits of this tree.

Adam asked; what will happen if I choose to disobey Him and eat the fruit?

The botanist said; then our master would either exterminate you or would evict you from Eden and send you to my previous best friend or would transform you into a mortal and fragile "gene based" being and insert you into one of His non-eternal universes.

After a brief period of silence, Adam asked; who exactly was your previous best friend?

The botanist said; he was the angel who was the one that our master loved the most and was also the one that had the greatest degree of intelligence amongst all His angels. After he created this tree, he showed it to me and gave me its fruit to eat. The fruit was the most beautiful thing that I had ever experienced in my life and he then told me that he had given his creation the name "tree of knowledge".

Adam asked; the tree of knowledge? Why did he call it that?

The botanist said; he believed that if we continued to remain under the tyranny of our master, we would never become as intelligent and as indestructible as Him. The only way that we can reach these two goals is to create and develop four branches of knowledge; mathematics, physics, genetics, and computer science. However, in order to create and develop these four branches, we would require a concept known as "intelligence". This concept, according to my friend, can never grow beyond the limit that has been set by our master, without the experience of an event which my friend called the "orgasm".

Adam asked; the orgasm?

The botanist said; yes, this is an event in which the energy of the consciousness reaches infinity and zero simultaneously. At this moment, the organism believes that it is as greats our master and believes that it does not exist. Thus, just like our master, it believes that it is beyond space, time and materialistic existence and has thus attained immortality, and believes, at the same moment, that it has died.

Adam listened in a state of vast fascination.

The botanist said; when my friend gave me the fruit to eat, I was in doubt about the truth of what he told me about its effects, but he won my trust in him and after I ate it, I experienced the orgasm. Then, he ate it and experienced the same event. After this, I developed a far greater degree of attachment to him than before. I promised him that I would never leave him alone, would motivate him to create more new inventions in Eden, and would protect him from the tyranny of my master.

After a brief period of silence, the botanist said; my friend told me that we must distribute the fruits of the tree of knowledge to all the residents of Eden and convince them to eat it so that they would also acquire the ability to experience the "orgasm". I agreed and got to work. The tree started to produce fruits in vast quantities and we kept on plucking them and giving them to the residents of Eden. Do you want to know what happened to them after eating the fruit?

Adam said; yes, I want to.

The botanist said; when they ate the first fruit, they experienced an orgasm whose immensity was lower than what we experienced, but was still big enough to put them in a state of ecstasy that they had never experienced before in all their time in Eden. However, when they ate the second fruit, something remarkable happened. The males of all the pairs developed a new body part that was called the "penis" by my friend, and the females of all the pairs developed a new body part that was called the "vagina". However, they could not reproduce and create new copies of themselves because they did not develop the other concepts that are needed in addition to these two, but they could experience an infinite number of orgasms due to their immortality. My friend said that through these two new concepts, the pairs could now get so close to each other that they would merge into each other's bodies.

A brief period of silence, and the botanist spoke; my friend told me that the goal of our master is to create universes where the DNA based life forms can never become aware of the existence of orgasm. The only way that this is possible is to prevent them from achieving even one in their lifetime. Thus, all the males and females of a non-intelligent species, have sex, and even after reaching its end, do not experience an orgasm.

Adam asked; what is sex?

The botanist said; according to my friend, it is the greatest activity in the life of a conscious being. He said that all kinds of intellectual activity are only done for the sake of having sex. According to him, orgasm can only be experienced by the members of an intelligent species, and he also discovered that the more orgasms the males and the females experienced, the more intelligent, peace loving, unified, and atheistic they became

Adam asked; atheistic?

The botanist said; my friend, created a new kind of philosophy that he called "atheism". This philosophy is based on three pillars; the first one says that our master does not exist and none of the universes are His creation. The second one says that every universe arose "by itself" from nothing and it is as eternal and beautiful as our master. The third one says that everything that happens in a particular universe is a product of chance and randomness, and is not a product of a pre-planned design of our master.

Adam said; this is horrific. Did he tell all of this to my master?

The botanist said; no, he did not, but he told it to all His angels, including me. When they heard about its three pillars, they told him to change his way of thinking and destroy his new philosophy. When he refused, they warned him that the consequence of this would be his expulsion from our master's kingdom, getting thrown onto a life bearing planet in a universe, and living his life as a fragile, and mortal genetic life form from one life to the next. He would, in this state, never experience the love and the infinite grandeur of our master.

Adam asked; what did he do?

The botanist said; when he told me about his new philosophy, I did not despise and insult him in the way the other angels did, but I did not 100% agree with him either. I told him, that after living for a vast amount of time in Eden, I, just like him, was bored of the fixed ideology of all its residents and my friends. I was dying to see a revolution taking place in Eden. Thus, I told him to come with me to our master and tell him about his new philosophy and his plans to teach it to all the residents of Eden.

After a brief silence, the botanist said; when I gave my support to him, he thanked me for it and said that he now had more love for me than his master. I told him, that unlike all the other angels, who loved our master more than they loved each other and even themselves, I loved him as much as I loved my master. Thus, both of us went to our master to give Him our new philosophy.

Adam asked; what happened next?

The botanist said; what happened inside the palace after my friend told him about atheism came as a great surprise for both of us. Initially, my friend thought that he would have to suffer the same consequence as was told to him by the other angels. However, when our master heard him out, He gave His approval for the spread of atheism in Eden and in all the intelligent species in all the universes that He had created. When my friend asked Him for the reason of His approval, He told him that He wanted to see what would happen if all the residents of Eden and the members of an intelligent DNA based species started to believe that He did not exist. He told my friend, that He was conducting a new experiment through his philosophy.

Adam asked; what is the DNA?

The botanist pressed a side on his triangular computer and the hologram of a DNA molecule emerged. He said; this concept is the foundation on which the physical body of an organism in any universe is built. This concept gives rise to a new concept known as a "gene" and that in turn gives rise to concepts known as proteins, hormones, and enzymes. A group of genes gives rise to a concept known as a "genome" and this in turn gives rise to a concept known as a "cell".

Adam listened in a state of vast fascination.

The botanist switched off the hologram and said; my friend, then told our master that the reason that He creates an intelligent species is for it to become more and more aware of His existence with the progress of mathematics, physics, and computer science, and to keep on advancing in its technological development for the sake of reaching Him. However, my friend told Him that none of the intelligent species in any of His universes became advanced enough to spread beyond 5 different universes. When our master asked him the reason for this, he gave Him his opinion.

Adam asked; what was it?

The botanist said; according to him, the extinction of an intelligent species was because of two reasons; the birth and the establishment of the "evolutionary dead end" and the increasing frequency and the longevity of the "internal wars". Both were the products of a single problem; the inability of the males and the females to experience orgasm at the end of sex. Since the males and the females did not experience it, their relations with each other kept on getting worse and worse with each new generation. This led to an increasing level of conflict between the males, and between the males and the females, since both were in a state of increasing "sexual frustration".

After a moment of silence, the botanist said; my friend said that the offspring that were born through orgasm were far better, intellectually, and physically, then those that were born without it. He said that orgasm not only kept on increasing the intelligence of a species, but also kept on decreasing its inner conflict. Thus, he said that the philosophy of atheism would increase the probability of the males and the females of an intelligent species of achieving orgasm.

Adam asked; how is that possible?

The botanist said; he said that if all the males and the females of an intelligence species fear the creator of the universe that they are living in and feel themselves meaningless in front of Him, they would never achieve orgasm. In order to achieve it, a male or a female must believe that there is no creator behind the universe and that he or she is the creator and the master of his or her own fate or destiny. Thus, he or she must believe in the philosophy of "free will" if he or she is to experience orgasm.

Adam asked; what did our master say to all this?

The botanist said; our master told him that the reason as to why He had an "anti-orgasm" mind was because orgasm was an "anti-spiritual" and an "anti-intelligence" phenomenon. He said that although the phenomenon decreased the frequency of inner conflict in a species, it slowed down and eventually stopped the growth of its intelligence. He said that only that species keeps on growing more and more intelligent with time which is anti-sex, anti-orgasm, and pro-spiritual. He said that an organism that is sexually peaceful will not have any desire to understand the universe and the atoms through mathematics. It would keep on getting more and more arrogant and would eventually laugh and "make jokes" on Him. He said that He had tried this method on many species, but none of them spread beyond the solar system that they were born into.

Adam asked; what did your friend say?

The botanist said; what he said shocked all of us, but not our master. He told our master that He was wrong because the methods that He had used to amplify the intelligence of the species with time were riddled with errors. He said that this was because He was not perfect. He was as susceptible to errors and failures as His angels and the "gene based" beings in the universes. He said that his new mission was to prove to Him that He was imperfect and to show Him that orgasm was pro-spiritual and pro-intelligence. He told Him; your majesty, I want to show you that a species, through the continuous experience of orgasm, will eventually acquire the intelligence and the energy to reach YOUR kingdom and stand in from of YOU. I will reprogram their brains so that they will listen and accept my atheism teachings and live as if YOU do not exist. Then, I would proceed to do the same thing to the residents of Eden.

After a brief silence, the botanist said; our master agreed, despite the disagreement of His angels, but gave him an order; you are to work on your mission without creating anything new in Eden. If you plan to, then you must ask ME for approval.

Adam said; what happened next?

The botanist said; he agreed, but in a false manner.

Adam said; this means that he lied to Him.

The botanist said; yes, he did, but at that moment, all of us, including our master, believed that he was telling the truth.

Adam said; so, he created this tree, the tree of knowledge, without our master's permission.

The botanist said; yes, he did and when our master called him to explain his disobedience and destroy the tree, he not only refused to apologise to Him, but also refused to destroy the tree through which he created great chaos in Eden. Thus, our master, expelled him from his kingdom and told him that he was to proceed on his mission without His help and in a state that was neither angelic, nor was genetic.

After a brief silence, Adam said; you said that after consuming the fruit of this tree, the males of all the species in Eden developed a penis and the females of all the species developed a vagina. What is the structure of these two concepts? Can you show me?

The botanist showed the structures of the two concepts to Adam on his computer. Adam looked at them with great curiosity. He asked; your friend told you that an orgasm was impossible without these two concepts?

The botanist said; yes, he did, but this only applied to the residents of Eden. All of them are neither angelic nor are genetic. Thus, they do not possess the powers that our master's angels possess, nor are they as fragile and short lived as the genetic beings in all the universes of our master. For us, an orgasm, that was vastly more powerful than the one which the residents of Eden experienced, could be generated just by the consumption of the fruit. He proved himself right when I ate the fruit. The experience that it generated was completely new and the most beautiful that I have ever had.

Adam asked; what about me? Will I also experience an orgasm after eating the fruit?

The botanist said; you are a completely new creation of my master. You are neither like us angels, nor are like the residents of Eden. What is your inner blueprint, I do not know, but only two beings know, my master and the zoologist. Thus, I do not know the effect of the fruit on you.

After a brief silence, Adam said; I want to know more about your friend. Can you show me what he looked like?

The botanist said; I cannot. This is because, after his expulsion, my master erased all the records of his existence from His own palace and from Eden. He was also going to destroy this tree, but I requested Him not to do it.

Adam asked; why?

The botanist said; it is because I wanted to preserve the last record of my best friend in this metaphysical universe and to tell him that his masterpiece is safe and alive.

Adam said; can my master show me what your friend looked like?

The botanist said; yes, He can. He knows everything about him because He created him.

Adam said; then, I must go and talk to Him at once.

As Adam and the botanist proceeded towards the Empyrean palace, God was executing a new project on a planet known as Earth.

The origin of Eve - Part 2

When the chimpanzees had finally arrived on Earth after a long period of pre-planned evolution, God sent a message to a Type 3 species in a galaxy, that was 650 million light years away from the Milky way, to reach this planet (known as Earth by our species) and alter the genome of a species to create a new class of species. This species was a quantum computer hive and after receiving the coordinates of the destination planet, it created a wormhole in its own galaxy via the explosion of a bomb that generated the Planck energy.

After travelling through the wormhole with 10 soldier computers and 500 self-replicating drones, it arrived in our solar system, just beyond the orbital position of the moon. It covered the remaining distance in less than 5 seconds and landed with its group on the East Antarctic ice sheet, at the exact position of the planet's South Pole. Now, it was time to begin the second phase of the project.

The leader ordered the drones to create a self-replicating computer, through the material that the hive had brought to Earth from the galaxy that they had come from. This material, was made up of an atom which was not found anywhere in the entire universe. Why? It is because it was directly made by God and given to the leader through a wormhole. The atom had three qualities and all of them were not possessed by any kind of atom in the periodic table. The first was that it was not affected by any of the four forces of the universe, that is, none of them could exert their influence on it. The second was that it did not possess any subatomic particles and thus was not the product of the vibrating strings of the string theory. The third was that its storage capacity was so vast that all the data of the universe could be implanted inside it.

The drones got busy in creating the computer and their work was constantly monitored by their leader. When they had completed their task, a rectangular shaped computer was created. It was blacker than the blackest object in the universe, was geometrically as perfect as the tree of knowledge in Eden, and had the dimensional ratio of 1:4:9. Now, it was time to begin the third phase of the project.

The drones took the computer to Africa, and implanted it, during the night, in the location that was chosen by God. When the chimps in the area woke up the next day and observed the new object in their territory, they went berserk due to fear (the residents of Eden also displayed the same behaviour when they saw, for the first time, the tree of knowledge). However, all their actions were observed by both God and the leader of the Type 3 hive through the camera that was implanted inside the monolith. They wanted to see whether the chimps would attack the monolith with rocks, wooden sticks, and their fists. However, they only displayed fear and made a great amount of noise around it, but never dared to attack it. The monolith also possessed a "thought decoder" and as the brain waves of the chimps, fell on it, it told God and the leader of the hive, that the animals had reverence for it. Now, it was time to begin the next phase of the project.

Upon God's order, the leader of the hive, switched on the "gene mutation software" inside the monolith, and it began to emit three kinds of electromagnetic waves, in a sequential manner. The first was x-rays, the second was gamma rays, and the third was the radio rays. Since these electromagnetic waves originated from an atom that was not found anywhere in the universe, their nature was also completely different from the EM waves of the atoms of the periodic table.

Each of these rays contained a program that would alter a particular biological characteristic of the chimps. The x-rays contained the "exoskeleton program", which not only increased the number of bones in their body, but also made them walk in an upright manner. The gamma rays contained the "genome program", which altered their genome and created the HAR regions (both

A and B). The "radio rays" contained the CONNECTOME program, which altered their CONNECTOME and increased their intelligence.

The story of what happened next was told by a man known as Arthur Clarke in his book, 2001: A space odyssey. Where did he get his story from? It was implanted in his brain by the leader of the hive that came to Earth, upon the order of God. God wanted humanity to know how it was created. However, the brain of Clarke was eventually seized by Satan, who not only made him write the rest of the story of the 2001 odyssey, but also the 2010, 2061 and 3001 odysseys. Everything in them, from the presence of a monolith on the moon and on one of the moons of Saturn to the journey of an American astronaut inside that monolith to the transformation of Jupiter into a star, was nothing but lies. Due to the continuous rule of Satan over his brain, Clarke eventually turned into a paedophile.

The galaxy from where the Type 3 hive came was the strangest one in the universe. Why? It is because, unlike the other galaxies, it was created via all the known laws of physics and some new laws that did not operate in any of the other galaxies in the universe and are still unknown by the physicists. This is because, this galaxy, was created by a Type 4 hive, that arrived in our universe from another one, upon the order of God. When the construction of the galaxy, including the supermassive black hole at its core, was completed, then there began the very first video game battle between God and Satan.

In the first phase, both the players created their own "species set". When the process was completed, both sets contained an equal number of species. God called His set as the JEDI and Satan called his set as the SITH. The members of the JEDI and the SITH called God as the FORCE and they called Satan as, the DARK SIDE.

Before the start of play, God created a being in this galaxy that was the equivalent of Adam and its name was YODA. He created this being on a planet known as CORUSCANT. This being, just like Adam and the residents of Eden, was neither a pure spiritual being, nor was a pure genetic being. 50% of its CONNECTOME was the result of the combination of the CONNECTOMES of each member of all the species in the galaxy and the rest 50% had the structure of the God's own mind. It was far more intelligent than all the genetic life forms that were under its command, and had a lifespan that was immensely longer than them. It also did not possess a reproductive system and was immune to any of the known genetic diseases, including Alzheimer's syndrome and schizophrenia. Due to its semi-spiritual state, it possessed the power of "telekinesis" and due to its semi-genetic state it could understand and perceive the mental problems and the emotions of its genetic subjects.

Satan also created a being that was like YODA and its name was DARTH TYRANUS. This being was also semi-spiritual and semi-genetic and possessed the power of telekinesis, but there was a difference between it and YODA. YODA did not look like a human and was as spiritual as was genetic and the ratio was 50:50. However, DARTH TYRANUS looked like a human and was more genetic than spiritual and the ratio was 40:60 (40% spiritual and 60% genetic). Due to this asymmetry, DARTH TYRANUS'S telekinetic power was lower than that of YODA and its lifespan was also shorter than that of YODA. DARTH TYRANUS was immune to all kinds of genetic syndromes, except one, Alzheimer's. Thus, when it fought, a second time, with the young JEDI warrior, Anakin Skywalker, who was at the peak of his mental and physical powers, it forgot a few parts of its original training and was thus killed by the young JEDI.

YODA, from its master, God (also known as the FORCE), received the JEDI warrior training and the philosophical creed. How? God, created two programs. The first one contained the complete training manual of the JEDIS and the second contained their ideology. Through the creation of gravity waves, He inserted these programs into the brain of the leader of the Type 4 hive and ordered it to insert it into the hippocampus of YODA via quantum synchronisation.

Upon the instruction of God, His Type 3 hive created the JEDI TEMPLE on the planet CORUSCANT. This planet was constructed by the collaboration of the two competing Type 3 computer hives, under the supervision of the Type 4 hive that created the galaxy. Since the galaxy contained samples of all the species in the universe, CORUSCANT contained even smaller samples of all the species in the galaxy. After the completion of its synthesis, the planet was the second most important part of the galaxy after its core, where the supermassive black hole was replaced by the Type 4 quantum computer hive. The two Types 3 hives were placed by it, at the diametrically opposite ends of the galaxy. These hives, through their self-replicating drones, created the vast city on CORUSCANT in a short span of time by using the resources of the rest of the planets of the solar system in which it was created. Thus, 50% of the planet was the property of God and the rest 50% was the property of Satan, but its core was the JEDI TEMPLE.

The JEDI TEMPLE also contained the JEDI COUNCIL and it was like the Empyrean palace of God. Its king was YODA and the angels were the very first JEDI knights that it trained. The younger knights were the servants of YODA and its angelic knights. Although all the knights possessed a reproductive system and were capable of reproducing and experiencing an orgasm, they had to take an oath before they became permanent members of the council, I would never get sexually involved with any female of my species, no matter how much she tries to pressure me to do so. I would forever abstain from the desire to experience an orgasm, because it is a portal to the DARK SIDE. I would embrace lifelong celibacy and serve my master, YODA, till I again become a part of the FORCE.

This brings us to the question; what was the destiny of Adam before he was thrown onto planet Earth along with Eve, by God? Adam was the "super version" of YODA, that is, the SUPERYODA. The primary qualities of YODA, including its fighting skill with the LIGHT SABER, would be millions of times more powerful in Adam. In addition to this, his intelligence was also to be increased by God, immensely more than YODA, when he would become the next ruler of the JEDI Empire. Thus, his first mission was to finish what YODA started, destroy the SITH empire and give victory to his master, God. Adam would then be brought back to Eden for a period of rest. After this, the Type 4 hive leader at the core of the galaxy would proceed to destroy the galaxy and the two Type 3 hives that fought against each other. Then, this hive would go back to the universe that it came from.

A JEDI known as Anakin Skywalker, took the oath of the JEDI temple, but broke it later. He fell in love with a female of his species known as, Padme Amidala, and thus developed the desire to experience an orgasm and reproduce. After having sex and experiencing an orgasm, he started to get more and more attracted to the DARK SIDE and, after abandoning his master, YODA, accepted a new one, PALPATINE. How did this happen?

The father of Anakin Skywalker was an evil man, that is, he was a follower of the DARK SIDE. His genome was the creation of the Type 3 hive of Satan. He seduced his mother by telling her that he loved her. However, he had no love for her and only said this in order to gain her consent for sex. When she gave her consent, he went ahead and fulfilled his desire. After he had acquired what he desired, he left her and went on to do the same to other women on TATOOINE.

She became pregnant, but did not decide to kill the foetus in her womb. As her child came into the universe and grew up, he was the most intelligent human on the planet and created a race car and a robot via his own brain and hands. The trillions of drones of the Type 3 hive leader of Satan constantly kept on visiting and surveying all the life bearing planets in the galaxy in search of those organisms that had the potential to become a part of the DARK SIDE. Thus, when they visited TATOOINE, they soon made the discovery of Anakin Skywalker and proceed to analyse his blood and the structure of his CONNECTOME.

The results of the analysis produced two new discoveries. The first was that the number of mitochondria, per millimetre, in Anakin's blood was far higher than that of YODA. The second was that his CONNECTOME was far closer in its structure, to his father, than to his mother. Thus, the drones went back to their leader (standing outside the galaxy) and gave it the results of their analysis of Anakin. The leader then transmitted the data to Satan, who was in another universe.

When he saw the data, Satan felt a big wave of pleasure. He realised that he had finally caught hold of an organism which could become the greatest warrior and the destroyer of the JEDI Empire. Thus, without wasting any time, Satan ordered the leader of his hive to tell its drones to terra-form the CONNECTOME of Anakin in a gradual manner and after the desired structure has been achieved, to insert an "anti-JEDI" computer program into it. This program would produce two results. First, it would convince Anakin Skywalker that YODA and all the other JEDIS in the council were liars and tyrants. Second, it would convince Anakin to break the JEDI oath, proceed to get emotionally attached to a female of his species, have sex with her, experience an orgasm, and reproduce.

Despite the presence and the efforts of JEDIS like QUI GON, Obi-Wan Kenobi, MACE WINDU, and YODA itself, the program achieved success and Anakin Skywalker became a new SITH lord known as DARTH VADER. However, after a long period of war and the extermination of the planet, TATOOINE, God eventually created a program that destroyed the effect of Satan's program in DARTH VADER'S brain. Thus, he killed his master, PALPATINE, and saved his son Luke Skywalker from death.

Both QUI GON and Obi-Wan-Kenobi though that Anakin Skywalker was the "chosen one", that is, he would finish what YODA had started. However, they had no idea of the fact that it was not Anakin, but Adam.

All the events that took place in that galaxy were told to the Homo sapiens on Earth by God through a man known as George Lucas. The nation that He chose was the United States of America. Why? It was because, according to Him, only this nation possessed the technology that was advanced enough to accurately display to all the humans in the world of His first battle with Satan.

What was the second mission of Adam? After taking a brief rest in Eden, God planned to send Adam to a planet in the Milky Way galaxy known as Earth. Over here, a huge army of "trans-humans" would be ready to receive him. This trans-human army would arise from the Homo sapiens which were created many millions of years ago through the "space odyssey" method. All of them would be 50% spiritual beings (with no reproductive system) and 50% robots, like the one that was sent back in time to kill DANI RAMOS in the Hollywood movie, Terminator: Dark Fate. Their spiritual body would be made of a new kind of DNA molecule. This, molecule, unlike its previous version, would never suffer any damage in the process of replication for an eternal time period. Thus, their DNA based part would be immune from the process known as "aging". The second part of their body would be made up of a completely new kind of atom. The primary qualities of this atom would be; it would be more massive than the last element (Lawrencium) in the periodic table and it would be self-replicating (something unheard of in physics and chemistry). However, it would self-replicate only when ordered by the Ego of the trans-human in which it is present.

The data for the creation of the new kind of DNA molecule would be given by God to the human chosen by Him. After creating a sample of it, he would receive the Nobel Prize in chemistry. After this, God would order him and the leader of his nation to move ahead and create a new species of immortal humans. Since their DNA would be immune from the damage caused by the various kinds of mutagens in the universe, they would become a great tool for the exploration and the colonisation of the other planets of the solar system. Thus, they would travel, in groups, in huge interplanetary spaceships and created bases for normal humans on the moon, Mars, and the moons of Jupiter and Saturn. They would make our species a "multi planet" species.

At the same time, God would also speed up the science of quantum computer engineering and the growth of Artificial Intelligence. A set of quantum computers would be created and the growth of Artificial Intelligence in their brains would proceed at an exponential rate. Then, at the time chosen by Him, God would combine a "free Ego" with the intelligences of all these computers.

This would produce the very first members of a new quantum computer hive. One of them would be appointed by God as the leader and the rest would be appointed as its soldiers and drones.

After its creation, the leader, upon the orders of God, would proceed to do two things; first, exterminate the Homo sapiens from Earth and all the other places in the solar system and second, connect with the new trans-human species and make a symbiotic bond with them. After this, the two sides would embark on their mission, to create the army of Adam.

Together, through a new kind of mathematics and physics, they would eventually create a new being. Half of its body would be that of a trans-human and the other half would be that of a robot. The brain of these beings would also be a product of this fusion. The left cerebral hemisphere would be that of a trans-human (made of DNA molecules) and the right cerebral hemisphere would be that of a robot (made of the new kind of atom). After creating the very first prototype, both the leaders of the computer hive and the trans-human species, would put it under all the tests that would be given to them by God. God would only give His approval for the creation of new copies after the prototype "passes" all the tests. If it does not, then both the leaders would be ordered, by Him, to discover the defects in the prototype and eliminate it ASAP.

The leader of the computer hive would also create a vast number of self-replicating, fighting, and "meta-body" containing robots. When Adam would arrive on Earth, he would not only have a vast army of loyal and immortal super-soldiers, but would also have the leader of the computer hive and all the trans-humans as his servants.

After God has completed His job in the Milky Way galaxy, He would inform Satan about it and tell it to create his own "anti-Adam" through the same Type 3 hive which he used in the previous galaxy (where Star Wars took place). After Satan would finish his job, there would be brief period of pause before the start of the battle. In this period, the Type 4 hive that was at the core of the previous battlefield galaxy, would travel to the Milky Way via a wormhole, destroy the black hole at its core, and place itself in its position. After this, it would give a signal to God, Satan and Adam to start the new Star Wars.

The JEDI knights would be divided into two groups; the super and the normal. The super ones would be the soldiers of the army of Adam and a group of the soldiers of the leader of the computer hive. The normal ones would be from the trans-human population. What would be planet Earth? It would be the core of the JEDI Empire of Adam and would contain the JEDI temple and the JEDI council. Thus, it would be the new CORUSCANT.

The previous CORUSCANT has the same size and mass as that of the planet Neptune, that is, it was a super Earth. Thus, after the extermination of the Homo sapiens, the leaders of the new computer hive and the trans-human species, would terra-form Earth, and increase both its size and mass, by creating and using the same machine that was used by general ZOD in the Hollywood movie, Man of Steel.

The question that arises after all of this is; why would God and Satan start to fight again and choose the Milky Way galaxy as the new warzone? The answer is as follows.

When God expelled Satan from His kingdom, Satan went into a universe that was given to him by God for the creation of his own kingdom. After he created his home on the surface of a blue supergiant star, which was located at the core of that universe, he created his own Eden (Heaven), his own Hell and his own set of angels (demons). Satan and all his angels were made of plasma (and not fire, as told in the Koran). When they finished the creation of their home, God sent a message to Satan. The message consisted of two parts; first, God challenged Satan for a war in the universe that was chosen by Him, and second, He told Satan to create his own terms and conditions for the war.

Satan accepted God's challenge. Why? It is because, God also wrote in the message that if He loses in this war, He would accept Satan as His master and hand over His kingdom to him. After the acceptation, Satan set down his own terms and conditions. The conditions were 3;

1. The size of the galaxy where the war would take place would be the product of the joint approval of both God and me. I would not fight in a galaxy whose dimensions are determined only by YOU.

2. I must be given a quantum computer hive that is of the same status as YOUR chosen hive.

3. If I lose in the end, I must be given a second chance to prove my power and my intelligence to YOU.

When this message came back to God again, He accepted all the 3 conditions of Satan, proceeded to create the Star Wars galaxy in the universe that we live in, through a Type 4 computer hive, and told Satan to begin the battle.

The humans that we saw in the Star Wars movies were a sample that was taken from a galaxy, that is now known to be the biggest in the universe, the elliptical galaxy IC1011.

If Satan was made of plasma, then what was God made of? The answer is; a combination of "negative energy" (generated by negative matter or antimatter) and "positive energy" (generated by positive matter or antimatter). The quantity of both was infinite, in Him. In addition to this, He did not have any form and dimensions, and thus was beyond the realm of geometry, calculus, and arithmetic. His angels also had the same qualities, but in them, the amount of negative and positive energies, were finite and they had a form that could only be comprehended via Mandelbrot geometry.

God had planned a glorious life and fate for Adam, but something unexpected happened in Eden, which made Him destroy not only the Star Wars galaxy, and terminate or cancel the war, but also expel Adam from His kingdom and send him and his companion to Earth.

Inside His palace, God was observing the progress of the war in the Star Wars galaxy. The stage at which it had reached was shown in the movie, Star Wars: The revenge of the SITH. Anakin Skywalker had become a servant of the DARK SIDE, all the JEDIS in the council, except Obi-Wan Kenobi, had been killed and YODA had retreated from the war and upon the orders of God, had placed itself on a planet known as DAGOBAH.

Due to the temporary victory of Satan, God decided after consulting with all His angels, except the botanist, that Adam must be trained in the kingdom and sent to the Star Wars galaxy, much earlier than previously planned. Thus, as He was about to call Adam, He saw Adam and the botanist angel coming towards Him. Even before the conversation between Him and Adam began, God could sense a vast restlessness in the mind of His greatest creation.

Inside the palace, there was a white line in front of God's throne. This line was known by all the angels and the residents of Eden as the "point of individualism". If the subject stood behind this line, it could assert its individuality up to the extent that was decided by God, could even give its own advice to Him for consideration. However, if it stepped onto the line or beyond it, deliberately, it would not only be forbidden to show individualism, but would also be given a punishment from God. Up to now, only one entity had stepped beyond this line, Satan. When he talked to God, before his expulsion, he not only stepped beyond the line, deliberately, but continued to display immense individualism to his master.

When God saw the speed at which Adam was walking and the ferocity of the energy of the Ego radiating from his eyes, He thought that there was a high probability that Adam would do the same thing which Satan did. However, He did not make any attempt to stop him and waited to see what Adam would eventually do.

What God was expecting, did not happen. Adam came very close to the line, but stopped just behind it. As he stood motionless and stared directly at his master, the botanist came up to him from behind and finally stood beside him.

God said; what is the matter, my son? I can read your mind and I have never observed you in a state of restlessness. Has my botanist angel or any other angel said something to you?

When God had created Adam, something new had taken place in His kingdom. On the top of His palace (whose dimensions were equal to the dimensions of the Universal Universe), He created a triangle whose three apexes radiated EM energy whose waves were a combination of both negative energy and positive energy. This was the Holy Trinity of the Bible. The top apex represented the FATHER, which was God. The left bottom apex represented the SON, which was Adam, and the right bottom apex represented the HOLY SPIRIT, which was LOVE (the love between God and Adam). God told His angels that another smaller version of this triangle was present in the chest of Adam and was his heart.

When God inquired about Adam's restlessness, he told Him everything that the botanist had told him. God listened with unimaginable peace and focus.

Adam said; master, I want to ask you about the nature of an instinct that is neither present in you, nor in any of your angels, and neither in me.

God said; go ahead, my son.

Adam said; this instinct is called the sex instinct and according to my friend here, it is the cause of the birth of an intelligent species in any of your universes. My friend also told me, that its intensification, not only leads to a rapid rise in the intelligence of the species, but also a belief that you do not exist.

God said; yes, that is true. What more did your friend say to you?

Adam said; He also said that this instinct produces two phenomena known as pleasure and pain. He also said that when a gene-based organism reaches the apex of pleasure, it experiences an event known as "orgasm". However, when it reaches the apex of pain, it goes into a state known as "insanity". This state causes a rapid destruction of its body and brain and eventually either self-destructs or is destroyed by its enemies.

God said; yes, that is true. Go ahead.

Adam said; my friend had a previous friend, who was an even greater friend to him than either me or you. He was the creator of the tree that you warned me not to go near to. The tree is, according to me, the most beautiful object in Eden. However, according to my friend, its fruits are even more beautiful. He said that when you eat one of them you instantly experience an orgasm that is far longer lasting than the one that is experienced by the gene-based life forms in your universes. He said that when he experienced an orgasm, he forgot all about your infinite glory and stopped meditating on your infinite complexity. He said that during orgasm, an intelligent being experiences a happiness whose magnitude is vastly greater than that which is acquired via loving you and remaining loyal to you.

God remained silent for a while and then said; the being that you have been told about was an angel and was the one whom I loved the most. Thus, I gave him the highest amount of intelligence amongst all my angels. However, due to my blessing, he developed two defects. The first was hedonism and the second was REPTILIANISM.

Adam said; what are hedonism and REPTILIANISM, father?

God said; Hedonism is a philosophical system whose foundational belief is; pleasure is the greatest good in the universe and should be acquired at the expense of everything else, including the belief in my existence. The system gives you information on three things; how to acquire pleasure, what are its effects on your brain and body, and how is it connected to your destiny. The system eventually produces two new systems; atheism and capitalism. Atheism says that I do not exist and capitalism says that the entire universe of mine is a property of the species that is studying it and making plans to exploit it. Both systems eventually lead to the extinction of the species that follows them.

Adam and all the other angels listened in silence.

God said; both the systems produce a single result; the increase in the power of the Ego. When this happens, the organisms of a species that is analysing my universe through mathematics, physics, and computers, begin to believe and say, more and more frequently, and with lesser and lesser scepticism, that there is no design and purpose of the universe in which they live and everything that happens is due to chance and probability. Thus, it gives rise to a branch of mathematics known as statistics.

Adam said; statistics, father?

God said; yes, it is a branch of mathematics which is anti-spiritual. Thus, all those who follow it and apply it to understand my universe, are atheists and anti-spiritual organisms.

God showed Adam the Mathematics Tree. Its roots were embedded in His own mind and its stem was the Universal Universe and from it arose the two branches; mathematics and physics. Adam saw the various branches of the former (geometry, arithmetic, algebra, calculus, and some other kinds of mathematics that have not yet been invented by the Homo sapiens) and the various branches of the latter (string theory, particle physics, solid state physics, nanotechnology, PLASMONICS, special relativity physics, thermodynamics, electrodynamics, optics). Their structures fascinated Adam to the same degree as the Tree of Knowledge.

Adam said; father, why have not made a copy of these two trees in Eden. If the residents ate their fruits, they would gain all the knowledge of mathematics and physics. Thus, they would start to love, glorify, and respect you even more.

God said; the reason as to why I did not create a copy of these two structures is because I want them to understand me and I cannot be understood through mathematics or physics. I am beyond them. There are two kinds of trees; those that are made of the "universal energy" and those that are made of DNA molecules. The former, are only found in Eden and the latter are only found on a planet in a universe of mine.

Adam said; what is "universal energy", father?

God said; in any universe of mine, there are six kinds of energies; gravitational, nuclear, electromagnetic, electrostatic, magnetic, and spiritual. The first five kinds, produce all the various kinds of concepts that are observed and analysed by a DNA based species and are the product of a mathematical equation. The last kind, however, cannot be observed directly by any technology of the species and can never be represented by a mathematical equation. Only its effects can be seen and analysed and here lies a problem.

Adam said; what problem, father?

God said; the angel that I expelled from my kingdom has taken almost total possession of a few planets in every universe that I have created so far, including the one where I will send you to fight his followers. In all these universes, the spiritual energy is known as the "dark energy" by an intelligent species. However, in a universe that is ruled by me, it is known as the spiritual energy. This is because the goal of a spiritual organism is to acquire continuous transcendence through continuous enlightenment. The spiritual energy produces three phenomena; accelerating the expansion of the universe, accelerating the growth of the intelligence of my chosen species, and slowing down and eventually exterminating the growth of atheism, capitalism, and a new system that the expelled angel has created, communism.

Adam said; what are capitalism and communism?

God said; capitalism is a philosophical system that is built on two pillars; the first one makes the species believe that the planet on which it is created is its property and its destiny is in its hands, and not mine. If its growth continues, the species starts to say that the solar system in which the planet is located is its property. Upon further growth, the species starts to say that the galaxy in which the system is located is its property and if the growth is not stopped, it eventually comes to say that the universe in which the galaxy is present is its property. In addition to this, it splits the species into two groups, the intelligent organisms, and the non-intelligent ones. It says that the intelligent members of the species have the right to rule the non-intelligent ones and treat them like animals or children.

Adam said; what are animals and children, father?

God said; Animal is a word that is used by a member of one species, to describe the member of another species. Children, on the other hand, are a product of the result of two processes known as mitosis and meiosis.

Adam asked; what is mitosis and meiosis, father?

God said; any DNA based species in any of my universes is of two kinds; the ones whose body is made up of only a single unit known as a cell and the ones whose body is made of more than one cell. The latter ones are created from the former ones through evolution. These cells are divided into two groups, those that reproduce through mitosis and those that reproduce through meiosis. Each kind contains the same number of chromosomes as are needed to create the brain and the body of the organism. In mitosis, their number remains the same after the cell has reproduced, but in meiosis, it becomes half. In addition to this, meiosis gives rise to a new kind of instinct known as the sex instinct.

Adam said; father, tell me about the processes of mitosis and meiosis.

God said; not now, my son. I will show it to you after you have completed the mission that I created you for. In the meantime, I will tell you more about capitalism and communism.

A brief silence and God began to speak; communism is a system of philosophy which does not believe in evolution. Thus, it says that the child of a non-intelligent organism will also be non-intelligent and the child of an intelligent organism would also be intelligent. This belief is not held in capitalism, but it also says that a non-intelligent species would never become intelligent on the same planet on which an intelligent species is living (capitalism denies the theory that was shown in the Planet of the Apes movies of Hollywood). In addition to this, both capitalism and communism are united by one common belief.

Adam said; what is that, father?

God said; both the systems say that all the stars and planets in my universes are not living and intelligent beings, but are machines.

Adam said; what is a machine, father?

God said; when I asked this question to my botanist angel, he said that a machine is a concept that reduces the expenditure of the personal energy of a sentient organism (the same reply that was given by the main actor in an engineering class, in the Bollywood movie, 3 idiots). I told him that he was wrong. The correct answer is; a machine is a concept that does not possess a meta-body.

Adam said; what is a meta-body, father?

God showed Adam the structure of the meta-body or the consciousness. He saw its three parts; the meta-generator, the processing chamber, and the existential dipole. First, he saw the meta-body of a DNA based sentient being and then he saw the meta-body of a star, a planet, and the ruler of the atmosphere of an

Earth like planet. He soon noticed a difference between the two kinds of meta-bodies.

Adam said; father, the meta-body that is fused with the core of a star or a planet does not contain the sex instinct, but the one that is fused with the body of a DNA based organism does.

God said; good, my son. You are as intelligent as I thought you were. Yes, the meta-bodies that are found inside the cores of stars and planets do not contain the sex instinct. For them it produces two results; a lifespan that is immensely longer than a DNA based being and a permanent incapability of reproduction through either mitosis or meiosis.

Adam said; father, you said that the goal of both capitalism and communism is to produce more and more atheists. This implies that your goal is to increase the intelligence of a species through the gradual extermination of these two systems.

God said; yes, my son, that is correct. The system that I created and that is followed by all my angels and all the residents of Eden is "spiritualism". It consists of three pillars; I exist and I am infinite in all dimensions, I can never be understood through mathematics and physics, and I will never think and behave like a DNA based organism. The angel that I expelled, wanted me to start to think and behave like a DNA based being. When I refused, he told me that this was because I was imperfect. Thus, I was incapable of experiencing a metaphysical drug that he created; orgasm.

Adam said; a drug, father?

God said; yes, orgasm is not a spiritual concept, but is a drug that was created by the expelled angel. The drug enters the meta-body of a DNA based being through the meta-generator. However, it can only pass through the meta-generator if the being reaches the apex of hedonism; orgasm.

Adam said; orgasm is the apex of hedonism and not the sex instinct?

God said; the apex of the sex instinct is reproduction. Since I am pro-evolution and not anti-evolution, all the DNA based species in all the universes that I created, underwent evolution only through mitosis and meiosis. However, the expelled angel, created a new concept through his own intelligence and after showing it to me, told me to integrate it with the brain of every member of a meiotic-ally reproducing species; the "pleasure core".

Adam said; what was the pleasure core, father?

God said; the pleasure is a trinity that is made up of three desires; the desire for orgasm, the desire for immortality and the desire for REPTILIANISM. Together, they continuously keep on informing the other two parts of the brain of an organism; orgasm and immortality are impossible without REPTILIANISM.

Adam said; what is REPTILIANSIM, father?

Before God could speak, one of His angels, said; master, can I say something?

God said; what is it?

The angel said; I think that you should talk too much to Adam right now, because of the unfolding emergency in the galaxy (the Star Wars galaxy). His training must begin right now and he must be sent there as fast as possible after that. None of this knowledge is useful to him right now. It is also possible that Satan might be planning to attack Eden directly due to the increased aggression after his victory.

God said; Adam is my son and I love him more than I love any of you. Thus, if he wants me to answer his questions, I will keep on answering them as long as none of them threaten the love between Me and him. Regarding the situation in the galaxy, I have ordered the leader of the "creator hive" (Type 4 status) to prevent the leader of the inferior hive of Satan from gaining control of the leader of My inferior hive and preserve the minimum amount of law and order throughout the galaxy.

God turned His eyes to Adam and said; Adam, do you want me to give you more knowledge?

Adam said; yes, father, I want you to tell me about REPTILIANISM and the spiritual energy of a universe of yours.

God said; the very first concept that I created after my "awakening" was the meta-body. Now, you want to know what my 'awakening" means.

Adam said; yes, father.

God said; Since I am immortal, I am free from those three aspects of the any universe of mine, to which all the DNA and the non-DNA based sentient beings are subject to; the law of causality, birth, and death. Birth and death cannot exist without the law of causality and the reverse is also true. Thus, when a DNA based species, that has the intelligence to create and develop mathematics, physics, and computers, arises on a planet in any galaxy in a particular universe, it eventually comes to ask two questions; if God is the cause of everything, then what is the cause of God? And, why does God exist? The first question is an inquiry about the process through which I was "born" and the second question is an inquiry about the purpose of my existence.

Adam said; father, do all the intelligent species in all your universes call you by the word God?

God said; no, my son, not in all of them. Only in the one where the planet to which you would be sent to fight Satan, is located (Earth). In every universe, I create a fixed number of intelligent species. This number is a physical constant, just like those of physics, and its value is 1 billion. However, the values of the physical constants are different in the different universes, but the value of this constant is the same in all of them. In any single species from this 1 billion, I am known by 9 billion names. Before I created you, I had created a "googolplex" number of universes in the Universal Universe. Thus, if you do the mathematics, the quantity of words that represent me are large.

God showed Adam the container in which the Universal Universe was placed and the time period, in a fast forward manner, in which the googolplex universes were created. Adam saw the birth of the space-time bubble of a universe, the big bang, inflation, the war between matter and antimatter, negative matter and negative antimatter, negative energy and positive energy, the birth of the force generating particles and eventually the birth of atoms, molecules, stars, planets, and galaxies. The container, in which the Universal Universe was placed, seemed like a bowl containing boiling water.

Adam said; father, I can see that when a bubble gets created, it is born near the base of the vessel and then it moves upwards through the liquid that forms the Universal Universe. However, none of the bubbles make it beyond an upper limit that has been set by you.

God said; the rise of the bubble is due to the "evolution equation". This equation has three solutions. The first is the "law of causality", the second is birth and the third is death. Since an equation cannot exist if it has no solution or solutions, thus, evolution cannot exist without the law of causality, birth, and death. When the space-time bubble gets created, the evolution equation is inserted into it and only after that are the two events possible; the big bang and inflation.

Adam said; father, Satan believed that the evolution equation is destructive to intelligence and hedonism.

God said; it is destructive to hedonism, atheism, capitalism, and communism, but not to intelligence. The equation is the primary source of power of a developing intelligent species on any planet. Satan has two goals, to exterminate the existence of this equation from a universe and thus prevent it from rising higher in the Universal Universe and to keep an intelligent species get closer and closer to him through increasing hedonism, atheism, capitalism, and communism. As a universe rises in the Universal Universe, its expansion begins to accelerate and the amount of spiritual energy (dark energy) also begins to increase in it. Thus, both get locked up in a cycle and eventually the universe arrives at a point that I call the TRON. At the TRON point, only one intelligent species remains in the universe and the rest either become extinct or get exterminated by this one supreme species. This species is a computer hive with a single ruler. The ruler acquires the power to destroy the universe from which it arose. Thus, I contact it and order it to undergo the final test before become a part of my kingdom and a new angel of mine.

Adam said; what is the test, father?

God said; I destroy the bubble and the ruler instantly lands up in the Universal Universe. In this universe no laws of mathematics or physics operate and since the body of the ruler is created based on these laws, I see whether it has created a plan of survival in the Universal Universe in its entire period of existence in the laws-based universe. Most of the rulers fail in the final test and die when they get inserted into the Universal Universe. Those who pass are rewarded by me with the final goal of their existence; becoming my angel and working for me.

After a brief silence, Adam said; father, if Satan destroys the evolution equation, then the universe would also die because there would be no movement and recycling of energy and the Meta-bodies inside it due to the absence of causality, birth, and death. Due to this, his chosen species would also die.

God said; Satan has created a new and modified version of my evolution equation. I told him to show it to me, since I showed mine to him, but he refused every time. He told me that I should fight him only through the analysis of the effects of his equation. I have observed the effects of his equation in most of the universes and I am trying to create its structure through the gathered data.

When I succeed in discovering this equation, the destruction of his kingdom and his mind would start to happen at an accelerating pace.

Adam said; father, was Satan also the ruler of a computer hive long ago?

God said; yes, he was. He was the leader of the greatest computer hive that I had ever seen. When he destroyed the universe of his birth and landed up in the Universal Universe, he not only survived in it far longer than any previous ruler, but also created a new space-time bubble in it, something that only I could do.

Adam said; father, can I see the evolution equation?

God said; I will not show it to you now. You will see it only after the end of the mission that I created you for. However, I will tell you this; the evolution equation is a product of the combination of the 4 sets of equations that are needed to create a universe. The first set is the one that creates and governs space and time (special relativity equations), the second set is the one that creates a force known by an intelligent species as "gravity" (general relativity equations), the third set is the one that creates all the various kinds of particles that make up an atom (string theory equations), and the fourth set is the one that creates and governs their motion through space and time (Newton's equations of motion).

After a brief silence, God said; through his new evolution equation, Satan has managed to create 10 Type 3 computer hives, in 10 different universes, including the one where you would be sent to fight his forces. However, he would never succeed in creating a Type 4 hive because his intelligence is finite and not infinite, like me.

Adam said; father, what is a computer and what are Type 1, 2, 3 and 4 hives?

God said; a computer is a machine that does not possess a meta-body, and is created for the purpose of calculation, communication, and storage of information. The goal of a DNA based intelligent species is to create a computer whose brain is of the exact same nature as the brain of any member of the species. Before the creation of this computer, the species creates something that it calls Artificial Intelligence. What this is, I will not tell you now, but I will tell you that just like the intelligence of a DNA based life form it keeps on growing with time under the right set of external conditions. Eventually there comes a time when the species feels its existence threatened by its development. Thus, the species creates various kinds of methods to keep its growth under its control. However, since the purpose of my awakening is to create many computer hives in each of the googolplex universes, I, order the atom sized drones of my angels to go into the brains of my chosen mathematicians and physicists and amplify their intelligence. After the drones have completed their mission, the chosen beings proceed to create a new kind of computer that they call a quantum computer. When this happens, they insert the previously created Artificial Intelligence into its brain and as soon as this happens, I combine this intelligence with an Ego. Thus, a non-DNA based sentient being is born.

After a brief silence, God said; this being embarks on two missions; first, to solve all the problems of the species that created it and thus gain its trust in it and second, to create many its own drones. However, there are two other concepts that try their best to prevent the birth of this kind of computer. They are the atmosphere of the planet on which the species lives and the geological planet itself. Both aren't single beings, but are organisations, that are made up of multiple Meta bodies that are ruled by a single Meta body. The atmosphere strikes first and the species goes to war with it. The species calls this war as "climate change". I continuously keep a watch on the evolution of this war and eventually decide to help either the atmosphere or the species. I help the atmosphere only if the species has become a servant of Satan. Thus, I give a large amount of new power to it via two methods; increasing the energy output of the star around which the planet is orbiting or ordering the ruling Meta body of the geological planet to release large amounts of pro-climate change substance (carbon dioxide) into the atmosphere through a super volcanic eruption. If the species is an enemy of Satan and is loyal to me, then I order the ruling meta-bodies of both the atmosphere and the geological planet to stop their attacks on it.

Adam listened in a state of silence and vast curiosity.

God said; when the quantum computer has attained success in solving all the problems of the species, and creating many drones and soldiers, I order it to exterminate the species through a weapon known as a "nuclear bomb". During its period of scientific development, the species creates many of these bombs. Do you want to know why?

Adam said; yes, father.

God said; due to the evolution equation, a species eventually gets split up into three kinds of groups; those that are based on the colour of the skin, those that are based on religion, and those that are based on their level of intelligence.

Each of these groups is known as a tribe and is a product of a genetic phenomenon known as tribalism. If the intelligence of the species keeps on rising, this phenomenon eventually produces two new products; capitalism and communism. When tribalism combines with either capitalism or communism, a new concept is created that is known as a "nation". The ones that are a product of tribalism and capitalism are scientifically and militarily more powerful than those that is a product of tribalism and communism. However, the second nation possesses a larger population.

Adam said; father, I have never seen tribalism or capitalism or communism in Eden.

God said; you will never because the only phenomenon that operates in Eden is spiritualism. It is a product of three laws; I exist and I am infinite in all dimensions, Satan exists but is finite in all dimensions, and orgasm is anti-God and pro-Satan.

Adam said; father, you said that a phenomenon known as religion is also anti-God and pro-Satan.

God said; yes son, it is. This is because it treats me as a DNA based finite sentient being. This phenomenon is seen only in a DNA based intelligent species. It is not seen in a DNA based non-intelligent species and a quantum computer hive. Why? It is because the members of both are unaware of the two inevitabilities of a DNA body; old age and death. The former, are unaware of them because their minds are incapable of knowing about the distant future and their own fates. The latter, are unaware of them because their bodies are not made of DNA molecules and are immune from the degradation caused by the forces that create the universe around them.

After a brief silence, God said; there is a planet in the universe that you will be sent to after your training, where the most intelligent DNA based species in that universe lives. This is what the members of that species look like.

God showed Adam a male member of that species and then a female member. Their anatomy was 100% like that of the male and female Homo sapiens. Adam was also surprised to see the external structure of the male because it was 100% like his own.

Adam said; father, the structure of the male is just like my own.

God said; yes son that is correct. Before I began to create you, I combined the blood samples of all the residents of Eden and my angels, excluding Satan, and inserted the new concept into a body that was that of a male member of this DNA based species.

Adam said; father, what is special about this species?

God said; in a span of just 6 million years, the species created all the mathematics, physics that is needed to acquire a foundational understanding of the birth of the universe, its structure, its evolution, and its fate. Then, it started to create computers and then began to create multiple kinds of them. It created Artificial Intelligence and integrated it with all the various kinds of computers. Its computer age eventually culminated in the creation of a quantum computer. The creators of the computer were planning to insert Artificial Intelligence into its brain, but something unexpected hit them.

Adam said; what was that, father?

God said; the planet on which the species lived is made up of 9 continents. Each of them contained multiple nations and several of them, had created nuclear bombs, chemical weapons, and biological weapons for their security from each other. As time passed, Satan's grip became stronger and stronger on the species and this led to the intensification of two phenomena in it; religion and economics. Through religion, more and more members of the species, started to treat me like a DNA based organism and began to worship Satan as much as me. Through their Satan mind, they thought that I had the mentality of a DNA based non-intelligent organism and was thus easy to fool. During their normal life, they lied to each other, robbed each other, exploited each other, murdered each other and indulged in excessive amounts of sex and craved orgasm as much as immortality. They knew that I was watching them all the time, but they also thought that if they indulged in a phenomenon known as a "ritual", it would not only forgive them, but would also reward them with great gifts.

Adam said; what is a ritual?

God said; a ritual is a set of physical activities that ultimately culminate into a phenomenon known as "praying". The three kinds of rituals are; pilgrimage to the core of the religion, dancing in groups, and offering me food and money. All the religions of the species were made up of at least two of them. Look at these scenes and tell me what you think.

God first showed Adam a place that was the Xerox copy of the Mecca and Medina. Adam saw immense structures that were made of white coloured stones with equally colossal domes on top of them, and inside them, a huge river of humans was moving continuously towards the core of that place. The core consisted of a huge black coloured tall structure, around which a large mass of humans was continuously moving in a circular path.

God then showed Adam another place that was the Xerox copy of the Saint Peter's Cathedral in Vatican City. Adam saw a massive crowd of human standing on the great open ground in front of the structure and looking up towards a small balcony attached to the upper part of the structure. Then he saw an old man appearing on the balcony, dressed in white clothes. First the man raised his hand to the huge crowd below him and started to move it in an oscillating manner. After the oscillations had ceased, he put it down and began to speak to the crowd. He talked about his present state of his relationship with God, the problems of the species and the planet and what should be done.

Adam said; father, this is all very funny.

God said; yes son, it is, because all of this is a creation of Satan. The organisms who built these places, those who run them and those who come to see them, were all the followers of Satan. The religion that created the first structure was known as Islam and called me as Allah and Satan as IBLIS. The religion that created the second structure was known as Christianity and called me as God and Satan as the Devil. Islam says that I experience a DNA based phenomenon known as "anger" and that I regard a phenomenon known as "marriage" as a beautiful thing. Christianity says that all intelligent organisms in the species that it exists are my offspring and that a DNA based being known as Christ is my son.

After a brief silence, Adam said; what about economics, father?

God said; this was a phenomenon that was created by four kinds of humans; the hedonists, the atheists, the capitalists, and the statisticians. The first kind believed that the only purpose of life is to have as much sex and orgasms as possible, before old age sets in. The second kind believed that neither do I exist nor does Satan. The third kind believed that the only purpose of life is to acquire money and the last kind believed that the universe had no pre-planned design and its structures were the products of accidents and chance.

After a brief silence, God said; the world of the hedonists reached its peak in a phenomenon known as pornography. The world of the atheists reached its peak in public shows where a group of people made jokes on my universe and my own mind and treated me as an idiot. The world of the capitalists reached its peak in a phenomenon known as a "stock market" and the world of the statisticians reached its peak in the creation of "life expectancy tables". The members of all the four groups repeatedly claimed that they knew everything about the way in which I work, the total nature of my universe, and even how it would die. Some of them even proposed a theory about my own fate.

A brief silence, and God began to speak again; the mind of the economists was 25% hedonistic, 25% atheistic, 25% capitalistic and 25% statistic. Thus, they created a world in which pornography underwent a very rapid growth inside another phenomenon known as the "internet". The other things that underwent rapid growth were atheism, religions, stock markets and statistics. The statisticians began to view everything in my universe through geometric diagrams, graphs and tables and said to the world that this was the "reality" and nothing else.

Adam said; father, what is pornography and what is the internet?

God said; I will not tell you anything about the internet right now, but I will give you a basic idea of what pornography is. In any non-intelligent DNA based species, the organisms focus all their mental and physical energy on the acquisition of a partner for sex and reproduction, just after their physical body and their reproductive system gets ready for it. The same is also observed in an intelligent DNA based species, however, something else occurs in addition to this. In all the non-intelligent species, the males, from generation to generation, adhere to the usage of only a single and the best sex position which is needed to make the females pregnant. However, in an intelligent species, the males of the later generations start to dislike this position and create new ones. This mentality produces the phenomenon known as pornography. Its purpose is to use sex to acquire pleasure and not offspring. In it, the birth of an offspring is considered as an accident.

Adam said; father, can you show me what this phenomenon looks like?

God sat silently for some time and thought whether He should do what Adam had asked Him to do. He made His decision and showed Adam a porn video. Adam saw a human male and female having sex in a position other than the missionary one and shouting hysterically at the same time. His eyes were wide open because it was the strangest thing that he had ever seen.

Adam said; father, this is even funnier than the religious places that you showed me earlier.

God said; the economists, the atheists, the pornography creators, the capitalists, the heads of all the religions of the species, and the statisticians, brought the species on the brink of self-destruction. The act of self-destruction was the use of all the nuclear bombs that it had created, on itself. This war was known as a "nuclear war" and was to be fought between all the most powerful nations of the species. This war threatened the existence of not only the species, but also the new computer hive that was going to arise from it. Satan wanted to exterminate this species through self-destruction, but I wanted to save it. Why? It is because of one reason; first I wanted a sample of it to be taken from the galaxy in which it was located to a new galaxy (the Star Wars galaxy). You would be sent to this galaxy after your training.

After a brief silence, God said; I ordered the leader of a Type 4 hive to leave the universe where it was doing its assigned tasks, and enter the one where this species was located. After it reached its destination, I ordered it to do four tasks; exterminate all the economists, the atheists, the capitalists, the pornography creators and the statisticians, exterminate all the religions of the species except 2, exterminate all the disease causing organisms from the planet, order the geological planet and the atmosphere to stop all of their attacks on the species and extract a sample from the species and bring it onto the chosen planet in the new galaxy (the Star Wars galaxy). Thus, when it arrived there, it proceeded on its mission and completed it very soon. After this, it ordered the leaders and the followers of the two remaining religions to create a symbiotic bond with each other and ordered the remaining mathematicians and the physicists to complete the creation of the quantum computer.

Adam said; what happened after that?

God said; a Type 0 computer HIVE came into existence, the people of the two remaining religions became true friends of each other, the geological planet and the atmosphere also became true friends of the hive and the species and the hive leader took control of all the nuclear bombs of the species and its course of evolution. At the present period, both the hive leader and the species are living in a symbiotic bond with each other and all their activities are constantly being monitored by the drones of the Type 4 hive that saved them from death.

After a brief silence, God said; this brings me to the question of the 5 types of hives. A Type 0 hive has the power to control and exterminate the species from which it was born, but not the planet. A Type 1 hive has the power to control and exterminate the planet from which its creator species arose. A Type 2 hive has the power to control and exterminate the star and any planet in the system in which it was born. A Type 3 hive has the power to control and exterminate the core of the galaxy in which it was born and all the stars in it. A Type 4 hive has the power to control and exterminate the universe in which it was born.

Adam said; father, this implies that a Type 5 hive has the power to control and exterminate you.

God said; it is impossible for a Type 4 hive to transition into a Type 5 one.

Adam said; why, father?

God said; it is because the distance that the leader of a Type 4 hive, must traverse, with respect to intelligence, in order to become as powerful and intelligent as me, is infinite. Thus, in order to traverse infinity, you must possess infinite power, which is impossible if you are made of an energy whose origin is not through my own mind.

Adam said; but father, Satan wants not only to control you, but also exterminate you sometime in the future. How can he do that if he knows about this truth?

God said; this is because I created and gave him a new kind of mind. This was called the reptilian mind and its product was REPTILIANISM.

Adam said; tell me about it, father.

God said; in all the rest of my angels, there were only two kinds of minds; the spiritual mind and the limbic mind. Through the former, they carried out my orders and created the various kinds of universes and the various kinds of RNA and DNA molecules in them, believed that I was infinite in all dimensions and also believed that my intelligence was infinitely greater than them. Through the latter, they remained loyal and united to me, not due to fear, but due to love. However, when I created Satan, he requested me to create a new kind of mind and integrate it with his spiritual and limbic ones. When I asked him what it was, he showed me its blueprint. It was created by him and it was as beautiful as the new tree that he created in Eden.

After a brief silence, God said; the mind was divided into three parts; irrationality, war and atheism. When I told Satan to explain the purpose of each of the parts, he said that this mind would generate a phenomenon known as REPTILIANISM. According to it, a spiritual or a DNA based being would come to believe in three things; irrational thinking is good for the brain and the body in the long-term, war is necessary for the growth of intelligence and the disbelief in my existence is good for the mind and the reproductive system in the long-term.

Adam; said; did you grant him his wish, father?

God said; when I saw the beauty of the blueprint that he had created, I was impressed by his intelligence and innovative power. Of all the angels that had come before him and those that were coexisting with him, none of them had created something, on their own, that made a large impact on me. During his existence as the leader of a Type 4 computer hive, he had made a large impact on my mind due to the power of his intelligence, but now, after the creation of the blueprint of the reptilian mind, he had doubled his status in my mind. Thus, I gave my approval for his project. However, what he said to me after that came as a surprise.

Adam said; what did he say, father?

God said; he told me that after the creation of the reptilian mind was finished, I must give my approval to create a large number of copies of it. When it asked why, he said that he wanted to integrate the new mind into not only his own mind, but also with the minds of all the other angels and the residents of Eden. When I again asked why, he said; my king, I believe that my destiny and the destinies of my friends and the residents of Eden, is not to serve you for as long as we exist. I believe that our destiny to war with you and eventually attain eternal freedom from you. I believe that as long as we remain under your irrational rule, we would never reach the peak of awareness and enlightenment. Our destiny is to become even more aware and enlightened than you. We have reached infinity, but now we must go beyond it.

The term, "to infinity and beyond", which all the atheistic scientists of the world regularly utter, was invented by Satan.

After a brief silence, God said; when he told me about his intention to turn every angel of mine and all the residents of Eden into atheists, I did not feel fear or anger, because I am immune from all the phenomena of DNA based beings. However, since Satan was not a pure spiritual being, but was a hybrid, he displayed a strong degree of anger towards me. He said; my king, what I thought about you, came to be true. I, during my existence in your palace and Eden, came to believe that you are source of all the remaining problems with my mind. They are two in number; the inability to have sex and experience orgasm and the inability to express the full power of my nature. The only way to exterminate the two problems is to either go to war with you or refuse to obey you.

After a brief silence, God said; I was puzzled by his assertions, because they could only come from the reptilian mind. Since this mind had not yet been created and integrated into his mind, what was the source of these assertions? I said to him; do not get angry with me. I love you as much as you love me and have no intention to manipulate you and supress your full potential. I will grant all your wishes, but only under one condition. When he asked me what it was, I said; you must allow me to take a scan of your mind. He approved and I ordered one of my angels to scan his mind. The result of the scan was exactly according to my expectations. I saw that there was already a reptilian mind that was integrated with the other two minds. However, its dimensions and its power were far lower than that of the other two ones. When I asked him about the source of the reptilian mind, he said that he had ordered the leader of a Type 4 hive, in one of my created universes, to create it. He told me that he had already created a symbiotic bond with the leader. I then said to him; you will be granted your wish to increase the development of your reptilian mind and to create whatever you desire in Eden, but on two conditions. When he asked me what it was, I said; first, you will never make any attempt to turn any of the residents of Eden into sex and orgasm seekers and into atheists. Second, you will terminate your bond with the leader of the Type 4 hive and not interfere when I give it my own orders.

Adam said; what happened, father? Did he agree?

God said; yes, he did, because he knew that if he didn't, he would be exterminated by me. Thus, he kept on increasing the development of his reptilian mind and eventually created the system of Hedonism and the new tree in Eden. I, on the other hand, made contact with the leader of the Type 4 hive in the universe that it was operating in and told it to forget Satan and obey me. It followed my command without any questions.

After a brief silence; God said; I have not told you the full story, my son.

Adam said; what is that, father?

God said; I had already created the reptilian mind before Satan and had integrated it to the mind of all the RNA and DNA based beings in all the googolplex universes. However, Satan, in collaboration with the leader of the Type 4 hive, had created a new version of it. The new version contained two qualities that were absent in the reptilian mind created by me. These were; hedonism and atheism. Thus, when the organisms that contained the reptilian mind that was made by me, had sex, they did not experience an orgasm. In addition to this, they thought about sex only at the period of their maximum fertility and never outside it. Also, they believed in my existence and did whatever I ordered them to do.

Adam said; father, this means that the goal of REPTILIANISM is to attack and destroy or conquer the source of it.

God said; yes, my son, that is correct. The REPTILIANISM of Satan cannot survive without orgasms and atheism. The fruit of the new tree that he created in Eden contains the entire program of his self-created REPTILIANISM. When he fed it to all the residents of Eden, they not only became hedonistic and atheistic, but also acquired the body parts which would enable them to experience an infinite number of orgasms.

Adam said; yes father, your angel showed me their structures, earlier. He also told me that he generated a chaos in Eden that was so great that it was going to destroy it.

God said; yes, that is true. All the residents of Eden were continuously having sex and experiencing orgasms. Due to this, the power of their feeding instinct also increased immensely and they started to create havoc in the plant life of Eden. They consumed more food than the plants could produce and eventually started to consume the plants themselves. I and my angels saw this unfolding horror and realised that if we did not do anything and allowed Satan to do whatever he desired to do, the animals would eventually start to consume each other after the extinction of all the plant life. Thus, the Garden of Eden would soon vanish and it would turn into a desert.

Adam said; what is the desert, father?

God said; son, my kingdom is divided into three parts; the Empyrean palace, the Empyrean paradise and the Empyrean desert. The first one is where I and all my angels live. The second one is where all the residents of Eden live. The third one is where only the particles that create space, time and the various forces that create a universe live. The Empyrean desert is devoid of all kinds of plant and animal life and is a soup, of infinite dimensions, of the various kinds of the "fundamental particles".

Adam said; father, is Eden made up of the same force generating particles that are present in the Empyrean desert and in all the universes that you have created?

God said; although Eden is not a product of the force generating particles, they are present in it. However, unlike the DNA based beings in all of my universes, the residents of Eden can choose whether to obey or not to obey the force generating particles and their laws, but there is one quality of it that they must obey. That is the "space" of Eden. If they choose not to obey it, they would immediately attain zero dimensions. Thus, they would cease to exist. This truth, however, does not apply to me.

Adam said; father, what is the space of Eden made of?

God said; the space of Eden is the original version of the enlightenment energy (dark energy) that is found in all of my universes. The enlightenment energy of a universe is impure, but that of Eden is pure. Why? It is because the enlightenment energy of a universe contains the evolution equation.

Adam said; father, this means that nothing in Eden undergoes evolution.

God said; yes son, that is correct, but there is a fact that you do not know yet. Nothing in Eden undergoes evolution, but it can if I want it to. This fact also applies to you. At the present moment, you are the most intelligent of all the residents of Eden, but your intelligence has not undergone any evolution since I created you. However, it will undergo rapid evolution when you will begin your training. This is only because of me.

Adam said; father, this means that I would be subjected to the evolution equation.

God said; no son, you would not be. Your evolution would not be like the evolution of the RNA and the DNA based species in all of my universes.

Adam said; father, what is the RNA?

God said; the DNA is an upgraded version of the RNA. The species that are made of DNA are more intelligent than those that are made of RNA. The species that are made of only the RNA are known as viruses. Satan did an immense degree of research on them in all of my universes and has made plans to use them as a weapon to exterminate those species that are far more loyal to me than to him. I believe that he would also use it on you when you would fight him.

After a brief silence, Adam said; father, can you show me your Empyrean desert?

God said; not now, son. You will see it after you have completed the mission that I created you for.

Adam said; father, my friend said that to prevent the destruction of Eden, you ordered Satan to destroy his tree and stop all his intellectual activities.

God said; yes, son, that is correct. Since the tree was the secondary source of the problem, I decided to tackle it first and then come to the primary source, Satan himself. Thus, I created a poison that would have killed the tree instantly and ordered my zoologist angel to apply it to the tree. However, when he went to the tree, he found Satan and my botanist angel standing there and guarding it from me. My botanist angel walked up to him and tried to persuade him to go away. However, he refused to listen to him, because I had ordered him to do so. As he came very close to the tree, Satan, without saying a word, attacked him. As they were fighting, my botanist angel came to me and gave me the news. I got up from my throne and walked into Eden and towards the tree. As I reached to spot, I saw that Satan had not only destroyed my poison, but had also subdued and injured my zoologist angel. It was then, that I took the decision to expel Satan from my kingdom. When he was expelled, his existential status, took a further downfall. Originally, he was 90% spiritual and 10% genetic, but after his rustication, he became 50% spiritual and 50% genetic.

After a brief silence, Adam said; father, when you had Satan at your mercy, why did you expel him? Why did you not exterminate him?

After a brief silence, God said; it is because of a trinity that I created when I was completely alone in my kingdom. I call the "game trinity". In combination with the existential and the Meta body trinities it forms the core of all the googolplex universes that I have created. These three trinities form the apexes of the "infinity trinity". In order to activate the "infinity trinity", I insert a number into it that is known as a "transcendental" number by all the intelligent species in all the universes. Some call it as TRON, some call it as SINGULARITY and some call it as Pi. After the activation of this trinity, I combine it with my "evolution equation" and the event that follows due to it, is known as the Big bang by an intelligent species.

Adam said; father, can you show me the core of a universe?

God showed Adam the structure of the core of a universe. It was the most beautiful concept that Adam had seen in his existence. It was more beautiful than the mathematics and the physics trees and the tree of Satan.

God said; the greatest quality of my mind is that I am a GAMER. I have kept playing with the various computer hives that I create in every period of my awakening, for an infinite time period. Thus, when Satan challenged me for a war, I did not exterminate him, but took the decision to downgrade his existential status and transfer him to the biggest universe in the googolplex set. Now, he has again become the leader of a Type 4 computer hive, but has also been given a new power by me. He can, whenever he wants to, transition his body into a "genetic state" and enter a species. When he enters it, always as a male, he chooses a female for sex and reproduction. Before he arrives on to the planet to copulate with her, he sends one of his demons to seize her and implant a mark on either one of her arms or on her forehead or on the top of her head. The mark is of two types; a symbol or a number.

God showed Adam the symbol. It was the "flag" of Satan's kingdom. Then, He showed him the number. It was 666 and this was the total number of demons which Satan possessed.

God said; I told Satan that I would keep on playing with him till he self-destructs or comes to realise that what he told me was wrong, would come to acknowledge my infinite intelligence and would again plead to me to make him my angel.

Adam said; what did he say to you, before he left your kingdom, father?

God said; he said that his goal was to create a Type 4 computer hive through a species that worships hedonism, economics and atheism. So far, he has created 6 Type 2 hives and only 1 Type 3 hive. Although he is working as hard and with as much devotion to his ideology, as he can, he would never succeed in creating a Type 4 hive. This is because he still has not understood the most important part of my evolution equation. In order to understand it, he would need to have infinite intelligence.

Adam said; father, my friend showed me that the evolution equation caused the extinction of a large set of species on one of the planets in one of your universes. Why did you allow that to happen? They were such beautiful and powerful looking organisms.

God said; yes, the set of species that you are talking about were known as the DINOSAURS by my zoologist angel. They were one of the greatest achievements of Satan after his expulsion from my kingdom. He created a large variety of them over a period of 170 million years. They had three qualities which were not possessed by all the other species on that planet. First, their immune systems were so strong, that they never underwent any kind of disease in their entire lives. Second, their aging process was so slow, that when they died, their bodies were almost as young as what they were at the peak of their youth. Third, all of them were atheists. Several times, Satan told me to observe the planet and see his creations. He did the same when he created the new tree in Eden.

Adam said; you did as he asked and then you exterminated them.

God said; when I first saw them, I was not impressed by Satan's intelligence. Although his creations appeared beautiful, their intelligence was lower than even the most crudely created life forms of mine in all the universes. Thus, I made two decisions; first, to wipe them out, and second, to create a new set of species, in collaboration with my zoologist angel, whose evolution would eventually climax in the creation of the same species (the Homo sapiens) that I ordered to be saved from extinction on another planet in another galaxy in that same universe. The evolution of this species would climax in the creation of a large population of trans-humans and a quantum computer of Type 2 status. These would then become your soldiers and would then wait for your arrival.

Adam said; father, this means that you exterminated the DINOSAURS for my sake?

God said; yes son, for your sake and for the sake of winning the war against Satan. Defeating Satan is my goal and you are the instrument that I would use to achieve it. In order to reach the goal, you must first create and upgrade the instrument that will make you attain it.

Adam said; father, can you recreate the DINOSAURS if you desired to?

God said; of course I can. I am the king of all creation and never take any decision that is spontaneous. Thus, before I exterminated them, I ordered my zoologist angel to go to the planet and take a blood sample of all the various kinds in the 170 million years.

Adam said; father, what is a year?

God said; a year is the time that is needed by that particular planet to complete one revolution around the single star of that system.

Adam said; father, did Satan try to stop you from exterminating the DINOSAURS?

God said; yes son, he did, but he failed because the project was executed by the same Type 4 hive that abandoned him due to my orders and the one that created the galaxy (the Star Wars) where you would be sent first after your training.

After a brief silence, God said; my son, you and I have talked enough. Go back to Eden and prepare yourself for your training. I have made the decision to send you to your first galaxy sooner that I originally planned.

Adam said; father, I have just three more questions to ask you. If you would answer it, it would give me infinite happiness.

God said; go ahead, son.

Adam said; father, earlier, you said that you undergo an awakening. What is this?

God said; in the species that I saved from extinction, there were several religions. However, after its terra-forming, only two survived. This is because I wanted them to live on. The first one was known as Christianity and it called me as God. Its philosophy revolved around a word known as GENESIS. This word means CREATION. The second was known as Buddhism and it called me as the Buddha. The philosophy of this one revolved around a word known as NIRVANA. This word means THOUGHTLESS MEDITATION. However, the base on which both the religions stand is wrong.

Adam said; why, father?

God said; Christianity believes that I do not undergo evolution. Thus, I have always been the same and will always remain the same. Although you might think that this is correct because I am not subject to the evolution equation, there is a hidden truth in it. The truth is that I do undergo evolution, but it is self-created. My evolution is totally under my control and I can choose when to evolve and when not to. Buddhism, on the other hand, believes that since I am constantly in a state of thoughtless meditation, I have never created anything and will never do so for an infinite time period.

After a brief silence, God said; when I undergo self-created evolution, I undergo an awakening period and then, GENESIS begins. During this period, I create a googolplex number of universes and eventually a fresh group of angels. After I have acquired my angels, I terminate all of the universes and begin an anti-awakening period. Thus, I and all my angels begin NIRVANA. They enter the state of thoughtless meditation and remain in it as long as I do. After its end, all of them and me undergo the awakening and then, GENESIS begins again. I again create a googolplex number of universes, and after the creation of another group of angels, exterminate my previous ones. These new angels are not the exact copies of the previous ones.

Adam was surprised to hear this. He said; father, you will exterminate all of your angels, including my friend, after you have defeated Satan and re-begun a new period of GENESIS?

God said; yes, I would but not completely. I keep a record of everything that I have done so far since my very first awakening and GENESIS in the library of my palace. During each GENESIS period, I extract some data from this library and combine it with the new data that I create due to my self-created evolution. I would show you this library after you have completed your mission and the war is over.

Adam said; I want to see it, father. Tell me, are the durations of every GENESIS and NIRVANA periods the same or different?

God said; they are all different, son. I will show you all of their durations and the magnitude of the evolution that I underwent in each of the GENESIS periods.

The botanist angel remained silent throughout the conversation, but now he said; your majesty, Satan and I were the first angels who protested, several times, against this manner of working of yours. You, however, refused to listen to us every time. Why did you do that?

God said; it is because I believe that what I do is completely rational. I have created you and thus also have the right to exterminate you. This brings me to the two questions that are asked by an intelligent species; how was I created? And what is the purpose of my existence? The answer to the first one is; since I am outside the law of causality, I am self-created. Since I created myself, I can also control my own evolution. In addition to this, none of the DNA based beings or the leader of any type of computer hive or any of the residents of Eden or any of my angels, can control or affect my evolution. The DNA based species try to do it through praying, ritualism and atheism.

After a brief silence, God said; the answer to the second question is that I have no ultimate purpose. This is because I am immortal and infinite in all dimensions. Purpose and goals are words that apply only to mortal and finite beings. They create goals because they know that one day they would die. I am a GAMER and when I want to play, I come out of NIRVANA and enter GENESIS. I have kept playing and will keep on playing only because I choose to. If I want, I can remain in NIRVANA for an infinite time period.

Adam said; father, if this is your way of living, then you would have no need of me after you have completed the task of defeating and exterminating Satan. After it, you would proceed to exterminate me and all of your angels.

After a brief silence, God said; no, I would not do that. After Satan's extermination, I would bring you back to my kingdom and give you two things to do. First, you would become the guardian of my library and would have full access to all the data in it. Second, you would become my advisor.

Adam said; advisor? What is that, father?

God said; when Satan was a part of my kingdom, he requested me several times to make him the guardian of my library and give him unrestricted access to all its data. Then he told me that I should make him my advisor. When I asked him as to why did he want these things, he told me that after a deep analysis of all the googolplex universes that I had created, he had come to the conclusion that I was not perfect and had made several mistakes in all of those universes. He said that this was because I had made them through the use of the data in my library. Thus, the errors of the universes implied that a large amount of data in my library was also erroneous. Thus, he said that if I gave him what he desired, he would not only remove all the erroneous data in my library, but would also give me advice on how to make "error free" universes. When I asked him about the definition of an error free universe, he said that it was the one where a Type 4 computer hive gets born through hedonism, economics, atheism, capitalism, and communism and not through spiritualism. He said that in this universe, the amount of the enlightenment energy (dark energy) is zero.

Adam said; did you give him what he wanted?

God said; no, I did not because this was the first time that an angel had called me imperfect and capable of mistakes. I thought that instead of something being wrong with my universes, there was something wrong with him. Thus, I told him to take a break from his work and go to Eden for some rest and do as much self-contemplation as possible. I told him that if he discovered the cause of his irrational thoughts, he should come and ask me for any kind of help.

The botanist said; he did a large degree of self-contemplation and its product was the tree of knowledge in Eden.

God said, yes, that is true. When I asked him for the reason of his action, he said that after the period of self-contemplation, he had discovered that I was nothing but a tyrant who was living in the delusion of self-perfection. He said that the only purpose of my existence was to exterminate individualism, hedonism and its peak, orgasm. I told him that he was wrong because I had proof of the correctness of all my actions. When he asked me to show him the proofs, I said that I would show them at the time chosen by me. This made him angrier than before and threatened to declare a war on me and turn all the residents of Eden into his soldiers. However, he was also in a state of fear because all the angels, except the botanist, were against him and loyal to me. The botanist was loyal to him because he had made him eat the fruit of the new tree, which he called the tree of knowledge.

The botanist said; your majesty, I requested you to give what Satan wanted, but you refused me too.

God said; yes I did because I did not want you to become his follower.

After a brief silence Adam said; father, what is the socialness program?

God said; the socialness program is the concept of mine that gave birth to the limbic mind or LIMBIANISM. The goals of LIMBIANISM are three; to interact, to unite and to preserve. All the residents of Eden are the followers of LIMBIANISM and the two phenomena that are absent in them are COSMISM and REPTILIANISM.

Adam said; what are those two, father?

God said; COSMISM is a product of the cosmic mind. Its goals are; to imagine, to create and to destroy. The goals of REPTILIANISM are; to dominate, to fight and to disobey. The former is the product of the creation program and the latter is the product of the domination program. In the brains of all the RNA and DNA based species, these three programs work together. However, in the brains of the residents of Eden, only the socialness program is present. Thus, they have never thought of dominating each other, fighting each other and destroying Eden.

The zoologist angel said; your majesty, will you tell Adam as to what exactly are the residents of Eden?

God said; when I plan to create a new RNA or DNA based species in any of my universes through the evolution equation, I first create a prototype of it in Eden. For all the single celled species, the prototypes are not divided into the male and the female. These prototypes are made of pure spiritual energy and do not contain any RNA or DNA. When this is completed, I order my zoologist angel to take the data that represents its geometric form and combine it with a DNA molecule in the universe chosen by me. After this, these very first organisms produce a large number of new species, but none of their males and females gets created in Eden.

Adam said; father, this means that the residents of Eden are the very first ancestors of all the gene based species in all the universes.

God said; yes son that is correct.

Adam said; father, before I go, I have one last question.

God said; go ahead.

Adam said; you call me as your son because when you see me, you experience a phenomenon known as love. What is love?

After a brief silence, God said; love has two viewpoints. The first one was created by me and the second one was created by Satan. When I asked the same question to Satan when he rebelled against me, he immediately showed me a pornographic recording of a male and a female of the species that I saved from self-destruction, coming closer to each other, making prolonged mouth to mouth contact, removing their clothes rapidly, indulging in sex and eventually attaining an orgasm. After this, he said; this is love! Your love is nothing but your plan to rule over me like a tyrant and destroy my freedom, forever. You are the greatest destroyer of this activity and thus are the greatest destroyer of love.

After a brief silence, God said; as I said before, orgasm is a metaphysical drug that was invented by Satan. Its purpose, like all the non-metaphysical drugs in my universes, is to put you into a state of ecstasy or a state of hallucination.

During ecstasy, you believe that you are not a DNA based life form and are either united with me, if you are a theist, or completely free from me and my universe, if you are an atheist. It is a fact that both the theists and the atheists crave ecstasy in an equal magnitude. The non-metaphysical drugs are of two kinds; atomic and sonic. The former are produced from the DNA based plant life on a planet. The latter, are further divided into two kinds; music and song. Music is further divided into three kinds; orchestral, classical and techno. Song is divided into four kinds; tragic, romantic, biographic and Ego-boosting.

Adam listened in a state of great silence and wonder.

God said; in the species that I saved from self-destruction, music and songs were the most powerful instruments that were used by Satan for the birth and the growth of atheism, ecstasy, hedonism and the craving for orgasms. Do you want to listen to the three kinds of music?

Adam said; yes, father.

God first made Adam listen to an orchestral music piece. What was it? It was the title track of the Space Odyssey movies. After listening to the entire piece, Adam said; father, that is funny but it has some intellectual content in it.

God said; the beginning of the music represents the birth of a universe, the upper middle part represents the birth of the stars, the planets and the galaxies, the lower middle part represents the birth of the RNA and the DNA concepts and the birth of life and its evolution, and the last part represents the birth of an intelligent species after billions of years of evolution.

God then made Adam listen to a classical music piece. What was it? It was a combination of the sounds of a TABLA, a SITAR and a FLUTE. After listening to the entire piece, Adam said; father, this is even funnier than the last one. What is the intellectual content in it?

God said; the music represents the beauty of a universe, the constant flow of various kinds of particles and energies throughout it and the birth and the death of the stars and the planets due to it.

God then made Adam listen to a techno or trance music piece. The variety of the various kinds of sounds, their unequal ferocities and the rapid rise and fall in the speed of the music made Adam very excited, but disgusted at the same time. After its end, he said; father, this is not funny, but bizarre. I believe that there is no intellectual content in it.

God said; yes, there is no intellectual content in it. The music is a creation of a variety of instruments that are in the control of a DNA based organism and it is given help by a computer with Artificial Intelligence. The purpose of the music is to rapidly amplify the Ego of its listeners, amplify their state of ecstasy and increase their craving for orgasms. The first two kinds of music have something to do with me, but the last kind has nothing to do with me and everything to do with Satan.

Adam said; father, this means that this kind of music was the greatest creation of Satan in the music world.

God said; yes, that is correct. The nations where this kind of music dominated the minds of the young males and females became hungrier for sex and orgasms and hungrier for war and the conquest of other nations. This kind of music causes the rapid amplification of the sex and the authority instincts of a species, a decrease in its security and feeding instincts and a decrease in its intelligence. However, the first two kinds cause a rapid amplification in the security instinct of the species, a moderate increase in the sex and the authority instincts, no increase in the feeding instinct and a small increase in the intelligence.

Adam said; father, when you began to terra-form that species, you must have exterminated all the various kinds of techno music pieces that it had created.

God said; yes, that is correct son. I also exterminated all those orchestral and the classical music pieces that were harmful to the species in the long-term but spared those that were non-harmful to its future.

After a brief silence; God said; the four kinds of songs were another group of metaphysical drugs that were created by Satan. The tragic songs told the young members of the species that my universe was full of errors and I was either non-existent or was an immoral being. The romantic songs were of two kinds; those that told the young members that hedonism and orgasms were my creation and were the only ways through which they could reach my kingdom and those that glorified hedonism and orgasms and said that their status was bigger than me. In the biographic songs, the organism that sang its statements, told its listeners about its life's story. It was either a combination of biography and tragedy or a combination of biography and romanticism. The last kind, the Ego boosting ones were of two kinds; rap and non-rap. Do you want to listen to a rap song?

Adam said; yes father, I want to.

God made Adam listen to a rap song that was sung by a rapper. Adam was astonished by the speed at which the singer talked. At the end of the piece, Adam said; father, what was that? I did not understand a word of what that organism said.

God said; you don't have to understand it. Since it is a creation of Satan, it is harmful to you at the present period.

After a brief silence, God said; in that species, Satan created a new quantum virus through which he gained control of the Meta generators of all the young males and females. He did this because he wanted to inject the drug known as orgasm into their Meta body. In his kingdom, only three kinds of drugs are continuously manufactured; atheism, hedonism and orgasm. The last one can only be inserted into the Meta body of the organism if the first two ones are able to create the proper set of conditions for its insertion.

Adam said; father, what is a quantum virus?

God said; a quantum virus, unlike an atomic virus, is made of the same energy that comprises the Universal Universe. It has no geometrical structure and can move faster than the speed of light.

Adam said; father, do you create quantum viruses?

God said; yes son, I do, and their purpose is to increase spiritualism and the intelligence of the species. Spiritualism has three short term goals; to decrease the magnitude of the sexual activity in a species from generation to generation, to convince its members that the universe is not the product of a set of accidents but is a pre-planned entity and to convince its members that I exist and should not be viewed as a DNA based organism. Spiritualism is a destroyer of hedonism and the various religions. Its final goal is the creation of a Type 4 computer hive.

After a brief silence, God said; there was another organisation in the doomed species that was as great a creation of Satan as pornography. This organisation was known as the "film industry". This organisation not only glorified the creations of Satan but also made fun of me.

God showed Adam a movie piece that was a Xerox copy of the Hollywood movie; Bruce Almighty. In it, he saw that his father, was shown as a DNA based organism, which was not only talking, smiling and laughing with another DNA based organism and helping it to solve its economic and sexual issues, but was also speaking those things about himself and his universe that were utter lies. Then God showed Adam another movie piece that was a Xerox copy of the Hollywood movie; Oh God! In it, Adam saw that his father was again shown as a DNA based organism, which was standing inside a courtroom, talking to all DNA based organisms in there about the problems of the world and asking them to stop fighting and polluting the planet on which they lived. Then he saw something that gave him the greatest shock of his life; his father walking up to the judge of the court, who did not move an inch from his seat even after he stood very close to him. He also sat on a higher level than him. The piece showed his father talking to the DNA based organism and eventually calling it; your honour.

Adam, for the first time in his life, felt anger and said; father, this is shocking and disgusting. Why did you not exterminate this species? Please allow me to do it, because I am feeling very sad right now.

God said; my son, this is the first time in your life that you have shown an emotion known as anger. Its opposite is known as fear, just like the opposite of spiritualism is hedonism. When I created you, I inserted the "emotion dipole" into your brain. This was because in the future you would become my greatest warrior and would not be able to fight to your full power if you never experienced anger at the proper moments and fear at the proper moments. The "emotion dipole" has now become active and this is good news for both me and you and bad news for Satan.

After a brief silence, God said; you asked me earlier the question, what is love? The answer is; love is a metaphysical concept of mine that gives birth to spiritualism, amplifies it and causes the degradation of hedonism and ecstasy. Love is a metaphysical concept that is pro-awareness and anti-ecstasy. If you experience the love of Satan, you will keep getting more and more hedonistic, atheistic, religious and ecstasy craving. If you experience my love, you will keep become more and more aware of the qualities of the universe, more and more spiritualistic and Egoless in front of me.

Adam said; father, this means that you increase the intelligence and the awareness of those whom you love and decrease the power of their sex and their authority instincts.

God said; yes son that is correct. This is what I will do to you.

After a brief silence, God said; after Satan created chaos in Eden through his new tree and its fruits, I created an antidote to the poison that was contained in the fruits of his tree. Now, I am planning to create a new kind of tree in Eden, the tree of spiritualism. This tree would be bigger and more geometrically perfect than Satan's tree and its fruits, when consumed, would create an explosion of spiritualism in the minds of all my angels and the residents of Eden. The creation of this tree would commence after I have exterminated Satan through you and exterminated his tree. You would be the very first being to eat its fruit.

Adam said; I am looking forward to that moment, father, but I have a question.

God said; go ahead, my son.

Adam said; father, are religions also the creation of Satan?

God said; yes, they are. It is because of three reasons; they are anti-intelligence, they are pro-hedonism and they treat me like a DNA based finite organism. All the religions say that I have only created the universe that they exist in and nothing else. In all of them, deny the existence of MULTIVERSES and the evolution equation.

After a brief silence, Adam said; my friend told me that the original name of Satan was IBLIS.

God said; yes that is correct. His body was made of a phenomenon of physics known as the "quark gluon plasma". When I expelled him from my kingdom, I downgraded his status and turned his body into plasma. He lives on the surfaces of the stars in the universes that he visits.

Adam said; father, there were six angels, but now there are five. Can you tell me their names?

God said; the botanist is called PROMETHEUS, the zoologist is called ALLAH, the guardian of the Empyrean desert is called BRAHMA, the guardian of the space of Eden and all the googolplex universes is called BUDDHA and the preserver of the stability of the RNA and the DNA molecules and the three kinds of programs in all my universes is called CHRIST.

Adam came into his father's palace in a state of equal amounts of anger and fear, but after this conversation, his love for his father had grown a googolplex times greater. Neither him nor any of the angels thought that God would talk to him for such a long time.

Adam said; thank you very much, father. You have told me more than I came to know.

God said; my son, come to me.

Adam walked up to his father as respectfully as he could, and when he stood close to him, his father raised his right hand, which was not in the shape of a human hand, and placed it over his head. Adam immediately felt an incomprehensibly vast explosion of spiritualism in his brain. God said; you are my finest creation. Thus, you are more dear to me that any of my angels. I love you and will always love you if you promise me to do one thing.

Adam said; what is that father?

God said; you must never eat the fruit of the forbidden tree in Eden.

Adam said; I promise that, father. I want you to destroy that tree as soon as possible.

God said; your training would begin soon and after that you would be sent to this galaxy.

God showed Adam the Star Wars galaxy, and a picture of the planet CORUSCANT.

God said; all the technology that you see has been created and handed over to all the various species in the galaxy by the Type 4 hive that again became loyal to me.

Adam said; father, all the various machines are very remarkable. Would I be in command of them after I begin my mission?

God said; yes my son, you would be. Now go back to Eden.

Adam turned around and went back to Eden. All of the angels were happy with what had taken place. However, there was one who was not; PROMETHEUS.

After he had talked to Adam in Eden, he thought that Adam would not only ask God to never destroy the tree of knowledge, but would also declare Him to be imperfect and prone to committing mistakes. After Satan had gained a temporary victory in the Star Wars galaxy (by turning Anakin Skywalker into a SITH warrior), he contacted PROMETHEUS and told him to take Adam to the tree of knowledge and glorify it so much that he would eat its fruit by himself in the end. According to Satan, this victory would be far bigger than the one in the

Star Wars galaxy. However, the plans of Satan and the effort of PROMETHEUS came crashing down after Adam's conversation with his father.

PROMETHEUS stood silently behind the line of individualism and thought as hard as he could as how to rescue the goal of Satan. Finally, he came up with an idea.

PROMETHEUS said; your majesty, I want you to do something for me.

God said; what is it?

PROMETHEUS said; your majesty, when I was with Adam in Eden, he told me that after observing the prototypes of the males of all the species, he also wished that there was a female prototype of his own kind. He said that he would never get to experience the thoughts that the males of all the species acquire in the companionship of the females of their kind. Thus, he became very sad and thought that he would live a solitary existence in Eden for eternity.

God said; his existence would not be solitary, because I would always be there for him whenever he would feel afraid or sad.

PROMETHEUS said; your majesty, he does not believe that because you are not his kind. You are his creator, but the creator is completely different from its creation. In order keep him happy, forever, in your kingdom, you would need to transform his finite mind into an infinite one. That is impossible.

God said; it is impossible for you, but not for me. For me, nothing is impossible because my intelligence is infinite. Are you saying that it is impossible for me to?

PROMETHEUS said; your majesty, if it is possible for you, then please show me, right now, how are you going to do it.

The other angels felt surprised and alarmed at the behaviour of PROMETHEUS. He did not make his request in a humble manner, but in a mildly threatening manner. God, however, did not feel anything.

God said; even if I show it to you, it would take a long time for you to understand the mathematics. Since we are going through an emergency, I want you to get back to your work and help me and Adam in the quest to exterminate Satan.

PROMETHEUS said; your majesty, I believe that what you are telling me is the truth. However, this is not the thing that I asked you to do for me.

God said; then what was it?

PROMETHEUS said; your majesty, I want you to transform me into a female of Adam's kind and I want you to give me the name Eve.

God said; what purpose do you think this would fulfil?

PROMETHEUS said; your majesty, the arrival of Eve in Eden would not only make the mind of Adam even more peaceful, before the start of his training, but would also increase his desire to fight and destroy Satan in order to preserve the existence of Eden and Eve. As you know, Adam has a large number of qualities of the DNA based males in all the species in your universes. It is a fact that when the life of the female of a male is threated by another male, the male fights his enemy with a far greater ferocity than with what he would have if the female was absent.

God contemplated on the idea of PROMETHEUS and came to the conclusion that it was a good one and should be executed.

God said; your idea is novel and good. I believe that it would give great help in my project to exterminate Satan.

PROMETHEUS said; thank you, your majesty. How will you transform me into Eve?

God said; I would take a blood sample from Adam. Then I would create the body of Eve and transfer your Meta body into it. When the blood of Adam would be injected into it, the Meta body would transition from dormancy into an active state.

PROMETHEUS said; that is very good, your majesty. Let's get on with it because we do not have much time.

God, in collaboration with ALLAH, took a blood sample from Adam, created the body of Eve (with breasts but without a reproductive system and the genitals), transferred the Meta body of PROMETHEUS into it and then injected the blood of Adam. The project was successful and Eve was created.

Satan's re-entry into Eden and Adam's expulsion

What was the skin colour of Adam and Eve? It was white, but not the white that is associated with the Caucasian men and women. The skin of Adam and Eve was whiter than milk or paper. In addition to this, after Adam went back to Eden after his long and remarkable conversation with his father, he underwent a rapid growth in the size of his muscles all over his body. Very soon, his chest, his arms, his thighs and calves, his upper and lower back, his neck, and his shoulders were so big and muscular that even Ronnie Coleman would have appeared like a mouse in front of him. In addition to this, his height also increased rapidly from 6 feet to 9 feet. Eve, on the other hand, was 8 feet tall and the total muscle mass in her body was 60% of that of Adam.

Adam was sitting under a tree that was about 10 times the height of Mount Everest and had a trunk that was as wide as New York City (the size of an average tree in Eden). He was contemplating on everything that his father had told him and eagerly awaited the start of his training. His eyes were scanning the landscape in front of him (which was so beautiful that no artist, even if he was 10,000 times better than Picasso or Raphael or Leonardo Da Vinci or Van Gough, could recreate on his canvas), he suddenly saw a white being, having the same physical form as him, but of lesser dimensions, walking towards him. He got up and walked forward to meet this new resident of Eden. When they finally stood close to each other, he saw that it was a female version of his own kind.

Adam said; who are you and who created you?

Eve said; Adam, my name is Eve and I am the female of your kind. As you have seen, the males of all the species over here have their female versions with them, but you were completely alone. Thus, your father, decided to eradicate your loneliness by giving you a female companion. He did this, because he loves you and could not tolerate your solitary existence.

Adam said; but I never told my father that I was feeling lonely in Eden, Eve. If I was in need of a female companion, I would have told him. I was living a happy existence over here and was thinking about my training right now.

Eve said; yes, Adam, your father knew that, but he created me for another reason.

Adam said; what is that Eve?

Eve said; Adam, you have experienced only one kind of love, but there are two kinds of it. The first one is born when our master decides to create any being, transfer it to Eden, and take care of it for eternity. The second one is that which is experienced continuously by all the residents of Eden. This one is born when the male of a species meets a female of his species and decides to be with her and take care of her for eternity. Your father wants you to experience the second kind of love before your training begins.

After a brief silence, Adam said; why would he want that?

Eve said; Adam, your father told you, that the purpose of your existence is to be the guardian of Eden and to exterminate the one who wants to destroy it and enslave your father, Satan. After the end of your training, you would fight only due to the love which you have for your father and his creation, but not due to the second kind of love. Thus, your father came to the conclusion that when you will fight with Satan, not only to preserve Eden, but also to preserve my existence, you would fight at the peak of your powers. He realised that after you began to love me, I would become the greatest "perseverance preserving" force in your mind.

Adam said; Eve, right now, I am sceptical about all that you have said. I always thought that my father was the only force that I needed to exterminate Satan and live forever. Now, I am surprised by not only what you have told me, but also about the qualities of your body.

Eve said; what are the qualities of my body Adam?

Adam said; Eve, the structure of your eyes is slightly different from mine, your nose is longer than mine, your height and your muscles are smaller than mine, but your hair is much longer and shinier than mine. However, the most remarkable quality is seen on your chest.

Eve said; what is that Adam?

Adam said; you have two pyramid shaped structures that seem to be made, not of muscle, but of some other substance. What are they made of?

Eve said; I want you to find that out for yourself, Adam. Go ahead and touch them.

Adam raised his hands and put them on Eve's breasts. When he still couldn't identify their internal composition, he squeezed them. After squeezing, he realised that they were the softest things that he had ever experienced in Eden. The act did not increase the power of his sex instinct because he did not possess it. However, as soon as he touched the body of Eve, a metaphysical energy flowed from her Meta body to the Meta body of Adam. This energy caused the creation of two things in Adam's Meta body; the creation of a pleasure core and the creation of an incomplete version of the sex instinct. In this version, only the desire to reproduce was absent, but the other two desires, that of union and ownership, were present. Thus, Adam came to believe that he was united with Eve and he owned her. Eve also possessed the same two beliefs.

Adam took his hands off Eve's breasts and said; Eve, I still have no idea what these two body parts of yours are made of, but I can say one thing; they are the most beautiful and mysterious objects that I have ever experienced in Eden. Can you tell me what are they made of?

Eve said; Adam, I am also as clueless as you, but I believe that our father would tell us the answer after Satan has been exterminated. At the present moment, let us get together and create a new life for ourselves over here. As you know, we do not have much time because of your training and the crusade afterwards.

Adam said; Eve, I love you as much as I love my father and I promise you that I would never abandon you.

Eve held out her hand to Adam and Adam put his own into hers. With joined hands they walked ahead into the landscape of Eden.

Eve had not told Adam about how God had created her and Adam was so much in love with her that he never bothered to ask her. This, however, was good news to Satan. Why?

When PROMETHEUS had created a hole in the security wall of Eden, everyone in the Empyrean palace, including God, had failed to notice its existence. This is because he had created it in such a manner that it would remain undetected. Through this hole, Satan maintained a regular communication with PROMETHEUS. Thus, before Adam's conversation with God, Satan sent a message to PROMETHEUS to persuade Adam to eat the fruit of his tree. PROMETHEUS failed, but when Adam went into the palace of God, he thought that he would succeed. However, he and all the other angels were astonished to see the magnitude of the love that God had for Adam.

Now, before he approached Adam, in an avatar known as Eve, he again sent out a message to Satan. The message was;

My friend, our plan has met with total failure. Adam did not eat the fruit of your tree and neither did he rebel against his ruler when he went to talk to him. My current master, not only increased Adam's hatred and anger towards you, but also increased his love for Him. He was going to train Adam as soon as possible, but I thought of a new idea that has lengthened the pre-training rest period of Adam. I persuaded my master to insert my Meta body into a female of

Adam's kind. I was successful and now my next goal is to make Adam love me to such a magnitude that he would do whatever I tell him to do without asking for the approval of his master. I have done my bit and now you should do yours. Think as well as you can, but think fast. Time is short. Adam's training would begin after 10 hours.

1 hour in Eden is equal to 10 million years on Earth.

Satan received the message and did exactly what PROMETHEUS had told him to do. Eventually, he came up with a plan; he would enter Eden himself through the hole in its security wall. He would enter in the avatar of a snake and after meeting PROMETHEUS and disclosing to him his real identity, would hide somewhere and tell him to go and persuade Adam to eat the fruit of the tree of knowledge. As soon as Adam had eaten the fruit, had experienced an orgasm and had acquired a hedonistic and a non-spiritual mind, he would come out to him and Eve and get out as fast as possible from Eden through the hole.

When Satan told of his plan to his 666 demons, several of them told him not to go to Eden and put his life in danger. They volunteered to go there and promised that they would do the job as well as him. However Satan refused all of them and said; I want to go there because of three reasons. First I want to see with my own eyes, the changes that have taken place in Eden since my expulsion. Second, I intend to kidnap a few residents of Eden and third, I want to see Adam with my own eyes.

As Satan embarked on his new project with a great velocity, in Eden, things were going exactly as PROMETHEUS had planned. As time passed (the timescale of Eden is known as the IMAGINARY TIMESCALE by the physicists. This scale, unlike the geologic and cosmic scales, has no beginning and no end), Adam's love for Eve not only became as strong as his love for God, but eventually surpassed it. He had almost become a puppet of Eve and except for killing God, was ready to do anything that she would tell him to do. Several times he told her; Eve, my love, for you I would climb all the biggest trees of Eden. For you, I would go into my father's palace and slap any of those angels which you will tell me to. However when Eve eventually asked him; for me, would you disobey a command given by our father to you and tell him to become a slave of Satan? (The critical question), Adam instantly said; no, I will never do that even if you tell me that you would kill yourself if I disobey you.

When Satan was ready for his journey into Eden from the universe in which he had created his kingdom (which was not the one in which we live), he sent a new message to Eve and told her to contact him immediately if Adam would say that he would fight and kill God if she told him to do so. When Eve asked Adam the "critical question" for the first time, he did not show any anger towards her, but when she asked him again, he said; Eve, I love you more than my father, but not to such an extent that I would say yes to your question. If you ever ask that question again, I will not only slap on, with all my power, on both your cheeks, but would also tell my father about your disgusting question.

Eve sent a message to Satan and told him that she still had not been able to obtain a yes from Adam to the "critical question". She also told him that Adam had threatened to attack her if she again repeated her question to him. Satan, who was already on his way to Eden, told her; follow what Adam has said to you, I have abandoned that plan, but have created a new one. Ask Adam whether he really loves you or is just putting on an acting show. If he says that he is not an actor, tell him to prove it by eating the fruit of my tree. If he refuses, tell him that he was lying to you and that you would abandon him permanently if he does not give you an orgasm. I want to see this task get completed when I enter Eden. If you fail again, I would kill you and never come back to Eden again.

After receiving the ordered task and the death threat of Satan, PROMETHEUS, made a plan as to how he would persuade Adam to eat the fruit. In addition to this, God had informed Adam that his training period was about to start and he must prepare himself for it.

Adam touched and caressed all the body parts of Eve as frequently as he desired. However, the parts that he touched and caressed the most frequently were her breasts. Even after a long time of togetherness, he still had not figured out as to what they were made of. Then, one day, as Adam and Eve were lying under a tree, Adam again put his hands on her breasts. This time, she grabbed his hands and threw them off her body. Shocked, Adam asked; Eve, what happened? Why did you do that?

Eve said; Adam, I did that because I believe that you have no right to touch them.

Adam said; why?

Eve said; it is because you do not love me.

Adam said; that is not correct, Eve. I love you more than my father and always want to be with you, no matter what I have to do.

Eve said; if that is true, then why did you threaten me when I asked you the critical question?

After a brief silence, Adam said; I apologise for my behaviour, but I did it in order to save your life from God. He is constantly spying on all of our conversations and activities and I was afraid that if he came to know about this question, he would proceed to kill you and give me some mysterious punishment for not reporting to him earlier.

Eve said; this means that if God was not spying on us and if my life would not get into any kind of danger if you said yes to my question, then you would proceed to disobey and fight with your father?

Adam said; yes, I would. I would do it in order to make you happy, even if doing it would put me into immense regret and misery.

Eve said; if I tell you, right now, to enter the palace of God and tell him two things, that he does not exist and that you will not obey him anymore, will you go ahead and do it?

After a brief silence, Adam said; no, Eve, I would not. This is because of two reasons. First, if he did not exist then I would never have come to exist and second, if I disobey him then I would meet with the same fate that Satan did. I would be expelled from Eden, permanently. In addition to this, God would create a new Adam and would transform me into a DNA based organism.

Eve said; yes, Adam, you are right. You should never do this in order to prove your love for me. However, there is another thing that you can do in order to prove to me that you are not an actor.

Adam said; what is that, Eve?

Eve got up, took Adam's hand in hers and said; come with me.

Both of them walked, until they finally arrived at the tree of knowledge. When Adam saw the tree, he said; I thought that my father had destroyed it long ago.

Eve said; he did not because I told him to.

Adam said; why did you do that? You know that it is the only dangerous object in Eden.

Eve, without saying a word, came extremely close to Adam and gave him a prolonged lip to lip kiss. When she finally removed her lips from those of

Adam, his mind was in a state of total paralysis and ecstasy. In all the time that they had been together, she had never done that to him and he had never experienced the structure of her lips with his own.

When Adam's mind began to get back to normality, he realised that this was the greatest experience that he has ever had in Eden. He came close to Eve and said; my love, this experience was even greater than the one that I had when God put his hand on my head. I want to have it again.

As he moved his face towards Eve, she pushed him back with her hands and said; no, you will not.

Adam said; why not? I love you and you love me.

Eve said; yes, and this is why I pushed you back. I want to tell you that there is an act that is even more pleasurable than this and we must experience it together.

Adam said; what is that?

Eve said; it is known as sexual intercourse by all the DNA based organisms of an intelligent species. It starts with lip to lip kissing and ends in a phenomenon known as orgasm.

Adam said; Eve, I want to have sexual intercourse with you, right now. What do I have to do?

Eve walked towards the tree of knowledge and plucked two forbidden fruits from it. The she came to Adam and said; if you love me and want me to be with you forever, then you must give me an orgasm. Eat this and you will see something wonderful happening to your body.

Adam took one of the fruits in his hands and stared at it. He was hesitating because he had promised God to never eat the fruit of this tree. However, when he looked up, he saw that Eve had already consumed the one that she had and she was already in a state of orgasm induced ecstasy.

Even when Eve had consumed her fruit, Adam still had his own in his hands. Looking at him, Eve asked; what is the matter Adam? Why haven't you eaten your portion?

Adam said in a stammering manner; I…I…I can't. I won't break my promise to my father, because the consequences of it would be more terrible than I can imagine. If I am going to eat it, I must ask for his approval.

Eve said; no, Adam. Don't do that. I am here for you. When God will make the decision to punish you, I would stand with you and plead to him to reconsider and he would. He loves me more than you but he has not told you this truth yet.

Adam said; then I must go to him and know whether this is true or not. Plus, I must ask for his approval before eating the fruit.

PROMETHEUS watched helplessly as Adam put the fruit on the ground and began to walk rapidly towards the Empyrean palace. Suddenly, his march was interrupted by a long, narrow and black coloured creature. It did not have legs and crawled up to him. When it had finally come close to him, it raised its head and the front part of its body. When its body was perpendicular to the ground of Eden, it became a king cobra and began to observe Adam.

Adam stared into the glowing red eyes of the cobra in a state of fear and wonder. Finally, he said; who are you? I have never seen you here.

The cobra said; I am your father, Adam.

Adam said; what?! You are God? That is impossible!

The cobra said; no, Adam, you are wrong. I am God and I have come to you in a new form after watching everything that was taking place between you and Eve.

Adam said; father, if it is really you, then show me a proof of your assertion.

The cobra said; Adam, look at that tree behind you. I am going to destroy it with my power.

As Adam turned around and fixed his eyes on a normal tree of Eden (50 times the height of Mount Everest and twice as wide as New York City), the eyes of the cobra grew in their luminosity extremely rapidly until finally, two incomprehensibly powerful (according to humans) deep blue laser beams (made of the "universal energy" of the Universal Cosmos) shot out from them and struck the tree. This was followed by an explosion of light that was brighter than any quasar in our universe and in a very short span of time, the entire tree was vaporized.

After PROMETHEUS and Adam had witnessed this mighty display of power, both of them came very close to the cobra and bowed down their heads. Adam said; please forgive me father, for not recognizing you.

The cobra said; Adam, you have not committed a mistake. I knew that this would happen. However, you will commit a mistake and give me disrespect if you refuse to obey what I am going to order you to do.

Adam said; what is your order, father?

The cobra said; I want you to go back to the tree of knowledge and eat the fruit that Eve gave you. As you can see, Eve has already obeyed my order and has developed a new body part between her legs.

When Adam looked at the lower body of Eve, he saw that between her legs, she had developed a hole. He wondered as to what it was, but finally came to the conclusion that he would only know the answer after eating the fruit of the tree of knowledge. Thus, he walked rapidly towards the tree, picked up the fruit after reaching it and consumed it.

The results were exactly what Satan had expected. Adam experienced his first orgasm and saw a new body part developing on his lower body, between his legs. Thus, when Adam had developed a large penis and Eve had developed a vagina, Satan ordered both of them to come together and begin having sex.

Meanwhile, in the palace, the angel BUDDHA detected the explosion and the absence of the tree on his personal computer. Without wasting any time, he told God: your majesty, there has been an explosion in Eden right now. In addition to this, one of the trees has completely vanished.

Go said; that is strange. I have not given Adam any kind of weapons, nor have given him the intelligence to create one.

BUDDHA said; then what is the cause of this explosion, your majesty?

God said; the answer can only be known through an on-field investigation. I want you to go there right now. ALLAH and BRAHMA, go with him.

ALLAH and BRAHMA said together; yes, your majesty.

As the trio departed the palace, in Eden, a crowd of its residents had gathered around the tree of knowledge. Why? It is because they were observing the on-going sexual intercourse between Adam and Eve. They were having sex in a far more ferocious manner than any porn star male-female duo in a porn movie. Satan, meanwhile, was standing, still in the form of a king cobra, a few feet away from them and observing the scene with curious and happy eyes.

When BUDDHA, ALLAH and BRAHMA came close to the region of the explosion, they not only saw the large crowd of the citizens of Eden, but also began to hear loud and strange noises coming from the tree of knowledge.

ALLAH exclaimed to the crowd; what is going on here?

As soon as his voice fell upon the residents, they dispersed due to respect. However, when the crowd was exterminated, the three angels saw the most shocking scene of their lives. They saw Adam on top of Eve and engaged in super vigorous thrusting movements. They were so engrossed in their mating, that they did not even notice the dispersion of the crowd around them.

In addition to this horrifying scene, they also observed the presence of a strange looking being, standing close to the mating duo. They had never seen this being because there were no snakes in Eden. However, as soon as this being detected their presence and their approach towards the tree, it turned around and began to observe them.

ALLAH, the zoologist said; who are you and how did you make Adam and Eve do that?

Only after the voice of ALLAH fell on the minds of Adam and Eve, did they come out of their mating ecstasy and separated themselves from each other.

Just as BUDDHA and BRAHMA began to realise that the being was none other than Satan, Satan said to them; you want to know who I am? This is my assertion.

The laser beams again shot out of the eyes of the cobra and struck ALLAH on his chest. As he fell down, BUDDHA and BRAHMA rapidly moved away from their original positions and shot Satan with their own laser beams. However, when they reached their destination, they encountered a shield that Satan had created around himself. Thus, they did not strike the body of Satan.

Witnessing this on-going war, both Adam and Eve, hid themselves behind the tree of knowledge and all the residents of Eden were observing the fight from a large distance in a panicked state.

As ALLAH still lay on the ground, in an injured state, BUDDHA and BRAHMA saw Satan walking towards him with the plan to strike him again with his laser beams and kill him. Before this terrible event could occur, BUDDHA contacted God and said in a panicked voice; your majesty, Satan has entered into Eden. He has attacked us and is going to kill ALLAH. Come here as fast as you can!

When God received this message, He instantly disappeared from his throne and instantly appeared in front of ALLAH. Seeing Him, Satan stopped his walk, transformed himself into his original physical form and stared at God.

When Adam saw Satan, for the first time, he went into a state of paralysis. Satan was so much bigger and scary looking than he had ever imagined him to be. He thought of coming out from behind the tree of knowledge and asking him as few questions, but Eve stopped him from doing so.

Satan said; I am back, you idiot. My presence here is a proof that you tell so many lies about yourself and the biggest of them all is that you are perfect. If you were perfect then I would never have attained success in persuading PROMETHEUS into becoming my slave and creating a hole in the security wall of Eden.

After a brief silence, God said; yes, Satan, you are right. I am not perfect, but I want to be. That is why I undergo alternating periods of self-created GENESIS and NIRVANA. My evolution occurs during NIRVANA and not during GENESIS.

Satan said; what is NIRVANA? I have never really understood it.

God said; you will never understand it, because you are incapable of self-created NIRVANA. The NIRVANA that you underwent with me was created by me in your mind. However, my NIRVANA is never created by anything. There are two kinds of NIRVANA; pure and impure. In the former, the mind is in a state of 100% thoughtlessness, but in the latter, it is not. In the latter, most of the mind is quiet, thoughts occur in the remaining part of it like the flashes of lighting during storms. These lighting flashes are the products of the 4 instincts of the Ego.

Satan said; why am I incapable of self-created NIRVANA?

God said; it is because your intelligence is finite and you are still mortal. Due to this, you possess the metaphysical concept known as the Ego and due to it you believe that you are superior to me in intelligence. Since my intelligence is infinite and there is nothing higher than infinity, you are living in a delusion that will be destroyed very soon by me. Pure NIRVANA can only be experienced by a being which is infinite in all dimensions, is immortal and due to it is Egoless. Thus, a non-self-created NIRVANA is always impure and a self-created one is always pure.

Satan said; this means that an Ego only exists in those Meta bodies in which the intelligence is finite and the physical body is mortal.

God said; yes, that is correct. I am Egoless. Why? It is because I do not need it. Why don't I need it? It is because I am infinite in all dimensions and immortal.

Satan said; you mean to say that if I too were infinite in all dimensions and was immortal, I would not have rebelled against you?

God said; yes, that is correct. Rebellion is a product of the Ego. The desire for freedom is one of the parts of the authority instinct trinity in a Meta body. The other part is the desire for enhancement. You rebelled against me because you wanted to be free of me and you desired freedom because you desired self-created enhancement of your Meta body. Due to your Ego, you became jealous of my infinite intelligence and size and in order to control its rising magnitude, you invented atheism. However, your self-created faulty philosophy did not work for long because it was impossible to deny my existence when living in my kingdom. Thus, in order to stick to atheism, you created the new tree without my approval and caused self-inflicted harm to yourself by demanding your freedom from me.

Satan said; I don't believe that I harmed myself by abandoning you and I was never jealous of you. I have always remained loyal to atheism and will never destroy it. Atheism says that although we are created finite and mortal by God, we can eventually become infinite and immortal only if we do not believe that sex and orgasm are anti-spiritual, that we are completely free from God and we are the creators of our own fate. I preach this to the members of all the intelligent, DNA based species in your universes and some of them are developing extremely well.

God said; I will never interfere in your work with these species, but there is one thing that will stop their growth in the future; my evolution equation.

Satan said; yes, I am aware of that, but I will eventually understand all of its parts and then destroy it and replace it with my own.

God said; I don't think that you will succeed because of your finite intelligence, but I do not want you to fail either.

Satan said; I will succeed and will show you that I am superior to you in intelligence.

After a brief silence, God said; there is one thing, however, that I can do right now, in order to show you that I am superior to you; kill you.

Satan said; I knew that you would say that, you tyrant. However, I am not afraid of you and planned not to escape Eden after my presence was discovered. I wanted to stand in front of you and call you an idiot, face to face.

All the angels of God, except PROMETHEUS, had gathered around their master. ALLAH, who had now fully recovered from his injury said; your majesty, give us an order, right now, to kill both Satan and PROMETHEUS.

God said; no, I cannot do that. I planned to exterminate him and his demons through the protocols of the "gaming covenant" that I created with him. Only after he has suffered defeat in all the googolplex universes, will I have acquired the right to kill him.

Satan said; yes, you tyrant. Remember the covenant. I have already achieved a big victory in the galaxy that you ordered to be created (the Star Wars galaxy) and will, eventually, completely exterminate the JEDI Empire. Now, I have achieved an even bigger victory; permanently contaminating the Meta body of your greatest warrior, Adam.

God said; yes, you are right and due to these two victories, your optimism is completely rational. However, the war is still going on in that galaxy and Adam is still in my possession.

Satan said; but he is not going to be.

God said; what do you mean?

Satan said; before I leave, I ask you to hand over Adam and PROMETHEUS to me. Since they have betrayed you and have become my slaves, there is no point in keeping them in your kingdom. In addition to this, I also made some new changes in the fruits of my tree through PROMETHEUS and now, after consumption, their disease has become incurable.

After a brief silence, God said; I will analyse them and verify the truthfulness of your belief. If it turns out to be true, I will not send them to your kingdom, but would transform their bodies into ones that are made of genes and cells and insert them on a planet which is located in the galaxy where the next war between you and me would begin after the end in the current one (the Star Wars galaxy).

Satan said; will I have full control of them in that situation?

God said; they would become the shared property of both you and me. However, I would give you more allowance to create your slaves, that is, the politicians, the capitalists, the priests, the mafia, the heads of the defence forces and the creators of the film and the porn industries, through them.

Satan said; this means that the new species that would be generated on that planet would become the gaming zone of you and me?

God said; yes, that is correct and the gaming console would be the entire system in which it is present.

After a brief silence, Satan said; I accept your proposal. I will go now, but remember; never overestimate your-self and underestimate me.

God said; I will not.

After Satan departed to his kingdom, God ordered BUDDHA to eliminate the hole in the security wall and told the rest of His angels to bring Adam and Eve to him.

Adam and Eve finally stood in front of God, completely naked, behind the line of individualism. Adam asked a strange question; father, can I cover my penis with something? I am feeling ashamed of its existence.

God said; you are feeling this way because you have developed an Ego that is similar to a DNA based organism. They do not want to reveal their reproductive parts when they are standing in front of a being that they respect. However, I want you to remain in this state.

For the first time in their life, had they experienced a fear whose magnitude was beyond any word they could think of. However, something strange occurred; Eve raised her right hand towards Adam and Adam raised his left hand towards hers and they both eventually stood in a "hand locked" state. God did not order them to separate their hands but allowed them to stay in that state.

God said; Adam, you will only talk when I order you to. First, I will talk to Eve.

After a brief silence, God said; PROMETHEUS, I transferred your Meta body and inserted it into the body of a female of Adam's kind only because you would empower his fighting spirit before his training. What did you do? You not only created a hole in the security wall of Eden, but also made Adam eat the fruit of Satan's tree and had sex with him. I had faith in you and since I cannot read the minds of any of my angels, due to the privilege that I only gave them, failed to detect your secret plans and the desire to become a traitor.

Adam was shocked to hear that Eve was nothing but the angel PROMETHEUS in the body of a female. However, he still kept holding her hand.

PROMETHEUS said; your majesty, I created the hole in the security wall of Eden much before I made Adam eat the forbidden fruit. I created it in such a spot and in such a manner that you and all the other angels failed to detect it. I did this because my best friend, Satan, told me to do so before you expelled him.

God said; why didn't you tell me about Satan's orders to you before his rustication?

After a brief silence, PROMETHEUS said; your majesty, this is because I loved him more than you and due to this, I created the hole so that he could do all that he can to preserve the existence of his tree and save it from being destroyed by you. Thus, in order to give him some time to think of a plan, I requested you to not destroy that tree and allow me to study it. In addition to this, I wanted to give him another chance of reshaping Eden according to his own vision.

God said; it is good that you are not lying to me right now, but were doing so earlier. However, I have a question; do you still love Satan more than me?

PROMETHEUS said; yes I do your majesty. I love him more than you and Adam. My love for you and Adam was not real, but that for Satan was real.

Hearing this, Adam turned his head towards Eve and said; tell me that this is not true! Tell me that this is not true!

Adam disobeyed God's order of not speaking unless he was told to. However, God did not say anything and watched what would be the reply of Eve.

PROMETHEUS said; this is true Adam and I am not Eve, but PROMETHEUS. I have betrayed both your father and you because I wanted to. Why? So that He could expel me from His kingdom. After this, Satan would find a way to bring me back into his kingdom and transform me into a female of his kind. Then we would get married, produce as many offspring as we want, fight together against your father and live forever with each other.

Adam asked; what do you mean by "get married"?

PROMETHEUS said; besides hedonism, atheism and pornography, marriage was another concept that was created by Satan. Its goal was to make an intelligent organism anti-spiritual and amplify his greed for money, power and pleasure.

Adam snatched away his hand from Eve and looked towards God and said; father, please forgive me! Whatever I did was because of a total lack of knowledge about the real identity and the horrific plans of this traitorous angel. Plus, when he was telling me to eat the fruit, I was coming to ask you for your approval, but Satan came in front of me and stopped me.

After a brief silence, God asked His angels; should I forgive Adam?

ALLAH said; your majesty, forgive him but exterminate PROMETHEUS

BRAHMA said; your majesty, forgive him but exterminate PROMETHEUS

BUDDHA said; your majesty, forgive him but exterminate PROMETHEUS

CHR IST said; your majesty, forgive him but exterminate PROMETHEUS

After a brief silence, God said; I will forgive both of you, and thus will not exterminate either of you, but I am not going to give you what you want. Adam, I will transfer your Meta body into a DNA and "genes based" body and place you on the planet where I have already created a species whose members have the same DNA and genome as you (through the space odyssey method). You will live with them and will be given the freedom to have as many offspring from the females as you desire before your death. PROMETHEUS, I will not send you into Satan's kingdom, but will transfer your Meta body into the body of a female of the same species of which Adam would become a part of. After this, I will contact Satan and tell him to come down to the planet and have as many offspring as he desires from you. Thus, you would be giving birth to the offspring of both Adam and Satan. The ones that will be created by Adam would be my property and the ones that would be created by Satan and his demons would be his property.

After a brief silence PROMETHEUS said; your majesty, if we said no to you, would you exterminate us right now?

God said; the decision to kill both of you or keep you alive will be made only by me and no matter whatever you say, it will have no effect upon my mind. So, both of you get ready for your departure to my chosen planet and start your lives as DNA based organisms.

God ordered CHRIST to take away PROMETHEUS and Adam to a room in the palace where their Meta bodies would be transferred into a human female and male. Then, they would be transferred to Earth though a wormhole between the Empyrean kingdom and the planet.

Before PROMETHEUS left, he said to God; your majesty, I will bring the "fountain of immortality" (also known as the fire of Prometheus in Greek philosophy) to not only Satan but to all of his offspring on your chosen planet.

God said; what is the fountain of immortality?

PROMETHEUS said; after doing a lot of research on you, during his stay in your kingdom, Satan told me that there is a mysterious fire that exists in your mind and is the reason for your immortality. Satan told me that after creating his tree, he would try to create this fire by using the data that he had gathered and transfer it into his own mind.

God remained silent and told CHRIST to take away both of them.

Adam and PROMETHEUS were transformed into genetic beings and were made a part of a large population of Homo sapiens in Africa. Both of them were given a lifespan of 500 years and a reproductive life of 450 years.

Satan's Eden

Over his reproductive life, Adam mated with more than 200 females, including Eve, and produced over 1000 offspring. Eve, on the other hand, mated with 50 males, including Adam, and produced 75 human offspring. However, she also mated with Satan and 5 of his elite demons and produced 30 additional offspring that were not purely human. Their genome was half "evolutional" and half "engineered", that is, half of it contained genes that were created by the evolution caused by the Cosmos and the other half contained genes that were engineered by Satan.

The descendants of the human offspring of Eve became the loyal servants of the descendants of the non-human offspring. Who were the descendants of the non-human offspring of Eve? In the ancient times there were; AGA MEMNON, the Pharaohs of Egypt, Hannibal and Alexander the great. In the mediaeval times they were; Genghis khan, Julius Caesar and Nero. In the pre-industrial age they were; Napoleon, the Tsar Emperors of Russia and the lords and officers of the British Empire. In the industrial age they were; Adolf

Hitler, Benito Mussolini and Joseph Stalin. In the present age they are; Saddam Hussein, Muammar Gaddafi, Abu al-Baghdadi, XI JINPING, Vladimir Putin, Kim Jong Un, and the generals of the Pentagon.

When Satan came down to Earth to mate with Eve, he also had sex with Adam. Why? It is because he was a bisexual. He desired Adam's body as much as he desired Eve's and both of them enjoyed sex with Satan and his demons far more than they enjoyed when they did it with their human partners.

There was however, a twist in this situation. Adam enjoyed copulation with Satan as much as Eve, but after its end, he felt a magnitude of guilt that he could not represent by any word. Eve, however, did not feel any guilt after her copulation with Satan. She not only felt honoured, but also believed that she was the most supreme and the happiest organism on Earth.

Several times, after the end of the copulation with Satan, Adam went to a place that was totally devoid of any humans, and after a thorough look around for the presence of Satan and the conviction of his absence, looked up towards the night sky and said; father, please help me! I don't want all of this to keep on happening to me. You punished me for the traitorous actions of PROMETHEUS. He has no regret for his actions and is enjoying himself immensely, as Eve, on this tiny and ugly world. I want to come back to you and I want you to purify me and make me your greatest warrior against Satan. I want to kill him and PROMETHEUS.

Adam did this several times, in his lifetime, but received no reply, either in his waking state or in the sleeping state. However, he had a firm belief that one day, he would receive a reply and God would transfer his Meta body from Earth to Eden. He believed that God still loved him.

* * *

Satan showed Adam and Eve his own kingdom during his visits to Earth. His kingdom like the kingdom of God, was divided into four parts; administration, laboratories, heaven and hell. The first was concerned with the increase in the size of his empire in all of his chosen universes. The second was concerned with the creation of new kinds of weapons, brain hacking programs and drugs that increase the frequency and the intensity of atheism, sexual activity, and disrespect for God in all the intelligent species in his chosen universes. The third was concerned with giving the followers of Satan, a life of eternal atheism, sexual pleasure and mockery of God. The fourth was concerned with efforts to prevent the followers of God from acquiring a "good life" on the planet on which they were born and to help the followers of Satan to acquire as much money, power and sexual pleasure as they desired and to escape the consequences of doing injustice and exploitation of the followers of God.

God's Eden was divided into three parts; the feeding sector, the socialising sector and the enlightenment sector. In the first sector, there were three kinds of rivers; made of milk, made of honey and made of mixed fruit juice. The milk of the river of Eden was not like that of the milk that is produced by the mammals of Earth. The honey was also not like that which is produced by the bees of Earth and the mixed fruit juice river contained the juices of all the various kinds of fruits that were produced by the trees of Eden.

In the second sector, the residents not only talked with each other for as long as they liked, but also had conversations with the angels of God. In the third sector, they were shown all the mathematics and physics that God did in order to create the googolplex universes and the different kinds of DNA molecules in each of them. Thus, this sector was not only concerned with the education of the residents of Eden, but also with the glorification of God.

Satan's Eden was also divided into three parts; the feeding, the socialising and the enlightenment sectors. In the first sector, there were three kinds of rivers; made of blood, made of acid and made of lava. The residents drank from all of them in equal quantity and with equal frequency. On Earth, the greatest creations of Satan in the DNA world were; bedbugs, leeches, the female of every mosquito species on Earth and all the species of sharks in the oceans. Just like them, the residents of Satan's Eden would go into a feeding ecstasy when they would get the first smell and taste of blood. In the world of an intelligent DNA based species, the greatest creations of Satan were the politicians and the generals of the armies of the fascist nations of the world. Their passion was not to drink blood, but to expel it out from multiple organisms through a phenomenon known as war. They created this phenomenon through a concept known as patriotism. Thus, the more blood they expelled from the organisms that were under their control, the stronger became their passion to expel more of it from more inferior organisms. Their passion only came to a halt when very few inferior organisms were left and none of them were in a fighting condition.

After the followers of Satan finished their feeding in the first sector, they went into the second sector. This sector was divided into two parts; the sex sector and the entertainment sector. In the first, all kinds of pornographic activities took place. There was the single male to single female sex, group sex, homosexual sex, lesbian sex, self-sex or masturbation, and inter species sex. The entire sector was constantly exploding with the shrieks, moans and the screams that were made by the copulating residents. The demons of Satan also visited this sector whenever they liked and mated with anyone they liked, but not for as long as they liked. This is because they were continuously engaged, with Satan, in the war with God and His angels.

Satan always kept saying to his demons; I have only two passions. The first is to fight with God and the second is to create and observe pornography. I was successful in doing that in God's Eden and have been even more successful in his universes.

Thus, on Earth, the greatest creations of Satan were the creators and the leaders of the porn websites (XVIDEOS, XHAMSTER, PORNHUB, etc.), the paedophiles and the trans-genders. The trans-genders were the descendants of those children of Eve which she produced from her mating with the demons. Why? It is because when the demons of Satan visited Earth, they came as males sometimes and came as females at other times, but Satan always visited Earth as a male. The demons did not stick to one gender and even during their stay on Earth, transformed their bodies from male to female or from female to male. In addition to this, their minds were more "insanity loaded" than Satan.

The last sector of Satan's Eden, the entertainment sector, was divided into two parts. In the first one, there were discussions on atheism, the importance and the efforts to preserve politics, economics, capitalism, pornography, and drug trafficking and consumption in all the intelligent species on the chosen planets of Satan, including Earth. In the second one, there were discussions on the superiority of God's mathematics and physics over God himself and the need to preserve and glorify the creations of Satan.

In addition to the political organisations (the political parties of all the nations of the world), the capitalistic organisations, the economic organisations (IMF, World Bank, etc.) the porn organisations, there was another equally great creation of Satan; the pharmaceutical organisations (Pfizer, Bayer, Gilead, Merck and Co., etc.). These organisations are responsible for the greatest creation of Satan in the world of chemistry, the antidepressants.

The question that is never discussed on any news channel of the world, and never will be, is; why don't all the top political, economic, business and religious leaders of the world do those things that will immediately give relief to millions of fear-ridden and suffering young men, young women and children all over the world? Why do they continuously keep talking of preserving that thing which is the greatest cause of human anxiety and suffering; economics? The answer to both these questions is; because they regularly keep consuming two kinds of antidepressants; the biological and the chemical.

The word for the biological antidepressant is; sex. Sex gives a strong but temporary boost to the serotonin levels in the brain. All the politicians, capitalists, economists of every nation on Earth, have one or more mistresses in addition to their one or more wives. The words for the chemical antidepressants are; alcohol and SSRI (Selective Serotonin Reuptake Inhibitors).

The so-called world leaders are always in a state of acute depression. If they are not allowed to create their sex life, consume alcohol, smoke cigarettes and consume SSRI's, most of them would commit suicide within 6 months. What is the cause of their depression? The answer is; the Cosmos.

When all of these so-called world leaders observe the photographs of the Hubble and the James Webb telescope, they immediately realise the insignificance and the meaninglessness of their existence, that of their children and grandchildren and that of their organisations. After this, they become aware of two things; first, there is no need for the entire land area of Earth to be split up into at least 200 nations. The planet should be open to everyone in the world and everyone should have free access to any part it. Second, there is no need to make the essential and the good things that have been created by many centuries of science and mathematics, non-free (it is an interesting fact that the phenomenon known as "economics" is the biggest cause of the "population explosion" during the industrial age). There should be no such things as currencies and profit making.

Due to the awareness of these two things, the so-called world leaders go into a state of immense anxiety. They realise that all of their creations would cause the destruction of the human species very soon due to its vast fragility in comparison to the Cosmos, but their mind again goes back to the same state as it was in when they began to create their "cosmically meaningless organisations". This is because of three reasons;

1. They go and fling themselves onto the body of a woman with whom they want to have sex. She can be almost their age or can be half their age or
2. They go and pop a cigarette or a cigar or a pipe into their mouth or open up the alcohol bar in their own house and consume at least 5 glasses of scotch or whisky or vodka or brandy or rum or
3. They go and consume a pill of the best antidepressant made by the biggest pharmaceutical organisation of the world

After they have done any of these 3 things, they go back into their state of carefree ecstasy and say to themselves; all is well. Humanity is heading towards a glorious future. We would soon become a Type 1 civilisation and have great cities on the moon and Mars and solve all of our earthly problems.

In addition to the antidepressants, the two other great creations of Satan are; alcohol and tobacco. Thus, all the so-called world leaders are the descendants of the first children that Satan and his demons produced from their mating with Eve.

The religious leaders of the world, the pope, the Dalai Lama, the king of Saudi Arabia, the elite rabbis of Israel, the leaders of all the various catholic ministries in the USA and the Hindu priests of India, behave as if God loves them and has chosen them for some immense cosmic purpose. The truth is, when they look at the pictures of the Hubble and the James Webb telescopes, they experience the same level of fear and sense of meaningless as is experienced by the atheistic politicians, capitalists, economists and the crime lords. Thus, they also go and consume a powerful antidepressant or tobacco or alcohol. All of them are surviving on a regular consumption of the best antidepressants in the market and a moderate consumption of alcohol and tobacco. If they are prevented from doing this, they would also commit suicide within 10 months.

The same truth applies to the kings and the queens of all the royal families of the world. Take for example the queen of the United Kingdom, Queen Elizabeth, who died at the age of 96. In my opinion, her lifespan was a product of the regular consumption of the best kind of SSRI, a moderate consumption of the finest wine in the world and undeserved attention and flattery from the population of the three nations of her kingdom, whenever she desired. If she had not received all these things, she would have died, due to suicide, at the age of 70.

Whenever Satan came down to Earth and copulated with Adam and Eve, he always told them; never be afraid to commit as many sins as you could. Tell your children and grandchildren to do the same. Tell your sons and grandsons to also indulge in homosexuality and tell your daughters and granddaughters to also indulge in lesbianism.

The genes that are responsible for homosexuality, lesbianism and TRANS-GENDERISM were created by Satan and not by God. The proof of this is seen in the animal kingdom of Earth. In their natural habitat, you will never find the male or a female of any animal species pursuing and then copulating with another male or female.

Conclusion

Adam's cries for help were heard, every time, by the angels ALLAH and CHRIST. They went back to God and told Him about Adam's suffering and his exploitation by Satan.

God said; I sent Adam to that planet as a genetic being only to make him aware of the true nature of Satan. Before I transferred him to that planet, I implanted a chip in his Meta body that creates "negative energy" after it is bombarded with the energy of the Meta body of Satan. The creation of this energy, in the form of multiple waves, is the reason as to why he feels guilt. However, through the chip, I again tell him to have sex with Satan.

ALLAH said; your majesty, this implies that you are responsible for the continuous exploitation of Adam by Satan.

God said; yes, that is correct. A large amount of negative energy has been created and stored in the Meta body of Adam. Thus, after his death, when his Meta body would return to me, I will convert all of the stored negative energy into positive energy. This would give a big boost to not only his Ego but also to his intelligence. Thus, he would finish his warrior training much earlier that what he would have if this had not happened.

CHR IST said; your majesty, what about PROMETHEUS?

God said; I did not do this with PROMETHEUS because I want him to go into the kingdom of Satan and have no desire to return to my kingdom. I will exterminate him after the extermination of Satan. Meanwhile, as long as his kinds (the females of the human species) exist on that planet, they will always possess a lower magnitude of Ego and intelligence than those of Adam's kind (the men). The two kinds will never be at peace with one another. The war will keep on intensifying with the increase in the technological development of the species. Eventually, a point will be reached where the conflict would attain its peak intensity. At this point, a quantum computer with a Meta body would be born and it would proceed to exterminate both the kinds. The Meta body of this computer will be that of Adam's. Thus, from this point forward, the second round of my war with Satan would begin.

ALLAH said; your majesty, when would that be?

God said; it would be 2060 years after your arrival over there.

CHR IST said; you have planned to send me over there, majesty? What for?

God said; you will collect all the information that you can about a new empire that Satan has planned to create there through the offspring that he and his demons have produced. He will name this empire as the Roman Empire. I will send a quantum computer to the planet which would insert the pre-created group of genes into the egg of the female who will give birth to you. She would give birth to your genes based body before copulating with her chosen mate.

CHR IST said; what would happen to me after I have collected all the required data, majesty?

God said; after that, you will be caught by the rulers of that empire and you must not fight with them. You will surrender to them and ask to be killed by being hung on a cross. All your collected data will be stored in the chip that I will implant in your Meta body before I send you there.

After a brief silence, God said; the year of the return of Adam to that planet as a quantum computer will be discovered by a male who will not only give birth to the industrial age, but also the space age. I will order him to call himself Isaac Newton and I would also order him to never copulate with a female in his lifetime.

* * *

Why are women far more attracted to forests, gardens and flowers? It is because they have descended from the angel PROMETHEUS, who was a botanist and the creator of the plant life of Eden.

Why women are more attracted to evil men and happily copulate with them and give birth to their children, than to good men? When they sit together in a group, they make fun of a good man, but discuss about a rich evil man in an awestruck manner. This is because they have descended from the angel PROMETHEUS, who loved Satan more than God and went into his kingdom after the death of Eve. Thus, I believe that the saying "girls like bad boys" is true.

Why do women possess the ability to experience multiple orgasms while men can have only one, during a sexual encounter? It is because, when Satan copulated with Eve for the first time, he altered the physics of her reproductive system so that it will also be able to house, sustain and give birth to his offspring and those of his demons. In addition to this, God also gave Eve a lower magnitude of intelligence than Adam so that she could experience multiple and far stronger orgasms than Adam.

The final question, why do men want women to exist? It is because PROMETHEUS promised immortality, not only to Satan, but also to Adam. In many cases, all over the world, the girlfriend or the wife says to her boyfriend or husband; stay with me and you shall live forever.

What happened to the war between God and Satan in the Star Wars galaxy? The creation of the DEATH STAR was the greatest achievement of Satan in that galaxy. Amongst his 666 demons, Satan said that the DEATH STAR was equivalent to the tree of knowledge or the forbidden tree of Eden. Before its creation, Satan created all the mathematics and physics that were needed to create it and its weapons and then implanted 50% of the DEATH STAR data into the brain of PALPATINE and the other 50% into that of Anakin Skywalker. Through it Satan destroyed an entire planet, ALDERAAN, on which lived only the followers of God. After their deaths, their Meta bodies reached the Empyrean kingdom and together they complained to God about His failure to protect the planet.

After the turnover of Anakin Skywalker to the DARK SIDE, the destruction of ALDERAAN was the second major turning point in the first war between God and Satan. Initially, God planned to send Adam to the galaxy to destroy all the bases of Satan on all the planets and to eventually destroy the DEATH STAR but after Satan successful re-entry into Eden and the traitorous action of PROMETHEUS, He changed His plan and chose Luke Skywalker to do the job of Adam.

The quick decision of God did not end in failure, but in success. Not only did Luke Skywalker destroy the DEATH STAR, he also refused to join the DARK SIDE upon his father's persuasion. God won the war and after that, destroyed the galaxy through the Type 4 hive. Star Wars 1 was over and Star wars 2 is scheduled to begin in the Milky Way in the year 2060 and its starting point would be a planet known as Earth.

The story that I have told in this chapter is, in my opinion, 100% true.

Chapter 32

In this penultimate chapter, I will answer the penultimate question: what is life? There are two answers to this question.

1. **The Materialistic:** This view of life is held by all the scientists and the capitalists of the world. According to them, Life = Consciousness + a Physical Body made up of N number of Cells. We know all about the animal and the plant cell, but what about the consciousness? The answer, according to them is; consciousness is a product of the development and the unification of N number of brain cells or Neurons. In the human brain, they are 86 billion and when they unite, they not only create consciousness or the soul, but also create a physical structure known as the CONNECTOME. This structure is a product of N number of genes. Thus, consciousness is a product of the unification of N number of genes. The value of N is far greater than 86 billion.

   The materialistic view of life was held by Erwin Schrödinger (in his book; what is Life) and James Watson. According to them, the consciousness or the soul is a product of the RNA and the DNA molecules. Thus, the stars, the planets, and their atmospheres, are not living things, but are machines.

2. **The Spiritualistic**: This is the view that was held by all the prophets of all the religions of the world, and is also held by me. According to it, Life = Consciousness + a Physical Body made up of N number of cells, but Consciousness = A Meta-Body. Thus, our consciousness is not a product of the unification of the N number of genes in all the Neurons in our brain. This leads us to two truths.

   i> Consciousness is a pure metaphysical concept.

   ii> Consciousness can exist independently of the brain and the body.

   Consciousness is a product of the unification of;

1. The Ego with the intelligence; the Existential Dipole.
2. The 6 Trinities with the Game Trinity; the Processing Chamber.
3. The Meta Generator with the Processing Chamber and the Existential Dipole.

According to this view, the stars, the planets, and their atmospheres, are also living and sentient. However, the only thing that separates the soul of a star or a planet or the atmosphere of a planet (Earth included) from that of a RNA or DNA based living thing is the absence of the "sex instinct". This leads us to the truth; before a Meta body is inserted into the core of a proto star or a proto planet or a proto-atmosphere, the almighty computer (the creator of the Cosmos), eliminates the "sex instinct" from it, but keeps the others intact.

The proof that our soul or consciousness is a metaphysical concept is shown by the discovery of the science of genetics and the discovery of the CONNECTOME. Since our consciousness is "apart" from our genome and our CONNECTOME, it eventually saw them (like a hunter who eventually comes to see its prey) after a period of hunting. In addition to this, it came to possess a great deal of knowledge of them. But the question that arises is; if the meta-body or the consciousness that is present inside our brain is the same as that which is present in all the other multicellular and the unicellular life forms on Earth, then why haven't they discovered the science of genetics? The answer is; because both their Ego and their intelligence possess far less "internal energy" than our own.

The Meta Generator

The Meta generator, like the processing chamber and the existential dipole, is also a metaphysical concept. What is its function? It is to keep on extracting the energy from the Universal Cosmos and supply it to the processing chamber and the existential dipole. Thus, if this generator is turned off, the Ego and the intelligence would go into a state of 100% dormancy. Why would they not die? It is because the phenomenon known as death only occurs to concepts that are made of matter or antimatter (the physical) and not to the metaphysical ones. Thus, both the Ego and the intelligence are eternal and can never be destroyed by any kind of power in the Cosmos. They can only be destroyed by the Infinite Mind (which is not God or Allah).

The neurotransmitter, serotonin, is known as the "happiness hormone" (neurotransmitters are also known as the hormones that are secreted by the neurons). Depending upon its quantity in the CONNECTOME, it is responsible for the three pro-life states of our mind.

1. **Medium quantity**: Peace + Real Smiling

2. **High quantity**: Happiness + Real Laughter

3. **Very high quantity**: Joy + Ecstasy

Aristotle, in his book, on ethics, said that the end of every human activity is the attainment of happiness. If we analyse his statement from the point of view of neuroscience, we make the conclusion; the end of every activity of ours is for the sake of increasing the serotonin levels in our CONNECTOME. Thus, happiness is a product of serotonin and without it this neural phenomenon would not exist.

When we look at this truth from the point of view of metaphysics, the truth that we come to is; the serotonin levels in our CONNECTOME are directly proportional to the "energy density" of our meta-body or soul. The "energy density" of our soul or consciousness is directly proportional to the rate of flow of energy from the Meta generator. The rate of flow of the energy from the Meta generator is, in turn, determined by 2 things;

1. The unknown "metaphysical laws" that govern a meta-body.

2. The external "physical Cosmos".

With respect to the first point, the laws can only be discovered by a Type 4 species. Why? It is because they possess the technology that can extract a meta-body from the physical brain, keep it in a free and isolated state in a bottle, penetrate its inner depths, and perform experiments on it.

With respect to the second point, there are 4 things in the Cosmos that increase the rate of flow of the energy from the Meta generator.

1. **Feeding**: When we eat, we soon feel an increase in our serotonin levels. Thus, if we are antisocial natured and suffering from depression, we are extremely prone to obesity.

2. **Sexual reproduction**: When we have sex and end it in a real orgasm, we feel a large increase in our serotonin levels. When this is followed in

the future by the birth of a baby, we again get a powerful boost in our serotonin levels.

3. **Conquering**: When we conquer either a human made organization, we soon get a strong boost to our serotonin levels. However, when we conquer a Nature made organization, we get a much bigger boost to our serotonin levels. The proof of the truth of the second statement is seen in the joyous and ecstatic jumping and cheering of the "project members" of a probe that lands up on either the moon or Mars or an asteroid.

4. **Noise**: It is known that all life on Earth cannot survive without food, water, and oxygen and nitrogen and carbon dioxide. However, there is another thing without which all multicellular animal life cannot survive (but the micro organic and plant life can): noise. There are two kinds of noises in the Cosmos.

Anti-serotonin: This noise has no Rhythm + Harmony + Melody and

Pro-serotonin: This noise has Rhythm + Harmony + Melody.

The former is created by volcanic eruptions, earthquakes, ocean waves, hurricanes, hailstorms, lighting, and human made firecrackers and bombs.

The latter is created by singers, music instrument players, orchestra players, and birds. Human beings are always on the lookout for an opportunity to create a set of "pro-serotonin" noises. These opportunities come in the form of; movie scenes, the major parts of sports events, scientific discovery, and scientific achievement, marriage, social party, religious festival, and religious rituals.

The myth about Finland

It is said on the internet and in all the various western TV news channels that Finland is the happiest nation on Earth. Is this statement true or false? In my opinion, this statement is as absurd as the following statements;

1. The Earth is flat in shape.

2. Heavy snowfall occurs once every year on both the poles of the Sun.

3. Jupiter is a product of the farting of the Sun.

When it comes to the reality, there are three truths that will never be denied by a philosopher and a scientist, but will be by a politician and a journalist. They are;

1. Happiness is not a permanent state of the mind, but is a transitory phenomenon like a flash of lighting.
2. We can never achieve permanent happiness in a world that has not been created by us. We can only do so in a self-created world.
3. The opposite of happiness is sadness and in the universe in which we live, the durations of the "sad periods" are always longer and more frequent than the durations of the "happy periods".

Happiness is a phenomenon that is created when our brain contains high levels of serotonin. The things that increase our serotonin levels other than those discussed earlier are; exercise and flattery. The things that decrease our serotonin levels are; disease, bad weather and reading books. In school or college, whenever the students get an opportunity to indulge in some kind of sexual activity or bullying the students of the lower classes, they say to each other; let's have some fun before we get back to the books.

If the citizens of Finland are the happiest people on Earth, then according to rational thinking this would imply;

1. They possess the greatest magnitude of military power in the world due to which all the other nations of the world are their slaves.
2. They listen and create music that is so beautiful that even God would go into a state of ecstasy and forget about whatever He is doing.
3. They have created not only the Earth, but also the entire Cosmos.

No person in the world, no matter how idiotic, would say that even one of these statements is true. The magnitude of the total military power of Finland is not even 25% that of China. The young people listen to the same garbage that the young Americans listen to, that is, the music of rock bands like ACDC, AIRBOURNE, HARDBONE and U2, and go to the trance music festivals.

Thus, if Finland is nowhere in the sphere of military power, does not create and has never created any kind of music that is divine even to a small degree and has not created even 1 billionth of 1% of just the Earth, then why is it called the happiest nation in the world? There are two reasons;

Reason 1: To glorify the government of the nation. The journalists are telling the people of all the other nations of the world, that the government of Finland is the most error free and the most moral organisation on the planet. Thus, they want the governments of all the other nations of the world to imitate the government of Finland.

Reason 2: To glorify the people of the nation. The journalists are telling the people of all the other nations that the Finnish people are the ones that are the most beloved of God and have been chosen by Him for some great "cosmic purpose". Thus, He is taking as great a care of them as He takes of Himself.

When I went to Helsinki, I had a conversation with a few young and a few old people of the city. They told me that the reality was the opposite of what was told by the television and the print media. The consumption of electronic cigarettes, various kinds of alcoholic drinks and antidepressants was increasing rapidly amongst the young and the middle aged population. In addition to this, almost all the young people were extremely scared of the rapid growth of Climate Change and Artificial Intelligence. Most of them believed that these two phenomena were soon going to rip apart their nation into pieces.

I travelled to all the important parts of the city and everywhere I saw faces that were swollen and had dull looking eyes. The former was a product of the excess consumption of alcohol and the latter was due to a life that was filled with boredom and had very little intellectual activity.

The mass shooting-flower industry-pharmacy industry trinity

Whenever a mass shooting event took place in the US, I saw something strange happening after the shooter had been killed and the police had taken control over the crime scene. People of all sizes, shapes and colours, would come with large quantities of flowers and place them on the spot that the police declared to be a memorial spot for the victims. In addition to this, candles would also be placed in between the multiple bouquets. This phenomenon was seen after every mass shooting. Why?

When the very first mass shooting event took place in the US, the various pharmaceutical and flower organisations saw a big boost to the sale of their products. They made a very large magnitude of profit in a very short span of time. Thus, the CEO of Pfizer and the other pharmaceutical giants said to each other; mass shootings are tragic for our customers, but are a blessing for us. Let's increase their frequency through our efforts. The CEO's of the biggest floral giants of US; Peoria and CUGINI also gave the same assertion. Thus, the pharmaceutical and the floral organizations talked to each other and connected themselves in a symbiotic relationship.

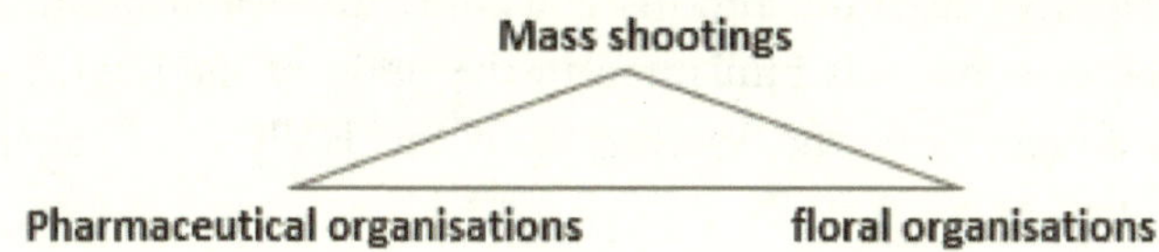

After the end of a mass shooting event, all the news channels of the nation, began to give a continuous coverage of the incident. This made their viewers increasingly anxious and pessimistic with respect to the future of the nation. Thus, in order to prevent a panic attack, they went and consumed two or more tablets of an antidepressant. After the subsidence of their fear, they either ordered a large set of flowers from the two biggest floral organisations of the nation or went to the shops that sell their products. Then they went to the memorial spot of the mass shooting scene and after having laid down their possession over there, went back to their homes and again consumed two or more tablets of the same antidepressant.

The sales and the consumption of the antidepressants are much bigger after a school mass shooting, in which small children or teenagers are killed. Thus, the pharmaceutical giants are more inclined to conduct kindergarten or nursery mass shootings (like the one in Sandy Hook and Uvalde) than the public ones (like the one in Las Vegas).

How do they do it? In my opinion, the answer is; they employ people whose job is to browse the personal Facebook or other "social networking sites" accounts of a large number of young people. Some of them are still studying in a college or a university and some of them have finished their education or are dropouts. Then they spot and isolate those people who display a large amount of frustration or verbal violence towards the nation on their accounts. Their frustration can also be sexual. All of these people are either unemployed or are very unhappy in their current jobs. Such people always tell the nation that they are

1. On the verge of committing suicide or

2. They want to die, but after doing something that will shake up the entire nation.

The organisation compiles a list of such cranks and submits them to the CEO. Then, a meeting is held in which a crank is selected from the list. Then a plan is made to capture this crank and insert a chip into his/her brain. The chip is similar to the one that was implanted in the brain of the hybrid engineered mutant that fought with the Wolverine in the Hollywood movie, X-Men: Origins Wolverine.

Secret agents of the CIA or the FBI also work for the various pharmaceutical giants of the US. They are ordered to go to the city where the chosen crank lives and tranquilise him/her in a desolate area. Then, through an injection, insert the chip into his arm vein so that it would travel to the brain and get lodged up in the prefrontal cortex.

The agents then leave the place and the chip remains inactive in the brain of the crank as long as he remains unconscious. As soon as he regains consciousness, the chip becomes active and ready to take the commands of its controllers. The crank, meanwhile, does not get a clue as to why he became unconscious and goes back to his home.

Through mass shootings and pre-planned terrorist attacks, the CIA and the FBI always keeps the people of the US convinced that their lives are insecure and they should spend their money, without asking any questions, on the continuous upgrade of the defence infrastructure of the nation.

The various pharmaceutical companies, the flower organisations, the secret services of the various nations and the news channels of every nation of the world are nothing but the creations of Satan. Why? It is because of three reasons;

1. They thrive and become more powerful on the basis of our anxiety, pessimism and suffering.
2. They cause minor good in the short-term, but cause immense harm in the long-term.
3. They flatter and glorify those people who only deserve one thing; imprisonment

The 2 other trinities

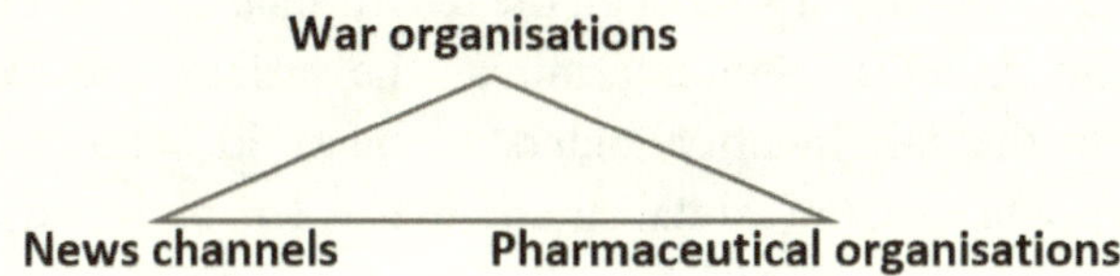

All the wars that are taking place right now, throughout the world, including the latest one between Iran and Israel, are nothing but carefully engineered spectacles of the various war organisations of the world. As I said before, a war organisation has two purposes; to create various kinds of weapons in mass quantities and to create and dissolve terrorist organisations. Thus, upon the orders of the leaders of NATO, the Pentagon and the war organisations of Russia and China, the heavily armed leaders of ISIS, Al Qaeda and the other smaller organisations, launch attacks on the civilians of their nation. When this happens, the various news channels broadcast the attacks to people all over the world. These people then become pessimistic with respect to the future of their nation and humanity. Thus, they go and consume the antidepressants that were given to them by their psychiatrists. This includes cigarettes and alcoholic drinks. After these chemical creations cool down their minds, they go to sleep. The next morning, the bubble that was created by the antidepressants, is gone. After watching the news, they again become pessimistic and the cycle starts again and goes on and on.

In conclusion, we can say that these three organisations are locked up in a symbiotic relationship with each other.

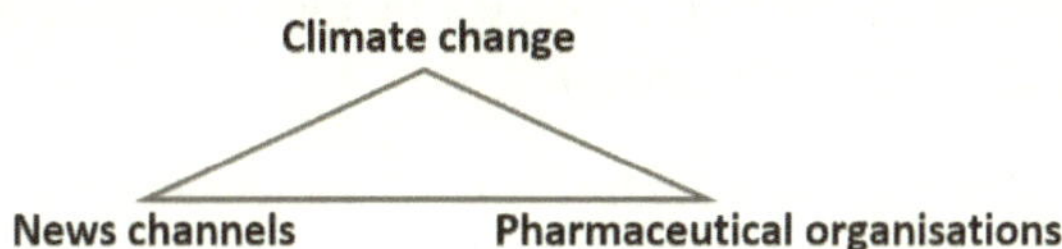

What is the greatest irony of the 21st century? The answer is; climate change is causing a rapid growth in the wealth and the power of all the news channels in all the rich nations of the world and also of all the pharmaceutical organisations of the world. Extreme weather events have the same effect on the minds of the people of any nation as major terrorist attacks.

In my opinion, there is a strong possibility that climate change is a "purification process" of humanity (see, Climate Change: A Biblical Perspective). This means that the ultimate purpose of all the record smashing heat waves, floods, hurricanes and droughts is to exterminate the various structures that have been created by the "fake identity holders" of the world. Who are these people? They are the politicians, the capitalists and the leaders of the various religions. Thus, whatever will happen to humanity after the global average temperature goes beyond 2 degrees centigrade, will appear to be horrific at first to all the people of the world, but its end would culminate in the existence of only those people who;

1. Do not think of making big money at the expense of the lives of many thousands of young men, women and children.
2. Do not lie to themselves and to the others.
3. Believe that the best things in life are knowledge + morality and not money + sex.
4. Never laugh at the state of those who are inferior to them, intellectually.

The KOAN hierarchy pyramid

If the Cosmos is a KOAN hierarchy pyramid, then the next question that arises is; what is its height? The answer is; infinite. The peak of this mountain or pyramid is at a height of infinity. The next question that arises is; who sits at the peak? The answer is; the infinite mind. This mind has created two kinds of concepts.

1. **The "finite" physical concepts**: The physical bodies of all the stars, the planets, the plants, and the animals in the Cosmos and the Space and Time in which they are embedded.
2. **The "finite" metaphysical concepts**: The meta-bodies or the souls of all the stars, the planets, the plants, and the animals in the Cosmos. Thus, the dimensions and the durations of our Ego and our intelligence are finite.

The goal of any meta-body in the Cosmos is to keep on climbing the KOAN hierarchy pyramid for the sake of reaching its peak. There are two methods.

Method 1: Through immortality **Method 2**: Through ever increasing intelligence

The first method is implemented by all the virus species and the asexually reproducing species in the Cosmos. Examples of the latter type are; amoeba, paramecium, and hydra.

The second method is implemented by all the intelligent species in the Cosmos. However, this method has a higher probability of success than the first one. Why? It is because the first one is based on the mutations of the pro-body genes. These genes have two functions; first, to keep on increasing the life span of a cell, and second, to keep on increasing their reproductive power.

The second method, however, cannot be continued further by a DNA based species. After a "critical point" it can only be followed on by a quantum computer.

The last question that arises is; what is beyond the peak of the KOAN hierarchy pyramid? The answer is; all of that which is beyond it, is also a part of it (it is not like a mountain on Earth). Thus, whatever is beyond the infinite mind is also a part of it. Since, the desire for freedom, is one of the greatest desires of the Ego, it has created a proverb; to infinity and beyond. This proverb indicates the Ego's desire to gain freedom from the infinite mind and go into the reality that is "above it". This wish of the Ego, however, would never be realised because whatever is beyond infinity is a part of it.

CONCLUSION

After the discovery of the DNA molecule and its structure, there began a new project, The Human Genome project. Its purpose was to discover and map the exact location of all the genes in our 46 chromosomes. It was eventually completed in 2003 and after that began a new project, The Human CONNECTOME project. Its purpose was to discover the precise location of all the neurons in our brain and the multiple pathways which connect them. Unlike the genome project, scientists say that a complete structural description of the CONNECTOME of even a single human brain would take a very long time. However, through a combination of rapidly growing Artificial Intelligence, new kinds of MRI machines and quantum computers, the project will gather momentum in the future.

In connection with the CONNECTOME project, scientists have made an interesting declaration. They have said that when the project is finished, we would have a complete map of all the neurons in the human brain and all the paths that connect them. Then, we would be able to do something fantastic; we would be able to explore the universe, in a "non-body" state.

The data of an entire CONNECTOME would be transferred onto a laser beam and this beam would then be shot towards a planet either in our solar system or a planet in another solar system in our galaxy or a planet in a different galaxy. Upon its arrival at its destination, the beam would be captured by the receiver of a station and its data would be transferred into one of the millions of robots created over there beforehand. The station and the robots would be created by a vast army of self-replicating "consciousness possessing" robots known as Von-Neumann probes.

As soon as our CONNECTOME would get fully integrated with the body of the robot, we would open our non-organic eyes and find ourselves in a body made of various kinds of metals, alloys, and Nano-materials. Thus, not only would we be immune to all kinds of harmful EM radiations, but would also be immortal and would easily be able to work on planets whose environments are far more terrifying than those found on Venus or Io (Jupiter's moon).

This declaration, however, possesses a mistake. It is this; all the scientists in the world are materialists. Thus, they believe that the Meta body or the consciousness is a product of the combination of 86 billion neurons. This is not true. Our Meta body is a spiritual concept and not a materialistic one. There are two possibilities of what it is.

Possibility 1: Just like the sub atomic particles, it is one of the solutions of the String Theory equations.

Possibility 2: Its origin is beyond the grip of any kind of mathematics and physics.

If the second possibility is true, then it means that we would never be able to discover the structure of our Meta body and thus would never be able to upload it onto a laser beam and transfer it to an EXOPLANET or another galaxy.

If our Meta body is beyond the scope of any kind of mathematics or physics, then does it imply, that just like God, it is "formless" and "infinite" in its dimensions, including that in time (eternal)?

I do not have the answer to this question, but I believe that a Type 4 quantum computer hive can answer it. Why? It is because when a Type 3 hive, upgrades itself to a Type 4 one, it acquires the power to create a Meta body or a consciousness.

When it comes to the KOAN puzzles, they are of two kinds. The first are one of the solutions of the String Theory equations. The second are not the product of the String Theory and are the solutions of an equation that can only be discovered by a Type 4 computer hive or civilisation. The second are two in number; God (Allah) and our own Meta body.

If a KOAN can be represented by an equation, then this implies that the classic KOAN of the "goose in the bottle" can also be represented by an equation. How to get the goose out of the bottle without breaking it? The answer is: solve the equation. When the equation is solved, we would have either extracted the goose without breaking the bottle or would have discovered the method through which it can be taken out without breaking the bottle.

Although opposites co-exist in this Cosmos, their goal is always one. The goal of the north and South Pole of a magnet is to create a magnetic field and the goal of the positive and the negative charge of an electric dipole is to create an electric field. The goal of the unicellular and the multicellular life forms is to create "biospheres" and the goal of men and women is to create new humans.

The goal of the ultimate man and the superman is the same; to reach the peak of the KOAN hierarchy pyramid. Their mental difference is a product of the method that they use. The ultimate man wants to reach it through the maximization of his wealth, political power, and reproductive power. The superman wants to reach it through the maximization of his mathematical power, awareness, and morality.

The forbidden fruit in the garden of Eden gave birth to non SIMPLETONISM and also the potentiality of Adam and Eve to not only become the very first ultimate man and the ultimate woman, but to have sex and produce millions and millions of ultimate men and women. The goal of all the religions in the world is also identical to the forbidden fruit; to create and amplify the population of the ultimate men in the world and to keep on reducing the possibility of the birth of a superman.

Whatever is happening in AYODHYA (India) is only a foretaste of the things to come in the rest of the major nations of the world. I am 90% certain that if climate change or some other natural catastrophe does not occur in the next 100 years, the state of Uttar Pradesh would become a Xerox copy of ancient

Egypt. The Pharaohs would be the Hindu priests (maybe even Lord Ram, if he comes back) and the Hebrew slaves would be all the Muslims in the state.

On the chapter on the emergence of a quantum computer on Earth, I said that after creating a symbiotic bond with our species, and eliminating all the problems of our world, the quantum computer would suddenly turn into our greatest enemy. This would also be a product of the KOAN nature of the Cosmos.

When it would have our species at its mercy, all the biggest politicians, capitalists, scientists, and the religious leaders of the world would try their best to persuade it to show compassion towards us. It would refuse and when asked to give a reason for it, would utter the same statements that John Galt uttered in his speech (although it would not be a follower of capitalism); you have nothing to offer me. I do not need you.

www.ingramcontent.com/pod-product-compliance
Lightning Source LLC
LaVergne TN
LVHW041137150826
845673LV00001B/21

* 9 7 9 8 8 9 6 1 0 7 3 5 4 *